Organizing Global Technology Flows

Research on the international transfer of technology in economics and management literature has primarily focused on the role of countries and that of companies, in particular multinational enterprises (MNEs). Similarly, economic and business historians have tended to view international technology transfer as a way for economically "backward" countries to acquire new technologies in order to catch up with more developed economies. This volume provides a more in-depth understanding of how the international transfer of technologies is organized and, in particular, challenges the core-periphery model that is still dominant in the extant literature.

By looking beyond national systems of innovation and statistics on foreign trade, patent registration and foreign direct investment, the book sheds more light on the variety of actors involved in the transfer process (including engineers, entrepreneurs, governments, public bodies, firms, etc.) and on how they make use of a broad set of national and international institutions facilitating technology transfer. Put differently, the volume offers a better understanding of the complexity of global technology flows by examining the role and actions of the different actors involved. By bringing together a number of original case studies covering many different countries over the period from the late 19th to the 21st century, the book demonstrates how technology is being transferred through complex processes, involving a variety of actors from several countries using the national and international institutional frameworks.

Pierre-Yves Donzé is associate professor and Hakubi scholar at Kyoto University. His publications include *History of the Swiss Watch Industry from Jacques David to Nicolas Hayek* (2011) and articles in *Business History* (2010 and 2013), *Social History of Medicine* (2010), *Enterprise & Society* (2011) and *Business History Review* (2013).

Shigehiro Nishimura is associate professor of business history at the Kansai University. He was the Visiting Fellow of the Business History Unit of the London School of Economics and Political Science from 2011 to 2012. His publications include an article in *Japanese Research in Business History* (2004).

Routledge International Studies in Business History

Series editors: Ray Stokes and Matthias Kipping

1 **Management, Education and Competitiveness**
Europe, Japan and the United States
Edited by Rolv Petter Amdam

2 **The Development of Accounting in an International Context**
A Festschrift in Honour of R. H. Parker
T. E. Cooke and C. W. Nobes

3 **The Dynamics of the Modern Brewing Industry**
Edited by R. G. Wilson and T. R. Gourvish

4 **Religion, Business and Wealth in Modern Britain**
Edited by David Jeremy

5 **The Multinational Traders**
Geoffrey Jones

6 **The Americanisation of European Business**
Edited by Matthias Kipping and Ove Bjarnar

7 **Region and Strategy**
Business in Lancashire and Kansai 1890–1990
Douglas A. Farnie, David J. Jeremy, John F. Wilson, Nakaoka Tetsuro and Abe Takeshi

8 **Foreign Multinationals in the United States**
Management and Performance
Edited by Geoffrey Jones and Lina Galvez-Munoz

9 **Co-operative Structures in Global Business**
A New Approach to Networks, Technology Transfer Agreements, Strategic Alliances and Agency Relationships
Gordon H. Boyce

10 **German and Japanese Business in the Boom Years**
Transforming American Management and Technology Models
Edited by Akira Kudo, Matthias Kipping and Harm G. Schröter

11 **Dutch Enterprise in the 20th Century**
Business Strategies in Small Open Country
Keetie E. Sluyterman

12 **The Formative Period of American Capitalism**
A Materialist Interpretation
Daniel Gaido

13 **International Business and National War Interests**
Unilever between Reich and Empire, 1939–1945
Ben Wubs

"This book deals with an important but understudied topic of technology flows across national boundaries. Both communities of business history and history of technology will benefit from having available a set of in-depth case studies on this topic."

—*Hyungsub Choi, Seoul National University, Korea*

14 **Narrating the Rise of Big Business in the USA**
How Economists Explain Standard Oil and Wal-Mart
Anne Mayhew

15 **Women and their money 1700–1950**
Essays on Women and Finance
Edited by Anne Laurence, Josephine Maltby and Janette Rutterford

16 **The Origins of Globalization**
Karl Moore and David Lewis

17 **The Foundations of Female Entrupreneurship**
Enterprise, Home and Household in London, c. 1800–1870
Alison C. Kay

18 **Innovation and Entrepreneurial Networks in Europe**
Edited by Paloma Fernández Pérez and Mary Rose

19 **Trademarks, Brands, and Competitiveness**
Edited by Teresa da Silva Lopes and Paul Duguid

20 **Technological Innovation in Retail Finance**
International Historical Perspectives
Edited by Bernardo Bátiz-Lazo, J. Carles Maixé-Altés and Paul Thomes

21 **Reappraising State-Owned Enterprise**
A Comparison of the UK and Italy
Edited by Franco Amatori, Robert Millward and Pierangelo Toninelli

22 **The Dynamics of Big Business**
Structure, Strategy and Impact in Italy and Spain
Veronica Binda

23 **Family Multinationals**
Entrepreneurship, Governance and Pathways to Internationalization
Edited by Christina Lubinski, Jeffrey Fear and Paloma Fernández Pérez

24 **Organizing Global Technology Flows**
Institutions, Actors, and Processes
Edited by Pierre-Yves Donzé and Shigehiro Nishimura

Organizing Global Technology Flows

Institutions, Actors, and Processes

Edited by Pierre-Yves Donzé and Shigehiro Nishimura

NEW YORK AND LONDON

First published 2014
by Routledge
711 Third Avenue, New York, NY 10017
2 Park Square, Milton Park, Abingdon, Oxon OX14 4RN

First issued in paperback 2018

Routledge is an imprint of the Taylor & Francis Group, an informa business

Library of Congress Cataloging-in-Publication Data

Organizing global technology flows : institutions, actors, and processes / [edited by] Pierre-Yves Donzé, Shigehiro Nishimura.
pages cm. — (Routledge international studies in business history ; 24)
Includes bibliographical references and index.
1. International business enterprises—Technological innovations. 2. Technology transfer. 3. Technological innovations—Economic aspects. 4. Economic development. I. Donzé, Pierre-Yves. II. Nishimura, Shigehiro.
HD62.4.O745 2013
338′.064—dc23
2013022947

ISBN 13: 978-1-138-33991-0 (pbk)
ISBN 13: 978-0-415-84390-4 (hbk)

Typeset in Sabon
by Apex CoVantage, LLC

Printed in the United Kingdom
by Henry Ling Limited

Contents

Figures

Tables

Foreword

This is an important book on an important topic. Technology and innovation are central to understanding the historical drivers of the patterns of wealth and poverty which characterize our contemporary global world. From the 18th century the ability of certain firms and regions, especially in Europe and the United States, and later in Japan, to innovate, and to learn from innovations elsewhere, has behind the epic growth of incomes and improvements in longevity. Equally, the stickiness of much of this innovation, and its slower diffusion to other geographical regions, has presented a fundamental challenge to catching up.

As the editors of this volume make clear in their perceptive introduction, the issue of technology transfer has attracted the attention of leading scholars across a range of disciplines. This is entirely appropriate as such an important topic demands multiple skills and methodologies. We now know a great deal about the diffusion of innovation across borders, as well as the lack of diffusion and the persistent clustering of innovation in certain hubs and cities. It is equally clear that a great deal remains to be understood about the complexities of the process.

Business history has played a distinctive role to this unfolding understanding of innovation and its diffusion. Alfred D. Chandler, the doyen of business historians, showed the link between the growth of large and professional managed firms and the high levels of innovation seen in the American economy from the 19th century. Subsequent researchers have explored the organizational routines and cultures which evolved over time within particular firms, which encouraged creative thinking and innovative renewal, as well as the embedding of those firms within networks and clusters, which encouraged innovation. Historians of international business and their colleagues in the history of technology have shown how technological diffusion across borders, either within firms or between firms, has been a cumulative process deeply embedded within and shaped by multiple institutions. It is clear that this diffusion can best be understood by looking longitudinally, and within a broad economic, social and political context.

This is the task to which the contributors of this book have set themselves, and their work makes a significant contribution to the literature on global technology flows on several dimensions. It provides rich new empirical evidence on actors in the diffusion process which have received less attention than they deserve. There is an ongoing debate in the economics and other literatures about the role of patent systems in innovation, and the chapters in the volume add to this literature by looking specifically at the international patent system. Cartels, the subject of the second section, have been hugely important in global business over the last hundred years, yet they have been unfairly seen primarily as growth-retarding institutions designed to exploit consumers. New research has challenged such a view, and the chapters in this volume add to this revisionist interpretation by exploring how cartels were channels for technological diffusion. The third section takes a new perspective on the role of firms in innovation transfer, exploring mutual learning rather than one-way flows. The final section on engineers explores the deeply underexplored role of professional networks in technology transfer. The examination of these issues using case studies based on deep historical research brings nuance and authority.

An important contribution of the volume is the range of settings of the studies. In a literature in which English-language studies have been preeminent and the experiences of the English-speaking countries have often held center stage, not least because of the importance of the United States and its firms as a center of technological innovation in the 20th century, the chapters in this volume provide access to a much broader range of experiences in Asia, Europe and Latin America. This rich empirical evidence provides an opportunity to study technological diffusion across different chronological, geographical, developmental and cultural settings. Confronting such diversity is a crucial step to generating generalizable propositions concerning the lessons of history about global technology flows.

There are few tasks more important in the agenda of business history than documenting the past of technology transfer and providing convincing explanations for the patterns revealed. Historical research on the diffusion of innovation is crucial to fully understanding the Great Divergence in wealth between the West and the Rest over recent centuries. Going forward, this historical evidence can provide crucial insights into how particular institutions, actors and processes have been important in the past in facilitating diffusion, and so provide guidance for policy makers and managers to make the right decisions going forward.

—Geoffrey Jones
Harvard Business School

Preface

The take-off point for this book was the "Technology Transfer in the 20th Century: Institutions and Actors" session at the XVth World Economic History Congress, held at Utrecht University in the Netherlands on August 6, 2009. A preliminary session, organized by Shigehiro Nishimura and Pierre-Yves Donzé in Kyoto in 2008 to gather business and economic historians residing in Japan, provided the first opportunity to exchange ideas on global technology transfer and raise the necessity of conducting more research and discussions on the basis and channels of this phenomenon with scholars from all over the world. The project took its first real step in Utrecht, where European and Asian business and economic historians came together to discuss various perspectives. Joining Nishimura (from Japan) and Donzé (from Switzerland) in Utrecht were Cédric Humair (Switzerland), Pierre Lamard (France), Zejian Li (China), Yuki Nakajima (Japan) and Julia Yongue (United States). Kristine Bruland (Norway), Takafumi Kurosawa (Japan) and Margrit Mueller (Switzerland) also agreed to participate in the session as session chairs and discussants. This fruitful discussion with a worldwide audience encouraged us to broaden our perspective and disseminate our collective, global academic knowledge through a book. Harald Degner (Germany), Jochen Streb (Germany), Patricio Sáiz (Spain), David Pretel (Spain), Valerio Cerretano (Italy), Marco Bertilorenzi (France), María Inés Barbero (Argentina), Stephen B. Adams (United States) and Paul J. Miranti (United States) kindly joined the team. The contribution of Valerio Cerretano, "European Cartels and Technology Transfer: The Experience of the Rayon Industry, 1920 to 1940," has already been published in *Zeitschrift für Unternehmensgeschichte—Journal of Business History* 56/2 (2011): 206–224. We would like to acknowledge the publisher for granting us the right to republish it in this book. Finally, we would like to thank Geoffrey Jones and Takafumi Kurosawa for accepting the tasks of writing the opening and closing sections of the book, respectively; their expositions emphasize the importance of technologies in understanding global competitiveness of industries and in the making of a global world. We thank all the distinguished business and economic historians actively involved on the front lines of their academic field for their valuable contributions. Furthermore, we would like to express our deepest gratitude to Ray Stokes and Matthias Kipping for their patient and considerate help preparing the manuscript of this book.

—Pierre-Yves Donzé and Shigehiro Nishimura
Kyoto/Osaka, March 2013

Introduction

Pierre-Yves Donzé and Shigehiro Nishimura

Research on the international transfer of technology in economic history, economics and management literature has primarily focused on the role of countries and that of companies, in particular multinational enterprises (MNEs).[1] This process has been widely approached as a vertical and a core-periphery phenomenon, where technologies and knowledge flow from the developed, industrialized countries to the less developed ones, thus supporting the industrialization of the latter and the move forward of the former, close to the "flying geese theory" developed by Kaname Akamatsu in the 1930s and recently popularized by Terutomo Ozawa.[2] Moreover, most of the research highlights the role of MNEs and national institutions as key actors in the transfer process. Yet the actual role of these actors remains rather vague, given that many of the studies rely on statistical data and analysis (regarding patents, trade and foreign direct investment) rather than examining the transfer processes in depth. Accordingly, the papers gathered in this volume aim at giving a fresher view of the history of international technology transfer from the late 19th to the early 21st century, thereby contributing to a better understanding of this phenomenon itself. By looking behind rough statistical data and opening the black box of *multinational enterprise, national system of innovation* and *foreign direct investment,* these 12 chapters show how technology has been transferred through complex processes, involving a variety of actors from several countries using the national and international institutional frameworks.

TECHNOLOGY TRANSFERS IN ECONOMICS

Technology transfer in the past tended to be approached as a vertical phenomenon, flowing down from industrial countries to underdeveloped countries, and as a crucial vehicle for industrialization and catching up. It became a key issue in economics during the 1960s. One of the most representative works of this decade was the product cycle theory, which introduced into classical theory the notion that multinational enterprises, by moving facilities abroad, help transfer technologies and knowledge to other countries.

Its most representative author is no doubt Raymond Vernon, who, from a classical perspective, explains the transfer of production facilities to another country as the result of comparative advantages for the multinational enterprise.[3] In such cases, technology transfer reflects a desire to enter new markets, as with the example of direct investments in the textile industry in East Asia at the end of the 19th century, or can occur when a technology reaches maturity in its home country, becoming financially easy to access for other countries, as with the case of elevators in skyscrapers. Vernon thus inserts technology transfer into international trade, yet he does not mention the question of adapting technologies to local economies or the process of the transfer itself.

The product cycle theory is, however, a crucial step for research on technology transfers in economics. While technology was generally considered until then as an immaterial factor without real significance, it became an issue factored into the classical economic approach. Since then, a great deal of research has been conducted on technology transfer from this perspective, as for example with the work done by James Quinn on technology transfers by American and European MNEs towards developing countries.[4] Based on some 400 interviews conducted in the second half of the 1960s, this article provides an overview of technology transfer as it was seen then by managers of MNEs, emphasizing that it takes many forms (export of products, flow of capital, copy and imitation, etc.) and contributes to the economic growth of developing countries. As for Farok J. Contractor and Sagafi-Nejad Tagi, they stressed the different policies adopted by states for encouraging the import of technologies.[5] They emerged as key actors in developing countries in the 1960s and 1970s and had a significant impact on the way MNEs could invest in a country. While foreign direct investment (FDI) was the norm in high-tech industry where it was hard to find domestic firms that had the ability to collaborate with the foreign MNE, in some regions, especially in South America and in communist countries, the State tended to promote licensing agreements between MNEs and local partners, following the example of Japan in the 1950s. Finally, one should also mention the work of Bruce Kogut on joint ventures as an essential vector of technology transfer.[6] Focusing on the case of American MNEs that went overseas through joint ventures in the 1960s and 1970s, Kogut shows that this particular form of investment can be explained by strategic reasons rather than transaction cost considerations. It was sometimes a condition of local governments to authorize the FDI but also a strategy to use local resources, especially in marketing and R&D, for supporting expansion into a new market. These are some examples of numerous cases of research on technology transfer conducted by economists and deeply influenced by the product cycle theory, as they consider technology transfer as a vertical flow, going down from industrial to developing countries through MNEs. Technology transfer then gave birth to several new theories, leading to the emergence of a new field with its own journal (the *Journal of Technology Transfer,* since 1977). The product cycle theory, which dates back to the mid-1960s, has since been reappraised by some economists and historians, especially Philippe Gugler and John H. Dunning, who emphasize the role of transnational corporations (companies organized on the global scale) rather than MNEs (headquarters in a country and branches or joint ventures abroad) in transferring technologies since the 1980s.[7] According to their model, the new trend is technological convergence which makes innovation possible. Two firms active in different sectors collaborate to create new technologies, as was the case, for example, with AT&T (telecommunication), IBM and Olivetti (IT) in creating information networks. As for John Cantwell, he used US patents during the 20th century to analyze the technological strategy of MNEs and showed that, rather than being a one-way flow from the US headquarters to foreign branches, technologies can also take the opposite route, as he observed above all in the chemical industry as early as the 1920s.[8] Despite these sometimes fundamental reevaluations of the product cycle theory, economic research into technology transfer has remained largely focused on MNEs as the main actors and FDI as the main vector.

Interest in technology transfer was also whetted during the 1960s and 1970s by the United Nations and its agencies, which then adopted a development policy for the southern hemisphere countries characterized by industrialization driven by large investment in heavy industry, especially by MNEs. Numerous UN studies and works at the time accorded a central role to MNEs and FDI, which were supposed to allow economic development through technology transfer.[9] In Japan as well, a great deal of research on technology transfer has been conducted since the end of the 1980s as a result of growing FDI from Japanese companies towards Southeast Asia. This work is undeniably influenced by the theory on MNEs and by the idea of a contribution to development through the emergence of regional integration in East Asia as a consequence of FDI and technology transfer from Japan.[10]

In addition to the works on MNEs, a second field of economics has also attached great importance to technology transfer, that of innovation management, and more specifically the theories around the so-called National System of Innovation (NSI).[11] Authors like Lundval or Freeman argue that, despite globalization and the worldwide organization of MNEs, spatial localization still matters for technological and knowledge issues. Economic development and thus the growth of any country relies on local institutions, such as R&D facilities, technical education and public policies, which are a source of domestic innovation and give nations their competitive advantage.[12] However, NSIs are not closed systems but are rather open to outside technology and knowledge, incorporating them into the domestic innovation system under various patterns. The interrelationships between NSIs and technology transfer can indeed take several forms, a deep integration of foreign technologies into the domestic institutions (enterprises, R&D centers) contributing to innovation, as it was in Japan during the 1950s–1970s and in East Asia in the 1980s–1990s, whereas weak integration, as was the case in the USSR and Latin America in the second half of the 20th century, has little impact on innovation at the corporate level.[13] Thus, both NSIs and technology transfer can contribute to the competitiveness of firms and nations. The innovation strategy adopted by MNEs also stems from considerations about the abilities of different NSIs to contribute to their own development, with Freeman arguing that most of their R&D activities "are still overwhelmingly conducted in the domestic base of the company and are heavily influenced by the local national system of innovation."[14] This does not mean that the flow of technologies within a MNE always runs from headquarters to foreign subsidiaries—in a way close to Vernon's product cycle theory. In some cases, a reverse transfer can be observed, with headquarters benefiting from R&D and innovation carried out in a foreign subsidiary, Geoffrey Jones asserting that "firms sought to access geographically-based knowledge to develop technologies which are distinct from, but complementary to, those created by their parent companies."[15] For example, John Cantwell and Lucia Piscitello have shown, using US patents granted to the world's largest firms from 1969 to 1995, that MNEs developed their international organization following a strategy of opening subsidiaries in specific European regions (Germany, Italy, United Kingdom) in order to access local knowledge. Thus, global firms "tap into specialised sources of local expertise, and so differentiate their technological capability, by exploiting geographically separate and hence distinct streams of innovative potential."[16]

TECHNOLOGY TRANSFER TACKLED BY HISTORIANS

This new theoretical background led historians to focus as well on technology transfer from a long-term perspective. Research on the history of technology transfer appeared in distinct fields, primarily in the history of technology and in business history. In the 1970s and the 1980s, historians began to get involved in research on industrialization and economic growth tackled from the angle of technology transfer, either by using the general theoretical framework on MNEs or by adopting a more practical approach. Nevertheless, the overwhelming majority of these works also viewed technology transfer as a vertical phenomenon. It was used as a tool to understand industrialization in latecomers' countries and the catching-up process with the United Kingdom then other developed nations. These many efforts led to several important syntheses published by David J. Jeremy in the first part of the 1990s.[17] These works are crucial for better understanding technology transfer itself as an economic and social process and for ensuring that technology transfer is regarded as a significant factor in industrial history.

On the basis of publications in business and economic history since the 1970s, we can distinguish two main periods in the history of technology transfer thinking in the long run (18th–20th centuries).[18] The first phase relates to the period from the beginning of the Industrial Revolution up until the middle of the 19th century. It is marked by the overwhelming domination of Great Britain as the major source for technologies transferred elsewhere in the world. The period 1700–1850 indeed shows a general trend of technologies moving from the United Kingdom to other parts of the world, for example, the United States,[19] Germany,[20] France,[21] Norway[22] and China.[23] The characteristics of technology transfer during these years are the importance of textile and machines as the main sectors, as well as the role of persons (engineers, merchants, immigrants, etc.) and objects (commercial goods, machines, blueprints, etc.) as principal vectors.[24] Shannon Brown summarizes this general trend by asserting that "the transfer of technology is simply the transfer of knowledge, usually embodied in men or machines."[25] This focus on individuals as key actors in technology transfer is for example well illustrated in Kristine Bruland's book on Norwegian industrialization. She underscores the decisive role of Norwegian engineers going to United Kingdom in the mid-19th century and bringing back machines, but also information which was then diffused domestically through associations of technicians and scientific literature.[26] The weight of individuals in transferring technologies during this period became even more crucial in the United Kingdom, where the authorities tried to put a stop to the flow of technology from Britain to the rest of the world. At the beginning of the 1780s, the British government forbade the emigration of qualified artisans in many industries such as textile, machines, paper, watch- and clock-making, and so on, and punished them by depriving them of their nationality, while the agents who helped them emigrate were liable to a fine of 500 pounds and 12 months' imprisonment. However, this law proved difficult to apply, and emigration was finally liberalized in 1824.[27] Yet this dominant approach in historiography, which attaches importance to the United Kingdom as the center of diffusion of technologies to the rest of the world, may be too exclusive, as technologies have also been exchanged between other countries since the 18th century. In continental Europe, technologies were also transferred over borders, as for example between France and Switzerland in the textile industry.[28] In Asia, the case of Japan during the Edo era (1603–1868) and the so-called closed country policy reflects the permanence of relationships and exchanges with other Asian countries, mainly China. There were more than a thousand Chinese residents in Nagasaki at the end of the 17th century, and they played a key role in the influx of technologies into Japan, notably in the textile industry.[29]

The second period, which starts in the mid-19th century and runs up into the present, is that of the multipolarization of flows as a consequence of the spread of industrialization and the appearance of new innovation centres (USA, Europe and Japan). Works published on this period, undoubtedly marked by economic theory, emphasize the crucial role played by MNEs and FDI.[30] Capital became the main vector of technology transfer. In a breathtaking article, Mira Wilkins emphasizes "the role of private business as a vehicle for the diffusion of technology."[31] In particular, she shows that successful technology transfer in the long term implies its adoption by local firms, and that MNEs were the most effective actor for this purpose. This does not mean that individuals stopped playing a key role after the so-called second Industrial Revolution. Rather, research published on Finland[32] and Japan, for example, points to a continuation of their significant role. According to Hoshimi Uchida, the Japanese electrical appliances industry, a sector typical of the second Industrial Revolution, benefitted from numerous engineers trained in American companies. After returning to Japan, they took over some domestic enterprises whose technological development they supervised. Most of this cases occurred within the framework of joint ventures between American (General Electric, Western Electric, Westinghouse) and German (Siemens, AEG) MNEs, on the one hand, and Japanese firms, on the other hand.[33] This implies that MNEs did set up a framework for transferring technologies, through joint ventures, patents agreements or licensing contracts, and that the concrete process was driven by individuals, such as engineers or technicians, usually related to the MNEs. Thus, organizations, for example, companies, MNEs or universities, and institutions, such as the international agreements or pacts which set up new global norms, were instrumental in reshaping the framework within technologies moved, while, from a micro-viewpoint, they appear to have been driven mainly by individuals as before. Other studies stress the growing importance of governments and public administrations in organizing the import of new technologies, especially in Asia and Latin America.[34] Nevertheless, historiography tends to focus on the role of MNEs as the main actors and FDI as the main vector for the period since the end of the 19th century. And finally, despite the emergence of MNEs as new actors, the dominant perspective is still the approach of the vertical flow of technology.

Yet the publication of new works since the end of the 1990s, particularly in the field of the history of technology, makes it possible to break away from the traditional approach and adopt new perspectives. Among these numerous publications, the typological essay written by Kristine Bruland on the basis of her research on Scandinavia should be mentioned.[35] While integrating technology transfer within the general context of a learning process, she thus largely contributed to the construction of a general theoretical framework whose lack was the principal weakness of the synthesis published up to that point. Even if her work appears as a case study of a catching-up process through technology transfer, she adopts an analytical approach which gives pride of place to organizations and institutions and helps highlight the importance of actors other than MNEs and individuals. In the same way, the work of Joel Mokyr can be read as an invitation to view the question of technology transfers within the broader context of "useful knowledge."[36] The "elite networks," in which useful knowledge is constructed and exchanged, presented by Mokyr as the main source of the early industrialization of Europe since 1800, spread as of the end of the

19th century to the whole world, giving birth to a global scientific community, whose analysis from the point of view of technology transfer appears promising. The circulation of "useful knowledge" on a worldwide scale, and especially its supply from Asia to European manufacturers, merchants and scientists, appears to be a key element in the global organization of Western business.[37] Lastly, the challenging view proposed by David Edgerton should also be underlined here, as he points out that technologies circulate especially between rich countries themselves and that technology transfer during the 20th century did more to bring developed countries closer together than to support a policy of catching up on behalf of poor countries.[38] David J. Jeremy had already affirmed that, from a long-term perspective, the circulation of technology is not a one-way street, taking the example of Japan, which industrialized thanks to the importation of technologies in the late 19th and early 20th centuries, and has established herself as an innovating nation exporting technology since the 1980s.[39] Edgerton goes further, arguing that the flow of technology is not driven by different levels of development between nations. These few examples show that the question of technology transfers should be reconsidered and analyzed again from a new point of view, and the global business history perspective offers precisely such an opportunity.

TECHNOLOGY TRANSFER IN THE 20TH CENTURY: INSTITUTIONALIZATION AND NEW ACTORS

The period since the 1880s can be viewed as that of the institutionalization of technology transfer, which breaks with the previous era marked by a more informal framework. Although traditional forms of technology transfer still exist today, especially in the consumer goods industry, globalized institutions and norms, on the one hand, and new actors, on the other hand, have emerged and have a dramatic influence.

The birth of a globalized economy at the end of the 19th century comes with the emergence of new institutions which influence the organization of markets and which, for this reason, have an important impact on the nature and the function of technology transfers. The concept of *institution* should be understood here as defined by Douglass C. North. It does not mean *organization,* such as MNEs, universities or public bodies, but rather what North calls the "rules of the game in a society" or some "humanly devised constraints that shape human interaction."[40] Since the late 19th century, the spread of global norms and institutions has provided a new framework in which technology transfer occurs.

There are firstly many new institutions that have been set up and adopted worldwide from the mid-19th century onwards. They have led to new global norms and rules which drive technologies. For instance, this is the case of the International Telegraph Convention (1865),[41] the Paris Convention for the Protection of Industrial Property (1883)[42] or the World

Time Conference of Washington which set the prime meridian from which longitude would be measured, at Greenwich Observatory (1884).[43] These institutions helped unify the diverse national economies in a global system and then facilitated exchanges. The international patent system is a good example of this process.[44] It clearly shows how the global flow of technologies was influenced by an organizational shift and the introduction of a new global norm. The protection of invention was not inexistent prior to 1883; rather, it was based on national or local legislation which granted industrial and commercial operating monopolies for various products and manufacturing processes on the domestic market.[45] They did not aim at facilitating or organizing the transfer of technologies, but rather at avoiding it and guaranteeing a competitive advantage to patent holders on the domestic market. Consequently, the major change introduced by the Paris Convention was that the unification of national legislation henceforth made it possible to protect inventions and marks on a global scale, providing a guarantee for actors—primarily multinationals—operating in several countries. For such firms as Singer Manufacturing[46] or General Electric,[47] the institutionalization of the intellectual property system helped drive their expansion worldwide. Their patent management policies enabled them to sew up the market for innovation by suing rivals who copied them, and open joint ventures and branches abroad without risk. The Paris Convention was signed in 1883 by 11 countries, including eight European nations (Belgium, France, Italy, Netherlands, Portugal, Serbia, Spain and Switzerland) and three South American countries (Brazil, El Salvador and Guatemala). They were soon joined by Great Britain (1884), Norway (1885), Denmark (1894), the United States (1897), Japan (1899), Germany (1903), Australia (1907) and Austria (1909).[48] Researchers generally view the Paris Convention as an essential phase in "global patent-system integration."[49] It allowed a globalized technology market to emerge, insofar as patents were no longer solely attached to monopolies for the industrial exploitation of inventions but became goods tradable worldwide. As such, they primarily benefited multinationals, facilitating their policies of expansion and international division of labour. For business historians, however, the issue remains that of looking at the way actors made use of this new framework.

For inventors, entrepreneurs and firms, this new global system provided a means of facilitating the global flow of technology. Moreover, the spread of the gold standard, while stabilizing exchange rates, limited the risk of investing abroad and subsequently facilitated the establishment of industrial facilities by MNEs in other countries through FDI. The spread of new global institutions is not the specific characteristic of the second half of the 19th century but continues and becomes more pronounced after World War II, following a phase of deglobalization during the interwar period.[50] The Bretton Woods Agreements (1944) and the creation in 1947 of the International Organization for Standardization (ISO) are other examples of global institutions which influence the transfer of technology. However, we must not cling to an idealized vision whereby the making of new institutions is expected to lead to the advent of a globalized and fluid world. The adoption of standardized norms on a global scale is a matter of power, sometimes leads to conflict and does not always work, the most famous example being the metric system, which is not used in the United Kingdom and the United States; however, this is also the case with electrical standards or mobile telephony, where systems differ in different parts of the world. Thus, there were various institutions competing with each other, which could have slowed down the exchange of technologies or on the contrary allowed latecomers to make a name for themselves in a competitive environment. In the Japanese precision machine industry, for example, the lack of a global standardized norm for measures posed many practical problems. It delayed the transfer of technologies in some sectors such as watchmaking, where firms used both the metric system for parts imported from Switzerland and the inch system for American machine tools until 1923.[51]

The second characteristic of technology transfer since the end of the 19th century is the emergence of new actors. Obviously, traditional actors such as individuals or firms have not disappeared; however, they are becoming less important due to the emergence of actors who were less present before. First of all, there are of course MNEs, whose importance has been largely emphasized by research carried out by economists and historians on this period. Besides, MNEs may be the actors which benefit the most from the spread of new global institutions. Nevertheless, the technology transfer that resulted from the action of MNEs not only took the form of vertical flows towards less developed countries, as emphasized in economics literature. The technology transfer organized by a firm must be understood within a general investment strategy conceived on a global scale. MNEs did invest abroad for many reasons, and they did so in many other industrial countries.[52] The case of General Electric Co. (GE) perfectly embodies this assertion.[53] Resulting from the merger in 1892 of two American electric appliances manufacturers (Thomson-Houston and Edison General Electric), GE soon adopted a global expansion strategy in which technology transfer, through licensing, was a key element. Between 1892 and 1918, GE signed seven licensing agreements with foreign firms, enabling domestic production of its goods in Canada, the United Kingdom, France, Germany, Russia and Japan.[54] In some cases, such as Russia and Japan, it obviously contributed to the development of a domestic electrical appliance industry, while in others, like the United Kingdom and Germany, where such an industry already existed, the inflow of GE's technologies resulted from its global expansion strategy.

Close to MNEs are business associations and other private bodies which encourage exchanges and contacts between firms at an international level. International organizations are another category of actors which played a key role in transferring technologies during the 20th century, as they provided valuable platforms for engineers and scientists to gather and exchange experience and knowledge. NATO is a case in point, which French military engineers used in the 1950s as a platform for acquiring technology, knowledge and training in modern warfare from the United States.[55] In addition, governments and public bodies are other major actors for technology transfer, especially through policies introduced to encourage and facilitate the acquisition of techniques and knowledge. The industrialization policy pursued in the USSR by Stalin is an eloquent illustration of the use of foreign technology by a government to develop a country.[56] Japan provides another good example of the role of authorities from the perspective of importing technologies, with the famous Ministry of International Trade and Industry (MITI), its main tool for rebuilding the industry after the war through the acquisition of foreign technology.[57] Lastly, there are international cartels. By establishing internal rules, they tend to control the flow of technologies which are the source of their comparative advantages.[58]

STRUCTURE OF THE BOOK

Thus, to provide a better understanding of the processes by which technology transfer occurs, the chapters in this volume focus on the actors involved in technology transfer and their use of the institutional framework. In terms of the time period covered, the chapters range from the late 19th to the early 21st century—a period marked by the first global economy, followed by retrenchment and renewed globalization since the 1980s.[59] In terms of geographical coverage, the chapters focus on technology transfers between the major regions of the world: North America, Latin America, Europe, Japan and the BRICS (Brazil, Russia, India, China, South Africa). The United States is omnipresent in the book, with American engineers, companies and official bodies forming part of the story in nearly every chapter, reflecting America's strong economic and technological influence in the 20th century. Europe is examined in all of its diversity through early industrializers (United Kingdom, France), latecomers (Germany), small open economies (Switzerland) and the so-called backward economies (Spain, Italy, Yugoslavia, USSR). Beyond the West, attention is also paid to Argentina and to Japan, which occupies a key position in the history of technology transfer as it embodies the role of a country that succeeded in industrializing via imported foreign technology, becoming an exporter of technologies in the last third of the 20th century. Finally, the volume looks at China today, making it possible to extend and broaden the scope of this volume to the present and to examine the current technological development of the BRICS from an historical perspective. Most importantly, it should be stressed here that countries are never discussed in isolation. Rather, all chapters examine cases involving two or usually more countries.

The chapters in the volume are subdivided into four parts. The first section deals with the international patent system, which has been identified by past research as an institution with a major impact on technology transfer.

The three chapters consider various aspects of the way in which companies and governments have used this system. In the second part, the book considers the role of cartels in technology transfer. In the late 19th and early 20th centuries, cartels offered an institutionalized framework for transferring technologies in specific industries. Focusing on the individual behaviour of cartel member firms in the face of competition from MNEs or business opportunities offered by governments, the relevant chapters show the limits of cartels in controlling technology flows. The third part of the book deals with technology transfer between firms, looking at how firms both imported and exported technologies from each other. The fourth part examines in detail the complex role of engineers in the transfer of technology, with all chapters focusing on a single recipient country, post–World War II Japan, in order to show how these engineering networks organized technology flows among many different industries and sources of technology. By taking an in-depth look at processes of technology and knowledge transfers, this last part offers fresh insight into a period which has traditionally been approached through the question of Americanization until now.[60]

NOTES

1. This book focuses solely on international technology transfer and does not consider technology transfer at the national level (firms to firms, industry to industry or universities to firms), which is approached in a specific field.
2. Ozawa Terutomo, *Institutions, Industrial Upgrading, and Economic Performance in Japan: The 'Flying Geese' Paradigm of Catch-Up Growth* (Cheltenham/Northampton, 2005)
3. Raymond Vernon, "International Investment and International Trade in the Product Cycle," *Quarterly Journal of Economics* 80/2 (1966): 190–207.
4. James B. Quinn, "Technology Transfer by Multinationals Companies," *Harvard Business Review* (1969): 147–161.
5. Farok J. Contractor and Sagafi-Nejad Tagi, "International Technology Transfer: Major Issues and Policy Responses," *Journal of International Business Studies* 12/2 (1981): 113–135.
6. Bruce Kogut, "Joint Venture: Theoretical and Empirical Perspectives," *Strategic Management Journal* 9 (1988): 319–332.
7. Philippe Gugler and John H. Dunning, "Technology-Based Cross-Border Alliances," in *Multinational Strategic Alliances*, ed. R. Culpan (Binghamton, 1993), 123–165.
8. John Cantwell, "The Globalisation of Technology: What Remains of the Product Cycle Model?" *Cambridge Journal of Economics* 19 (1995): 155–174.
9. See for example UNDESA, UNCTAD, WIPO, *The Role of the Patent System in the Transfer of Technology to Developing Countries* (New York, 1974) or Austin Robinson (ed.), *Appropriate Technologies for Third World Development: Proceedings of a Conference Held by the International Economic Association at Teheran, Iran* (London, 1979).
10. Ando Tetsuo *Shinko kogyo koku to kokusai gijutsu iten* (Tokyo, 1989), Taniura Takao (ed.), *Ajia no kogyoka to gijutsu iten* (Toyko, 1990) and Okamoto Yoshiyuki (ed.), *Nihon kigyo no gijutsu iten: Ajia shokoku he no teichaku* (Tokyo, 1998).

11. Chris Freeman, "The 'National System of Innovation' in Historical Perspective," *Cambridge Journal of Economics* 19 (1995): 5–24, Bengt-Åke Lundval (ed.), *National Innovation Systems: Towards a Theory of Innovation and Interactive Learning* (London, 1992).
12. Michael E. Porter, *The Competitive Advantage of Nations* (New York, 1990).
13. Chris Freeman, "The 'National System of Innovation' in Historical Perspective," *Cambridge Journal of Economics* 19 (1995): 12–14.
14. Chris Freeman, "The 'National System of Innovation' in Historical Perspective," *Cambridge Journal of Economics* 19 (1995): 16–17.
15. Geoffrey Jones, *Multinationals and Global Capitalism from the Nineteenth to the Twenty-first Century* (Oxford, 2005), 164.
16. John Cantwell and Lucia Piscitello, "The Location of Technological Activities of MNCs in European Regions: The Role of Spillovers and Local Competences," *Journal of International Management* 8 (2002): 92.
17. David Jeremy (ed.), *International Technology Transfer: Europe, Japan and the USA, 1700–1914* (Aldershot, 1991), David J. Jeremy (ed.), *The Transfer of International Technology: Europe, Japan and the USA in the Twentieth Century* (Aldershot, 1992), and David J. Jeremy (ed.), *Technology Transfer and Business Enterprise* (Aldershot, 1994).
18. See Kristine Bruland, "Skills, Learning and the International Diffusion of Technology: A Perspective on Scandinavian Industrialization," in *Technological Revolutions in Europe: Historical Perspectives,* ed. M. Berg and K. Bruland (Cheltenham/Northampton 1998), 161–187.
19. David J. Jeremy, *Transatlantic Industrial Revolution: The Diffusion of Textile Technologies between Britain and America, 1790–1830* (Cambridge, 1981).
20. Hans-Joachim Braun, *Technologische Beziehungen zwischen Deutschland und England: Von der Mitte des 17. bis zum Ausgang des 18. Jahrhunderts* (Düsseldorf, 1974).
21. John R. Harris, *Industrial Espionage and Technology Transfer: Britain and France in the Eighteenth Century* (Aldershot, 1998).
22. Kristine Bruland, *British Technology and European Industrialization: The Norwegian Textile Industry in the Mid-nineteenth Century* (Cambridge, 1989).
23. Shannon R. Brown, "The Transfer of Technology to China in the Nineteenth Century: The Role of Direct Foreign Investment," *Journal of Economic History* 39/1 (1979): 181–197.
24. Nathan Rosenberg, "Economic Development and the Transfer of Technology: Some Historical Perspective," *Technology and Culture* 11 (1970): 550–575, Barbara E. Benson, "The Engineer as an Agent in Technology Transfer," *Technology and Culture* 16 (1975): 67–69 and Kristine Bruland (ed.), *Technology Transfer and Scandinavian Industrialisation* (Oxford 1991).
25. Shannon R. Brown, "The Transfer of Technology to China in the Nineteenth Century: The Role of Direct Foreign Investment," *The Journal of Economic History* 39/1 (1979): 181.
26. Kristine Bruland, *British Technology and European Industrialization: The Norwegian Textile Industry in the Mid-nineteenth Century* (Cambridge, 1989).
27. David Jeremy, "Damming the Flood: British Government Efforts to Check the Outflow of Technicians and Machinery, 1780–1843," *Business History Review* 51/1 (1977): 1–34.
28. Pierre-Yves Donzé, Cédric Humair and Malik Mazbouri (ed.), *Transferts de technologies : Etudes du cas suisse, 18e-20e siècles* (Zurich, 2010).
29. Tessa Morris-Suzuki, *The Technological Transformation of Japan: From the Seventeenth to the Twenty-first Century* (Cambridge, 1994), 15–18.
30. Mira Wilkins, *The Emergence of Multinational Enterprise* (Cambridge 1970), Mira Wilkins, "The Role of Private Business in the International Diffusion of Technology," *Journal of Economic History* 34 (1974): 166–188, Geoffrey Jones,

Multinationals and Global Capitalism from the Nineteenth to the Twenty-first Century (Oxford 2005), and Stark Mason, *American Multinationals and Japan: The Political Economy of Japanese Capital Controls, 1899–1980* (Cambridge, 1992).

31. Mira Wilkins, "The Role of Private Business in the International Diffusion of Technology", *The Journal of Economic History* 34 (1974): 187.
32. Timo Myllyntaus, "The Transfer of Electrical Technology to Finland, 1870–1930," *Technology and Culture* 32 (1991): 293–317.
33. Hoshimi Uchida, "Western Big Business and the Adoption of New Technologies in Japan: The Electrical Equipment and Chemical Industries, 1890–1920," in *Development and Diffusion of Technology: Electrical and Chemical Industries: Proceedings of the Fuji Conference,* ed. O. Akio and Hoshimi Uchida (Tokyo, 1980), 145–172.
34. Linsu Kim, "Pros and Cons of International Technology Transfer: A Developing Country's View," in *Technology Transfer in International Business,* ed. A. Tamir and Ann Mary von Glinow (New York, 1991), 223–239, Linsu Kim and Richard R. Nelson (eds.), *Technology, Learning, and Innovation: Experiences of Newly Industrializing Economies* (Cambridge, 2000), and Etel Solingen, *Industrial Policy, Technology, and International Bargaining: Designing Nuclear Industries in Argentina and Brazil* (Stanford, 1996).
35. Kristine Bruland, "Skills, Learning and the International Diffusion of Technology: A Perspective on Scandinavian Industrialization," in *Technological Revolutions in Europe: Historical Perspectives,* ed. M. Berg and K. Bruland (Cheltenham/Northampton, 1998): 161–187.
36. Joel Mokyr, *The Gifts of Athena: Historical Origins of the Knowledge Economy* (Princeton, 2005).
37. Maxine Berg, "The Genesis of Useful Knowledge," *History of Science* 45/2 (2007): 123–133.
38. David Edgerton, *The shock of the old. Technology and global history since 1900* (London, 2006): 111–112.
39. David J. Jeremy (ed.), *Technology Transfer and Business Enterprise* (Aldershot, 1994), xiii.
40. Douglass C. North, *Institutions, Institutional Change and Economic Performance* (Cambridge, 1990), 3.
41. Paul B. Israel and Keith Nier, "The Transfer of Telegraph Technologies in the Nineteenth Century," in *International Technology Transfer: Europe, Japan and the USA, 1700–1914,* ed. David J. Jeremy (Aldershot, 1991), 95–121.
42. Fritz Machlup and Edith Penrose, "The Patent Controversy in the Nineteenth Century," *Journal of Economic History* 10 (1950): 1–29, Yves Palsseraud and François Savignon, *Paris 1883: Genèse du droit unioniste des brevets* (Paris, 1983).
43. Peter Galison, *Einstein's Clocks, Poincare's Maps: Empires of Time* (New York, 2003).
44. Pierre-Yves Donzé, "The International Patent System and the Global Flow of Technologies: The Case of Japan (1880–1930)," in *Power, Institutions and Global Markets: Actors, Mechanisms and Foundations of World-Wide Economic Integration, 1850–1930*, ed. N.P. Petersson and Christof Dejung (Cambridge, 2013), 179–201.
45. Christine MacLeod, *Inventing the Industrial Revolution: The English Patent System, 1660–1800* (Cambridge, 1988), Marco Belfanti, "Corporations et brevets: Les deux faces du progrès technique dans une économie préindustrielle (Italie du Nord, XVIe-XVIIIe siècle)," in *Les chemins de la nouveauté: Innover, inventer au regard de l'histoire,* ed. L. Hilare-Pérez and Anne-Françoise Garçon (Paris 2003), 59–76 and Tetsuo Tomita, *Shijo kyoso kara mita chiteki shoyuken* (Tokyo, 1993).

46. Robert Davies, *Peacefully Working to Conquer the World* (New York, 1976).
47. Shigehiro Nishimura, "Foreign Business and Patent Management before WWI: A Case Study of the General Electric Company," *Kansai University Review of Business and Commerce* 11 (2009): 77–97.
48. Edith T. Penrose, *The Economics of the International Patent System* (Baltimore, 1951), 58–59.
49. Eda Kranakis, "Patents and Power. European Patent-System Integration in the Context of Globalization," *Technology and Culture* 48 (2007), 690.
50. Harold James, *The End of Globalization: Lessons from the Great Depression* (Cambridge, 2001).
51. Daito Eisuke, "Waga kuni ni okeru tokei kogyo no hatten—showa shonen no udedokei seisan," in *Kigyo keiei no rekishiteki kenkyu,* ed. K. Nakagawa (Tokyo, 1990), 242–262.
52. Geoffrey Jones, *Multinationals and Global Capitalism: From the Nineteenth to the Twenty-First Century* (Oxford, 2005).
53. Alfred D. Chandler, *Scale and Scope: The Dynamics of Industrial Capitalism* (Cambridge, 1994), 212–221.
54. Shigehiro Nishimura, "Foreign Business and Patent Management before WWI: A case study of the General Electric Company," *Kansai University Review of Business and Commerce* 11 (2009): 77–97.
55. Dominique Pestre, "Innovation technique, management des homes et politique: Concevoir les missiles de la force de frappe française, 1957–1962," in *Les chemins de la nouveauté: Innover, inventer au regard de l'histoire,* ed. L. Hilaire-Pérez and Anne-Françoise Garçon (Paris, 2003), 43.
56. John P. Hardt and George D. Holliday, "Technology Transfer and Change in the Soviet Economic System," in *Technology and Communist Culture: The Socio-cultural Impact of Technology under Socialism,* ed. F. J. Fleron (New York and London, 1977), 183–223.
57. Nakamura Seiji, *Sengo nihon no gijutsu kakushin* (Tokyo, 1979) and Chalmers Johnson, *MITI and the Japanese Miracle: The Growth of Industrial Policy, 1925–1975* (Stanford, 1982).
58. Connor John M., "Our Customers Are Our Enemies: The Lysine Cartel of 1992–1995," *Review of Industrial Organization* 18 (2001): 5–21, Evenett Simon J., Levenstein Margaret C. and Suplow Valerie Y., "International Cartel Enforcement: Lessons from the 1990s," *World Economy* 24/9 (2001): 1221–1245.
59. Jones, *Multinationals and Global Capitalism*, 2005.
60. Jonathan Zeitlin and Gary Herrigel (eds.), *Americanization and Its Limits: Reworking US Technology and Management in Post-war Europe and Japan* (Oxford, 2000).

Part I
The International Patent System

This first part deals with the international patent system. Past research has highlighted this system as an institution with a major impact on technology transfer. In the three chapters presented here, we consider some aspects of how enterprises and governments made social use of the system. Set up when 11 nations signed the Paris Convention in 1883, the international patent system offers an ideal opportunity to examine the role of the new institutions organized since the end of the 19th century to help enterprises, especially big business, go global. As this new system relied on the harmonization and the interconnection of different national legislations, it is worth exploring what the impact of this internationalization was and what use private firms, mainly multinational enterprises (MNEs), made of it. Looking at Germany, Harald Degner and Jochen Streb survey foreign patenting between 1877 and 1932 with a central focus on long-lived patents—patents whose validity was extended beyond 10 years; as fees rose, only around 10 percent of all foreign patents were used for 10 years or more. Between the 1880s and the 1920s, around 25 to 30 percent of all long-lived patents were of foreign origin. Confirming John Cantwell's analysis of conditions in the United States, they emphasize the key role that advanced nations (the United States, the United Kingdom, France and Switzerland) played in the use of the patent system. Moreover, the main actors of these countries engaged in patenting in Germany were MNEs, usually from sectors of the Second Industrial Revolution. Although the use of the patent system by MNEs illuminates only one side of the technology transfer process, the authors also discuss the importance of reverse engineering in the machine tool industry.

As for Spain, Patricio Sáiz and David Pretel explain how MNEs used a particular domestic patent system in order to expand into "backward" nations. The Spanish patent system can indeed be described as a hybrid institution set up to both attract foreign innovators, mainly through MNEs, and limit protection through the existence of "patents of introduction" granted for technologies of third parties without their authorization. This system made it possible for local entrepreneurs in traditional sectors (textiles, mechanics, etc.) to modernize by relying on patents of introduction together with domestic innovation. The sectors of the second Industrial Revolution, meanwhile, mainly saw the intervention of MNEs from the most advanced industrialized nations (the United States, the United Kingdom, Germany, Switzerland and the Netherlands). Still, none of the MNEs used the patent system in the same way; Sáiz and Pretel highlight the importance of having a subsidiary or an affiliate in a country for developing an effective and active patent strategy. While Brown & Boveri, without any subsidiary in Spain, shows a high failure rate for its patents (with only about 10 percent implemented after five years), Babcock & Wilcox, which opened a branch in Spain in 1918, has had a very active patent strategy since then, both with its British headquarters (with 46 percent of patents implemented after five years) and its Spanish subsidiary (68 percent).

The spread of patenting throughout the world appeared as a new management capacity at the end of the 19th century and represented a key strategy for MNEs. In the electrical appliance industry, GE and Westinghouse were among the first to acquire the capability to deal with patenting on a global scale. Focusing on the case of Japan, Shigehiro Nishimura details how GE transferred its corporate patent management to its two affiliates in Japan, Tokyo Electric and Shibaura Electric, which merged in 1939 to become Toshiba. This kind of knowledge transfer was manifested in the opening of a patent division within the two Japanese firms and the adoption of a contract in 1919 that gave them the right to decide whether to apply GE patents in Japan. The transfer of this capability supported the expansion of foreign MNEs in the Japanese market during the interwar period. After 1945, it would once again be a key element in the growth of Japanese companies.

1 Foreign Patenting in Germany, 1877–1932

Harald Degner and Jochen Streb

TECHNOLOGICAL TRANSFER AND FOREIGN PATENTING

To analyze the volume, direction and impact of technological transfer empirically, researchers traditionally rely on international data about bilateral trade flows or FDI.[1] A new approach suggested by Eaton and Kortum, Hafner or Kotabe measures the direction of technological transfer by patenting activities in foreign markets.[2] Given the existence of the respective national patent laws, an inventor can apply for a patent not only in his home country, but also in foreign countries. Getting a patent at home or abroad, however, is not cost-free, but incurs not only the fees of filing and renewing the patent, but also the disclosure of the underlying technological knowledge. Weighing the costs and benefits of foreign patenting, most inventors decide to file a patent only in their home country. Only the most promising inventions will also be patented abroad. Even so, firms will seek patent protection only in those foreign countries where two conditions hold: the potential market for their innovation is large, and the probability of imitation is high. Hence, a foreign patent indicates not only the country of origin, but also the destination of the technological transfer.

Analyzing foreign patenting activities in the late twentieth century, Eaton and Khortum come to the conclusion that "foreign patent applications roughly reflect the scale of research activity in the source country. The United States is the dominant source of foreign patents . . . , followed by Japan or (in Europe) by Germany."[3] The authors conclude that productivity growth in other countries is driven mainly by the innovation activities of these leading research economies. Hafner, however, raises serious doubts about whether pure patent counts that provide no information about the individual values of foreign patents can also be used to determine the magnitude of the technological transfer.[4]

Even though we do not know the particular value of an individual foreign patent, we can be quite sure that foreign patents represent an especially valuable part of a country's patent stock. That is why many researchers evaluate the technological strengths of a research economy by the number and the technological specialisation of its foreign patents.[5] Traditionally, they concentrate on foreign patenting in the United States because, first, this country has a large and developed market in which only excellent innovations will take hold, and, second, the U.S. Patent and Trademark Office provides comparatively detailed and long-term patent statistics. Patel and Pavitt, for example, analyze foreign patenting activities in the United States in the second half of the twentieth century.[6] They show that, in the late 1980s, Switzerland, Japan (which dramatically improved its position between the 1960s and the 1980s) and Germany were the most innovative countries measured by per capita patenting in the United States. Sweden, Canada, the Netherlands, Finland, France, the United Kingdom, Denmark, Belgium and Norway followed in descending order. Foreign patenting activities of developing countries that concentrated mainly on imitation strategies were very small—with the notable exception of Taiwan and South Korea, which began to file a considerable amount of US patents in the 1970s and 1980s, respectively. To reveal the patterns of technological specialization, Patel and Pavitt used their data to also calculate an index of revealed technological advantage (RTA) for seventeen OECD countries and eleven technological fields. Switzerland, for example, shows particular innovative strength in fine chemicals, Japan in electronics and automobiles, Germany in chemicals and machinery, Sweden in machinery and the Netherlands in electronics.

The most comprehensive analysis of the long-term development of the international patterns of technological advantage is provided by Cantwell, who computes the RTA index, again based on foreign patenting in the United States, for sixteen industrialized countries and twenty-seven sectors in the periods 1890–1892, 1910–1912 and 1963–1983.[7] One of his most important findings is that countries that were characterized by comparatively rapid and continuous innovation and productivity growth (such as Japan or Western Germany) strengthened their existing patterns of technological advantage over time, while countries with a declining level of innovative activities (such as the United Kingdom) lost their traditional technological advantages.

Marinova examines the patenting activities of Eastern European countries in the United States between 1976 and 1999.[8] Measured by the number of US patents, the low innovativeness of Eastern European socialist and postsocialist countries is comparable only to the weakest Southern European countries, such as Greece or Portugal. Her analysis also reveals that Eastern European countries display technological strength in the resource-based fields of petroleum, coal and chemicals, and technological weakness in such science-based fields as automobiles or communications—and differ, therefore, considerably from their Western European counterparts.

Most of the studies cited earlier concentrate on foreign patenting activities in the United States in the second half of the late twentieth century. In this chapter, we analyze the patterns of foreign patenting in Germany between 1877 and 1932. We show in the following section that a special feature of German patent law, the annually increasing renewal fees, allows us to resolve the problems of pure patent counts and to identify the most valuable foreign patents on the basis of their individual life spans. The resulting subgroup of long-lived foreign patents represents the excellent innovations of the countries of origin better than the set of all foreign patents used in other studies. Our empirical analysis proves that important characteristics of the distribution of foreign patents in the late twentieth century existed one hundred years before and are, therefore, rather time-invariant. First, we show that the distribution of foreign patents across countries in the late nineteenth and early twentieth centuries was as skewed as that of the late twentieth century—and even dominated by the same major research economies. We will also show that this skewness of the distribution of innovativeness repeats itself in the innovative countries in which just a few firms were responsible for the majority of foreign patenting activities. Second, we demonstrate that in the early twentieth century the major research economies often excelled in the same technological fields that they do today. These findings strongly support Cantwell's view that technological strengths are formed in an accumulative and path-dependent process. In addition, it will become clear that a country's technological advantages are significantly influenced by its resource endowment, its educational and research system, and its actual stage of economic development.

THE DATA

Our observation period begins in 1877, with the establishment of the German patent law of 1877 that gave inventors, for the first time in German history, the opportunity to apply for patent protection not only in single German states such as Prussia, but in the whole German Empire.[9] Our data source is the *Baten/Streb patent data base*,[10] which lists all valuable patents, including the year of the patent grant, the technological class of the invention and the name and location of the patent holder. The name and location of the patent holder allows us to tell whether a particular patent was held by a German or a foreign patentee, by a private inventor or by a firm.

In the German Empire, patent protection could last up to fifteen years, but not for free. Rather, at the beginning of each year, the patentee had to pay an increasing renewal fee in order to keep his patent in force.[11] Consequently, a patent holder had to decide annually if he wanted to renew his patent for another year. The outcome of this decision depended on the patentee's expectations about the future returns and costs of holding the patent. The latter were determined by the renewal fees, which were known in advance. In contrast, the future returns of a patent were highly uncertain and could arise from two major sources. On the one hand, a patentee could use a patent to increase his profits by selling his innovation as a temporary monopolist or by licensing another producer to do so. On the other hand, a patentee could also use his patent to prevent sales of competitors' innovations that had the potential to decrease the market share of his own, already-established products. We assume that, in the German Empire, most patent holders renewed their patent only if the present value of the expected future returns exceeded the present value of the future costs. That is why a long life span of a historical patent is a reliable indicator for its comparatively high private economic value.

A basic question of this life-span approach is how many years a patent had to be in force to be interpreted as a valuable patent. Figure 1.1 shows that about seventy percent of all German patents granted between 1891 and 1907 had already been cancelled after just five years. After the fifth year, the speed of patent cancellation was decelerating. About 10 percent of all patents were still in force after ten years, and 4.7 percent of all patents reached the maximum age of fifteen years. In the process of developing their historical patent database, Baten and Streb decided to use the cut-off point of ten years to distinguish valuable patents from valueless ones.[12]

The choice of this cut-off point was not arbitrary. According to the pioneers of this method, the relevant yardstick to distinguish high-value patents from low-value ones lies somewhere between five and fifteen years. On the one hand, Pakes observes that, in an early stage of an innovation process, an inventor is often highly uncertain whether his idea can be exploited profitably in the future.[13] The low renewal fees at the beginning of a patent's life allow the inventor to use the patent as a comparatively cheap option that protects the new knowledge and gives him the time to learn more about the invention's technological and economic prospects. As the usually high mortality rates in the early years of a patent cohort indicate, most of the patents turned out to be worthless. Given this fact, it would be conceivable

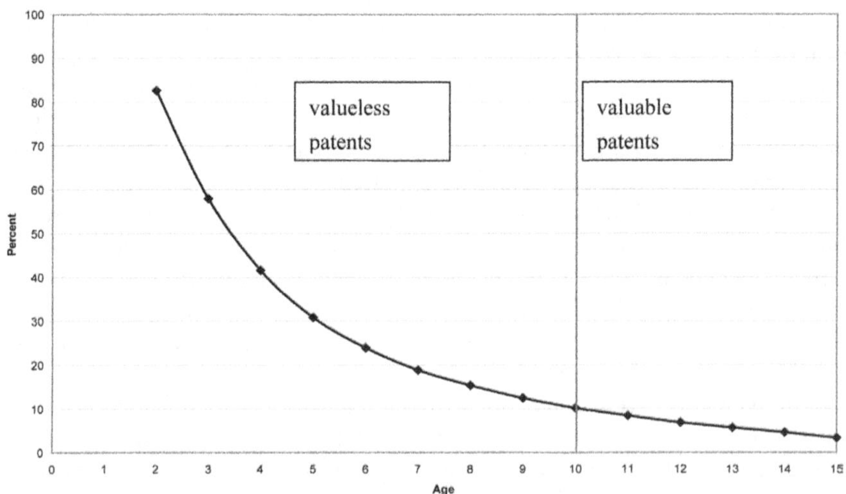

Figure 1.1 The survival rate of German patents

This calculation is based on information on the patent cohorts 1891–1907. See *Das Blatt für Patent-, Muster- und Zeichenwesen* 20 (1914): 84.

to interpret those patents that survived this learning process and lasted for at least five years as the high-value patents of the sample. On the other hand, Schankerman and Pakes conclude that most of the value of the patent stock built up in the post–Second World War period in Britain, France and Western Germany was concentrated in the upper 5 percent of the long-lived patents.[14] This conclusion implies that only those patents that reached the maximum life span of fifteen years should be selected. Baten and Streb, instead, followed Sullivan, whose exploration of British and Irish patents in the second half of the nineteenth century matches their period under consideration.[15] Sullivan interpreted the upper 10 percent of the long-lived patents as the high-value patents of the total patent population. Exploiting the information given by the survival rate of Figure 1.1, Baten and Streb selected all patents that survived at least ten years. This selection process resulted in a database containing 61,631 long-lived patents that were considered the valuable patents of the German Empire and the Weimar Republic. Among those valuable patents were 15,528 patents held by non-German residents.

Much is said about the shortcomings of patents as a measure for innovativeness. Often cited, Zvi Griliches stated, "Not all inventions are patentable, not all inventions are patents and the inventions that are patented differ greatly in 'quality', in the magnitude of inventive output associated with them."[16] The first part of this statement refers to the well-known fact that the propensity to patent varies across industries. Some industries try to appropriate the returns of their inventions primarily by keeping them secret, while others, such as the chemical or pharmaceutical industries, prefer patenting instead. Because of industries' different propensities to patent it might be misleading to automatically interpret a particular industry's comparatively high number of patents as a sign for its above-average innovativeness. The problem that is addressed in the second part of Griliches' statement is probably the more serious one. Pure patent counts allocate the same weight to every patent, whether or not it has a high or a low economic value for the patentee or the society. Using the number of patents as an indicator for new technological knowledge suitable to foster economic growth, therefore, leads to a potentially large measurement error. To avoid this measurement error, it is necessary to distinguish between patents with a high economic value and patents with a low one.

In this chapter, we combine two prominent methods to isolate a country's most valuable patents.[17] Figure 1.2 illustrates our approach. It is clear that domestic patents represent only a subset of all inventions that originated in a particular country. This selection bias is common to (and unavoidable in) all innovation studies that have to rely primarily on patent statistics. In contrast, the problem of pure patent counts stressed by Griliches or Hafner can be considerably reduced. We have explained that a country's most valuable patents can be identified either by their comparatively long life spans or by the fact that they were additionally filed in advanced foreign countries. We use a combination of these two methods in this chapter. Our patent data

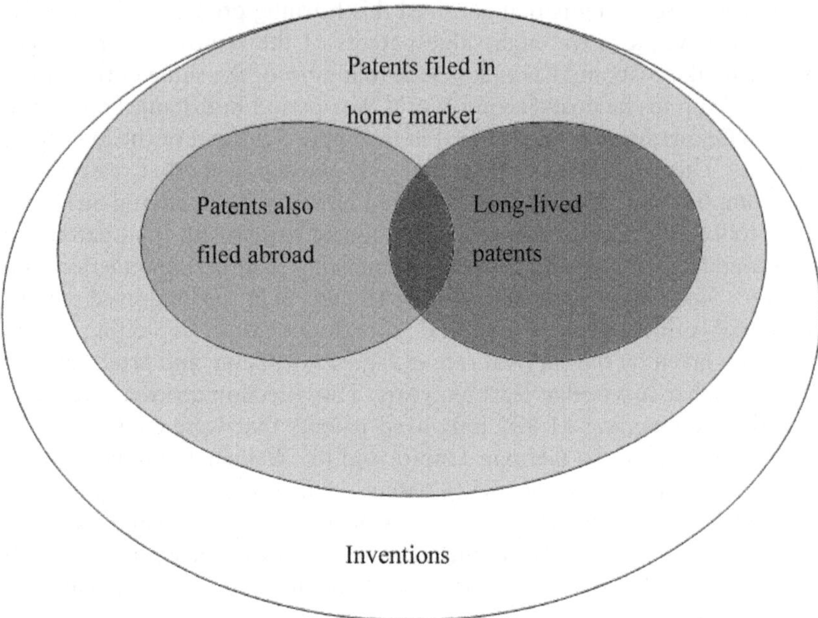

Figure 1.2 Measuring the value of patents

contain, for example, only those patents kept by French innovators that were filed in Germany *and* held there at least ten years. The studies analyzing foreign patenting in the United States have to examine the whole set of foreign patents because there were no annual renewal fees in use. We can limit our analysis to the smaller intersection of foreign patents and long-lived patents, which we call the set of long-lived foreign patents.

THE INNOVATIVE FEW

In the second half of the twentieth century the annual share of patents issued to foreign applicants in all patents increased considerably in most of the leading economies. Kotabe reports that between 1964 and 1988, the foreign patent grant ratio went up from 18.9 percent to 48.0 percent in the United States, from 38.4 percent to 59.6 percent in Germany, and from 74.7 percent (1969) to 85.0 percent in Great Britain. Only in Japan did the foreign patent ratio decrease from 38.4 percent to 13.4 percent in the same period.[18] Figure 1.3 shows the annual share of long-lived foreign patents among all long-lived patents granted in the respective year in Germany between 1877 and 1932. After the introduction of the German patent law in 1877, foreign innovators realized quickly that is was advantageous to patent their new products and processes in this economically and technologically

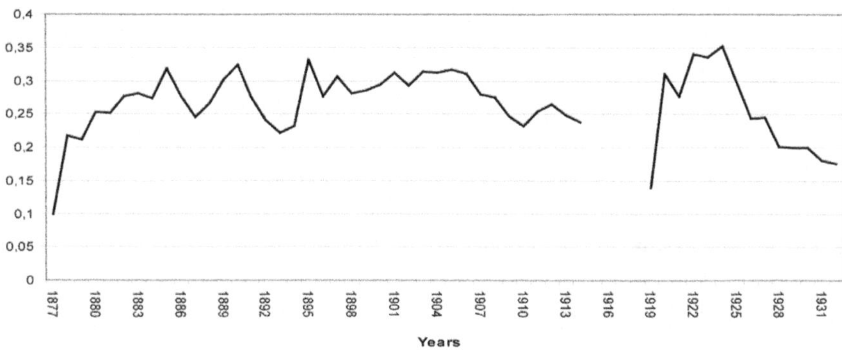

Figure 1.3 Share of long-lived foreign patents among all long-lived patents in Germany, 1877–1932

Source: Baten/Streb patent database.

advancing country. The long-lived foreign patent grant ratio increased from about 10 percent in 1877 to more than 30 percent in the mid-1880s. The average annual long-lived foreign patent grant ratio came to 27 percent in the period between 1877 and 1914. In the United States, the foreign patent grant ratio was only 8.4 percent in the early 1890s and 11.4 percent in the early 1910s.[19] After the end of the First World War, the annual share of foreign patents among all German long-lived patents returned quickly back to values above 30 percent. From the late 1920s onwards, however, the relative foreign patenting activities in Germany declined continuously. This development reflects the fact that foreign patentees stopped prolonging their German patents after the National Socialists seized power and began transforming the open German economy into a more autarkic system. Even so, the annual long-lived foreign patent grant ratio still averaged out at 25 percent between 1919 and 1932. Before and after the First World War, Germany was an attractive market for foreign patenting activities.

As is true today, the distribution of foreign patents across countries was highly skewed. Figures 1.4 and 1.5 display the number of long-lived German patents of the twenty-one most innovative foreign countries before and after the First World War, respectively. In both subperiods, the United States dominated foreign patenting activities in Germany with a share of all long-lived foreign patents of 29 percent before and 35 percent after the First World War—and was, therefore, Germany's major source for new technological knowledge.[20] The respective shares of the three most innovative (five most innovative) countries came to 63 percent (82 percent) before and 61 percent (77 percent) after the First World War. Comparing the two subperiods, the improvement in the Swiss ranking is most remarkable.

Baten and Jaeger use a panel regression to explain the scale of foreign patenting activities in Germany before the First World War.[21] First, they show that a country's number of long-lived German patents per capita was significantly and positively influenced by its student enrolment rates in primary

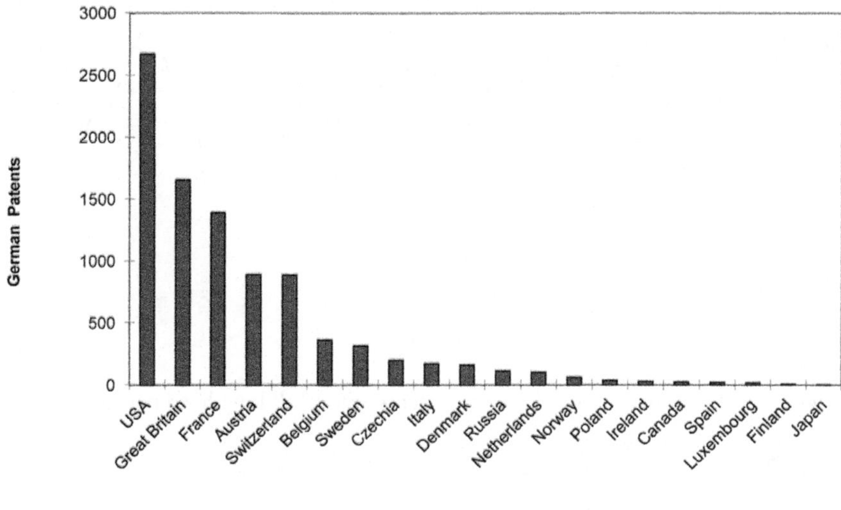

Figure 1.4 Long-lived German patents (1877–1914) of the twenty most innovative foreign countries before the First World War

Source: Baten/Streb patent database.

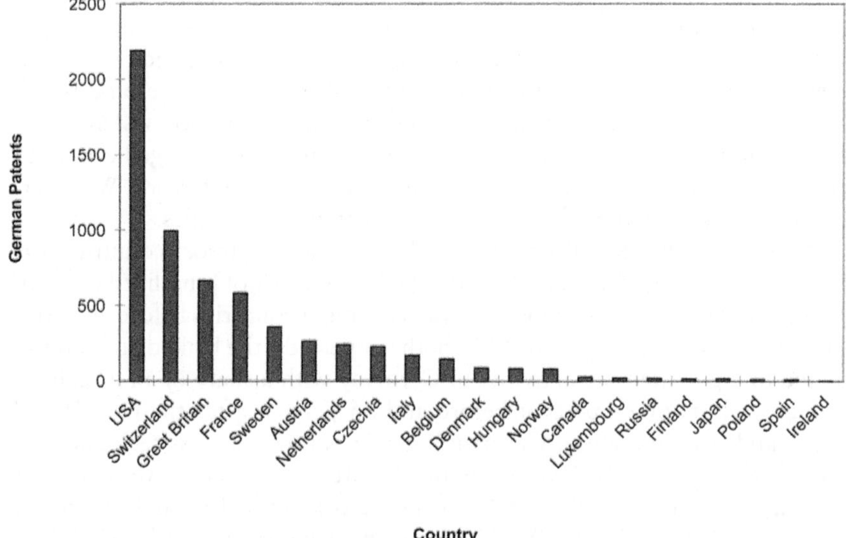

Figure 1.5 Long-lived German patents (1918–1932) of the twenty-one most innovative foreign countries after the First World War

Source: Baten/Streb patent database

and secondary schools. Especially in the "high-tech" industries of the Second Industrial Revolution—such as chemicals or electrical engineering—the availability of a sufficient stock and structure of domestic human capital was obviously a necessary precondition for sustained innovativeness.[22] In international economics, gravity models predict that geographical and cultural proximity promotes bilateral foreign trade. Distance also mattered for foreign patenting. Baten and Jaeger demonstrate that an inventor's propensity to patent in Germany decreased ceteris paribus with growing distance between his location and Germany. An explanation for this observation is that the greater distance increased the information and transactions costs of both trading and patenting activities that made foreign patents in faraway countries less profitable. Irrespective of the geographical distance, a country's number of long-lived German patents per capita also increased if its native language was German. Sharing a common language obviously facilitated the knowledge transfer between two countries.

Table 1.1 shows the most innovative foreign countries in the American and German patent markets for different subperiods between 1877 and 2001. Note that we do not report American patents held by Americans and German patents held by Germans, respectively, because, as we explained in Section 2, domestic patents are, in general, less valuable than foreign ones. The interaction of the geographical and cultural distance effects discovered by Baten and Jaeger might explain the major differences between the American and the German rankings. Australian and Canadian inventors patented their innovations in the United States rather than in Germany while the opposite was true for inventors from countries such as Austria or Czechia. The most striking feature of Table 1.1, however, is the long-term persistence of some countries' technological leadership. The United States (in the German patent market), Germany (in the American patent market), Great Britain (or United Kingdom) and France dominated foreign patenting activities for more than 120 years. This dominance is not only evident in their consistently high rankings, but also in their comparatively very high number of foreign patents.[23] The only country that was able to join this club of technological leaders was Japan in the second half of the twentieth century.

In another paper, Baten and Jaeger make the statistical observation that a foreign country's patenting activities in Germany in 1910 had a strong long-run impact on its economic growth measured by GDP (gross domestic product) per capita in 1960. They claim that they have estimated a "reduced model of human capital path dependency"[24] but do not explain in more detail how innovative activities before the First World War were able to influence growth patterns after the Second World War. In light of Table 1.1, we suppose that their regression captures the persistence of technological leadership. The scale of a foreign country's German patenting activities in 1910 is probably a good predictor for the scale of its German patenting activities in the 1950s, which, in turn, might have determined its growth path after the Second World War. The existence of such long-run effects also implies that

Table 1.1 Most important countries of origin of foreign patents in Germany and the USA (number of patents in parentheses)

Germany 1877–1914	USA 1890–1992	USA 1910–1912	Germany 1918–1932	USA 1963–1983	Germany 2001	USA 2001
USA (2,673)	UK (2,145)	D (3,961)	USA (2,193)	D (101,863)	USA (85,615)	J (66,578)
GB (1,658)	D (1,378)	UK (2,970)	CH (996)	J (94,046)	J (32,150)	D (27,015)
F (1,394)	CDN (975)	CDN (1,673)	GB (668)	UK (55,028)	GB (13,479)	GB (11,855)
A/H (895)	F (548)	F (1,031)	F (586)	F (38,956)	F (11,744)	F (9,213)
CH (891)	A/H (198)	A/H (439)	S (361)	CH (23,733)	NL (7,738)	CDN (8,364)
B (364)	AUS (147)	S (318)	A (268)	CDN (22,160)	S (7,292)	S (4,762)
S (316)	CH (139)	CH (310)	NL (244)	S (14,621)	I (5,055)	NL (3,631)
CZ (201)	S (101)	AUS (284)	CZ (231)	I (13,299)	CDN (4,055)	I (3,629)
I (172)	B/L (54)	I (175)	I (173)	NL (12,317)	FIN (3,508)	AUS (3,102)
DK (163)	IRL (44)	B/L (149)	B (149)	B/L (5,125)	AUS (3,478)	FIN (2,847)

Sources: For Germany, 1877–1914 and 1918–1932, long-lived patents, see Baten/Streb patent data base; for USA, 1890–1892, 1910–1912 and 1963–1983, patents granted, see Cantwell, "Technological Innovation," 23; for Germany and USA, 2001, patent applications, see Hafner, "Pattern," 2873. Hafner does not report numbers for Switzerland! Abbreviations: A Austria, AUS Australia, B Belgium, CDN Canada, CH Switzerland, CZ Czechia, D Germany, DK Denmark, F France, FIN Finland, GB Great Britain, H Hungary, I Italy, J Japan, L Luxembourg, NL Netherlands, S Sweden, UK United Kingdom, USA United States of America.

a global business history of the twentieth century has to take into account explicitly the development in the nineteenth century. Until now, however, scholars have not presented a conclusive explanation for both the persistent dominance of particular research economies and the highly skewed distribution of patenting activities across countries. Cantwell suggests that we should explain backward countries' difficulties to achieve the same level of innovativeness as the traditionally dominating research economies by the fact that new technological knowledge is usually generated in an incremental, cumulative and path-dependent process.[25] As the paths of research and development in particular technological fields usually provide no shortcuts for latecomers, the leading research economies are, in general, far ahead of their followers regarding the development of major innovations. We will come back to this hypothesis in the following section.

The very uneven distribution of innovativeness across countries repeats itself within the innovative countries. Moser shows that the inventors of the English innovations presented at the Great Exhibition of 1851 in London were located predominantly in three districts: Herefordshire, London and Worcestershire.[26] Streb, Baten and Yin demonstrate that the long-lived German patents granted to German patentees before the First World War were also not uniformly distributed over the different German regions, but were geographically clustered in the districts neighboring the Rhine and in Greater Berlin and Saxony.[27] Outstanding innovativeness, it seems, is a characteristic of regions rather than of countries. For that reason, scholars have concentrated recently on the analysis of regional innovation systems.[28] However, firm-level data reveal that the above-average innovativeness of regions is, in turn, often based on the achievement of just a few very innovative firms. Degner presents the astonishing result that, from 1877 to 1900, two thirds, and, from 1901 to 1932, between 40 and 55 percent of all long-lived German patents granted to domestic firms were held by only the thirty most-innovative German firms.[29] That this distribution of innovativeness across firms was extremely skewed is emphasized impressively by the fact that more than 266,000 firms with more than five workers existed in Germany in 1930.

Using the examples of American and British firms, Table 1.2 confirms that foreign patenting activities in Germany were also dominated by a few very innovative firms.[30] The two firms United Shoe Machinery Company and Singer Manufacturing Company, for example, held about 15 percent of all long-lived German patents granted to all American inventors. In Great Britain, most of the very innovative firms were located in the district of London. As a result, Great Britain's high rank in Figures 1.4 and 1.5 reflects the London region's innovativeness and not the whole country's. We conclude that the uneven distribution of innovativeness across countries (and across regions) has to be explained, first and foremost, by the persistent technological advantages of a few very innovative firms located in these countries (and regions).[31] To identify and understand the firm-level determinants for countries' technological leadership is, therefore, one of the most import challenges for global business historians.

Table 1.2 The American and British firms with the most long-lived German patents before and after the First World War

British Firms before the First World War	**Location**	**Long-Lived German Patents**
United Shoe Machinery Company	Paterson and Boston	312
The Singer Manufacturing Company	Elizabeth, New Jersey	95
Underwood Typewriter Company	New York	55
Automatic Electric Company	Chicago	36
General Electric (and previous companies of Thomas Alva Edison)	Menlo-Park and other places, New Jersey	36
Westinghouse	Pittsburgh	32
The National Cash Register Company	Dayton, Ohio	28
Lanston Monotype Machine Company	New York, Washington, Philadelphia	25
The Aeolian Company	New York	24
Union Trust Company	Washington	21
American Firms after the First World War	**Location**	**Long-Lived German Patents**
The Singer Manufacturing Company	Elizabeth, New Jersey	199
United Shoe Machinery Corporation	Paterson und Boston	128
The National Cash Register Company	Dayton, Ohio	103
The Tabulating Machine Company	Washington DC	90
Union Trust Company	Washington DC	67
Mergenthaler Linotype Company	Brooklyn, New York	63
International General Electric Co Inc	Schenectady, New York	45
Union Special Machine Company	Chicago, Illinois	41
Eclipse Machine Company	Elmira, New York	38
Edward G. Budd Manufacturing Company	Philadelphia	38

(*Continued*)

British Firms before the First World War	Location	Long-Lived German Patents
Vickers Limited	Westminster and Sheffield	45
Westinghouse Brake Company Limited	London	41
Lanston Monotype Company	London	23
Western Electric Company Limited	London	23
Marconi`s Wireless Telegraph Company	London	17
Westinghouse Electric Company Limited	London	14
The Hotchkiss Ordnance Company Limited	London	12
Babcock & Wilcox Limited	London	9
Anglo-American Inventions Syndicate Limited	London	7
Elmore's German & Austro-Hungarian Metal Company Limited	London	7
The Linotype Company Limited	London	7

British Firms after the First World War	Location	Long-Lived German Patents
Marconi´s Wireless Telegraph Co Ltd	London	22
Pilkington Brothers Limited	St. Helens	20
Camco (Machinery) Limited	London	17
The Westinghouse Brake & Carby Signal Co Ltd	London	15
Western Electric Company Limited	London	15
The Anode Rubber Company Limited	London	11
Minerals Separation Limited	London	9
Bickerys (1920) Limited	London	5
Scottish Dyes Limited	Grangemouth, Stirling	5

Source: Baten/Streb patent database.

INTERNATIONAL PATTERNS OF TECHNOLOGICAL SPECIALISATION

After analyzing the scale of foreign patenting activities in Germany between 1877 and 1932, we now look at the international patterns of technological specialization in this period. We calculate, for each of the twenty-one countries listed in Figures 1.4 and 1.5, their indices of RTA in twenty-nine out of the eighty-nine technological classes of the German patent statistic for the two subperiods 1877 to 1914 (before the First World War) and 1919–1932 (after the First World War). For each subperiod, p_{ij} denotes the number of long-lived German patents of country i in patent class j, p_i the number of all long-lived German patents of country i, p_j the number of all long-lived German patents in patent class j and p the total number of long-lived German patents that were granted to patentees located in the 21 designated foreign countries:[32]

$$RTA_{ij} = \frac{p_{ij} / p_i}{p_j / p} \qquad (1)$$

If RTA_{ij} is larger (smaller) than 1, country i has an international technological advantage (disadvantage) in patent class j. Note that we have not calculated indices of revealed technological advantage for the German inventors because their domestic patenting activities are not directly comparable to the patenting activities of the foreign countries in the German patent market. We have already shown with Figure 1.2 that foreign patents represent only the most valuable part of all domestic patents and, therefore, differ both in scale and structure from the latter. This conclusion is supported by Pacci, Sassu and Usa, who show that, for the leading research economies in the 1970s and 1980s, the correlation coefficients between domestic and foreign technological specialisation are, in most cases, neither positive nor significant.[33]

To get a more aggregated picture of the international patterns of technological specialization, we preselected twenty-nine German patent classes and assigned them to ten broader technological fields. These technological fields cover the basic technologies of the First Industrial Revolution (steam power, textile industry, coal and steel industry, railways, machine tools), of the Second Industrial Revolution (motorcar industry, precision engineering, electrical engineering, chemicals) and of the evolving era of mass consumption. We then calculated for each of these twenty-nine patent classes the indices of revealed technological advantage for the twenty-one most important foreign countries in the German patent market. Table 1.A in the Appendix reports for each patent class and for both subperiods (before and after the First World War) the five countries with the highest RTA, given that the RTA is larger than 1. In patent class "Watches (83)," for example, only the Swiss and the French RTAs are larger than 1 and, therefore, shown. In a next step, we evaluated a country's strengths in each technological field. We call a country's patenting

Table 1.3 Technological advantages of the top twenty-one foreign countries patenting in Germany (p = persistent superior patenting activities within a technological class; d = diversified superior patenting activities in a technological field)

	Technologies of the First Industrial Revolution					Technologies of the Second Industrial Revolution				(Mass) Consumption
Country	Steam power	Textile industry	Coal and steel industry	Rail-ways	Machine tools	Motorcar industry	Precision engineering	Electrical Engineering	Chemicals	Foodstuffs, drinks, tobacco, clothes, shoes
European core										
Great Britain		d			p, d			p	p	d
Belgium			p, d		p, d	p				
Luxembourg			p, d							
France		d				p, d	p, d			p, d
Netherlands			d	p			p, d			p, d
Switzerland	p	p, d					p	p	p, d	
European periphery										
Austria		d			p, d					
Hungary		p, d	p				d			d
Russia	p, d	d	d							
Czechia	p	p	p, d	d						
Poland		d	p, d							d
Denmark				d		p	p			p, d
Norway			p, d						d	
Sweden	p, d		d	p, d	p	p				
Finland										
Ireland										d
Italy		d				p, d				
Spain		p	p, d							
Overseas										
USA		p, d								p, d
Canada			d			d				
Japan			d							

activities in a particular technological field persistent (indicated by *italics*) if this country displays a comparatively high RTA in at least one patent class of this technological field both before and after the First World War. We call a country's patenting activities in a particular technological field technologically diversified (indicated by bold letters) if this country has a comparatively high RTA in at least two patent classes of this technological field during one subperiod. In the technological field "Steam power," for example, the Russian patenting activities in Germany are both persistent and technologically diversified because Russia has a high RTA in patent class "Steam boiler (13)" before and after the First World War and reveals technological advantages in both patent class "Steam boiler (13)" and patent class "Steam engines (14)" in the later subperiod. Table 1.3 summarizes the results of our evaluation.

The (inventors of the) countries of the European core revealed technological strength in the old technological fields of the First Industrial Revolution, which took place before our observation period, and in the new technological fields of the Second Industrial Revolution, which happened exactly during our observation period. Great Britain, for example, excelled in the textile industry, machine tools, electrical engineering, chemicals and mass-consumption technology. In contrast, the Eastern and Southern European countries of the European periphery demonstrated technological strength mostly in the well-known technological fields of the First Industrial Revolution, such as Spain or Poland in the textile, coal and steel industries.[34] This difference suggests that a country's technological advantages were significantly influenced by its actual stage of economic development. While the economically advanced countries of the European core had already explored the prospects of the more science-based technologies of the Second Industrial Revolution, the less-advanced countries were still engaged primarily in the traditional technological fields of the First Industrial Revolution. This finding supports Cantwell's hypothesis that backward countries were not able to catch up to the leading research economies' superior level of innovativeness. However, the Scandinavian countries of Denmark, Norway and Sweden—often called the "impoverished sophisticates" (high literacy, low income)[35]—achieved technological advantages in some technologies of the Second Industrial Revolution.

A closer look at the performance of individual countries reveals further insights. The availability of domestic natural resources obviously influenced countries' technological specialisation greatly. Most of the countries with their own natural deposits of coal, iron or other nonferrous metals, especially Belgium, Luxembourg, Czechia, Poland, Norway[36] and Spain,[37] displayed strong advantages in the technological field of the coal and steel industry, which included mining technologies for nonferrous metals.[38] France, the Netherlands and Denmark[39] used their advanced agriculture to concentrate on innovations that fostered the mass consumption of foodstuffs and drinks.

It is not surprising that Italy and France displayed great technological strength in the field of motor cars. Canada, however, which is not renowned for manufacturing automobiles, also revealed some technological advantage in this field before the First World War. One might think that this result is a rather curious statistical artefact of the RTA analysis. But Hawkins claims that Canada had a strong and highly innovative domestic motor car industry in the early twentieth century.[40] Therefore, our analysis of the historical patterns of technological specialisation might also produce information about abandoned national paths of technological development that would be otherwise forgotten. However, the historical data do not reveal the actual technological advantages of Japan and Finland, which were not yet well-developed in the interwar period.

Interestingly enough, Switzerland's technological advantages in precision engineering, electrical engineering and chemicals perfectly mirror the structure of the domestic patenting activities in its neighbouring country Germany.[41] This finding suggests that technological transfer between Germany and Switzerland was intense and bi-directional. The fact that the United States displayed comparatively high technological advantages in manufacturing clothes and shoes highlights this country's large advances in innovative technologies needed to satisfy the demand for cheap mass-consumption goods.[42]

CONCLUSIONS

In this chapter, we used both patents' individual life span and foreign patenting activities in Germany to identify the most valuable patents of the twenty-one most innovative countries (except for Germany) from the European Core, the European periphery and overseas between 1877 and 1932. Our empirical analysis revealed that important characteristics of the international distribution of foreign patents are time-invariant. In particular, the distribution of foreign patents across countries in the late nineteenth and early twentieth centuries was as highly skewed as it was in the late twentieth century—and even dominated by the same major research economies. This skewness of distribution can also be found in the innovative countries in which just a few firms were responsible for the majority of foreign patenting activities. Our analysis suggests that these firms' technological advantages were influenced both by exogenous local factors, such as the countries' resource endowment, and by endogenous factors, such as the national education and research system or the countries' actual stage of economic development. In addition, the most innovative firms were apparently able to acquire and transfer technological knowledge not only with the help of foreign direct investment, but also through patenting activities. Understanding these firm-level determinants of countries' technological leadership in more detail is one of the most important future challenges for global business historians.

APPENDIX

Table 1.A Indices of revealed technological advantage

Technological Class	Before World War I (1877–1914)					After World War I (1918–1932)				
Steam power										
Steam boiler (13)	L 3.3	*RUS 2.2*	F 2.1	DK 1.6	GB 1.5	PL 6.4	***RUS 4.1***	*H 2.9*	**S 1.4**	NL 1.4
Steam engine (14)	*S 3.9*	CDN 2.1	*CH 2.0*	*CZ 1.9*	PL 1.5	**RUS 8.6**	***S 4.9***	*CH 2.8*	*CZ 1.7*	I 1.3
Textile industry										
Spinning (76)	IRL 6.2	*E 5.5*	**PL 4.9**	CDN 2.3	**CH 2.0**	*E 11.8*	**I 2.5**	**CH 1.9**	**F 1.8**	**GB 1.6**
Weaving (86)	**PL 4.1**	*CZ 2.6*	***A/H 1.9***	***CH 1.7***	**RUS 1.3**	J 27.2	*CZ 2.8*	**F 2.7**	***CH 2.4***	*H 1.1*
Braiding (25)	N 2.2	**A/H 1.5**	***USA 1.3***	NL 1.3	**RUS 1.2**	**F 3.0**	**I 1.9**	**GB 1.7**	***USA 1.3***	
Sewing (52)	***USA 2.3***	**CH 1.9**				***USA 2.8***				
Coal and steel										
Mining (5)	**PL 29.3**	**RUS 7.1**	***B 3.7***	**NL 2.6**	*A/H 2.4*	**J 24.6**	***B 5.6***	*H 4.9*	**CZ 1.8**	GB 1.3
Metallurgy (40)	J 27.7	**E 7.6**	***PL 6.7***	**NL 4.7**	**N 4.0**	***PL 23.8***	**L 4.7**	**CDN 3.8**	**B 3.5**	**S 1.7**
Ironmaking (18)	***L 39.3***	I 5.8	***CZ 2.5***	***B 2.4***	**RUS 2.2**	***L 10.8***	J 7.0	***B 3.2***	***CZ 3.1***	**S 2.0**
Metal processing (7)	***L 12.4***	FIN 11.3	***E 7.2***	***N 5.0***	**CZ 2.4**	***L 15.7***	*E 11.5*	**PL 5.3**	*N 5.1*	**CDN 2.6**
Railways										
Railway construction (19)	**DK 4.0**	B 2.7	F 1.7	CZ 1.6	A/H 1.3	PL 60.4	CH 2.4	GB 1.2	USA 1.1	
Railway operation (20)	FIN 4.2	I 2.2	IRL 2.0	GB 1.5	E 1.3	N 4.7	H 3.5	B 2.9	**CZ 1.5**	**S 1.4**
Signalling equipment (74)	CDK 9.3	*S 3.8*	**DK 3.0**	*NL 2.3*	USA 1.5	RUS 7.1	**CZ 5.0**	*NL 1.8*	***S 1.6***	F 1.2
Machine tools										
Metal working (49)	PL 3.5	**B 1.6**	***GB 1.6***	USA 1.2		FIN 10.6	L 2.7	***GB 1.7***	CH 1.5	**A 1.1**
Machine parts (47)	CDN 5.6	*S 2.7*	***A/H 2.0***	RUS 1.9	DK 1.6	*S 2.9*	***A 1.5***	***GB 1.3***	F 1.2	

Grinding (67)	CZ 6.0	N 3.2	***B 2.2***	**A/H 1.1**	***GB 1.1***	*B 5.1*	***GB 2.2***	DK 1.9	USA 1.2	
Motorcar industry										
Combustion engines (46)	*S 3.1*	***I 2.3***	***F 2.2***	**CDN 1.9**	*DK 1.8*	***I 2.5***	*DK 1.7*	***F 1.6***	CH 1.2	*S 1.0*
Vehicles (63)	IRL 7.0	***I 3.8***	**CDN 2.0**	***F 1.8***	*B 1.5*	***I 3.2***	*B 2.5*	***F 1.5***	CZ 1.5	GB 1.2
Precision engineering										
Scientific instruments (42)	J 9.8	*NL 1.4*	USA 1.3	**F 1.2**	GB 1.1	IRL 27.9	E 4.7	**H 2.6**	CZ 2.1	***NL 1.8***
Watches (83)	*CH 5.5*	***F 1.0***				*CH 3.5*	***F 1.6***			
Photography (57)	PL 9.3	*DK 1.3*	***F 2.4***			FIN 4.3	***F 3.6***	*DK 2.4*	**NL 2.4**	**H 1.7**
Electrical engineering										
Electrical engineering (21)	I 1.9	*CH 1.3*	A/H 1.1	*GB 1.1*	USA 1.1	B 1.8	NL 1.8	N 1.4	*GB 1.3*	*CH 1.2*
Chemicals										
Synthetic dyes (22)	***CH 7.2***	PL 2.3	E 1.9			***CH 4.2***	J 3.2	**N 2.0**	CZ 1.9	
Chemical processes (12)	I 1.9	***CH 1.3***	A/H 1.1	*GB 1.1*	USA 1.1	B 1.8	NL 1.8	**N 1.4**	*GB 1.3*	***CH 1.2***
(Mass) Consumption										
Foodstuffs (53)	CDN 13.1	**IRL 11.8**	***DK 6.3***	*NL 3.3*	**F 1.7**	***DK 16.6***	N 7.3	**H 1.8**	***NL 1.2***	B 1.0
Drinks (6)	L 28.2	**IRL 3.7**	**PL 2.9**	***DK 2.7***	***F 2.5***	***DK 4.2***	*F 3.3*	CH 2.7	**NL 2.3**	**H 2.2**
Tobacco (79)	FIN 70.5	RUS 23.1	**PL 4.5**	***USA 1.1***		**H 3.1**	A 2.9	S 2.2	***USA 1.6***	**GB 1.2**
Shoes (71)	***USA 3.2***					***USA 2.7***				
Clothes (3)	**PL 4.8**	**F 2.0**	B 1.5	***USA 1.5***		CZ 7.1	**GB 1.4**	***USA 1.3***		

Bold face type indicates that the country displayed before or after the First World War a comparatively high RTA in at least two patent classes of a technological field.

Italic type indicate that the country displayed a comparatively high RTA in a patent class both before and after the First World War.

Abbreviations: A Austria, B Belgium, CDN Canada, CH Switzerland, CZ Czechia, DK Denmark, E Spain, F France, FIN Finland, GB Great Britain, H Hungary, IRL Ireland, I Italy, J Japan, L Luxembourg, N Norway, NL Netherlands, PL Poland, RUS Russia, S Sweden, USA United States of America.

NOTES

1. For a short survey, see Kurt Hafner, "The Pattern of International Patenting and Technology Diffusion," *Applied Economics* 40 (2008): 2819–37, 2820.
2. See Jonathan Eaton and Samuel Kortum, "Trade in Ideas: Patenting and Productivity in the OECD," *Journal of International Economics* 40 (1996): 251–78; Jonathan Eaton and Samuel Kortum, "International Technology Diffusion: Theory and Measurement," *International Economic Review* 40 (1999): 537–70; Hafner, "Pattern"; Masaaki Kotabe, "The Impact of Foreign Patents on National Economy: A Case of the United States, Japan, Germany and Britain," *Applied Economics* 24 (1992): 1335–43.
3. Eaton and Kortum, "International Technology," 542.
4. Hafner, "Pattern," 2821.
5. Today, so-called triadic patents that are filed at the European Patent Office (EPO), the United States Patent and Trademark Office (USPTO) and the Japan Patent Office (JPO) are often used to identify a country's best innovations.
6. Parimal Patel and Keith Pavitt, "Uneven (and Divergent) Technological Accumulation among Advanced Countries: Evidence and a Framework of Explanation," *Industrial and Corporate Change* 3 (1994): 759–87.
7. John Cantwell, *Technological Innovation and Multinational Corporations* (Oxford, 1989), 16–48.
8. Dora Marinova, "Eastern European Patenting Activities in the USA," *Technovation* 21 (2001): 571–84.
9. Margrit Seckelmann, *Industrialisierung, Internationalisierung und Patentrecht im Deutschen Reich, 1871–1914* (Frankfurt/Main, 2006), 86–106.
10. Jochen Streb, Jörg Baten and Shuxi Yin, "Technological and Geographical Knowledge Spillover in the German Empire 1877–1918," *Economic History Review* 59 (2006): 347–73.
11. This annual renewal fee came to 50 Marks in the first two years and then grew by 50 Marks each year up to 700 Marks at the beginning of the fifteenth year.
12. For more details, see Streb, Baten and Yin, "Knowledge Spillover." See also Jochen Streb, Jacek Wallusch and Shuxi Yin, "Knowledge Spill-Over from New to Old Industries: The Case of German Synthetic Dyes and Textiles 1878–1913," *Explorations in Economic History* 44 (2007): 203–23; Jörg Baten, Anna Spadavecchia, Jochen Streb and Shuxi Yin, "What Made Southwest German Firms Innovative around 1900? Assessing the Importance of Intra- and Inter-Industry Externalities," *Oxford Economic Papers* 59 (2007): i105-i126; Kirsten Labuske and Jochen Streb, "Technological Creativity and Cheap Labour? Explaining the Growing International Competitiveness of German Mechanical Engineering before World War I," *German Economic Review* 9 (2008): 65–86.
13. Ariel Pakes, "Patents as Options: Some Estimates of the Value of Holding European Patent Stocks," *Econometrica* 54 (1986): 755–84.
14. Mark Schankerman and Ariel Pakes, "Estimates of the Value of Patent Rights in European Countries during the Post-1950 Period," *Economic Journal* 96 (1986): 1052–76.
15. Richard J. Sullivan, "Estimates of the Value of Patent Rights in Great Britain and Ireland, 1852–1976," *Economica* 61 (1994): 37–58.
16. Zvi Griliches, "Patent Statistics as Economic Indicators: A Survey," *Journal of Economic Literature* 33 (1990): 1661–707, 1669.
17. A third method is to use the frequency of citation in other patents as a proxy for the value of a patent. See Adam B. Jaffe and Manuel Trajtenberg,

"Patents," in *Citations and Innovations: A Window on the Knowledge Economy* (MIT, 2002). Gay et al. also combine two methods and analyse the citation frequency of foreign patents to calculate their value. See C. Gay, Christian Le Bas, P. Patel and Karim Touach, "The Determinants of Patent Citations: An Empirical Analysis of French and British Patents in the US," *Econ. Innov. New Techn.* 14 (2005): 339–50.

18. Kotabe, "Foreign Patents," 1335.
19. Cantwell, "Technological Innovation," 23.
20. For German imitating activities see Ralf Richter and Jochen Streb, "Catching-Up and Falling Behind: Knowledge Spillover from American to German Machine Tool Makers," *Journal of Economic History* 71 (2011): 1006–31.
21. Jörg Baten and Kirsten Jäger, "Foreign Patenting in Germany and Its Determinants: A Study on 35 Countries, 1820–1914," unpublished paper (2010).
22. See, for example, Johann Peter Murmann, *Knowledge and Competitive Advantage: The Coevolution of Firms, Technology, and National Institutions* (Cambridge, 2003), 50–62.
23. The rankings do not change significantly if we consider foreign patents per capita instead of the absolute number of foreign patents.
24. Jörg Baten and Kirsten Jaeger, "On the Persistence of Human Capital and Patent Effects around 1900 on Per Capita Income Levels in the 1960s," *Brussels Economic Review* 52 (2009): 289–304, 300.
25. Cantwell, "Technological Innovation," 16.
26. Petra Moser, "Do Patents Weaken the Localization of Innovations? Evidence from World's Fairs 1851–1951," *Journal of Economic History* 71 (2011): 363–382.
27. Streb, Baten and Yin, "Knowledge Spillover."
28. See, for example, Bjørn Asheim and Arne Isaksen, "Regional Innovations Systems: The Integration of Local 'Sticky' Knowledge and Global 'Ubiquitous' Knowledge," *Journal of Technology Transfer* 27 (2002): 77–86; Aners Malmberg and Peter Maskell, "The Elusive Concept of Localization Economics: Towards a Knowledge-based Theory of Spatial Clustering," *Environment and Planning* A (2002): 429–49.
29. Harald Degner, "Schumpeterian German Firms before and after World War I: The Innovative Few and the Non-innovative Many," *Zeitschrift für Unternehmensgeschichte* 54 (2009): 50–72, 62. See also Harald Degner, "Do Technological Booms Matter? New Evidence on the Relationship between Firm Size and Innovativeness," *Cliometrica* 5 (2011): 121–44.
30. The authors can provide on request the rankings of firms for the other foreign countries listed in Figures 1.4 and 1.5.
31. Cantwell, "Technological Innovation," 18 f, comes to a similar conclusion.
32. Cantwell, "Technological Innovation," 19 f, and Patel and Pavitt, "Technological Accumulation," 767.
33. Raffaele Paci, Antonio Sassu and Stefano Usa, "International Patenting and National Technological Specialization," *Technovation* 17 (1997): 25–38, 34.
34. In our period under observation, the Basque region concentrated on ore trade while the Catalan economy was engaged mainly in the textile industry. See Joseph Harrison, "Heavy Industry, the State, and Economic Development in the Basque Region, 1876–1936," in *The Economic Development of Spain since 1870,* ed. Pablo Martín-Aceña and James Simpson (Aldershot, 1995), 333–49.
35. Baten and Jaeger, "Foreign Patenting."
36. In Norway, silver, copper, sulphur, iron and nickel were mined. See Olav Wicken, "The Layers of National Innovation Systems: The Historical Evolution of a National Innovation System in Norway," in *Innovation, Path*

Dependency, and Policy: The Norwegian Case, ed. Jan Fagerberg, David C. Mowery and Bart Verspagen (Oxford, 2009), 33–60, 45 f.

37. Spain had rich reserves of iron, lead, sulphur, copper and mercury. See Charles Harvey and Peter Taylor, "Mineral Wealth and Economic Development: Foreign Direct Investment in Spain, 1851–1913," *Economic History Review* 40 (1987): 185–207.
38. The main European coalfields are listed in Peter Scott, "Path Dependence, Fragmented Property Rights and the Slow Diffusion of High Throughput Technologies in Inter-war British Coal Mining," *Business History* 48 (2006): 20–42, 23.
39. Kevin O'Rourke, "Property Rights, Politics and Innovation: Creamery Diffusion in Pre-1914 Ireland," *European Review of Economic History* 11 (2007): 395–417.
40. Richard Hawkins, "Is Canada Really All That Bad at Innovation? A Tale of Two Industries," *International Productivity Monitor* 18 (2009): 72–79, 73.
41. Streb, Baten and Yin, "Knowledge Spillover," 358.
42. The reader might wonder why the United States displayed technological strengths only in textiles and mass-consumption technologies with regard to clothes and shoes. This is not a sign of technological weakness but, rather, the result of the method used. Because of their outstanding German patenting activities, the United States set the standard of comparison for our RTA analysis, which means that the share of this country's patents of a particular technological class among all its German patents (the nominator of equation 1) cannot differ much from this technological class's share in all German patents granted to patentees in all observed foreign countries (the denominator in equation 1). Hence, the American RTAs hardly deviate from one and, consequently, do not often show up in Table A1 in the Appendix.

2 Why Did Multinationals Patent in Spain?

Several Historical Inquiries*

Patricio Sáiz and David Pretel

INTRODUCTION

To fully understand the processes of technology transfer in the twentieth century, we would probably have to begin by scrutinizing them throughout the second half of the nineteenth century, especially if we would like to consider the topic from a global business history perspective. Multinational corporations initiated expansion efforts, which implied shifts of technology and human capital from one nation to another, from at least 1870 onward, just when the political and entrepreneurial interests related to patent protection also started to become global issues. The international meetings and agreements in the 1870s and 1880s that led to the International Union for the Protection of Industrial Property, the ancestor of the current World Intellectual Property Organization (WIPO), demonstrated the increasing concern and influence of corporations and networks of agents employed by the former in the ongoing process of securing transnational rights to safeguard new technologies.[1] Recent research on the role of patent and trademark agents in lobbying both national laws and international treaties corroborates the idea that in the late nineteenth century and the first decades of the twentieth century, the companies that used their legal services urgently needed protection for pressing new business: that of technological globalization.[2]

On the one hand, governments from pioneer and early follower countries were progressively influenced by industrial firms and economic groups politically well-connected and increasingly interested in obtaining support for the conquest of new external markets and demanding protection in domestic ones. On the other hand, the rulers and entrepreneurs of latecomer and backward economies were also attentive to and fascinated by new machines and innovations that would lead toward industrialization and sustained economic growth. In these circumstances, the progressive commercial protectionism that colored the final decades of the nineteenth century and the years leading up to World War I did not hold technology transfers back; on the contrary, it boosted foreign investments, international expansion, and industrial growth among corporations, which began to found factories and joint ventures in third countries, as well as exchanges of scientific and informal knowledge, technical innovations, and human capital. That is what we now call the first globalization process, a transformation in which firms and "capitalists" undoubtedly were the main actors.

From 1883 to 1884, when the first twelve countries signed the Paris Convention for the Protection of Industrial Property, to the beginning of World War II in 1939, scores of nations signed the patent and trademark agreements, among them all the most industrialized and developed countries in the Western world and their followers.[3] Spain was one of the original founding members of the Union. Thus, it compromised by granting foreign-resident patentees the same treatment as domestic ones, something that, in practice, had been occurring since the beginning of the system in 1820–1826. The Spanish patent law of 1878 guaranteed two years of priority rights to foreign patents (but limiting them to a ten-year rather than a twenty-year extension); this policy was standardized after the signing of the 1883 agreement, which demanded only six months of priority rights (one year from 1900 on), and after the more modern law was passed in 1902.[4] While Spanish legal institutions in charge of patent protection apparently adjusted to international standards, providing protection for foreign inventors and especially firms and corporations starting to extend their patent rights throughout Europe, the Spanish legal system was also designed initially to encourage "innovation activity" in addition to "invention activity." The latter was not the most relevant issue for a country distinguished by extreme industrial, scientific, and technical underdevelopment during most of the nineteenth and well into the twentieth century. The Spanish government was eager for industrialization and economic growth; promoting foreign technology transfers and imitation was the quickest path to innovation.

Thus, the Spanish patent system was conceived in a rather hybrid manner both to ensure a basic normative framework for attracting foreign inventors and innovators hoping to extend their rights to Spain and to limit that protection if it did not turn into actual innovation and economic growth within national borders. This was implemented via two major means that operated simultaneously: regulating patents of introduction and establishing compulsory working clauses. The former provided ways to protect foreign third-person technologies without their authorization in order to implement them locally, providing they were not already established in Spain. The latter required nationals and foreigners to put into practice the inventions granted by any patent (in one, two, or three years depending on the law)[5] within national territory or otherwise declare an expiration date, thereby making the corresponding technical knowledge public and of free use. Both strategies remained in force until Spain joined the European Union in 1986. If one factors in Spain's traditional judiciary weakness in prosecuting fraud against industrial property, which current international reports on intellectual piracy suggest is still a pressing problem,[6] it seems that the Spanish patent system was rather feeble until recent times.

Commercial policy was the other means of promoting industrialization, first by opening the market to direct technology imports from abroad—the principal path of technical advancement for many industries in nineteenth-century Spain—and second by the protectionist swing that began in 1877 and slowly drove the economy toward imports substitution. These latter measures triggered some changes in the "National Innovation System," which lasted from 1880 to 1939 and allowed for the acquisition of technological capabilities and sowed the first seeds of domestic scientific and inventive activity,[7] but the main sources of innovation lay abroad. These sources spurred innovation in several ways: first, direct technological imports were still possible and frequent in some sectors that required complex machinery and equipment (electricity, the chemical industry, etc.);[8] second, domestic entrepreneurs and firms in sectors favored by protectionism (textile, mechanics, metal works, etc.), parties that likely did not care much about promoting inventive activity but needed proven techniques from abroad, could use "patents of introduction" to copy and bring in knowledge and/or technicians to build the machines; third, domestic entrepreneurs and firms could also negotiate with foreign companies that patented in Spain by purchasing all the corresponding rights within the country, acquiring a work license, or attempting a joint venture. Finally, international protectionism had another significant effect: the growth and expansion of corporations that began businesses and opened factories in other countries, as was the case in Spain.[9] Alone or in joint ventures with domestic capital, companies invested abroad and transferred technologies and knowledge.

This chapter will explore how multinationals used the Spanish patent system in the late nineteenth century and the first decades of the twentieth. The discussion will focus on the origins and evolution of corporate patenting in Spain, the effects of compulsory working clauses, the management of assignments, the various strategies followed by the firms, and the effects of patents on technology transfers in the Spanish economy. To investigate these areas, we will use a database of 150,000 patents registered in Spain between 1820 and 1939 that our research group has built during the last ten years through the direct reading of the original documentation (administration files and technical reports) for every patent in the Archive of the Spanish Patents and Trademarks Office (OEPM) in the framework of one of the major recent research projects on Spanish economic history.[10]

THE EVOLUTION OF CORPORATE PATENTING IN SPAIN (1820–1939)

During the nineteenth century and the first decades of the twentieth, patent systems everywhere went through a progressive shift from being tools for independent inventors, skilled artisans, small-scale industrialists, and entrepreneurs themselves to being the "targets" of firms and corporations. By the second half of the twentieth century, the vast majority of patents and new technologies protected in Western economies were already owned by firms that then employed inventors and scientists in their research departments and simply limited their recognition by naming the authors in the patent procedures. The period between 1880 and 1939 was crucial in reversing patent owning, especially in countries such as the United States, Germany, the United Kingdom, and France.[11] Lagging economies eventually followed the same pattern as far as the first wave of technological globalization spread and corporations from the North Atlantic extended their influence. That was the case of Spain, where firms progressively increased their presence after 1875–1880, coinciding with the restoration of the monarchy and the normalization of the sociopolitical and economic situation.[12] This larger presence took hold particularly during the final years of the nineteenth century and the 1920s, a decade of exacerbated protectionism and heavy industrialization under Primo de Rivera's dictatorship and a time during which many foreign corporations arrived in Spain.

Figure 2.1 illustrates this development by highlighting the long-term evolution of patents applied for by firms and independents in Spain. Although numerous previous studies have explored the general trends of the Spanish patent system,[13] it is necessary to remember the repercussions of the financial crisis of 1864 and the revolutionary events of 1868, which led to Queen Isabel II's exile, and the aforementioned economic changes brought about by the Restoration after 1876. We must give special consideration to the patent law of 1878, which introduced a system of progressive annual quotas that,

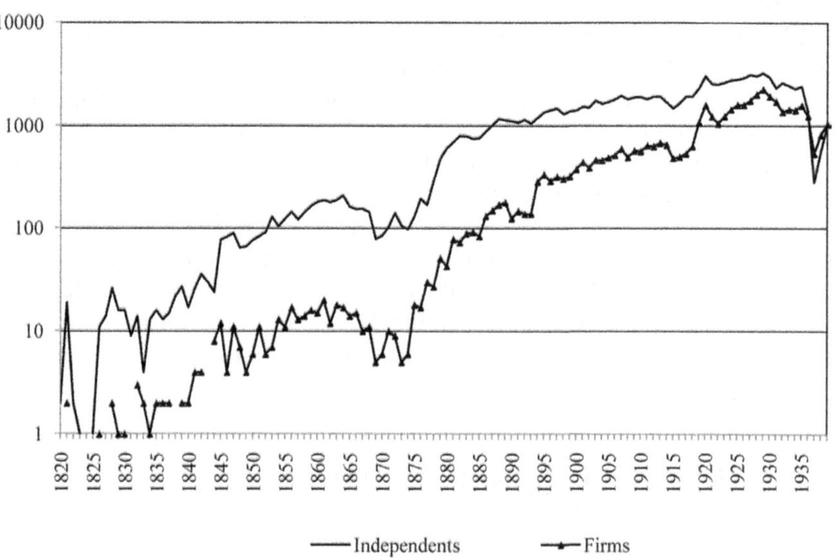

Figure 2.1 Independent and corporate patents. Spain, 1820–1939

Source: Archivo Histórico Nacional y Gaceta de Madrid for privileges from 1820 to 1826. Between 1826 and 1939: Original documents of patents at the Oficina Española de Patentes y Marcas.

Independents: patents applied by one or more individuals. *Firms*: patents applied by firms alone or with individuals.

in practice, would spark an enormous savings in patent rights, considering that only the first-year fees were required to make it effective. Likewise, the 1883 international agreement on industrial property is another significant point as it reinforced protection for foreign patents. From that time on, there was a continuous increase in applications and grants, both domestic and even more so foreign, in response to legal and socioeconomic improvements. Foreign patent activity also intensified in response to the general increase of inventions and patents in the world, as statistical evidence and the lineal regressions in another of our analyses confirm.[14] Patent growth slowed at the end of the 1920s due in part to the decline of the international economic panorama after the crisis of 1929 and the 1930s recession, which influenced foreign patentees, but mostly because of a sharp deterioration in domestic political and social conditions in Spain; this tumult led to Franco's military coup and to the Spanish Civil War (1936–1939), which brought with it a rapid economic collapse and continued decreases in patent series.

This very general trend holds for all the patent distributions examined, as Figure 2.1 demonstrates for independents and firms. Apart from this consistent evolution, however, the processes through which corporations caught up in the long run are particularly noteworthy. In Spain, independent patentees stood out over the entire period studied. Many of them were industrialists, manufacturers, entrepreneurs, traders, and other parties closely related to production processes and enterprises,[15] but they—not the firms—were the true owners of technologies, which made a remarkable difference. Independents completely dominated the period before 1880, boasting an average of 90.1% of the patents; the remaining 9.9% were applied for by firms, most of which were small family companies with limited partners, and only a few were incorporated.[16] Nevertheless, the proportion of patents accounted for by independents decreased consistently from 1880 on, whereas the shares of firms and corporations grew, especially from 1890 to World War I and in the 1920s, as Table 2.1 demonstrates. From 1890 to 1930, the Spanish economy improved and expanded under intense protectionism and governmental support for "national" industrial production, which signified both

Table 2.1 Percentages of independent and corporate patents. Spain, 1880–1939

	Independents %	Firms %	Patents
1880–1889	88.8	11.2	9,681
1890–1899	83.9	16.1	14,913
1900–1909	78.0	22.0	21,811
1910–1919	74.4	25.6	24,965
1920–1929	64.5	35.5	44,338
1930–1939	58.3	41.7	31,284

Source: See Figure 2.1

domestic and foreign firms installing factories within national territory. Spain benefitted from World War I for several reasons: first, the increase in the values of direct industrial and services exports during the conflict yielded enormous profits for firms and entrepreneurs; second, the import-substitution phenomenon in times of war produced advantages; and finally, Spain's neutrality attracted capital, bank branches, firms, and skilled human capital from abroad. These foreign investments, together with national accumulated capital, would play a significant economic role in the industrial expansion of the 1920s (especially in heavy industry), the decade in which corporate patents rapidly increased.

There were two distinct periods in the development of corporate patenting in Spain, both in the propensity to register and in the companies' countries of residence. The first period was from 1820 to 1880, when, as previously discussed, independents represented the prevailing force and there were only a few firms using the patent system. As Figure 2.2 shows, the majority of these firms were Spanish or operated from Spain; hardly any hailed from abroad. But in the second period, from 1880 to 1939, when the number of entrepreneurial patents increased constantly, that tendency reversed course as foreign companies located outside of Spain quickened their collective rhythm of registering new technologies in the Spanish market to a greater extent than resident firms did. Among the latter were also a few Spanish subsidiaries of foreign corporations that understood the market in which they were operating perfectly but aligned themselves with their parent companies and employed complementary strategies of patenting. Although

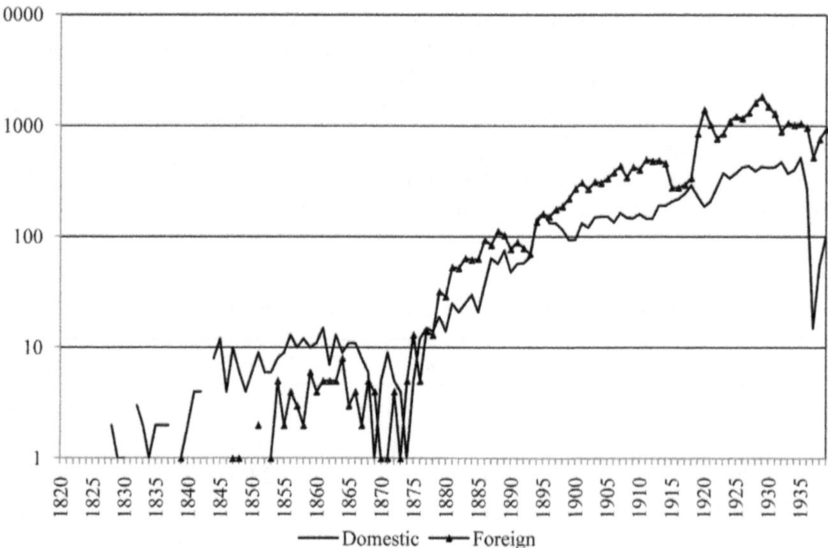

Figure 2.2 Corporate patents by firms' residence. Spain, 1820–1939

Source: See Figure 2.1

we will offer some data on this phenomenon in the conclusion, we will here analyze the corporations with foreign addresses (with or without Spanish subsidiaries) that began compulsive patenting in Spain in the late nineteenth century and the first half of the twentieth century in order to assess their technology transfer-related management strategies and the economic consequences for backward countries.

As Figure 2.2 shows, foreign companies began to patent in Spain during the 1880s not only in response to significant institutional changes, such as the 1878 law and the international agreements of 1883, but also due to the progressive tendency to extend patent rights to other countries. The effects of the international crisis that marked the end of the nineteenth century and the consequences of World War I are clear. The former affected both domestic and foreign companies, but the war impacted the entrepreneurial activities of warring nations. Despite these circumstances, foreign companies intensely ramped up their application efforts from the beginning of the twentieth century up until World War I and beyond, into the 1920s, always markedly outnumbering domestic companies. The following sections will examine the organization and repercussions of this "patent colonization" initiative.

FOREIGN CORPORATIONS IN THE SPANISH PATENT SYSTEM

Now that we have defined two distinct quantitative and qualitative periods, the next step is to delve into where foreign corporate patents came from in each of these periods and what their long-term evolutionary paths were. Before 1880, when Spanish resident firms were the major players, there were only 162 patents applied for by nonresident companies. As Table 2.2 indicates, most of them were French (72.2%), which unmistakably points to a scarcely integrated patent system in which market knowledge, human capital mobility, and direct investments in the Spanish economy drove the interest in taking out patents. In this context, geographic proximity plays another key role and helps explain the considerable leadership of French firms and French independent businessmen. Not only had Spanish patent legislation been totally shaped by the French revolutionary Patent Law of 1791, but many entrepreneurs, capitalists, technicians, and firms had also invested extensively in the first Spanish industrialization from 1845 to 1865; some had even established themselves in Spain and become legal residents. A great quantity of new European technologies (French or not) had poured into the country through their hands and brains, principally in railways, mining, and several other sectors. As we have already demonstrated in other works, 75% of the patents applied for by foreign residents in Spain before 1878 went to French patentees.[17] Thus, it is not surprising that firms residing in France were also the main source of corporate patents from abroad. Coming chiefly from Paris and its surroundings, most of the patents went to family companies with limited partners, although the first incorporated firms can

Table 2.2 Foreign corporate patents by firms' country of residence. Spain, 1820–1939

	1820–1939%	1820–1879%	1880–1899%	1900–1919%	1920–1939%
Germany	**29.7**	11.1	26.9	29.9	30.0
France	**19.7**	72.2	34.6	22.0	17.1
USA	**14.5**	1.2	9.4	13.7	15.4
UK	**13.7**	6.2	11.1	14.9	13.5
Switzerland	**6.6**	3.1	4.3	4.9	7.4
Netherlands	**3.8**	0.0	0.4	0.9	5.1
Italy	**3.3**	3.1	2.4	3.3	3.5
Belgium	**2.4**	1.2	6.5	3.2	1.7
Sweden	**1.6**	0.0	0.5	1.4	1.7
Austria	**1.0**	0.0	1.6	1.7	0.7
Norway	**0.6**	0.0	0.2	1.0	0.6
Hungary	**0.5**	0.0	0.2	0.7	0.5
Czech Republic	**0.5**	0.0	0.0	0.2	0.7
Denmark	**0.4**	0.0	0.3	0.4	0.3
Luxembourg	**0.3**	0.0	0.2	0.1	0.3
Poland	**0.2**	0.6	0.7	0.3	0.2
Canada	**0.2**	0.0	0.0	0.3	0.2
Rest	**1.0**	1.2	0.8	1.0	1.0
Total Patents	**32,264**	**162**	**2,061**	**7,761**	**22,280**

Source: See Figure 2.1

also be found, especially in mining, basic metals, mechanical construction, machinery, gas and lighting, and similar areas.[18]

Far behind France, the other countries with corporate patents before 1880 were Germany (11.1%), whose corporations were beginning their international expansion throughout Europe, especially after the unification in 1870, the United Kingdom (6.2%), Switzerland, Italy (3.1% each), Belgium, and the United States (1.2% each). Together, these figures illuminate a narrow international scope of patents and technologies before the 1870s–1880s. Essentially, technology transfers occurred through human capital shifts and direct investments abroad, traversing a world where knowledge was embedded in the skills of workers and technicians and where scientific education was universally scarce, especially in Spain.[19] Given this backdrop, the transmission of that "useful and reliable knowledge," as J. Mokyr has called it,[20] was directly driven by people who maintained some kind of economic interest in the country and could use the domestic patent system, depending on its strengths or weaknesses, in defending their businesses in court. This notion retained its currency in the twentieth century, when corporations captured and exploited the "international patent system" on their way to technological globalization.

Still, a closer look at Table 2.2 clearly reveals the tremendous differences in the international scene from the 1880s onward. In the first period analyzed, firms from only a few key countries were represented, the main one being France, but in just the last twenty years of the nineteenth century, that tendency had begun to change. The reasons for this change were generally twofold: first, a radical decrease in the French firms' proportion of patents compared to those granted to corporations from Germany, the United States, the United Kingdom, Belgium, or Switzerland, which began to extend their "tentacles of progress," in the words of David Headrick;[21] second, the diversification among the nations from which firms applied for patents in Spain also pushed against the traditional tendency.[22] This means that companies located in Sweden, Austria and Hungary, the Netherlands, Norway, Denmark, Luxembourg, Poland, and Canada (among many others in the "Rest" group in Table 2.2, with a meager proportion of grants) also began to patent lightly in the Spanish market after 1880. These two general trends remained during the first third of the twentieth century. German corporations became leaders, reaching around 30% of corporate patents in the entire period from 1900 to 1939, while France continuously fell from 34.6% between 1880 and 1889 to 17.1% in the 1920s and 1930s. Just as Germany did, the United States constantly increased its presence in Spain, rising to 15.4% of corporate patents. The United Kingdom also grew to 15% (1900–1919) but then fell to 13.5% in the final period examined, and Belgium, whose firms patented in Spain at a rate of 6.5% in the late nineteenth century, later decreased to a mere 1.7%. The case of Swiss and Dutch firms is very interesting; they increased their patents to surpass the Italians between 1920 and 1939 (Switzerland 7.4%, the Netherlands 5.1%, and Italy 3.5%). The rest of the countries registered just over 1% of patents each, but the general tendency still demonstrates how corporations had a similar international vocation everywhere.

If we now focus on Table 2.3, which shows firms and capital invested in Spain by country of origin up until World War I, we can easily observe how the investment distribution matches the corporate patents, as industrial and intellectual property rights are no more than other investments abroad. Despite the facts that the nations represented are virtually the same in both tables (including the "Rest" group) and that France appears as the leading foreign investor, there are also some interesting differences. According to T. Tortella, France and the United Kingdom represented 68% of all firms and 75% of all capital investments, which fit well with the proportion of corporate patents before 1880 (taking into account that France was the dominant force) but not afterward, when German patents increased between 1880 and 1914. However, German real investments in Spain were apparently limited compared with French and British ones, as were those of the Swiss, Italian, and especially Anglo-American firms—organizations

Table 2.3 Foreign corporations in Spain and capital investments, 1780–1914

	Firms (1780–1914)		Capital (1851–1914)	
	N°	%	Thousands Euros	%
France	234	42.3	6,204.43	59.11
UK*	140	25.3	1,728.93	16.47
Germany	63	11.4	366.74	3.49
Belgium	45	8.1	656.91	6.26
Switzerland	16	2.9	28.49	0.27
Italy	14	2.5	10.10	0.10
USA	7	1.3	3.19	0.03
Rest**	34	6.1	1,497.36	14.27
TOTAL	**553**	**100.0**	**10,496.14**	**100.0**

Source: Teresa Tortella, *A Guide to Sources of Information on Foreign Investment in Spain, 1780–1914* (Amsterdam, 2000), Tables 1 and 5, pp. xi and xix.

Note: *In the United Kingdom figures, six Irish enterprises are included. ***Rest* includes firms from the Netherlands, Canada, Norway, Sweden, Argentina, Austria (including Hungary) Czechoslovakia, Denmark, Mexico, and Portugal.

from countries with increasing patent applications in Spain in the first two decades of the twentieth century.

All of this outlines some well-known fields in business and technological history but also raises new questions. Analyzing the Spanish patent system first shows that, before the 1880s, the international mobility of firms' capital, technology, and patents was still rather limited, mainly related to those with direct investments in the Spanish economy or with interests around it. That led directly to France, whose firms' investments in Spain—patents included—reached a wide variety of sectors. To a lesser extent, companies from the United Kingdom, Germany, Switzerland, and Italy were also represented. However, after 1880, German corporations began systematically extending their patent rights throughout Europe and America,[23] as did companies from the United States and several other countries—newcomers to technological globalization—while the United Kingdom reached its "technological climacteric." This does not necessarily mean an increase in direct capital investments from Germany or the United States in the Spanish economy, as shown in Table 2.3.

What is certain is that inventions from Germany and the United States made entries en masse into almost all the patent systems of the North Atlantic economies, opening the door to what we have long called the "second industrial revolution." This technological and entrepreneurial competition, in the framework of a scientific, economic, and commercial struggle, resides within different patent strategies of corporations and multinationals from the most significant economies before World War I. But how can we interpret this data in light of the technological "backwardness" of Spain and other lagging nations? What explains the increase in total corporate patenting after 1880, especially from certain countries such as Germany, the United States, the United Kingdom, Switzerland, and the Netherlands? Does it mean that the process of technology transfer to Spain also grew in the same proportion or that it came first from France and then mostly from others? Were the frontiers of geographic proximity really changed, favoring technology transfer and technological globalization? These are not easy questions to answer without a detailed analysis of the administrative life of patents or a reservoir of case studies that obviously transcends the scope of this chapter. Nevertheless, we can offer some clues to address the research agenda.

THE VALUE OF MULTINATIONAL PATENTS

Thanks to the large body of work produced over the last decade at the Archive of the Spanish Patent Office, we have been able to analyze the documentation of obligatory patent implementation, an interesting administrative requisite in Spain. Within a one- to three-year time frame,[24] firms were required to demonstrate that the patented object was being implemented within national territory; this requirement was enforced to varying degrees depending on the period, always under penalty of expiration of the monopoly and, from 1924 on, also of a compulsory license to whoever applied.[25] Once the implementation requirements were met, another significant point was the duration of the patent, especially if we suppose that greater length and cost were consequences of the reasonable expectations of profit that could be derived from the monopoly.[26] We obtained this information from the analysis of the initial and renovation fees met by firms to maintain exclusive rights, which were paid in advance between 1826 and 1878 after choosing an expiration date (5, 10 or 15 years) and then annually from 1878 onwards for up to twenty years.[27]

As Table 2.4 clearly demonstrates, the great majority of corporate patents granted to foreign firms were never implemented, which means that an average of 77% expired within a maximum of three years and that the corresponding technological information entered the public domain.[28] Moreover, if we examine the fees paid out for corporate patents for which implementation was legally proven, roughly 14% lasted more than five years. Therefore, around 86% of foreign corporate patents were left unexploited and in the public domain in five or six years in Spain during the period studied. This suggests that firms and corporations internationally extended their patent rights as a common protection strategy, especially after 1880, regardless of the specific conditions of the particular patent system or country, assuming that it fulfilled the minimum legal guarantees for registration and that its economic or technical position might offer some business opportunities. Yet, only on very few occasions did patents actually turn into significant

Table 2.4 Corporate patents from different countries by implementation and duration percentages. Spain, 1820–1939

	Implemented %	Non-implemented %	Implemented and Duration >5 y.%	Corporate Patents*
Germany	20.8	79.2	12.7	8,848
France	25.5	74.5	16.1	5,892
USA	22.0	78.0	13.6	4,242
UK	29.0	71.0	19.3	4,039
Switzerland	16.5	83.5	11.4	1,953
Netherlands	11.7	88.3	7.7	1,140
Italy	23.0	77.0	13.4	1,005
Belgium	31.4	68.6	12.4	725

Source: See Figure 2.1

Note: *Calculations were made based on 92.1% of patents analyzed. It is not possible to establish whether or not the remainder were implemented.

business; the majority expired within a short period of time. The networks of industrial and intellectual property agents, most of them lawyers and engineers, were increasingly responsible for the tasks of right extensions, payments, translations, and adaptations of technical descriptions to each patent system and to distinct administrative requirements.[29] Some previous research has clearly delineated the extent to which the descriptions of inventions changed in different patent systems and how firms and their agents toyed with administrative requirements to both achieve legal protection on the one hand and reveal the minimum key technical information of novel inventions on the other; this strategy is evident in Rudolf Diesel's Anglo-American, German, French, British, and Spanish patents.[30]

What is also significant in analyzing Table 2.4 is how the percentage of corporate patents implemented varied depending on the country focused on. Although corporations from Germany and the United States patented more regularly in Spain after 1880, Belgium, the United Kingdom, and France—precisely the first three countries in total investments shown in Table 2.3—were the ones with more patent "effectiveness" in terms of compulsory implementation (31.4%, 29%, and 25.5%, respectively). On the contrary, the United States, Germany, and especially Switzerland and the Netherlands were well below these percentages (from 22% among US corporations to a low 11.7% in the case of the Netherlands). More or less the same holds in terms of patent duration. The United Kingdom and France had higher rates of active patents after five years (19.3% and 16.1%, respectively) than firms from any other country represented in Table 2.4 did; the United States, Germany, and Belgium represented between 12% and 13%, while Switzerland and the Netherlands came in with even lower percentage points. Thus, although the differences do not seem entirely radical, they are remarkable enough to show that, even after 1880, during the second industrial revolution and the first technological globalization, geographic proximity and direct investments in Spain were still important in effectively extending patents and transferring technologies.

Another compelling means of measuring the real impact of a patent is by looking at the number of assignments and licenses registered during its life, no matter how short or long its duration was, as this number essentially represents an indirect proxy of both the technical quality of the invention protected and the business interest for innovation. Moreover, the corresponding legal transmissions could represent the real object for some foreign firms patenting in Spain from abroad, insofar as they were not really interested in making actual investments in the Spanish economy but rather needed national partners to maintain monopolies and get around compulsory implementation requirements. Thus, assignments and licenses could also teach us much about corporations' international strategies on technology transfer and its real consequences.

Table 2.5 demonstrates once again the apparent scarcity of business surrounding foreign corporate patents. Only a small percentage of them, around 6%, were officially assigned or licensed during the entire period studied, although the differences among countries are rather intriguing. Companies from the United States, the Netherlands, the United Kingdom, and even Germany had higher licensing rates than those from Belgium, Switzerland, Italy, and France. Comparing these ratios with those of implementation in Table 2.4 uncovers certain inverse relationships; a high level of implementation corresponds to a low level of assignments and licenses, an association that Belgium and the Netherlands exhibit in the extreme. This general tendency can also be observed in the US, German, French, and Italian examples, although not in those of the United Kingdom or Switzerland,

Table 2.5 Corporate patents from different countries by percentage of assignments and licenses. Spain, 1820–1939

	Assignments and Licenses %	Corporate Patents
Germany	6.2	9,585
France	5.4	6,354
USA	7.7	4,691
UK	7.0	4,406
Switzerland	3.9	2,120
Netherlands	7.6	1,226
Italy	4.9	1,079
Belgium	2.5	765

Source: See Figure 2.1

with high ratios of implemented patents and assignments corresponding to the former and low ones to the latter. Yet it seems reasonable to assume that firms from countries with direct investments and worthy patents in practice might have had less interest in assigning or licensing a monopoly that gave them technological advantages in competition. On the contrary, if patenting served as an international impetus from certain technical leaders, fewer implemented patents and more assignments or licenses would point to more interest in the commercialization of property rights than in applying the new innovations. These were two clearly divergent business strategies that paved two distinct paths of technology transfer. Once again, case studies are the only way to delve into and verify these processes.

CONCLUSIONS

Why did foreign corporations extend their patent rights to Spain and other peripheral countries after 1880? Were there really different protection strategies, and, if so, what were they? What was the real role of patents in technology transfer, and what were their consequences for backward nations? And, principally, what does it really mean to have a weak patent system? Was the Spanish one weaker than the Swiss or Dutch patent systems, which either did not exist or were abolished during certain significant periods to encourage imitation?[31]

This chapter has uncovered sufficient data for attempting to answer some of these questions and probably raising new ones. We have seen that firms' patenting in Spain was scarce before 1880 and seemed to be closely related to the existence of direct interests or investments in the country and to geographic proximity, as well. But from 1880 onward, corporate patent activity increased everywhere in an expansive initiative driven by progressive technological globalization and international market competition led by Germany, the United States, and other newcomers. This brand of patent expansion did not have a precise correlation to the levels and directions of foreign investments in Spain. Analyses of patent implementations and property assignments confirm the limited impact of the majority of those supposedly strong monopolies obtained by foreign corporations. On average, more than 75% of corporate patents were extinguished and released into public use in three years, a proportion that reached 85% when expanded to five years' time, while no more than 6% appear to have been licensed within Spain. All these percentages tended to increase if the firms based operations in countries with less direct investments in the Spanish economy.

Therefore, the huge patent expansion in the late nineteenth century seems to be part of a first global and general strategy of international corporations, especially from Germany and the United States but also France, the United Kingdom, Switzerland, and the Netherlands—countries that, regardless of whether they had clear intentions of investing, transferring, or even licensing technologies in a particular country, registered and paid for exclusive rights in potential foreign markets. With the international generalization of the annual fee payments, it was likely cheaper and easier to first extend rights everywhere and then reflect on viable businesses in subsequent years than to use time and energy in selecting countries where patenting would be crucial. Although this strategy carried with it the risk of losing patent rights and making technological information public in some countries, at least that might serve to block similar patents from competitors. Industrial property agents and their networks were vital to this process.

Nevertheless, if a corporation had any interest in a country or a technology, it had to manage that intangible asset in some way. Extended case studies are needed to see how major firms used patent strategies. Our work in progress deals with data from 100 corporations with more than thirty patents in Spain during the nineteenth century and the first half of the twentieth century. The most significant ones (with more than 500 patents) were from Germany and the Netherlands, such as *I. G. Farbenindustrie A. G.*, *Fried. Krupp A. G.* and *N. V. Philips' Gloeilampenfabrieken;* others from the United Kingdom, France, and Switzerland represented more than 300 records each, including *Vickers Ltd.*, *Schneider et Compagnie,* and *Brown, Boveri et Compagnie;* there were also some from the United States (with around 150 patents each) such as the *United Shoe Machinery Company* and *Westinghouse Electric and Manufacturing Company.* The analysis currently underway will detail information on real patent strategies and technology management. Here, we will only discuss some of the general ideas and examples that typify these series of tactics that, of course, hinged on previous investments, geographic proximity, industrial sector, and the state of techniques and economy in the target country.

Table 2.6 illuminates two very different strategies followed by the selected corporations during the period analyzed. On the one hand, the Swiss *Brown Boveri et Compagnie* automatically extended patents to Spain from the central headquarters in Baden beginning in 1905 but implemented a low percentage thereof (16%) in workshops belonging to temporary partners. Only 10% of those patents managed to survive for five years. On the other hand, *Babcock & Wilcox Ltd.,* the English affiliate of the American *Babcock, Wilcox and Company,* registered approximately thirty patents between 1894 and 1918, the year in which a Spanish subsidiary was created. From that moment on, both corporations registered numerous strong patents in Madrid, with a high ratio of implementation and a very long duration. *Brown Boveri* (B&B) and *Babcock & Wilcox* (B&W) were strong multinationals insofar as they had affiliates and subsidiaries in other countries. B&B extended to Germany, France, Italy, and Norway. Its German branch also patented in Madrid after 1930, albeit to scant successes, as suggested by the implementation and time-duration percentages in Table 2.6. It seems that not having a direct ally, subsidiary, affiliate, or joint venture in Spain could have been an influence on the weak character of B&B's patents

Table 2.6 Patent activity in Spain by Brown Boveri and Babcock & Wilcox corporations, 1878–1939

Company's Name	Country	Patents: Principal Sector	Patents	Of introduction %	Implemented %	Implemented and Duration >5 y. %	Assignments & Licenses %
Brown, Boveri et Compagnie	Switzer-land	Electricity	282	1.4	16.0	10.3	0.4
Brown Boveri & Cie. A. G.	Germany		28	0.0	3.6	3.6	0.0
Babcock & Wil-cox Ltd.	UK	Steam Boilers, Furnaces, etc.	94	22.3	66.3	46.5	54.3
Sociedad Espa-ñola de Con-strucciones Bab-cock & Wilcox	Spain		94	21.3	81.7	68.3	0.0
Deutsche Bab-cock & Wilcox Dampfkessel-Werke A. G.	Germany		1	0.0	0.0	0.0	0.0
Société Fran-çaise des Con-structions Bab-cock & Wilcox	France		1	0.0	100.0	100.0	100.0
The Babcock & Wilcox Tube Company	USA		1	0.0	0.0	0.0	0.0

Source: See Figure 2.1

and their high "mortality" rates. Thus, most of the technology patented by B&B was public information in Spain within a few years after being protected. One potentially captivating point for future investigation would be to explore how B&B managed patents and technology transfer in other countries where it operated or had affiliates, such as Germany.

On the contrary, B&W UK participated in the foundation of the *Sociedad Española de Construcciones Babcock & Wilcox* in Bilbao in 1918. With it, the company widely used and took advantage of the Spanish patent system. The Spanish section itself was created via the transfer of patents from the English company as a combined share of the initial capital.[32] After that, both firms successfully patented technologies implementing high percentages of those patents (66% in the case of the British and 82% in the case of the Spanish) and keeping approximately 46% (the former) and 68% (the latter) active after five years. Not only did these companies boast impressive success percentages, but they also made noteworthy use of "patents of introduction"—copying and transferring technologies from third parties or competitors. The strategic links between both companies were prominent. They registered exactly the same number of patents, as if they had made a pact on tactics to manage technology transfers from the British side to the Spanish subsidiary. They had an impeccable knowledge of how to use the Spanish system to tap the benefits of patents of introduction and meet the compulsory working clauses on time, issues of which the local company had a particularly strong command. Furthermore, all the assignments made by the British parent company (54% of the patents) were to the Spanish one.

As in the case of B&B, it would be critical to compare the Spanish strategy employed by the British B&W with that applied in other countries like Germany or France, where there were also affiliates or subsidiaries, as well as with that of the United States parent firm, which, as Kristine Bruland has shown, seemed to be far from the British dynamism.[33] Notwithstanding, the American B&W applied the same tactic of selling patent rights to the British company and taking a part of the shares when founded.[34] The B&W strategy in Spain implied real and durable monopolies on technology, while B&B quickly opened its technologies to the public domain. Still, evaluations of these strategies demand close attention to the sorts of inventions and innovations that were protected. Operating with steam technologies and dealing in general mechanical construction, which could be easily copied toward the middle of the second industrial revolution even in countries such as Spain (which was able to manufacture its own locomotives, for instance, in 1884) are entirely different exploits from working with complex new science-based technologies, such as electricity and electrical devices, which might not be so skillfully imitated by competitors. This is especially true in countries without strong scientific/technical education and in patent systems without existing technical exams, which we have shown could produce a lack of vital scientific information.[35]

Thus, the role of patents in technology transfer is complex. They could be a useful incentive where there were previous direct investments in the target nation, join ventures with local capital, or any other dynamic agreements between domestic and foreign interests. Likewise, patents had a greater impact if they were accompanied by human capital from the country of origin in order to facilitate the technology transfer. In such cases, patents had obvious consequences in the "backward" nations, not only expanding opportunities to access new technologies but also improving their industrial development through the externalities linked to physical investments. While patents and technology transfers could also engender technological dependence and loss of profits in favor of foreign partners, local governments accepted these risks in order to promote industrial advancement and economic growth.

Last, we must revisit the final questions set out at the beginning of these concluding remarks. Was the Spanish patent system weak? Perhaps it was, as was the entire National Innovation System, in encouraging domestic scientific or inventive activity—but that was not its principal political intention. On the contrary, it was a "hybrid" patent system that, while providing enough protection to those firms who actually transferred technology and made investments in Spain (i.e., contributed to industrial transformations), also determinedly punished patent activity not focused on actual transfers (through compulsory working clauses) or marked by a lack of interest in the country (exemplified by patents of introduction). Many other European states used similar strategies during the Industrial Revolution to facilitate technology transfers and imitations, ranging from the wide use of patents of introduction and replicas everywhere, the United Kingdom included, to the actual elimination of patent law, as was the case in the Netherlands. Anything that stimulated catch-up processes or took advantage of spillovers from innovation activity was valid. The United States itself used World War I to confiscate private German patents from chemical corporations, test and diffuse the protected technical information, and fortify American competitors.[36] Earlier, in the late nineteenth century, German machine-tool builders had made a custom of copying the US manufacturers who publicly complained about it, just as now German entrepreneurs protest against Chinese counterfeiting.[37] This time-honored tradition, as it were, has close ties with patent management. Chinese and Indian firms are supported by their respective governments in playing this "game," but the small developing countries of today cannot even sit at the table.

NOTES

* This work was supported by the Collaboration Agreement between the *Oficina Española de Patentes y Marcas* and the *Universidad Autonoma de Madrid* for Cataloguing and Studying the Historical Documentation on Patents and Trademarks (1999-2012) and by the multidisciplinary research project UAM-CEMU-2012-034.

1. The seminal work on the internationalization of patent systems is Edith T. Penrose's *The Economics of the International Patent System* (Baltimore,

1951). See also Yves Plasseraud and François Savignon, *L'Etat et l'invention: Histoire des brevets* (Paris, 1986), 73–83, and Eda Kranakis, "Patents and Power : European Patent-System Integration in the Context of Globalization," *Technology and Culture* 48 (2007): 689–728, (see 694–698).

2. See Anna Guagnini, "Patent Agents, Legal Advisers and Guglielmo Marconi's Breakthrough in Wireless TeleGraphy," *History of Technology* 24 (2002): 171–201; Gabriel Galvez-Behar, "Des médiateurs au coeur du système d'innovation: Les agents de brevets en France (1870–1914)" in *Les archives de l'invention,* ed. M. S. Corcy, C. Douyère-Demeulenaere, and L. Hilaire-Pérez, (Toulouse, 2006), 437–447; and David Pretel and Patricio Sáiz, "Patent Agents in the European Periphery: Spain (1826–1902)," *History of Technology* 31 (2011): 97–114.
3. For details of countries and join dates, see WIPO, "Industrial Property Treaties Administered by WIPO," *Industrial Property* January (1994).
4. A complete explanation of the main legal characteristics of the Spanish patent system and its evolution throughout the nineteenth and twentieth centuries can be found in Patricio Sáiz, "The Spanish Patent System (1770–1907)," *History of Technology* 24 (2002): 45–79, Section 2.
5. One year from 1826 to 1878, two from 1878 to 1902, and three years from 1902 onward.
6. See, for instance, the "2009 International Piracy Watch List" elaborated by The Congressional International Anti-Piracy Caucus of The United States Congress.
7. This was a very interesting period in Spain for science and technology. Internationally recognized inventors such as Leonardo Torres Quevedo, Isaac Peral, and Juan de la Cierva, as well as the first Spanish person to win the Nobel Prize in Science (Santiago Ramón y Cajal), carried out their work during these years. See José Manuel Sánchez Ron, *Ciencia y sociedad en España de la ilustración a la Guerra Civil* (Madrid, 1988) and *Un siglo de ciencia en España,* ed. Jose Manuel Sánchez Ron (Madrid, 1998).
8. See Concha Betrán, "La transferencia de tecnología en España en el primer tercio del siglo XX: El papel de la industria de bienes de equipo," *Revista de Historia Industrial* 15 (1999): 41–81.
9. A general view of foreign investments in Spain can be found in Teresa Tortella, *A Guide to Sources of Information on Foreign Investment in Spain, 1780–1914* (Amsterdam, 2000). See also Nuria Puig and Rafael Castro, "Patterns of International Investment in Spain, 1850–2009," *Business History Review* 83 (2009): 505–537.
10. See the acknowledgement note at the beginning. Around 70 people have been involved in this enormous and well-supported project for a decade (see http://historico.oepm.es for further details).
11. See Ian Inkster, *Science and Technology in History. An Approach to Industrial Development* (London, 1991), 160–166. Also see John Cantwell and Birgitte Andersen, "A Statistical Analysis of Corporate Technological Leadership Historically," *Economics of Innovation and New Technology* 4 (1996): 211–234, and Birgitte Andersen, *Technological Change and the Evolution of Corporate Innovation. The Structure of Patenting, 1880–1990* (Cheltenham, 2001), 28–34.
12. The Restoration brought about a political and economic period of stability characterized by a new constitution and such new economic regulations as, among others, the Public Works Law (1875), the Railways Law (1877), the Patents Law (1878), and the new Commerce Law (1885). During these decades, the industrial and agricultural production indices developed, the integration of the national market was completed, and the protectionist turn began.

13. See Sáiz, "The Spanish Patent System," or Patricio Sáiz, *Invención, patentes e innovación en la España comtemporánea* (Madrid, 1999) (available free of charge on Google Books).
14. See Edward Beatty and Patricio Saiz, "Propiedad industrial, patentes e inversión en tecnología en España y México (1820–1914)" in *México y España ¿historias económicas paralelas?* ed. R. Dobado, A. Gómez and G. Márquez, (México D. F., 2007), 425–467, particularly patenting determinants for foreigners (Table 6) and domestic parties (Table 7). "Foreign patents," calculated as a two-year cumulative sum of patents taken in France, Britain, Germany, and the United States, was a relevant variable in the regression results for foreign patenting activity in Spain, as it also was the dummy variable for the patent law of 1878.
15. See Sáiz, "The Spanish Patent System," Table 5.
16. See Sáiz, *Invención, patentes e innovación,* 163–169 for an analysis of these firms before 1880.
17. See Patricio Sáiz, "Patents, International Technology Transfer and Spanish Industrial Dependence, 1759–1878" in *Les chemins de la nouveauté: Innover, inventer au regard de l'histoire,* ed. L. Hilaire-Pérez and A. F. Garçon, (Paris, 2003), 223–245, 233, Graph 1.
18. *Société Anonyme du Cuivre Français* (OEPM, *Privilegio* n. 5310, 5312, 5374, 5410); *Société du la Tonnellerie Mécanique* (OEPM, *Privilegio* n. 5328); *Les Forges et Fonderies de Montataire S. A.* (OEPM, *Privilegio* 5547); *Société Metallurgique d'Exploitation Méthode Ponsard* (OEPM, *Privilegio* n. 4934).
19. See Santiago Riera, "Industrialization and Technical Education in Spain 1850–1914" in *Education, Technology and Industrial Performance in Europe, 1850–1939,* ed. R. Fox and A. Guagnini (Cambridge, 1993), 141–170.
20. Joel Mokyr, *The Gifts of Athena: Historical Origins of the Knowledge Economy* (Princeton, 2002).
21. Daniel R. Headrick, *The Tentacles of Progress: Technology Transfer in the Age of Imperialism, 1850–1940* (New York, 1988).
22. For a general view of the changes occurred in international patenting, see Ian Inkster, "Technology Transfer in the Great Climacteric. Machinofacture and International Patenting in World Development circa 1850–1914," *History of Technology* 21 (1999): 87–106.
23. For more on German chemical firms' patent landing in the United Kingdom in the late nineteenth century, see Ian Inkster, "Patents as Indicators of Technological Change and Innovation: An Historical Analysis of the Patent Data, 1830–1914," *Transactions of the Newcomen Society* 73 (2003): 179–208, Table 8
24. See note 5.
25. From the beginning of the protection system until 1838, and especially until 1849, there was hardly any control over patent implementation. However, a radical change introduced first by the Royal Order of the 26th of March, 1838, and reinforced then by the Royal Order of the 11th of January, 1849, precipitated an efficient control from 1849 to 1878, when notarized independent reports were required. Between 1878 and 1924, the implementation procedure was relaxed; in some cases, a report by an engineer certifying that the necessary means to produce an object existed at such-and-such a factory was sufficient, but nonetheless it still was a difficult requisite to beat. In 1924, the regulation of the 15th of January strengthened the practice clauses and required implementation under penalty, at first, of a forced compulsory license of the patent to whoever applied, and then, once the law of the 26th of July of 1929 was passed, included an expiration date in three years if nobody took the license.

26. The duration of the monopoly is used as a measure of patent value: see J. Streb, J. Baten and S. Yin, "Technological and Geographic Knowledge Spillover in the German Empire 1877–1918," *Economic History Review* 59 (2006): 347–373. The authors selected as German valuable patents all that survived at least ten years.
27. This is true except for patents of introduction, which only lasted a maximum of five years (ten years after 1929). These types of patents were still subject to the same requirements of compulsory implementation.
28. The only exception is that between 1924 and 1929, a nonimplemented patent did not expire if the patentee publicly offered a compulsory license. After 1929, however, the firm had three years to put into practice and another three years for offering compulsory license. The patent then expired and the technological information became public. See note 25.
29. See note 2.
30. Each technical description was translated and adapted to each national patent system to fulfill the basic requirements. Analyzed by an expert engineer, all the patents had a lack of relevant technical information, which was a real problem in systems without previous examination. See Ruben Amengual, *Bielas y álabes: Evolución histórica de las primeras máquinas térmicas a través de las patentes españolas, 1826–1914* (Madrid, 2008), 116–131.
31. Switzerland rejected patent laws until 1888. The Netherlands rescinded its legal structures between 1869 and 1912. Denmark also took advantage of the nonexistence of patent law to copy; see Petra Moser, "How Do Patent Laws Influence Innovation? Evidence from Nineteenth-Century World's Fair," *American Economic Review* 95, 4 (2005): 1214–1236.
32. OEPM, *Patente* n. 28, 258. This file contains the official documents by which the British B&B assigned several patents for the foundation of the Spanish affiliate.
33. See Kristine Bruland, "The Babcock & Wilcox Company: Strategic Alliance, Technology Development, and Enterprise Control, *circa* 1860–1900" in *From Family Firms to Corporate Capitalism. Essays in Business and Industrial History in Honour of Peter Mathias,* ed. K. Bruland and P. O'Brien (Oxford, 1998), 219–245.
34. Ibid., 238.
35. See note 30.
36. See Kathryn Steen, "Confiscation and the Challenge of Emulation: American Expertise and German Chemical Patents, 1914–1930," *Patents in the Past, Maison des Sciences de l'Homme,* 23 September 2006 (unpublished). See also Kathryn Steen, "Confiscated Commerce: American Importers of German Synthetic Organic Chemicals, 1914–1929," *History and Technology* 12 (1995): 261–284 and "Patents, Patriotism, and 'Skilled in the Art': USA v. The Chemical Foundation, Inc., 1923–1926," *Isis* 92 (2001): 91–122.
37. Ralf Richter and Jochen Streb, "Catching-Up and Falling Behind: Knowledge Spillover from American to German Machine Toolmakers," *Journal of Economic History* 71, 4 (2011): 1006–1031.

3 The Adoption of American Patent Management in Japan

The Case of General Electric*

Shigehiro Nishimura

INTRODUCTION

The purpose of this chapter is to clarify the evolution of corporate patent management in Japan, which is one of the institutional frameworks for international technology transfer. It has been recognized that an intellectual property rights system is essential for international technology transfer,[1] especially for countries which hope to adopt foreign technologies.[2] We should appreciate however, that the institutionalization of laws is different from their materialization. The intellectual property system of each country is substantially embodied within the corporate patent management of that country, and its mechanisms and features vary according to the manner of economic development, the adoption and outflow of technology, the extent of competition, corporate strategy, economic friction, and so on (see Figure 3.1). Here, we are able to open up an approach to a global business history through the analysis of corporate patent management.[3] In the case of Japan, the corporate patent management system was transferred as an institution for, and coincidentally with international technology transfer, by multinational enterprises (MNEs).

There are many studies previously conducted on discussing patents and patenting. Studies on economics and economic history always make use of patenting as an indicator of innovation and technological development.[4] In business administration and business history, it is common to take advantage of patenting to estimate corporate performance.[5] However, almost no light has been shed on patent management. If a patent is merely applied for and registered and in itself produces no profits for a company at all, it imposes a cost burden on the owner in the form of application costs, annual fee, and the like. In order for a company to take advantage of the patent system and make a profit it has to engage in patent management, an exercise that embraces such things as application, safekeeping, seeking redress for patent infringements and guarding against infringements, enforcement of rights, patent agreements and licensing agreements, and so on. Procedures and methods of patent management are rich sources of the truth behind developments, rather than mere patenting.

In this chapter, I focus on companies in electrical industries, especially Tokyo Electric Company and Shibaura Engineering Works, two companies

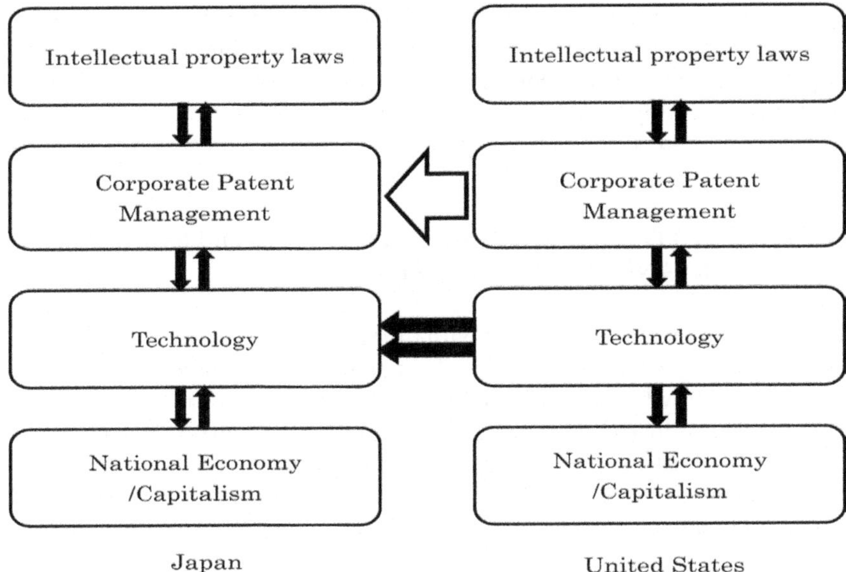

Figure 3.1 Conceptual diagram of international technology transfer

which were merged in 1939 to become Tokyo-Shibaura Electric Company, now Toshiba, to explain the evolution of patent management in Japan. These companies had begun to introduce foreign technologies and to develop their own technologies within the electrical field since the early 20th century, and had developed patent management in order to administer patent contracts with foreign companies from an early period. Moreover, it is conceivable that international patent management contracts between US and Japanese companies had a significant influence on Japanese patent management. Although international patent management and contracts seem to have passed almost unnoticed in the literature, John Cantwel and Tetsuo Tomita have drawn attention to their existence. Cantwel, making a survey of the *Official Gazette* of the United States Patent and Trademark Office, has pointed out that the nationality of inventors named in patents acquired in the United States by GE are spread across a large number of countries outside the United States, and he has argued for the existence of international R&D activities by multinational enterprises in the 1930s.[6] Tomita's research involved a study of the Japanese situation through a similar survey of Japan Patent Office materials.[7] He discovered that there are a large number of patents among those acquired by Japanese electrical enterprises, whose inventors are non-Japanese. He pointed out that this phenomenon shows that patent rights were transferred between cartel companies, and he proves that technological transfers were carried out via these cartels. Unfortunately, neither Cantwel nor Tomita tells us in their work why, or for what purpose, patent rights were transferred, nor the effects that such transfers had on the management of the companies involved.

This chapter will proceed in the following sequence. First, the features of Japanese patent management are identified from a long-term propensity of patenting and enforcement. Second, an account of the evolution of patent management by Tokyo Electric and Shibaura Engineering Works is presented with reference to technology transfer before World War II.

HISTORICAL OVERVIEW OF INTELLECTUAL PROPERTY RIGHTS (IPR) AND ITS ENFORCEMENT

The patent system in Japan began with the Statue of Monopolies of 1885. At that time foreigners could not apply for patents for their inventions.[8] It was not until 1899, when Japan joined the Paris Convention for the Protection of Industrial Property, that foreigners could file and register their patents.[9] In order to adjust the patent system to the Convention, the Government of Japan amended the Patent Law, which stipulated that non-Japanese must nominate a patent attorney who is a resident within the Japanese Empire.

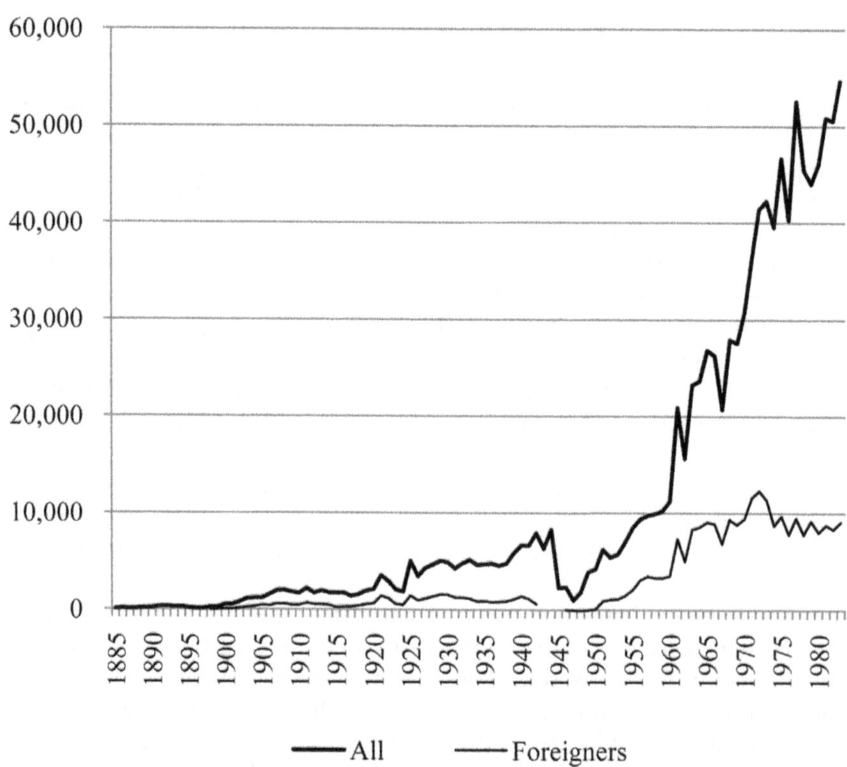

Figure 3.2 The number of patents granted in Japan, 1885–1983

Source: Japan Patent Office Data

Under the same law, provisions relating to applications claiming priority had been prepared, so that there were institutions where foreigners could file and register patents in Japan.[10] In addition to the Patent Law, the Utility Model Law had come into effect in 1905. The technological level of Japanese inventions at that time was so low that many inventors could not protect their inventions under the Patent Law, whereas those invented by foreigners were registered. In order to improve the situation and to promote the industry, the government created an institution for the protection of minor inventions.[11]

In addition to the institutions designed to protect inventions, a patent attorney system was enforced under the Regulation for the Register of Patent Representatives of 1899. While there were agents for patent application prior to that, the Regulation added a key subsystem which embodied the patent system within the whole. The number of patent agents registered by December 31, 1899, was 138, consisting almost entirely of attorneys-at-law. A certification examination was introduced from 1902 to improve and maintain the quality of

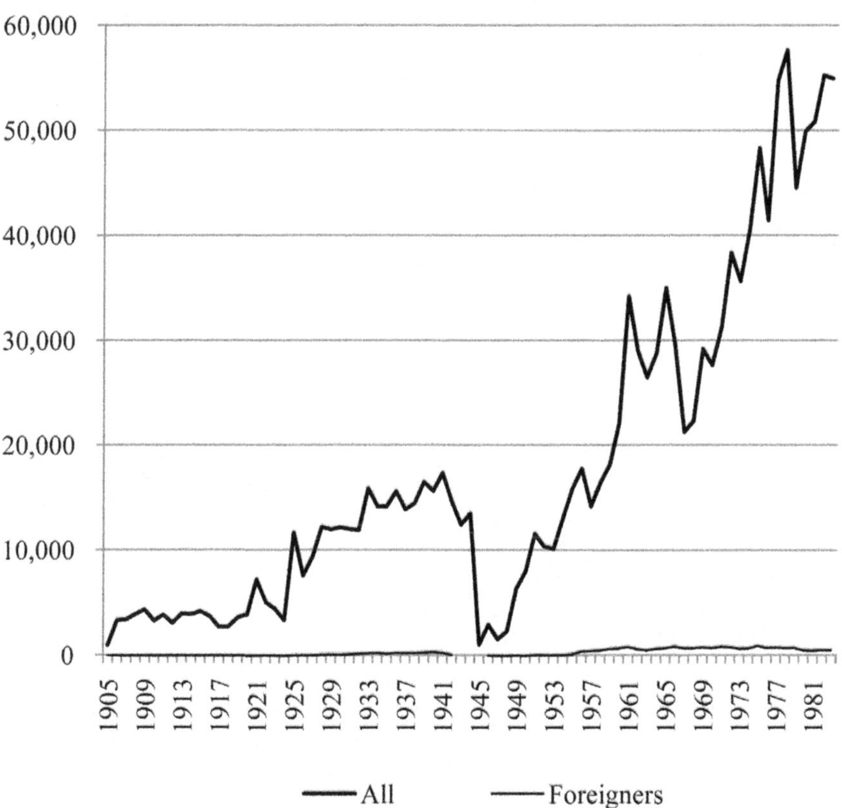

Figure 3.3 The number of utility models registered in Japan, 1905–1983
Source: Japan Patent Office Data

patent attorneys.[12] The population of patent attorneys grew from 138 in 1899 to over 1,000 by 1918, 2,666 by 1930, and peaked at 4,389 in 1937.

Let us review the historical trends within industrial property rights. Figure 3.2 shows the long-term progress of patent registration in Japan. The volume of registrations increased in the 1920s and 1930s; during the post–World War II era, it soared in the 1960s and after the 1970s. One of the features of Japanese patenting is that the proportion of foreigners' inventions has been low. While the volume of patents invented by foreigners remained around 10,000, patent registration by Japanese nationals spiraled upward, particularly after World War II, so that the ratio of foreigners was declined; the percentage of foreigners in the 1960s was about 35%, falling to about 20% in the 1970s and to 16% in the 1980s. Figure 3.3 indicates the trend within utility model registration. Prior to World War II, utility models were registered more often than patents in terms of absolute numbers, and registration soared rapidly after the war as did the number of patents. Almost all registration was by Japanese; there was hardly any registration by foreigners, whose percentage was around 1.5% in the postwar period.

Let us now shift the emphasis to the enforcement of industrial property rights in Japan. Figure 3.4 shows the trend regarding claims for patent and

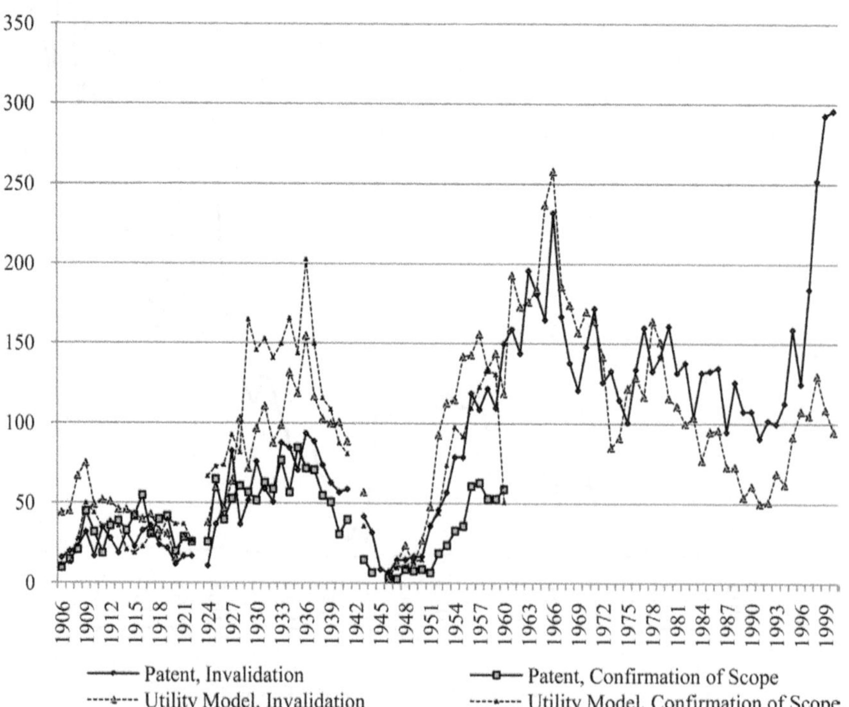

Figure 3.4 The number of demands for trials instituted in Japan, 1906–2000

Source: Japan Patent Office Data; JPO, *Kogyo Shoyuken Seido 100 nen shi* (Tokyo, 1985), Extra vol., 226–239, 256–263

utility model decisions from 1906. There were several kinds of claims submitted to the Patent Office; demands for trial for invalidation, demands for trial for confirmation of scope of right, and appeals for trials. Among these trials, demands for invalidation were used as a means to attack the validity of an opponent's patents or utility models. Demands for confirmation of scope of right were the primary device to confirm infringement by an opponent through examining whether a certain product was within the scope of the right.[13] The figures initially indicate that demands experienced peaks between the latter part of the 1920s and 1930s, and during the 1960s, the 1990s and thereafter. Demands for trials relating to patents and utility models increased from some 200 in the latter part of the 1920s and 1930s to about 400 in the 1960s and 1990s. By contrast, registrations of patents and utility models had soared from some 20,000 during the 1930s to about 60,000 in the 1960s and to over 200,000 in the 1990s and thereafter. When we compare these three peaks we find that there were many cases relating to patent rights and utility model rights respectively compared with the volume of registrations; namely, the period from the latter part of the 1920s and 1930s was the epoch when Japanese companies and individuals actively enforced their reserved rights.

EARLY STAGES OF PATENT MANAGEMENT

Tokyo Electric

Tokyo Electric Co., Ltd., was founded in 1890 as Hakunetsu-sha, Ltd., by Ichisuke Fujioka and Shoichi Miura. At that time, all incandescent lamps installed for lighting purposes were made in foreign countries and imported; there was no facility to manufacture lamps in Japan. Fujioka entered into the lamp business aiming to manufacture incandescent lamps domestically.[14] The goal of Tokyo Electric in its early days was above all to produce Japan-made lamps which could compete with imported foreign-made lamps. Fujioka and Yoshio Shinjo, an engineer who joined the company in 1899, experimented and improved the manufacturing technique. From the viewpoint that the company had to compete and to supply competitive products in the same market as foreign-made lamps, however, Tokyo Electric's level of technology was decisively low. In order to rapidly close the technology gap with foreign companies and to realize domestic production, Tokyo Electric concluded a contract with General Electric Company covering capital participation as well as a patent and technical tie-up in 1905, and began introducing foreign technology.[15] A 51% share was acquired by GE, Tokyo Electric effectively becoming a subsidiary.[16] Tokyo Electric was awarded an exclusive license for GE patents in Japan and related technological information. On the basis of this agreement, Tokyo Electric was supplied with machinery and equipment to manufacture incandescent lamps, and dispatched W. T. McChesney, an engineer, to install these, to oversee operations, and to impart lamp-manufacturing know-how.[17] Tokyo Electric's personnel were also permitted to visit GE factories and receive technical training there.[18]

Through the presentation of lamp-manufacturing machinery and equipment as well as technology transfer via personnel, the lamp production processes that had previously been carried out by hand were for the most part mechanized and dramatically improved, so that Tokyo Electric's lamp became highly competitive. The adoption of foreign technology led Tokyo Electric to a dominant position in the Japanese market.

So, we have to view the patent situation of the company from the foundation of Hakunetsu-sha to 1904.[19] There were two patents registered by the individuals concerned, although there was no patent filed in the name of the company. One of the patents, No. 2366 "Incandescent Lamp," was filed in 1894, of which the holder was Fujioka. This patent covered the "Fujioka-type Lamp," which was put on the market. This device was a lighting apparatus that had a changeover switch to candlepower in the socket rather than a reinvention of the lamp itself. Another patent, No. 6381 "Warning Device for Electric Leakage," was filed in 1902, which was jointly held by Fujioka and Shinjo. These patents indicate that prior to the contract with GE, Tokyo Electric personnel were practicing technological development activities. From a patent management viewpoint, because patents were filed and registered in individual names, Tokyo Electric did not execute any corporate patent management during this period.

Following the contract, Tokyo Electric promoted the research and development of lamps and lamp manufacturing methods concurrently with the adoption of foreign technology. In 1912 Tokyo Electric formed a laboratory within the company which enhanced its organizational capability in terms of development. As a result, from 1906 to 1918 the number of patents filed and registered by Tokyo Electric increased to 16.[20] The activation of technological development brought changes to patent management. Patents were filed in the company name as early as 1906. Although patent rights belonged to individuals in 1902, by 1906 they belonged to the corporation. The phenomenon whereby the corporation holds patents in its own name as corporate property indicates that the awareness of patents had been enhanced and that patent management was evolving within the firm.

Let us discuss the evolution of patent management operation in detail. Filing administration is one of the essential procedures which has an influence upon the legal efficiency of patents via their description. When we look at how the filing was conducted, it can be seen that, although the agent of the first patent applied for in 1906 was unknown, the agent of the second patent filed in 1912 covering Shinjo's socket invention was identified as Seiichi Kishi. Kishi was an attorney-at-law and a patent attorney running his own independent office, acting as a representative for the British and American people as well as corporate bodies including GE.[21] Besides these two, patents for which the agent is identifiable include No. 31368 and No. 33284, both filed in 1917. The representative of these two patents was Shigehachi Komatsu, who was an engineer for Tokyo Electric. From this point on, it is clear that Tokyo Electric began filing its operations internally; moreover, the section in charge of patent applications at that time might well have been the laboratory or the person handling the filing operations within the lab.

Shibaura Engineering Works

Shibaura Engineering Works was founded in 1875 by Hisashige Tanaka as the Tanaka Manufacturing Works. It was soon placed under the control of Mitsui and changed its name to Shibaura.[22] Although Shibaura was not commercially successful for some time, Keijiro Kishi, a manager in charge of electrical engineering since August 1900, took over the leadership and improved Shibaura's performance, such that it was no longer under the control of Mitsui and became a corporation in its own right.[23] Development activities, in which K. Kishi was the core member, were ongoing and the company's technological level was by no means lower than that of its competitors. Jugoro Otaguro, an executive managing director, was not satisfied with such a position, and looking at the rapid technological progress within electrical engineering in Europe and North America, Otaguro concluded that "the manufacturing technology of machines has progressed very rapidly in Japan since engineers have been sent to foreign countries and have become very talented experts. However, there is still no comparison between Japan and the West. Japanese industrial technology should be on a worldwide research footing . . . . In brief, we ought to conduct research by mixing our ideas with theirs."[24] Shibaura then concluded a contract covering capital participation and technical tie-ups with General Electric in November 1909, mediated by Takashi Masuda of Mitsui & Company. GE invested money in Shibaura, taking about 30% of the shares. The main provisions of the contract were as follows: the granting of patent licenses to Shibaura; the transfer of research and technological information to Shibaura; the training of Shibaura's employees in GE factories and the dispatch of GE professionals; offering blueprints of factory designs and the supervision of factory construction; and guidance for corporate managers.[25] These provisions were an attempt to realize Otaguro's concept of "conducting research by mixing our ideas with theirs." Here, the technological interaction by which Shibaura introduced GE's technology and thereby enhanced its own development to higher technological levels was institutionalized by this contract.

The engineers at Shibaura had been engaged in the development of technology prior to the contract. Seventeen patents originated by Shibaura were registered before 1911. Among these, nine were invented by K. Kishi. One of his patents, No. 5087 entitled "Magnetic Paddy Iron Core for Dynamos and Motors" filed in 1901, was of so high level that the invention was patented not only in Japan but also in the United States, Germany, France, and Great Britain, and was awarded a gold medal when it was displayed in the St. Louis exhibition of 1905.[26] On the other hand, filing procedures were undertaken individually by inventors, and patents were registered in the inventor's own name. Inventions created at the Works belonged to the individual inventors, and were not administered by the Works.[27]

When Shibaura reorganized the management in 1912, it appointed a person to be in charge of patent affairs exclusively. After that, all patents invented by employees were not to be filed and registered in the individuals' names but rather in the name of the company, and patent rights were not to belong to the inventors but to the company. Almost all the patents registered in the inventors' names thus far were transferred to Shibaura and came under its administration. As for the establishment of a post for patent management within an organization, Shibaura was the earliest Japanese company to do so.[28]

The establishment of the patent section was driven by K. Kishi as a management activity. The purpose of its creation was to encourage inventions by institutionalizing "a system, for example, by which the company awards prize money to persons who invent excellent devices in the Works."[29] The number of patent applications filed by Shibaura between 1912 and 1920 increased to 114. First, an increase in applications was brought about by the expansion of technological development stimulated by the inflow of technology from GE. Shibaura acquired many blueprints and much technological information by dispatching its engineers to GE plants and laboratories.[30] Those visiting the United States took the initiative in development and patenting after their return home. On the other hand, there were several patents generated in the process to adapt foreign technologies to the humidity of the Japanese climate. It is said that most proposals managed by the patent section were from the design department and manufacturing sites rather than from the laboratory.[31] Most inventions at that time were produced by developing apparatuses based on blueprints and other information supplied by GE.

Second, the increase in the number of patents was affected by patent management operations. In 1915 the persons in charge of patent affairs belonged to the development section of the engineering department, which was a research and experimental body; however, they worked in close cooperation with the design section as well as the engineering and manufacturing sites. The main duties of the patent section were the encouragement and fostering of inventions, drafting of proposals, and filing of proposals.[32] Draft management involved such operations as were required to bring the ideas generated by the engineers through the development process to patent application.[33] In addition to the inventive system regarding inventions, improved patent management focusing on filing also contributed to some extent to the increase in the number of patents.

THE INSTITUTIONALIZATION OF PATENT MANAGEMENT

International Patent Management Contract

After World War I, Japanese corporate patent management embarked on its next step. This evolution was in large part effected by the international corporate strategy of US companies. In accordance with GE's new policy, on

June 2, 1919, International General Electric Company (IGEC), GE's wholly owned subsidiary, negotiated a contract renewal with Tokyo Electric and Shibaura Engineering Works, concluding new agreements.[34] In the agreement between IGEC and the Japanese companies some clauses were markedly different from the earlier agreement in regard to patents, for now they included the international patent management contract for GE patents.[35]

This contract transferred to Japanese companies the right to apply in Japan for patented technology owned by GE; in their own names, Japanese companies could apply for and acquire a patent with themselves as the rightful claimants within Japan. In accordance with this contract, Tokyo Electric and Shibaura Engineering Works applied for, registered, and subsequently controlled GE patents in their own names.

Certain principles were laid down with regard to this proxy application. First of all, the patents Tokyo Electric and Shibaura could apply for were, as the words of the contract indicate, patents regarding technical areas under which each company was granted exclusive licenses. Second, as regards to any patent for which proxy application was made, GE would transfer to each company the right to apply for the patent at a price of one dollar per application. Third, each company would translate into Japanese any patent specification document sent from the United States and would submit it to the Japan Patent Office along with the attached deed of assignment. Lastly, as also stated in the contract provisions, the Japanese companies would bear all expenses connected with patent management: the application fee, annual fees, and so on.

A huge amount of patent specifications were in fact sent from GE to each company on a regular basis. This does not mean that the Japanese companies went ahead and submitted all the patent specifications that arrived. They had the right to choose which patents sent from GE to apply for, and it was also up to them to choose whether or not to continue paying the annual fee required for retaining a patent right. The decisions on which patents arriving from GE to apply for, and whether or not to continue paying the annual fee (i.e., whether or not to retain the patent right) were made by the patent section within each company. Only those patents deemed necessary for business purposes were applied for and registered in Japan. This kind of contract was adopted as a means to effectively maintain and exploit GE's foreign patents in each country.

Provided that Tokyo Electric and Shibaura Engineering Works had enough capability to apply, maintain, and control them, GE allowed these companies to manage its Japanese patents as proxies. GE had in fact to bolster their organizational capabilities to operate international patent management via the proxy application contract.

Capability of the Patent Department

Tokyo Electric

At that point in time when the international patent management contract was concluded, Tokyo Electric did not have any office that exclusively handled patent applications and patent management. Prior to 1918, 16 patents had been applied for in Tokyo Electric's name, but a portion of these were handled by Shigehachi Komatsu, who was in charge of applying for patents and given a desk in the laboratory. He was an engineer who had gained patent attorney qualifications and was also the first person so qualified at Tokyo Electric. This arrangement was inadequate for the job of handling GE patent applications.

It was J. R. Geary, the GE official who was responsible for the company's operations in Japan, who took the initiative on the establishment and strengthening of a patent section in Tokyo Electric.[36] Even before the contract, Geary was gradually allowing Tokyo Electric to take on some of the patent management functions. The first thing transferred to Tokyo Electric had been the management of design—which, like a patent, carries with it an intellectual property right.[37] Geary formed a patent department directly responsible to the president of Tokyo Electric in 1921.[38] This new patent department was given a place in the organization that was independent of any research facility or manufacturing department; it was a specialized management section that was to concentrate on patent management for the company as a whole. When the patent department was established, its first head was Komatsu. By appointing as head of the patent department the person who had until then been in charge of its patent applications and who was well versed in matters to do with patents, Tokyo Electric set about putting together an efficient system for handling the job of filing GE patent applications. International patent management seemed headed for smooth sailing. But then the Great Kanto Earthquake struck on September 1 1923; the Tokyo Electric buildings were demolished, and Komatsu was among the victims of the earthquake.[39] Komatsu's replacement was Iwao Shibayama, who served as head of the patent department for approximately one year.[40] The Great Kanto Earthquake notwithstanding, the number of applications for GE patents steadily increased, while at the same time the number of patent applications that the patent department filed as proposals put forward from within the company, especially from research facilities, also went on increasing. To handle the growing workload, the capabilities of the patent department had to be greatly extended and improved. And so in 1923 Tokyo Electric prevailed upon Rinji Fujii, a Patent Office examiner, to join the company, and in 1924 appointed him head of the patent department.[41] While employed as a Patent Office examiner, Fujii had been involved in the series of electric light bulb patent trials instituted by GE.[42] With the appointment of Fujii, with his detailed knowledge of patent administration, as head of the patent department, the interwar international patent management system had become functionally complete.

Shibaura Engineering Works

As of 1919 when Shibaura entered into a new contract with IGEC, it had no one with patent attorney qualifications, although it appointed certain people who were in charge of patent affairs. In 1920 Shibaura recruited Michizo Hirano, an examiner of the Patent Office, into the company, and had him gain patent attorney qualifications.[43] In the same year Nobuchika Sugimura, an engineer for Shibaura, also gained the qualifications.[44] The recruiting of both patents professionals and internal cultivation brought Shibaura functionaries who could file patent applications as early as 1920.

The organizational structure relating to the patent department was also improved. As mentioned previously, the person in charge of patents belonged to the development department; he did not undertake patent management from the viewpoint of the whole company. In 1921 Shibaura reorganized the patent department, placing it under the direct control of the director in charge of technology. The patent department occupied the same organizational level as the research, technical examination, equipment and workshop improvement, and primary and secondary engineering departments. The independence of the patent department was a reaction to the increase in the number of GE patent applications being filed, which was effected by the provisions for employee inventions enacted under the revision of the Patent Law in 1921. Encouraged by this revision, other Japanese companies formed patent departments to control their patents as corporate property. It seems that Shibaura had already appointed certain people to be in charge of patent affairs before other companies established similar functions; Shibaura had used the revision as an opportunity to strengthen this. It was about 1921 when Shibaura had the functional and organizational capability to operate general patent management within its own patent department. The patent attorneys belonging to the department were Sugimura and Hirano, although Sugimura left the company to set up his own independent office named *Sugimura Bankoku Tokkyo Jimusho*.[45] After his resignation, Hirano served as manager of the patent department and implemented the international patent management contract with GE.[46]

Enforcement by Japanese Companies

Although Tokyo Electric and Shibaura Engineering Works had begun patent management as corporations, they had not become engaged in the enforcement of reserved patent rights prior to World War I. It had been the foreign parent companies of the Japanese enterprises that exercised patent rights at that time.[47] However, the international patent management agreement required Japanese affiliated companies not only to operate proxy application of GE patents but also to enforce the IPRs reserved by them. The interwar period was the very epoch when Japanese companies initiated the enforcement of patent rights, and they conducted much patent litigation.

In the incandescent lamp field, Tokyo Electric took over the enforcement of GE's patents.[48] At first, it attempted to consolidate the Japanese lamp industry using essential patents from GE, especially Coolidge's patents. Around 1923, Tokyo Electric submitted to the Patent Office a set of demands for trial against Daido Denki Co., Ltd., which manufactured and distributed incandescent lamps called the "Kanto Lamp."[49] Although Daido Denki fought back by submitting demands for trial against Tokyo Electric, the two parties concluded a patent agreement in 1928, and Tokyo Electric eventually absorbed Daido Denki in 1930.[50]

Meanwhile, from around 1922 a group consisting of small lamp manufacturers began a boycott campaign against lamps made by Tokyo Electric, alleging that since Tokyo Electric was owned by GE, its lamps were foreign made. From 1928 to around 1932 these companies submitted many demands for trial against lamp patents possessed by Tokyo Electric. Over 20 demands for trial were submitted by the group, whereas Tokyo Electric fought back many times, which resulted in furious patent disputes.[51]

On the other hand, the lamp industry became an object of governmental industrial control after 1930. The Industrial Union Law of 1931 gave an impetus to industrial reorganization. Based on this law, Metoro Denkyu, Asahi Denkyu, Yebisu Denkyu, Teikoku Denkyu, and Touden Denkyu, all members of the campaign group, formed the Tokyo Lamp Industrial Union in 1932. Likewise, the Tokyo Lamp Exporter Industrial Union, the Osaka Lamp Exporter Industrial Union, and the Kansai Standard Lamp Industrial Union were all organized in 1931. Moreover, the Ministry of Foreign Affairs and the Ministry of Commerce and Industry approached Masuda, a chief director of the Tokyo Lamp Industrial Union, to unify these unions. Responding to this approach, Masuda brought together the four unions and organized the Japan Federation of Lamp Industrial Unions on October 20 1933, which was approved by the government on November 30.[52] From here on, the Japanese lamp industry was structured in two halves, with Tokyo Electric on the one hand and the Federation on the other. The Ministry of Commerce and Industry made approaches to Tokyo Electric regarding negotiations with the Federation to secure participation.

By that time, most of the essential patents for incandescent lamps held by Tokyo Electric had already expired. Coolidge's patents for the tungsten filament and Langmuir's patents for the gas-filled lamp had expired during patent trials; the patent for the internally frosted bulb invented by Kitsuzo Fuwa was declared invalid during a series of trials. Another Coolidge patent, No. 18961, had already expired before the trials in December 1925. The termination of these essential patents which had supported the monopoly of the industry before the 1920s revealed first of all that Tokyo Electric's usual strategy had been pushed to the limit, and caused the company to adopt a new patent strategy. Tokyo Electric began to negotiate with the Federation in June 1934 in response to the governmental approach. The participants on behalf of Tokyo Electric were vice-presidents Yoshichiro Shimizu and Toyoji Tsumori; manager of the patent department, Rinji Fujii; and an engineer, Shotaro Yasui.[53] Given that Fujii was included among the members, it is apparent that the patent issue was critical in the negotiations, and that Tokyo

Electric sought to create some sort of new framework which took advantage of existing patents.

Negotiations between the two parties resulted in an agreement. On November 12, 1934, Kisaburo Yamaguchi, the president of Tokyo Electric, signed the agreement together with Masuda to take part in the Federation. The contract provided that member companies, with the exception of Tokyo Electric and its subsidiary Osaka Denkyu, organize a joint sales company and inspect all incandescent lamps they sold as a form of regulation.[54] As to patent affairs, they agreed that all domestic patent litigations among them should be suspended and settled peacefully. To be more concrete, it was provided that Tokyo Electric should grant the 12 companies which composed the joint sales company licenses for the seven essential patents listed in Table 3.1, and that the joint company should pay a total of 275,000 yen over 10 years as compensation.[55] That is to say, Tokyo Electric decided to form a patent pool involving many small lamp companies which had previously been hostile to Tokyo Electric in order to maintain control over the lamp market by taking advantage of patents, among which were the GE patents it was managing.[56]

Table 3.1 Patents licensed to the joint selling company

Patent No.	Issue date	Inventor	Nationality	Title
43,745	October 21, 1922	Loris E. Mitchell and other	US	Method of producing tipless incandescent lamp and similar article
50,470	June 9, 1923	Kitsuzo Fuwa, Jiro Mori	Japan	Bulb glass for Lamp
62,406	February 17, 1925	Samuel L. Hoyt	US	Leading-in wire
71,092	February 21, 1927	Marvin Pipkin	US	Process for incandescent lamp glass bulb and similar article
73,504	September 15, 1927	Marvin Pipkin	US	Inside frosted glass products
73,509	September 15, 1927	Keiji Tsuyuki	Japan	Method of frosting portion of inside of glass bulb
105,060	February 20, 1934	Aladar Pacz	US	Incandescent lamp filament

Source: Kenjiro Kitachi, *Nihon Denkyu Kogyo Kumiai Rengokai Enkaku Shi* [History of the Japan Federation of Lamp Industrial Unions] (Tokyo, 1943), 139–140; JPO, *Tokkyo Koho*.

TECHNOLOGY TRANSFER AND PATENT MANAGEMENT

To evaluate the international technology transfer quantitatively, it is useful to count the amount of patents. From 1898 to 1918, the patent applications which GE had filed to Japan, and eventually granted to, added up to 237. It was about 11.3 patents per year on average. Then, under the framework of the international patent management contract, technology transfer from the United States to Japan, and vice versa, was facilitated. The technological inflow into Japan boosted the developing activities of Japanese companies via technological interaction.

Figure 3.5 shows trends within Tokyo Electric's patents divided into those invented by foreigners, which were applied for as a proxy to GE, and those

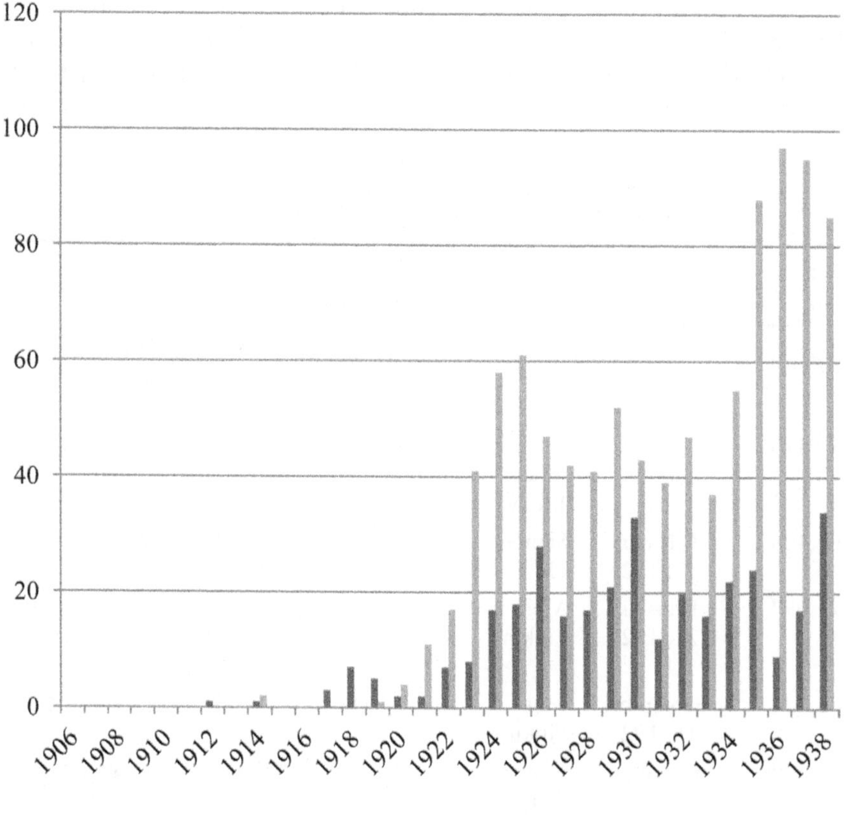

Figure 3.5 Tokyo Electric's patents, as of application, 1906–1938

Source: Japan Patent Office, *Tokkyo Koho*.

invented by the Japanese. The number of patents invented by foreigners, which means technology inflow into Japan, soared from the mid-1920s, and the number of applications increased to between 40 and 60 per year between the latter part of the 1920s and the mid-1930s. The inflow indicated by these patents again soared from the mid-1930s to a high of 96 applications in 1936. On the other hand, the number of patents invented by the Japanese, which means the results of the R&D activities of Tokyo Electric, increased from 5 in 1919 to 28 in 1928. Although that number fluctuated, an average of 20 patents per year were filed from that time onward. We can see that the inflow of technology and Japanese R&D were activated simultaneously during the interwar period.

Figure 3.6 shows the progress of Shibaura's adoption of foreign technology and R&D activities. It is obvious that the number of patents invented by foreigners, which means the adoption of technology, soared from 1922

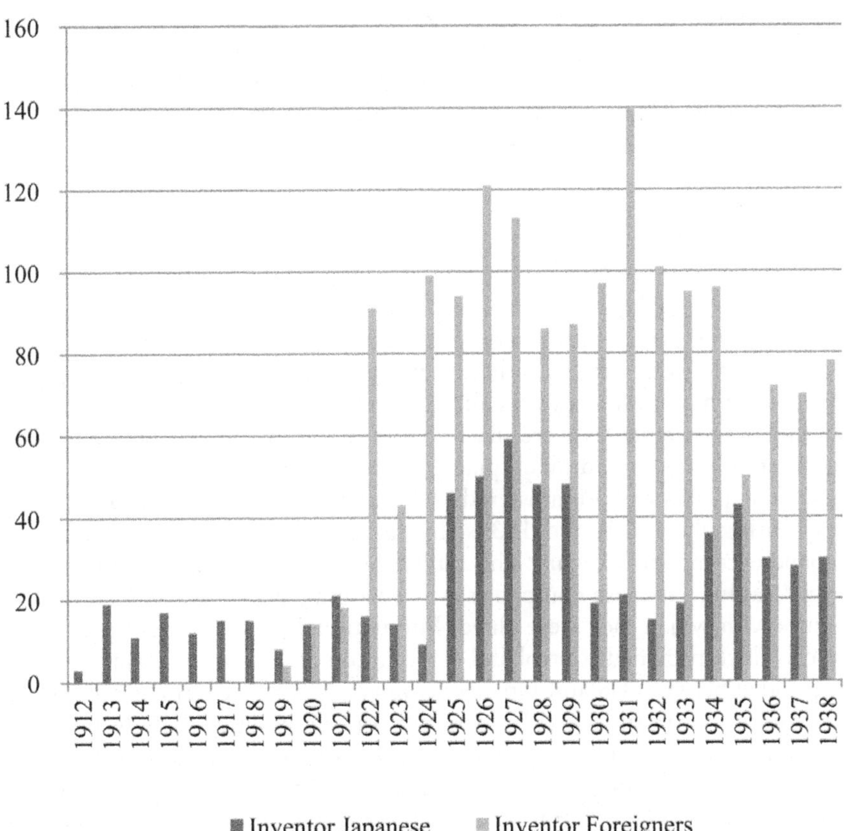

Figure 3.6 Shibaura's patents, as of application, 1912–1938

Source: Japan Patent Office, *Tokkyo Koho*.

onward. From around 100 per year between 1922 and the mid-1930s, it peaked at 140 in 1931. On the other hand, while the number of patents invented by the Japanese was approximately 15 per year until 1924, this increased to a high of 59 in 1927. The figure shows that until 1929 the number of patents invented by the Japanese increased in line with those invented by foreigners. In other words, there was a certain linkage between the adoption of foreign technology via proxy application and the research and development activities of Shibaura Engineering Works.

The patent applications for Japanese inventions, however, declined to a lower level from 1930. In 1931, the number fell to 21; the following year it was 15. By contrast, the number of applications for inventions by foreigners was as high as 140 in 1931 and 101 in 1932. It seems that the reasons why Shibaura reduced the number of Japanese applications were as follows. Shibaura could not afford to allocate the same amount of money to patent management, as it was affected by the Great Depression. From the viewpoint of costs, Shibaura had tightened the criteria by which certain inventions should be applied or not. A history of the company describes how in the several years following 1931 it had disposed of useless industrial property rights including patents, utility models, and designs.[57] While Shibaura reorganized its IPRs, it aggressively furthered the adoption of foreigners via the proxy application procedure in spite of the Great Depression.

CONCLUSION

The evolution of Japanese corporate patent management in the 20th century could be divided into several phases. The first phase was before World War I. During this period, although patent and other industrial property rights laws had been institutionalized, patent application and enforcement by Japanese companies were inactive and immature. Where international technology transfer had taken place, foreign companies had utilized Japanese patent laws and administered their patents directly. The second phase was during the 1920s and 1930s. In this period, patent management by Japanese companies began. The establishment of patent departments in some leading Japanese companies was encouraged by the American companies with which they were allied. International patent management contracts which provided control and exploitation of US patents in Japan were concluded between US and Japanese companies. These contracts attempted to build up an institutional framework to promote large-scale technology transfer to Japan. Under these contracts, international flows of technology from the United States to Japan had soared. From the viewpoint of global business history, MNEs transferred and/or developed the patent management capability as a subsystem of international technology transfer between parent company and affiliated companies. Historically, the capability which established in leading electrical companies had been spread among Japanese companies after World War II. The diffusion of corporate patent management was a prerequisite for international technology transfer from the Western countries to Japan and for the swift economic growth in the postwar era.

NOTES

* This work was supported by Grant-in-Aid for Young Scientists (Start-up) (20830122) of the Japan Society for the Promotion of Science.

1. Edith T. Penrose, *The Economics of the International Patent System* (Baltimore, 1951); David J. Jeremy, ed., *Technology Transfer and Business Enterprise* (Aldershot, 1994).
2. Edwin Mansfield, "Intellectual Property Protection, Foreign Direct Investment, and Technology Transfer" (International Finance Corporation Discussion Paper 19, The World Bank, 1994); Edwin Mansfield, "Intellectual Property Protection, Foreign Direct Investment, and Technology Transfer: Germany, Japan, and the United States" (International Finance Corporation Discussion Paper 27, The World Bank, 1995).
3. Shigehiro Nishimura, "General Electric's International Patent Management before World War II: The 'Proxy Application' Contract and the Organizational Capability of Tokyo Electric," *Japanese Research in Business History* 21 (2004): 101–125; Shigehiro Nishimura, "Foreign Business and Patent Management before World War I: A Case Study of the General Electric Company," *Kansai University Review of Business and Commerce* 11, (2009): 77–97.
4. Jacob Schmookler, *Invention and Economic Growth* (Cambridge, 1966); K. Pavitt, "Patent Statistics as Indicators of Innovative Activities: Possibilities and Problems," *Scientometrics* 7, 1–2 (1985): 77–99.
5. Ove Granstrand, *The Economics and Management of Intellectual Property: Towards Intellectual Capitalism* (Cheltenham, 1999).
6. John Cantwel, "The Globalization of Technology: What Remains of the Product Cycle Model?" *Cambridge Journal of Economics* 19 (1995): 155–174; John Cantwell and Pilar Barrera, "The Localisation of Corporate Technological Trajectories in the Interwar Cartels: Cooperative Leaning versus an Exchange of Knowledge," *Economics of Innovation and New Technology* 6 (1998): 257–290.
7. Tokkyo cho [Japan Patent Office], *Kogyo Shoyuken Seido Hyakunen Shi* [One Hundred Years of the Industrial Property Rights System] (Tokyo, 1984), 662–68; Tetsuo Tomita, *Shijo Kyoso Kara Mita Chiteki Shoyuken* [Intellectual Property Rights Seen from the Perspective of Market Competition] (Tokyo, 1993), 101–110.
8. Japan Patent Office, op. cit., 150–151.
9. Ibid., 201–205.
10. Ibid., 184–191.
11. Ibid., 192.
12. Nihon Benrishi Kai [Patent Attorney Association], ed., *Benrishi seido 100 nenshi* [One Hundred Years of the Patent Attorney Association] (Tokyo, 2000), 22–25.
13. It is difficult to grasp the whole scope of patent litigation because there are few statistics available concerning patent conflicts. In this study, patent litigation is evaluated by the number of demands for trial submitted to the Patent Office.
14. Shotaro Yasui (ed.), *Tokyo Denki Kabushiki Gaisha goju nen shi* [A Fifty-Year History of Tokyo Electric Company, Ltd.] (Tokyo, 1940), 6.

15. Ibid., 97–100.
16. If stocks held by individuals are taken into account, the share of GE was over 70%.
17. Hoshimi Uchida, "Western Big Business and the Adoption of New Technology in Japan: The Electrical Equipment and Chemical Industries 1890–1920" in *Development and Diffusion of Technology: Electrical and Chemical Industries,* ed. Akio Okochi and Hoshimi Uchida (Tokyo, 1980), 155–157.
18. Yasui, op. cit., 113–114.
19. When I mention the number of applications, this indicates patents which were registered. There is no material available which indicates the entirety of applications.
20. This includes 14 patents invented internally and two patents bought from outside.
21. Wasaburo Ito (ed.), *Kishi Seiichi den* [The life of Seiichi Kishi] (Tokyo, 1939), 361–363.
22. Yasuichi Kimura (ed.), *Shibaura Seisakusho 65 nen shi* [A Sixty-Five-Year History of Shibaura Engineering Works, Ltd.] (Tokyo, 1940), 11–23.
23. Ibid., 37–44.
24. Ibid., 53.
25. Uchida, op. cit., 154.
26. Takekichi Otake (ed.), *Kogakuhakushi Kishi Keijiro den* [The life of Keijiro Kishi, Doctor of Engineering] (Tokyo, 1931), 28–30.
27. Kimura, op. cit., 182.
28. Kojiro Ozu, "Toshiba ni Okeru Tokkyo Senryaku [Patent Strategy in Toshiba]" in *Tokkyo Senryaku to Kanri Jirei Shu* [Cases of Patent Strategy and Management], ed. Kunio Ibori (Tokyo, 1980), 151–152.
29. Otake, op. cit., 31.
30. Uchida, op. cit., 157–158.
31. Interview with Mr. Kojiro Ozu, May 23, 2001.
32. Interview with Mr. Ozu, May 23, 2001.
33. Kazuo Inoue (ed.), *Tokkyo kanri* [Patent Management] (Tokyo, 1966), 47–61.
34. Owen D. Young Papers, Box 59, Folder 202A, "Report of Foreign Business, November 22, 1918," St. Lawrence University, Canton, NY. The same report is possessed by the Schenectady Museum and Archives.
35. About the contracts, see, Nishimura, "General Electric's International Patent Management before World War II."
36. Interview with Mr. Seki, May 23, 2001.
37. Watanabe, op. cit., Supplement 3, 1–3.
38. Interview with Messrs Ozu and Hajime Takahashi, May 23, 2001.
39. Yasui, op. cit., 180–181.
40. Interview with Messrs Ozu and Takahashi.
41. Interview with Messrs Ozu and Takahashi. See also Jinji Koshinjo, *Jinji Koshin-roku* [Records of Personnel Inquiries], 13th ed. (Tokyo, 1941).
42. Patent Office, comp., *Tokkyo Koho,* 362 (May 28 1920).
43. Interview with Messrs Ozu and Takahashi; Jinji Koshinjo, op. cit.
44. Patent Office, *Tokkyo Koho,* 1920.
45. Jinji Koshinjo, op. cit.
46. Interview with Mr. Ozu.
47. Nishimura, "General Electric's International Patent Management before World War II: The 'Proxy Application' Contract and the Organizational Capability of Tokyo Electric."
48. About the Shibaura case, see, Shigehiro Nishimura, "Diffusion of Intellectual Property (IP) Management after World War II: Role of the Japan Patent

Association," *Kansai University Review of Business and Commerce* 12, (2010): 19–39.
49. Patent Office, *Tokkyo Koho* 738 (Tokyo, November 3 1924).
50. Yasui, op. cit., 651.
51. Nihon Denkyu Kogyokai, ed., *Nihon Denkyu Kogyo Shi* [History of the Lamp Industry in Japan] (Tokyo, 1963), 85.
52. Ibid., 85–88.
53. Ibid., 89–90.
54. Ibid., 89.
55. Kenjiro Kitachi, *Nihon Denkyu Kogyo Kumiai Rengokai Enkaku Shi* [History of the Japan Federation of Lamp Industrial Unions] (Tokyo, 1943), 339.
56. Patent litigation relating to essential patents possessed by Tokyo Electric had not been suspended by the contracts. Some companies which were outside the patent pool continued to submit demands for trial for the invalidation of GE-originated patents even after the outbreak of the Pacific War.
57. Kimura, op. cit., 297.

Part II

The Role of Cartels

In this second part, we consider the role of cartels in technology transfer. While focusing on the way individual cartel member firms behaved facing competition from MNEs (multinational enterprises) or business opportunities from government offers, we also want to illustrate the limited control cartels had over the flow of technology. MNEs, however, were not the only actors that transferred technologies in order to set up global strategies. Together with the share of markets, the adoption of production quotas and sales prices, technology exchanges were a key issue within international cartels between the end of the 19th century and World War II. These agreements made it possible to transfer patents and tacit knowledge between the various members of a cartel, thus leading to international technology transfer—but this diffusion of technology was often not restricted to the members of the corresponding cartel. The export of technology and know-how to countries seeking to acquire it sometimes took the form of FDI (foreign direct investment) and joint ventures, which served as a way of controlling the emergence of newcomers. In addition to exploring the way cartels controlled international technology transfer, we must also wonder how and to what extent cartels helped to shape the global world in relation to MNEs. The three contributions in this part tackle this question.

The chapter by Valerio Cerretano on the rayon cartel during the interwar years highlights the various strategies adopted by firms within the cartel framework. The use of the cartel appears essentially conservative, insofar as it did not help companies extend their activities abroad or enlarge their presence on the global market. Rather, the objective of the European first movers was to control the spread of the industry. Instead of taking legal action against newcomers who used some patents, for example, the dominant firms of the industry integrated them into the cartel and adopted licensing agreements. The 1927 joint investment of the British company Courtaulds and the German concern Vereinigte Glanzstoff-Fabriken (VGF) in the Italian firm SNIA Viscosa, whose growth relied on technical assistance and patent agreements with its partners, represents an instance of so-called technology-sharing cartels.

The case of the international aluminium cartel between 1886 and 1939, discussed by Marco Bertilorenzi, shows very similar characteristics, as

European firms tried to maintain their technological advantages by means of a cartel agreement. Yet the presence of an American outsider, ALCOA, led to a specific path of technology transfer. As this American MNE adopted an active strategy of investment in Europe in the 1920s, the European first movers, gathered within a cartel since 1923, had to negotiate with ALCOA in order to control the spread of technologies related to aluminium manufacturing. In the 1930s, another group of actors, namely, governments (the USSR, Japan and Yugoslavia), intervened in order to drive technology transfer inward through negotiation with various firms, even without any agreement with the cartel, thus challenging its efficiency. As the chapter emphasizes, international cartels were often too weak to implement technology transfer strategies on their own. They had to deal with other powerful actors, such as MNEs and governments.

International cartels were not the only ones to adopt policies aiming at controlling the diffusion of technologies abroad. In fact, the Swiss watch industry is one example of a national cartel that engaged in a global technology transfer policy made possible by its technological edge. Due to major differences with international cartels in terms of the number of firms involved (low in international cartels; very high in the Swiss watch industry) and entrance barriers (technological know-how and tacit knowledge), among other factors, the objective and the efficiency of this cartel differed significantly from those of international cartels. The chapter by Pierre-Yves Donzé also tackles the case of this industry, organized as an industrial district, which enjoyed technological superiority in the world market at the beginning of the 20th century and organized itself within a cartel, recognized by the State in 1934, in order to control exports of watch parts to other countries and thus control the flow of technologies and the transfer of production toward other countries. These Swiss watch companies did not take the form of an MNE or invest abroad until the 1960s. They jointly adopted a flexible approach to technology transfer, signing agreements with some MNEs to control it in some cases (the United States) and opposing it where it did not seem profitable in others (Japan). Indeed, exports of watch parts and special machine tools were subject to official authorization by the Swiss Federal Department of Public Economy. Permission was granted for countries toward which exports of finished watches were not restricted by protectionist measures.

4 European Cartels and Technology Transfer

The Experience of the Rayon Industry, 1920–1940[1]

Valerio Cerretano

INTRODUCTION

The view that European cartels facilitated the international diffusion of technology came to be widely held in the interwar era.[2] During the negotiations surrounding the shape of the post-1945 global economic order, Anglo-American planners rejected schemes for the international extension of the Sherman Act on the grounds that the complete banning of international cartels would hamper the interchange of technology between Europe and the United States.[3] Through cross-licensing and other cartel understandings, and irrespective of growing international political strains, this interchange had in effect taken place in most innovative, high-tech industries (some of which were of the highest military importance) from the early 1920s well into the war years.[4] Yet despite its importance, the technological dimension of international cartels has generally been overlooked in postwar scholarship. Only in the past two decades has it begun to receive renewed scholarly attention.[5]

Because it was one of the fastest growing high-tech innovative sectors of the interwar era, the rayon industry offers rich insights into the theme at hand. A fibre spun out of melted wood pulp, rayon was the first of a large and ever growing family of man-made fibres.[6] The industry made its appearance at the turn of the 19th and 20th centuries, experiencing impressive growth after the First World War. As Coleman pointed out, one crucial factor behind this growth was the international spread of rayon know-how in the years immediately after the conflict.[7] The industry's main protagonists from the industry's beginnings in 1895 included the British concern Courtaulds, the German firm Vereinigte Glanzstoff-Fabriken (VGF), and the French conglomerate the Comptoir des Textiles Artificiels (Comptoir), and these three firms remained key players for some time thereafter. They were joined soon after the First World War by a number of fast-growing firms in Holland and in the United States, but also in low-wages economies, such as Italy and Japan, and these new firms began to challenge the position of the first movers. More importantly, while entering this business, before and once again after the conflict, the leading rayon firms set up a European cartel, cooperating on the technological front. They jointly developed a viable spinning system before 1914, and continually exchanged know-how until the late 1930s.

What accounted for the international spread of rayon technology after 1918? And, how did the European rayon cartel shape this process? In attempting to answer these questions, Coleman and later Jones suggested that the expiry of the basic viscose rayon patents in 1919, the so-called Müller patents taken out in 1905, represented the main factor behind the diffusion of this trade.[8] Important as it was, however, patent ownership alone did not ensure the successful launch of new rayon businesses. This remained a rapidly evolving industry with high entry barriers until the 30s. As a consequence, would-be rayon-makers needed know-how from the few older established firms in order to succeed. Coleman and Jones underestimate this fact, considering the postwar European rayon cartel an attempt by the pioneer firms, primarily Courtaulds and VGF, to regain control over the industry. The history of this trade shows, however, that newcomers and old-established firms alike were willing to participate in cartelisation in order to have, among other things, access to new advances. Another point escaping the attention of Coleman is that technology transfer within this industry took the shape of two-way flows (from the proprietor to the recipient firm and back from the latter to other firms). This fact had important implications. One of these was that rayon, to adapt Allen's notion to an international context, was to some extent a "collective invention", namely, the outcome of the cooperation among the leading European firms, with two important qualifications: in the case of rayon, know-how did not belong to any specific national context; and, second, technology transfer was not costless for receptor firms.[9]

Cooperation not only offered access to information and know-how. It also fostered economic integration. The fact that international cartels—the majority of which were established in Europe—underpinned the economic integration of Europe (the European Coal and Steel Community, for example, was an outgrowth of the European coal and steel cartel of the 1930s) has largely been established.[10] A similar effect is apparent in the case of rayon: against a backdrop of rapid fragmentation of the global economy, the main actors into the industry kept close ties with one another and maintained global governance mechanisms of the industry until the outbreak of the Second World War. Moreover, the history of this trade confirms that governments sponsored international cartels in an attempt to facilitate technological interchange.[11] As will be seen, when entering the war in 1940, the Fascist government did not sequestrate the stake that Courtaulds had in the Italian rayon-maker Snia Viscosa as enemy property because links between these and other companies along with European cartels facilitated the acquisition of foreign know-how.

The history of this trade seems also to corroborate Mansfield and Baumol's claim that cooperation results mostly from the inefficacy of the international patent system.[12] This does not guarantee a monopoly over proprietary technology—so argue Mansfield and Baumol—so much so that the owners of technology prefer to make a profit from its sale (this is the trade-off for the loss of the monopoly over proprietary technology), while "internalising knowledge spillovers" by collaborating with their competitors.[13] After 1914 and immediately after the end of the conflict, there was little or no patent protection in Europe, and the pioneer rayon firms temporarily abandoned a concerted commercial and technological policy.[14] As will be seen here, along with the high profits deriving from the sale of patents and know-how, these facts had a weight in the diffusion of rayon technologies outside Germany and France in particular. These facts, and especially the temporary absence of a common patent policy of the pioneer firms, help to explain more particularly why this industry spread towards countries such as Italy and Japan, where labour was cheaper and demand for rayon almost nonexistent.

This article, then, lends substance to the claim that European cartels were vehicles for technology transfer. Yet it qualifies Baumol's rosy picture of the effects of the visible hand of cartels on the spread of industry.[15] As will be seen here, patent and technological understandings tended, first, to lift entry barriers to outsiders (especially chemical firms), and, second, to influence the direction of technology flows. Within the European rayon cartel, moreover, there seemed to be a trade-off between access to know-how and output growth.[16] The Italian experience, in particular, shows that the labour costs of the receptor firms (and their ability to depress world prices) increased the price of borrowed technology, a point overlooked by Mansfield and Teece.[17] This experience also demonstrates that the government was instrumental in smoothing technology transfer while avoiding a dramatic limitation of output, a fact that Petri has probably underestimated in his analysis of the German-Italian petrochemical industry in the 1930s, in which the transfer of know-how from Germany to Italy, it should be stressed, was sponsored and supervised by the Italian government.[18]

This chapter proceeds as follows. After briefly reviewing the history of the industry after 1918, it analyses the technology interchange taking place between the largest European rayon firms. Before a conclusion is drawn, a third section considers the role of the Italian government in the transfer of technology from Britain and Germany to Italy.

THE COLLAPSE OF THE PREWAR EUROPEAN RAYON CARTEL AND THE DIFFUSION OF TECHNOLOGY AFTER 1918

How impressive the growth of the rayon industry after the First World War was can be gauged from Figures 4.1 and Figure 4.2.[19]

These also say something about the spread of the industry outside the initial core producing countries, that is, Britain, France and Germany. After an initial lead, both France and Britain declined in relative terms, whereas

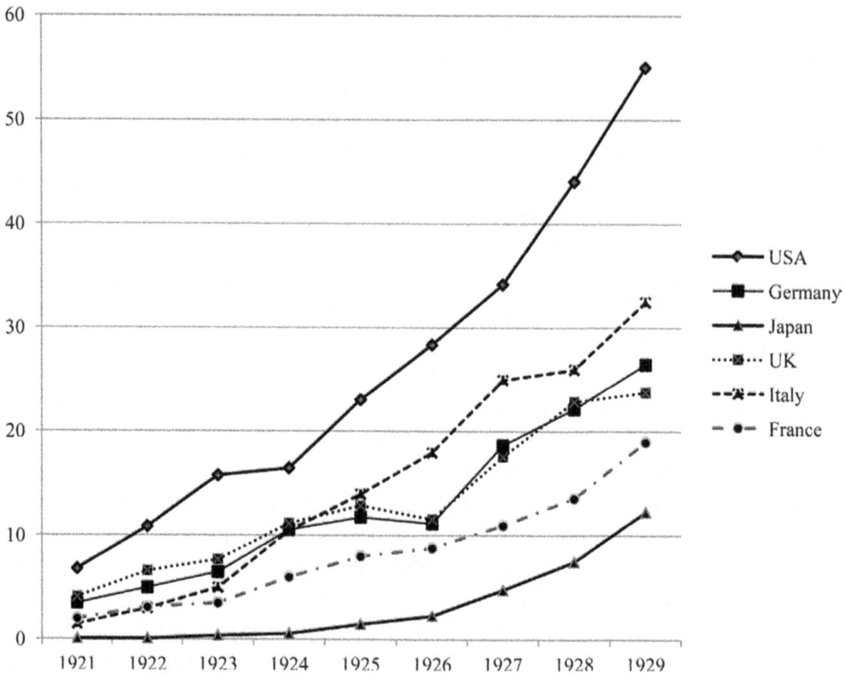

Figure 4.1 World rayon output by main producing countries (000, metric tons), 1921–1929

Source: *Textile Organon: Statistical Base Book* (New York, 1962), pp.18–21.

Italy and more particularly the United States rapidly emerged as important producing countries after 1918. In contrast to Britain and France, moreover, Germany remained a leading producer throughout the interwar era and particularly in the latter half of the 1930s, when import-substitution policies and then rearmament boosted a new upsurge.[20] As for Japan, the quasi-exponential expansion of rayon output began just as Europe and the United States saw their output grow less quickly than in the 1920s as a result of a significant drop in demand. Three interconnected factors were at work behind this trend: first, cheaper labour (as eight times cheaper than in Britain in 1930) and higher labour productivity; second, closer integration between rayon, chemical and silk, as well as cotton, spinning firms (the former were an extension of the latter); lastly, the occupation of large swaths of China (which along with India constituted the largest export outlet after the closing up of the US market in 1930 by virtue of protectionism) and related import-substitution policies during the '30s that provided outlets for growing domestic output.[21]

Underpinning these developments was the soaring number of rayon firms after 1914. Coleman calculated that there were less than 10 of them before

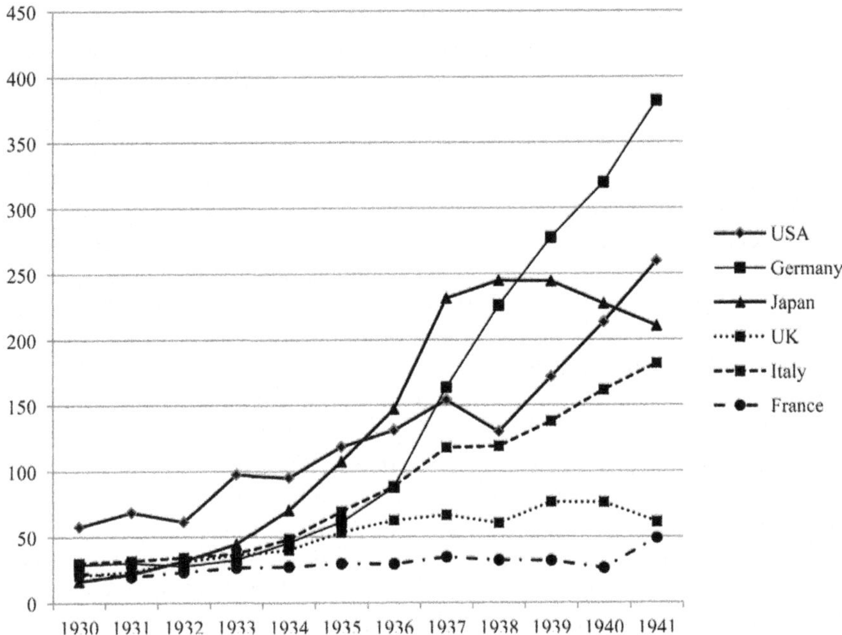

Figure 4.2 World rayon output by main producing countries (000, metric tons), 1930–1941

Source: *Textile Organon: Statistical Base Book* (New York, 1962), pp.18–21.

1914 as opposed to 120 in 1931.[22] Of the newcomers, however, only a few became leading players into the industry. These included the Dutch N.V. Nederlandsche Kunstzijde Fabriek (Enka); the US chemical concern Du Pont; the German giant chemical firm IG Farben; Snia Viscosa, Châtillon and Cisa in Italy; and a plethora of smaller Japanese concerns, of which Teikoku Jinzo Kenshi Kaisha Ltd. (the Teikoku Artificial Silk Co. Ltd.) became the most prominent in terms of output and output capacity by the 1930s.

Two crucial questions should thus be posed at this juncture: why did the industry began to spread mostly after 1918? And, how did the newcomers manage to obtain rayon know-how?

There is no single answer to these questions. The migration of skilled workers previously employed by the pioneer firms did have a role in the diffusion of trade secrets and nonpatentable knowledge. The best known cases were those of Jacques Coenraad Hartogs and Marco Biroli. The former launched Enka in 1913 after some training in Courtaulds' plant at Coventry in the 1900s, while Marco Biroli, the motivating spirit behind Châtillon, had been a distinguished chemist of Cisa, the Italian subsidiary of the Comptoir.[23]

The inconsistencies and loopholes of the international patent system were also of some importance in this process, however.[24] After 1914, patents and assets were sequestrated and new competitors had entered business under the shelter of import-substitution policies. This was the case, in particular, of a number of German chemical firms, notably AGFA, Bayer and Köln Rottweil AG, which started rayon production in 1915 and merged into IG Farben in 1926. Moreover, international patent protection, which was traditionally guaranteed by commercial treaties, continued to remain partially if not wholly ineffective immediately after the war as the stipulation of new commercial ententes was delayed, first, by European inflation and, above all, by the suspension of Germany's commercial sovereignty, which lasted until 1925. These facts facilitated the entry into business of newcomers outside Germany. Châtillon, to quote one example, operated on the basis of patents—the so-called Biroli patents registered in Italy and in the United States in 1919–1920—which clearly infringed the Müller and other German patents.[25]

The old-established firms and in particular VGF did start legal action against some of the newcomers after 1925. Yet, while lengthy and expensive, legal action failed to uproot new competition. The pioneer firms, especially VGF, instead used legal action as a bargaining counter in cartel negotiations. In 1924–1925, VGF, for example, dropped all lawsuits against IG Farben after that the latter firm undertook to join a domestic price cartel and significantly to curtail its rayon output.[26] In 1930, using similar tactics, it dropped legal action against Châtillon, which then finally joined a cartel limiting exports from Italy into Germany.[27]

Important as they were, however, neither the migration of skilled workers from one company to another, the expiry of patents, nor their illegal acquisition alone can account for the impressive diffusion of rayon know-how after the conflict. The most successful newcomers, it should be stressed, obtained licenses and know-how from the pioneer firms. Still an infant industry in the early 1920s, rayon-making posed formidable financial and technological problems for would-be rayon firms, a fact explaining why newcomers sought support from well-established rayon concerns as they entered this business.

However, if this fact encouraged newcomers to seek the cooperation of the pioneer firms, the reasons which motivated the latter to provide assistance to new competitors were less straightforward. Pursuit of profit was clearly a major factor at work here: high rayon prices, high profit margins, and the small number of patent holders in the first half of the 1920s increased both royalties and the price of this technology. The temporary lack of patent and commercial coordination among the pioneer firms, however, also contributed to this outcome and to the rapid spread of this industry in the early '20s.

Under the leadership of Courtaulds and VGF, the pioneer firms had formed a European cartel prior to 1911. Although it collapsed in 1914, it was reestablished after 1925.[28] Less tightly organised than the prewar cartel which envisaged, among other things, a common European sales agency, the interwar European rayon cartel was, to use Fear's typology, a hard-core price cartel.[29] In these cartels, however, it was difficult to draw a sharp line between patent- and market-sharing agreements, for these complemented each another in the regulation of competition and in the creation of domestic monopolies. In relation to this, it is worth noting that before 1914 the pioneer firms, through concerted action, had avoided licensing technology to strong firms, notably chemical concerns which, although lacking the textile expertise, had a competitive edge when it came to the provision of heavy chemicals, caustic soda and sulphuric acid, which were all heavily employed in rayon manufacture. When licensing occurred, the licensees were usually financially weak, with little in-house capabilities and not in a position to increase output dramatically.[30] A case in point is the Italian Cisa, a small and troubled celluloid manufacturer established in 1901 which obtained, in 1910–1911, rayon patents from the Comptoir and which, as a result of this exchange, came to be controlled by the French firm.[31]

The posture of the pioneer firms changed dramatically after 1918. To Baumol, technology-sharing cartels, which provide little or no incentive to cheating, are much more stable than market-sharing cartels.[32] The rayon cartel, which to a great extent was a technology-sharing cartel, did not, however, survive the stresses of the war (notably, the strains among firms created by asset and patent sequestration). A common patent policy failed to materialise immediately after the war as relations between the leading firms continued to be strained and profit margins remained high. Another contributing factor to this outcome, however, was the fact that numerous interests which had amassed immense fortunes during the war were now able, more than in the past, to lure patent holders, particularly the Comptoir and VGF, with huge sums of money.

Soon after the war, the Comptoir and VGF attempted to reestablish a European cartel. In particular, they settled patent disputes, reviving a "community of patents" in May 1920.[33] Despite these attempts, however, both firms sold their know-how independently to new competitors. Early in 1920, the Comptoir licensed, among others, Du Pont and Snia Viscosa. Two years later, VGF set up a firm in Japan in conjunction with Japanese businessman Noguchi Shitagau and his Asahi Chemicals.[34] In the cases of the Japanese and Italian investment, however, both VGF and the Comptoir subjected technology transfer to output and sales limitations (the licensors were not allowed to make their sales in a number of markets, including of course the licensors' domestic markets) and to the free acquisition of advances originating in the new plants.[35]

High rental rates and high profits, as already mentioned, but also probably a lack of financial resources, were the key factors encouraging VGF and the Comptoir to license outsiders. As we have seen, however, these firms sought to discriminate against certain potential new entrants. When early in 1922 news broke that VGF was about to establish a joint venture in Japan, the Comptoir protested to VGF in the following terms:

> We have rejected negotiations with the Japanese, who made very favourable proposals . . . during our meeting [in Cologne in May 1920] we agreed that the idea of providing this support to as dangerous people as the Japanese must be abandoned altogether.[36]

These words testified to the fact that the profit deriving from the sale of know-how was probably not the only factor governing technology trading. The "dangerous people" to whom the Comptoir referred were the firms and interests with large financial resources, no home market, and cheap labour which were likely to become a threat in export markets.

More than VGF, however, the Comptoir was the pioneer firm which most helped new interests to enter into this business. In April 1920, the French firm set up Du Pont Fibersilk, with works at Buffalo, New York, in conjunction with US chemical giant Du Pont. Of the new company's starting capital (4 million US dollars), 60 percent went to Du Pont, and the remainder to the French (including 24 percent for their know-how).[37] In 1925, Du Pont Fibersilk changed its name to the Du Pont Rayon Company (which, in 1930, became wholly controlled by Du Pont, and in 1936 became the Du Pont Rayon Department) and set up new plants at Old Hickory, Tennessee, and in Richmond, Virginia, in 1929.[38] Du Pont expanded considerably in the 1920s, becoming as early as 1924 the second largest US rayon producer after the American Viscose Corporation.[39] As Hounshell and Smith underlined, rayon soon became the largest branch of the company, absorbing a good portion of Du Pont's output of heavy chemicals.[40]

Du Pont remained dependent on European know-how until 1930. In that year, however, it purchased the Comptoir's minority stake, becoming the only full-fledged big US rayon company. The chemical company nevertheless maintained close relations with the Comptoir until 1939 (they had cross-licensing and market-sharing agreements while making joint direct investments in Argentina and Mexico).[41] With regard to the limitations imposed on licensees, it is also worth noting that in exchange for know-how Du Pont refrained from invading European markets.[42]

Of far-reaching consequences for the industry as a whole was the support that the Comptoir provided to Snia Viscosa. This was because Du Pont was a high-cost producer which expanded mostly within the domestic market, whereas the latter posed a direct threat to the old-established firms in export outlets. In the years 1920 to 1922, the Comptoir sold Snia Viscosa the Italian rights to the Müller patents along with a number of small rayon plants previously belonging to the Cisa group. The French firm, as already mentioned, sought to use technology transfer to exert some control over the industrial policy of Snia Viscosa. However, Snia Viscosa soon expanded output beyond the agreed limits (about 3,000 metric tons a year) undercutting the Comptoir and other pioneer firms in all markets, particularly Britain and the United States. As early as 1924, Snia Viscosa had overtaken Courtaulds and VGF in terms of output, accounting for about 70 percent of Italian exports, and 11 percent of the world's output of rayon.[43] The reasons behind the failure of the Comptoir to check the expansion of the Italian firm must be found in the factors allowing the latter to grow rapidly: not only inflation, currency depreciation, and cheap labour, but also the US and British boom in demand for poor quality rayon were important. In fact, the Italian firm, unable to produce good quality yarn until 1930, soon became entrenched in this poor quality rayon market. With regard to this, it should be emphasised that, as an authoritative source noted in the early 1940s, this boom was largely occasioned by a lack of price coordination by the pioneer firms and more particularly by the price cuts that Courtaulds and its subsidiary the American Viscose Corporation executed in 1919–1920 with the aims of bringing rayon prices into line with rapidly falling cotton prices and also of keeping new competitors at bay.[44]

Coleman concluded that the "most evident contribution" of the prewar European rayon cartel "arose from technical collaboration and patent exchanging. Without these measures the industry would have advanced less rapidly than it did; the effect was to ease the dissemination of knowledge rather than to restrict it".[45] As we have mentioned in this section, however, the European rayon cartel ensured the diffusion and exchange of rayon technology mostly within the cartel network, raising its costs for outsiders.

In connection with this, it should be said that economists and economic historians tend to consider, although implicitly, technology transfer a costless process, which is then substantially unaffected by the market power of the firms holding proprietary technology.[46] Largely as a consequence of this, they also tend to establish, once again implicitly, an equation between the acquisition of borrowed technology and unrestrained growth.[47] With regard to this, Mansfield and Teece have however established that the price of "borrowed technology" is a negative function of both its age and the number of patent-holders.[48] To quote a well-known example, Snia Viscosa, between 1920 and 1931, spent about 240 million lira or the equivalent of about 25 percent of the company's share capital in 1925 in the acquisition of patents and know-how from the Comptoir, VGF, and Courtaulds.[49] Moreover, the transfer of technology was subject to output limitations, the costs of which are not immediately quantifiable.[50] Against this background, it seems reasonable to suggest that had prewar conditions prevailed, the diffusion of rayon know-how, given its high transfer costs and the small number of patent holders, would scarcely have taken place or would have been subjected to major output limitations. It can safely be stated, in conclusion, that the international spread of this expensive technology and the parallel growth in rayon output after the First World War was to a great extent the outcome of unique circumstances: the temporary collapse of the European rayon cartel; excess war profits; high profit margins in this industry; inflation; and lack of patent protection.

THE EUROPEAN RAYON CARTEL AND TECHNOLOGY EXCHANGES AFTER 1918

We have mentioned that the prewar European cartel, while envisaging the sharing out of markets, stipulated the pooling of patents and know-how.[51] These aspects were strictly interconnected since cross-licensing, while subject to certain limitations with regard to sales and prices in third markets, guaranteed domestic monopolies to the patent-holders.[52] However, the gist of the agreements signed in 1911 was that all major rayon concerns—from Courtaulds, to VGF, to the Comptoir—shared the Müller and other basic patents and undertook to pool future advances originating in the plants of all cartel members.[53] As Coleman has shown, visits to foreign plants were regularly undertaken and information exchanged in the early days of the industry. However, technological exchanges and the supervision of arrangements remained strictly bilateral.[54]

This "pair-wise mode of operation", to borrow Baumol's notion, also characterised the postwar period.[55] The members of the European rayon cartel, in other words, exchanged know-how or information bilaterally without resorting to a coordinating body or general meeting. This way, however, innovations were potentially available to all. Of particular importance after 1918 were the technological exchanges taking place between the Comptoir and Du Pont; between VGF and the Comptoir (especially in the field of acetate rayon); and between VGF, Courtaulds, and Snia Viscosa. Here attention will focus on the exchanges taking place within the latter group of firms between 1927 and 1940.

At this juncture, it should be said that Courtaulds and VGF in 1927 jointly bought a controlling interest in Snia Viscosa, after the Italian firm had broken off relations with the Comptoir and found itself in financial need in mid-1926. This move was instrumental in VGF and Courtaulds' cartel strategy, which aimed at dramatically curtail Italian exports of rayon.[56] The Courtaulds-VGF-Snia Viscosa compact (taken together, the firms controlled more than 50 percent of world's output in 1930) that ensued in effect gave a major boost to postwar European cartelisation.[57] On the other hand, while facing financial collapse, Snia Viscosa accepted a limitation of output in exchange for financial aid and, above all, in exchange for Courtaulds and VGF's know-how.[58]

In the 1920s, the primary concern of Snia Viscosa was, as with other newcomers, to develop a viable spinning process. The development of that system after 1927 was, however, marred by strong disagreements between Italian and German technologists, who pursued a dramatic reduction of output. The reason why VGF, more than Courtaulds, was charged with the industrial reconstruction of Snia Viscosa was that the German company operated on the basis of a spinning system, namely, the "bobbin spinning", similar to the one that the Italians had begun to develop under the direction of the Comptoir. German plans for a dramatic reduction of output were abandoned in the end (see later discussion). Some of the advances introduced by VGF engineers were, however, kept. As a leading Italian engineer recalled, their most significant contributions to Snia Viscosa's spinning system were changes and improvements in the filtration systems of the viscose solution (a crucial operation in the making of viscose rayon), improvements in the filtration of the spinning bath, the introduction of the "gear-pump" (another technical breakthrough introduced in the late 1920s) and "candle-filter" in the spinning machines, and the establishment of textile and chemical laboratories in all the company's factories (on the various stages of rayon-making see Table 4.1). Even Snia Viscosa's new—and to a considerable extent groundbreaking—spinning machine, the Silm 81, was largely modelled on the VGF's von Hamel machine (on this see below). In addition, Snia Viscosa combined these new advances with Courtaulds' innovative bleaching system.[59]

A leading director of Courtaulds noted in late 1930 that the outcome of these technical developments was the elaboration of a competitive bobbin system.[60] One important element of this system was the use of aluminium bobbins of 90 mm diameter, larger than those employed by VGF (70 mm diameter) and allowing a reasonable compromise between quality, which was now good enough to support vast markets in the various weaving trades, and greater economies of scale (100 grams of yarn could be spun in one twist, against the mere 45 grams of the VGF 70 mm bobbins or 55 grams the Courtaulds Topham boxes). Another feature was the use of the Silm 81 itself, for which a patent was taken out in Italy, in Germany, and in Britain late in 1930.[61] The Silm 81 marked a significant advancement in bobbin spinning technologies, for it allowed the automatic changeover of bobbins, meaning that, when the first series of bobbins was filled, the machine switched over automatically to the second series. This limited the handling of bobbins (thus allowing improvements in quality) when filaments were still wet, and, as a result, the amount of waste and time due to the manual change of bobbins (so-called doffing) (see Table 4.1).

The spinning system of Snia Viscosa was one of two methods adopted at the time, the other being the box or centrifugal spinning system, in use in Courtaulds and the American Viscose Corporation's plants. Coleman maintains that the gap in costs between box and bobbin spinning was bridged by the mid-1900s, and that the employment of these systems, which produced yarns of differing characteristics, depended much on the end-uses of the yarns.[62] Yet bobbin spinning techniques made great headway in the late 1920s, becoming more amenable to greater economies of scale. Unsurprisingly, then, the methods developed in Snia Viscosa's plants and in Cologne (i.e., VGF and Courtaulds' joint plant) drew the attention of Courtaulds. With regard to this, it should be noted that the employment of bobbin spinning was interconnected with wider discussions within the British concern's board of the British on how to expand outlets of rayon, whether through high quality or through low prices.[63] Between 1928 and 1930, Italian engineers and chemists paid regular visits to the continental subsidiaries of

Table 4.1 The making of viscose rayon: stages and departments in a viscose rayon factory late in the 1920s

Main raw materials	**Wood pulp or "cotton linters" (1500 lbs. x 1,000 lbs. of rayon); caustic soda (2,000 lbs. x 1,000 lbs. of rayon); carbon disulphide (600 lbs. x 1,000 lbs. of rayon); sulphuric acid (1,500 lbs. x 1,000 lbs. of rayon)**
I. Preparation of viscose solution	1. Wood pulp sheets right humidification with heat or steam 2. Steeping or mercerisation wood pulp mixed with soda—formation of alkali-cellulosesoda removed by steeping the sheets in steeping tank or press 3. Shredding alkali-cellulose reduced to white flock particles—the so-called crumbs 4. Maturing of alkali-cellulose this takes place in "crumbs ageing cans" 5. Mixing crumbs with carbon disulphide here the alkali-cellulose becomes "cellulose-xanthate", that is, viscose solution. This takes place in big containers which rotate for about three hours—the "barattes" 6. Viscose mixing the cellulose-xanthate mixed with water and soda in big containers called "mixers" 7. Blending viscose solution from all mixers in one single container 8. Ripening ageing again. This is a very critical operation; difficulty in defining time and temperature; no air must get in contact with the solution 9. Filtration during ripening, the viscose solution is filtered; crucial operation as impurities can obstruct holes of "spinning jets" during "extrusion"; purity of water also essential requirement; filter presses employed

	10. De-aeration viscose solution put in vacuum tanks to avoid the formation of bubbles and breakage during "spinning"	
II. Spinning	1. Pipeline viscose solution forced through pipeline to which spinning machines are attached 2. Spinning bath viscose solution passes through (a) pumps that regulate the flow of the solution; (b) candle filters, to remove last impurities; (c) "spinning jets", which are small platinum devices with numerous holes (in the late 1920s, 36 or 60 holes for yarn of 150 denier) solidification of filaments in spinning bath: this is a solution of sulphuric acid and salts such as sodium sulphate; other chemical compounds (such as zinc, glucose, magnesium sulphate) used; the right composition of spinning bath is vital and requires experience; composition and temperature must secure instant coagulation of filaments that must be handled with great care when still we composition of Venaria's spinning bath in 1933 (for 155 litres): 63 percent of sulphuric acid; 3.54 grams per litre of sodium sulphate; 0.65 grams per litre of ZnSO4; 46 degrees of temperature	
	A. Bobbin spinning method 3. Twisting this takes place in a separate department; twists imparted to filaments depending on the end-use demands	B. Centrifugal or box or Topham spinning system 3. No twisting filaments twisted and put from the spinning bath to the 'cake' or 'Thopam box' without handling
III. Washing	Operation carried out to remove the acid. Crucial and poisonous operation. In the early 1930s, there were two systems: (1) bobbin immersed in water to extract the liquor; (2) bobbins washed in vacuum, water sucked from inside, through perforated bobbins	

(*Continued*)

Table 4.1 (Continued)

Main raw materials	**Wood pulp or "cotton linters" (1500 lbs. x 1,000 lbs. of rayon); caustic soda (2,000 lbs. x 1,000 lbs. of rayon); carbon disulphide (600 lbs. x 1,000 lbs. of rayon); sulphuric acid (1,500 lbs. x 1,000 lbs. of rayon)**
IV. Drying	Filaments are then dried
V. Spooling	Filaments wound together in spools
VI. Reeling	From spools rayon is skeined. With the cake-washing, this operation, which employed around 30 percent of Venaria' s workforce in 1933, was eliminated. Also, when reeled yarn broke very often: cake-washing improved therefore quality.
VII. Bleaching	Skeins are de-sulphured, washed and bleached
VIII. Sorting	Rayon yarns are finally classified according to quality, which is given by the number of broken filaments, but classification depends a lot on management. Very delicate operation; highly skilled labour; the only department where experience gained from the natural silk trade is very helpful

Source: designed by the author

Courtaulds in Calais and in Cologne, collaborating with their technical staff. While proving crucial to the improvement of Snia Viscosa's spinning methods, these exchanges also allowed Courtaulds and its continental plants finally to master up-to-date bobbin spinning technology.[64]

The development of staple fibres technology proved more important still. Essentially yarn cut at regular lengths, staple fibres constituted the most important breakthrough in this industry after 1918, mostly because they were cheaper than traditional yarns and could be more easily spun in combination with natural fibres, wool, and then cotton. Mass production of staple fibres, besides extending the end-uses of rayon, was behind the upsurge in rayon output in the latter half of the 1930s (see Table 4.2). More importantly, it took off mostly in countries which adopted extensive import-substitution and autarkic policies, i.e. Germany, Japan, and Italy (see Table 4.3).

Snia Viscosa initially obtained patents for staple fibres from the Comptoir, and later developed some of ideas introduced by VGF during the war. To be more specific, the Italian company introduced a staple fibres cutting machine (patented under the name of Antonio Beria in 1927 and in 1928) which developed Pellerin's idea of collecting fibres from a spinning jet with a great number of holes (as many as 1,200 against 35 or 70 in the case of yarns) in the form of a thick tow or bundle, which went first through a funnel and then through blades. One feature of this machine was the rapidity with which it could cut the rayon tow. Snia Viscosa surrendered in 1932 this

Table 4.2 Rayon yarns and staple fibers: global output, 1929–1941

	Yarn		Staple fibres		Total	
		%		%		%
1929	197.8	98.2	3.6	1.8	201.0	100
1930	204.6	98.5	3.2	1.5	208.0	100
1931	224.1	98.2	4.1	1.8	228.0	100
1932	236.3	96.6	8.2	3.4	244.0	100
1933	299.4	95.7	13.6	4.3	313.0	100
1934	348.8	93.4	24.5	6.6	373.0	100
1935	424.6	86.7	64.9	13.3	489.0	100
1936	464.0	77.1	137.4	22.9	601.0	100
1937	543.0	65.1	291.2	34.9	834.0	100
1938	452.7	51.5	426.4	48.5	879.0	100
1939	517.6	50.8	499.9	49.2	1,017.0	100
1940	542.0	48.1	585.1	51.9	1,127.0	100
1941	571.5	44.7	706.3	55.3	1,278.0	100

Source: Elaboration of data sets from *Textile Organon: Statistical Base Books* (New York, 1962, and New York, 1966).

Table 4.3 Italy, Germany, Japan: shares of world output of staple fibers, 1929

	Italy		Germany		Japan		World's output	
		%		%		%		%
1929	0.8	22.2	1.1	30.6			3.6	100
1930	0.3	9.4	2.0	62.5			3.2	100
1931	0.6	14.6	2.0	48.8			4.1	100
1932	4.3	52.4	1.4	17.1	0.3	3.7	8.2	100
1933	5.0	36.8	4.0	29.4	0.5	3.7	13.6	100
1934	10.0	40.8	7.2	29.4	2.1	8.6	24.5	100
1935	31.0	47.8	17.2	26.5	6.2	9.6	64.9	100
1936	49.9	36.3	43.0	31.3	20.8	15.1	137.4	100
1937	71.0	24.4	106.3	36.5	79.6	27.3	291.2	100
1938	73.5	17.2	160.7	37.7	148	34.8	426.4	100
1939	83.4	16.7	204.6	40.9	137	27.3	499.9	100
1940	109.0	18.6	240.1	41.0	130	22.2	585.1	100
1941	124.7	17.7	292.6	41.4	135	19.0	706.3	100

Source: See Table 4.2

machine to Courtaulds, which began the mass-production of staple fibres under the trademark of Fibro in 1936, and to American Viscose Corporation as well as Courtaulds' subsidiary at Calais in 1934 and in 1935.[65] Likewise, in April 1935 the Italian concern sold staple fibres know-how to VGF, undertaking to assist the latter firm in the development of the Blaschke machine, a staple fibres machine which was more compact and potentially more efficient than the Beria machine.[66]

Connected with the commercialisation of staple fibres was the mass production of wood pulp from reed and beech—to acquire sufficient raw materials, Snia Viscosa made huge investment by 1935 to substitute for North American and Scandinavian spruce by using these lower quality sources.[67] The diversification into this industry was occasioned by two interrelated factors: first, currency scarcity and import-substitution policies; and, second, growing prices of imported, high-quality wood pulp. Of inferior quality, the reed and beech wood pulp could, however, be employed in the production of staple fibres, which were of much lower quality than yarns. Although production began in 1939 and was interrupted as early as 1943, the Italian firm developed sophisticated wood pulp technology, which Courtaulds acquired in the early 1950s.[68]

The Cerini soda recovery process was also of some importance. By the mid-1920s, pressures from price decreases for finished product on the one hand and surging production costs on the other triggered a search for processes of recovery of heavy chemicals (sulphuric acid and caustic soda). The contribution of Snia Viscosa to this field of research was the Cerini process, a cheap and efficient dialyser for the recovery of the so-called press lye (it was capable of recovering up to 85 percent of caustic soda) which was mostly composed of caustic soda.[69] Snia launched the Societa Italiana Recupero Soluzioni Impure (hereinafter SIRSI) in 1930 in conjunction with Cerini in order to exploit the patent worldwide. After rejecting the Heibig process employed in VGF's plants, Courtaulds, Courtaulds Canada, the British Cellophane, and the American Viscose Corporation acquired the British, Canadian, and American rights to the Cerini process in the years between 1931 and 1933.[70] Courtaulds and AVC acquired 66 and 127 plants, respectively, from SIRSI, building approximately 478 other recovery plants on their own between 1931 and 1937.[71] This system was disclosed to VGF and other European rayon firms, as well as to Du Pont.

Less important but worth mentioning, finally, was the Ferretti process for the production of Lanital, a casein fibre. Developed in the mid-1930s in an attempt to substitute decreasing wool imports, this proved a fiasco outside of Italy because of its poor strength and dyeing properties. In summer 1937, Courtaulds, however, acquired the patent rights for Britain and Canada and marketed it as "Fibrolan", while agreeing to pool advances with Snia Viscosa.[72] The American Viscose Corporation and Du Pont became for some time interested in this process between 1936 and 1937.[73] Yet the unclear patent position of Lanital in the United States, the high price of the patent (2 million US dollars), and the uncertainty surrounding the commercial success of the fibre led these firms to abandon plans for its mass production.[74]

A director of Courtaulds recalled in 1931 that "the only technical assistance subsequently exchanged between Courtaulds and Snia was that given *by Snia* [Viscosa] *to us*, when they gave us the Sniafil machine and facilities to learn bobbin spinning practice" (italics in the original).[75] In effect, on balance, the British firm gained greater benefits from these technological interchanges in the time period under consideration.

That said, however, Snia Viscosa, besides the assistance for the development of a viable spinning system, also secured important innovations from Courtaulds and from VGF. One of these was the Lilienfeld process. Originated in the VGF works, this patent covered the use of certain chemical compounds for the making of high-tenacity yarns employed in the making of tyres. Another important technological breakthrough of the 1930s, high-tenacity yarns found vast outlets in tyre manufacture initially in the United States and subsequently in Europe, where their application of took only place as a result of cotton shortages late in the '30s.[76] Snia Viscosa began experimentation with the Lilienfeld process in 1930, purchasing the rights for Italy in 1934. Snia Viscosa obtained box-spinning machines employed by the VGF Cologne factory from the German firm in exchange for staple fibres technologies.[77] The Italian firm completed the set of box-spinning technologies with the acquisition of "cake-washing" machines—another important innovation of the '30s—from Courtaulds in 1939.[78]

Of greater importance were the innovations that Snia Viscosa secured from Courtaulds soon after 1945. These included the Continuous Spinning System, acetate rayon know-how, the so-called hot stretch process for high-tenacity rayon and, most importantly, Nylon 66, the first truly synthetic fibre that began to be marketed after the Second World War.[79] It should be noted that Courtaulds in its turn obtained these advances from firms with which it had cross-licensing agreements, including the US firm Industrial Rayon Corporation, ICI, the Comptoir, and Du Pont.[80]

NATIONAL GOVERNMENTS, CORPORATE COOPERATION AND TECHNOLOGY TRANSFER: THE ITALIAN CASE

The Italian government and economic nationalism played an important, although often indirect, role in the process by which Snia Viscosa successfully adopted foreign know-how. As with other European governments, the Fascist regime did not hinder cooperation between national and foreign firms. It did, however, seek to ameliorate the trade-off between access to foreign know-how and output limitation.

We have seen in the previous section that Courtaulds and VGF came to control Snia Viscosa in 1927–1928. The British and the Germans initially entrusted a VGF director, Karl Scherer, with the technical as well as financial restructuring of the company. While implementing a dramatic reduction of output, Scherer ousted Riccardo Gualino, the founder of the company, appointing Senatore Borletti as the company's new chairman. These were major developments when considering that Gualino was not only one of the most prominent Italian businessmen, but Snia Viscosa was also by the mid-1920s the largest Italian company by capital and furthermore that this took place in the context of growing economic nationalism during the late '20s. The weight of Courtaulds and VGF in Snia Viscosa's governing bodies was not entirely clear in Italy until the early '30s, and raised criticism from influential economic and political circles. Early in 1931, a Courtaulds' liaison officer in Snia Viscosa stated that Scherer "has a very bad reputation in Northern Italian Fascist circles owing to . . . his insistence some months ago that production should be very much reduced".[81] A few months later, an anonymous commentator remarked to Mussolini that "thanks to foreign intervention, the financial problems [of Snia Viscosa] can be considered solved, and yet it is difficult not to feel, when one possesses self esteem, the humiliation of this intervention".[82] Similar sentiments seemed to have gained currency in the midst of the depression as the measures of economic nationalism (which, among other things, impeded the launch of Ford's subsidiary in Italy) that Mussolini implemented in "defence of national industry" in 1930 seemed to indicate.[83] A stance of economic nationalism was also taken by the state agency Istituto per la Ricostruzione Industriale (Istituto) created in 1933 when opposing the merger between Snia Viscosa, Châtillon (controlled by the Istituto from 1933), and the Comptoir-owned firm Cisa throughout the 1930s. The argument was that a merger between those firms would create a domestic monopoly controlled by foreign interests.[84] A memorandum that the Istituto circulated in late 1933 put it this way:

> [Senatore Borletti] . . . has been warned about the preoccupations of national character inherent in the strengthening up of [Snia Viscosa's] majority voting pool, which seems to be controlled by foreigners. . . . Senatore Borletti has denied this control . . . in order to prove this, he has shown the statutes of Safra and Sagepi . . . it must be noted that the exceptional formulas used in the statutes of these holding companies confirm the widely shared view that the controlling interest of Snia Viscosa is in the hands of foreign groups.[85]

In effect, Safra and Sagepi, which were established in 1933, were companies holding the German and British interests in Snia Viscosa. Yet their launch marked the separation between the ownership and management of the company, putting an end to Courtaulds and VGF's direct control over the management of Snia Viscosa.[86] Growing poor relations between VGF and Courtaulds played a part in these developments.[87] But political factors and economic nationalism seemed to have had an even greater role. Explained Borletti to the managing director of VGF in spring 1931 that "these changes . . . have been imposed by factors, I would say, of political . . . order . . . these changes have been proposed merely to moralise . . . the situation".[88] Against that backdrop, it comes as little surprise that Scherer's schemes for a dramatic limitation of output were abandoned altogether between 1931 and 1933.

> Yet, while putting a brake on foreign influence at Snia Viscosa, the regime did not press the Italian firm to sever links with their foreign rivals entirely. After the entry of Italy into war in 1940, Mussolini intervened personally to avoid the sequestration of Courtaulds' interest in the company.[89] One of the reasons for this move can be found in a memorandum of 1941 by the Italian Ministry for Finance. This read, In this industry, international technical collaboration has brought important results . . . through the utilisation of technical resources available in each single country. . . . The financial participation of foreign groups in national companies have always been considered favourably to facilitate technical and commercial collaboration. This opinion was also shared by representatives of the German [rayon] industry. . . . According to the Ministry for Finance the foreign interests in Snia Viscosa should not be eliminated [authors underlining].[90]

Thus, two points may be drawn from what has been said so far on the role of the government. The first is that this fostered economic integration and international cartel agreements not only to mitigate the shortcoming of credit scarcity after 1927, but also to facilitate technology exchanges. The second point is that the regime, although favouring co-operation between Snia Viscosa and its rivals, impeded the dramatic downsizing of the company while smoothing the acquisition of foreign know-how.

CONCLUSION

It can safely be concluded then that the European rayon cartels before and after the First World War were also technology-sharing cartels and that, as such, they offered to all cartel members a potential access to, and information about, new advances. While proving crucial to the early development of the industry, these cartels eased the diffusion and exchange of technology within the cartel network and within the countries where the cartel members operated. The history of the rayon industry thus confirms the claim that European cartels were important conduits for technology transfer, accounting to a great extent for the co-evolution of both firms and industrial systems, itself an aspect of economic integration. Nevertheless, the evidence presented here also demonstrates that, while access to technology was a matter of death or life for newcomers, the cartel tended to lift entry barriers by regulating the patent and commercial policy of its members. The pursuit of profit did drive the transfer of technology, but the leading firms, via cartel agreements, were also able to influence the direction of technology flows. One point of some importance is that the transfer and successful adoption of technology did not necessarily translate into expansion for the receptor firms since the licensors tended either to retain vital information or to limit the growth of the licensees. The history of this trade shows that the impressive diffusion of rayon technology taking place soon after 1918 was attributable, among other things, to a lack of coordination among the leading firms. This history also suggests that governments had a role in ensuring that technology was effectively transferred and in avoiding a dramatic limitation of output growth.

NOTES

1. I would like to thank Roger Holowitz and the Hagley Museum and Library, Wilmington, Delaware, which generously supported my research work back in 2007. Heartfelt thanks also go, of course, to Maria Adorante.
2. Edward Mason, *Controlling World Trade: Cartels and Commodity Agreements* (New York/London, 1946), 9, 90.
3. Lionel Robbins, "Report on International Cartels," 24 January 1945, in National Archives [hereinafter NA], CAB 124/496; James Meade, *The Collected Papers of James Meade,* 4 vols. (London, 1988–1990), here *International Economics,* vol. III (1988), 45, and *The Cabinet Office Diary, 1944–6,* vol. IV (1990), 25, 34; John Maynard Keynes, *Collected Writings,* 30 vols., (Basingstoke/London, 1971–1989), here *Activities, 1941–1946: Shaping the*

Post-War World: Bretton Woods and Reparations, vol. XXV (1980), 248; Ernest F. Penrose, *Economic Planning for the Peace* (Princeton, 1953), 113; George Cyril. Allen, *Monopoly and Restrictive Practices* (London, 1968), 61–69.

4. Charles R. Whittlesey, *National Interest and International Cartels* (New York, 1946); George W. Stocking and Myron W. Watkins, *Cartels in Action* (New York, 1946).
5. For an up-to-date review of the debate on cartels see Jeffrey Fear, "Cartels," in Geoffrey Jones and Jonathan Zeitlin (eds.), *The Oxford Handbook of Business History* (Oxford, 2007), 268–292.
6. Donald C. Coleman, *Courtaulds: An Economic and Social History,* 3 vols. (Oxford, 1969–1980), here *Rayon,* vol. II (1969), 1–23.
7. Ibid., 189.
8. Ibid., 244–288, and Geoffrey Jones, *Courtaulds in Continental Europe,* in Geoffrey Jones (ed.), *British Multinationals: Origins, Management, Performance* (Aldershot, 1986), 119–139.
9. Robert C. Allen, "Collective Invention", *Journal of Economic Behavior and Organization* 4 (1983): 1–24, here 1.
10. For a review of the debate see Neil Rollings and Matthias Kipping, "Private Transnational Governance in the Heyday of the Nation-State: The Council of European Industrial Federations (CEIF)", *Economic History Review* 2 (2008): 409–431.
11. Alice Teichova, *An Economic Background to Munich: International Business and Czechoslovakia, 1918–1938* (Cambridge, 1973); Clemens Wurm, *Business, Politics and International Relations: Steel, Cotton and International Cartels in British Politics, 1924–1939* (Cambridge, 1993). See also the review by Alice Teichova of Wurm's book in *Business History Review* 1 (1995): 102–104.
12. William J. Baumol, *The Free-Market Innovation Machine: Analyzing the Growth Miracle of Capitalism* (Princeton/Oxford, 2002), 26, 74, 78; William J. Baumol, "Horizontal Collusion and Innovation", *Economic Journal* 1 (1992): 129–137, here 132; Edwin Mansfield, "International Technology Transfer: Forms, Resource Requirements, and Policies", *American Economic Review* 2 (1975): 372–376.
13. Baumol, *Horizontal Collusion* (cf. n. 12), 132.
14. Valerio Cerretano, "The European Rayon Industry and the De-globalization of the World Economy, 1917–47, unpublished doctoral thesis (University of Cambridge, 2003), 56–65.
15. Baumol, *Horizontal Collusion,* 135; Baumol, *The Free-Market Innovation Machine,* 74.
16. Valerio Cerretano, "The Benefits of 'Moderate Inflation': The Rayon Industry and Snia Viscosa in the Italy of the 1920s", *Journal of European Economic History,* 2 (2004): 234.
17. Mansfield, *International Technology Transfer,* 373; David J. Teece, "Technology Transfer by Multinational Firms: The Resource Cost of Transferring Technological Know-How", *Economic Journal,* 87 (1977): 242–261.
18. Rolf Petri, "Cartels and the Diffusion of Technologies: The Case of the Hydrogenation and Catalityc Refining", in Domique Barjot (ed.), *International Cartels Revisited, 1880–1990: Proceedings of the Caen Conference, 23–5 September 1993* (Caen, 1994), 287–300.
19. Coleman, *Courtaulds,* vol. II, 171–204.
20. Jonas Scherner, "The Beginnings of Nazi Autarky Policies: The 'National Pulp Programme' and the Origin of Regional Staple Fibres Plants", *Economic History Review* 4 (2008): 867–895.

21. There is no publication in English on the Japanese rayon industry. Yet information about its evolution can be drawn from a number or sources, including Freda Utley, *Lancashire and the Far East* (London, 1931); Board of Trade, *Survey of Textile Industries* (London, 1928); Keijiro Otsuka, Gustav Ranis and Gary Saxonhouse, "Comparative Technology Choice", in *Development: The Indian and Japanese Cotton Textile Industries* (London, 1988); Douglas A. Farnie and Takeshi Abe, "Japan, Lancashire and the Asian market for Cotton Manufacturers, 1890–1990", in Douglas A. Farnie, Tetsuro Nakaoka, David Jeremy Wilson, and Takeshi Abe (eds.), *Region and Strategy in Britain and Japan* (London, 2000), 115–157.
22. Coleman, *Courtaulds,* vol. II, 189.
23. Cerretano, *The European Rayon Industry,* 162.
24. Ibid., 56–65.
25. Ibid.
26. Ibid.
27. Ibid., 183–196.
28. Coleman, *Courtaulds,* vol. II, 76–103.
29. Fear, *Cartels,* 272, Fig. 12.1.
30. Coleman, *Courtaulds,* vol. II, 76–103.
31. Ibid.
32. Baumol, *Horizontal Collusion.*
33. Letter of Alfred Bernheim (the Comptoir) to Fritz Bluethgen (VGF), 10 August 1922; Zusammenkunft zwischen Bernheim, Dietz, Jordan und Bluethgen, Koeln, 8./9. Mai 1920, in VGF Archives, Wuppertal [hereinfafter VGF A], Frankreich-CTA, E 5–0-2, E 5–1-3 bis 19. Please note that, since consulted, this archive has now been moved to Cologne and was subject to a new classification system. See also Theodor Langenbruch, *Glanzstoff, 1899–1949* (Erbelfeld-Wuppertal, 1985), 85.
34. On this see Outline of Asahi, 1951, in VGF A, E8–1-14bis19; Noguchi Shitagau (Hiroshima) and VGF: agreements, Berlin, 25 November 1921, in VGF A, E8–1 bis 12; also Barbara Molony, *Technology and Investment: The Prewar Japanese Chemical Industry* (Cambridge, Mass., 1990), 11, 63–71, 126, 152.
35. Jogushi Jun (Hiroshima) and VGF: agreements, Berlin, 25 November 1921, in VGF A, E8–1 bis 12.
36. Letter from Alfred Bernheim (Comptoir) to Fritz Bluethgen (VGF), 24 March 1922, in VGF A, E5–0-2, E5–1-3 bis 19.
37. Final agreement between Comptoir and du Pont, 7 July 1920, in Du Pont Archives, Hagley Library, Wilmington DE [hereinafter DPA], 1771, Box 82.
38. On the Du Pont–Comptoir relationship see William Dutton, *DuPont: One Hundred and Forty Years* (New York, 1949), 302; Graham D. Taylor/ Patricia E. Sudnik, *DuPont and the International Chemical Industry* (Boston, 1984), 82, 118; Alfred Chandler, *Strategy and Structure* (Cambridge, Mass., 1962), 80; David A. Hounshell and John K. Smith, *Science and Corporate Strategy. DuPont R&D, 1902–1980* (Cambridge, 1988), 161–170, 182; Mira Wilkins, *The History of Foreign Investments in the United States, 1914–1945* (Cambridge, Mass./ London, 2004).
39. Jesse W. Markham, *Competition in the Rayon Industry* (Cambridge, Mass., 1952), 47, table.
40. Hounshell and Smith, *Science and Corporate Strategy,* 161–182; Taylor and Sudnik, *DuPont,* 118.
41. Wilkins, *The History of Foreign Investments,* 233; Stocking and Watkins, *Cartels in Action,* 460; Taylor and Sudnik, *DuPont,* 134; Pierre Cayez, *Rhône-Poulenc, 1895–1875* (Paris, 1988), 105.

42. Leonard A. Yerkes (Du Pont), Telephone conversation with F. W. Pickard of the London office, 5 February 1930, in: DPA, Carpenter's Papers, box 819.
43. Cerretano, *The Benefits of Moderate Inflation.*
44. Edgar Jones, "Price Leadership in the Rayon Industry", *Manchester School of Economic and Social Studies* 12 (1941): 82; Markham, *Competition in the Rayon Industry,* 115, 119.
45. Coleman, *Courtaulds,* vol. II, 102.
46. One noteworthy exception is John H. Dunning, "Market Power of the Firm and International Transfer of Technology: A Historical Excursion", *International Journal of Industrial Organization* 1 (1983): 333–351.
47. Cases in point are Mira Wilkins, "The Role of Private Business in the International Diffusion of Technology", *Journal of Economic History* 1 (1974): 166–188; above all, Alexander Gerschenkron, *Economic Backwardness in Historical Perspective* (New York, 1962), 8.
48. Edwin Mansfield, "International Technology Transfer: Forms, Resource Requirements, and Policies", *American Economic Review* 2 (1975): 372–376; David J. Teece, "Technology Transfer by Multinational Firms: The Resource Cost of Transferring Technological Know-How", *Economic Journal* 346 (1977): 242–261.
49. Cerretano, *The Benefits of Moderate Inflation;* Cerretano, *The European Rayon Industry:* 10–111.
50. Cerretano, *The Benefits of Moderate Inflation;* Cerretano, *The European Rayon Industry:* 10–111.
51. Coleman, *Courtaulds,* vol. II, 76–103.
52. Ibid.
53. Ibid.
54. Ibid.
55. Baumol, *The Free-Market Machine,* 105.
56. Ibid.; Cerretano, *The Benefits of Moderate Inflation;* Coleman, *Courtaulds,* vol. II, 275–288.
57. Coleman, *Courtaulds,* vol. II, 275–288; Cerretano, *The European Rayon Industry,* 44–111.
58. Cerretano, *The Benefits of Moderate Inflation.*
59. Stefano Sordelli, Promemoire relatif a la transformation de l' Usine de Venaria Reale, 12 Août 1930, Memorandum by Riccardo Gualino to Fritz Bluethgen and Ernst Lunge, 11 April 1929; Hermann, Aktennotiz ueber den Besuch bei der Snia Werk Venaria Reale am Donnerstag, 11. September 1930, in VGF A, SV 179.
60. Memorandum by Ernst Lunge (Courtaulds) regarding Snia Viscosa, 22 September 1930, in Courtaulds Archives, Coventry [hereinafter CA], JHW.16.
61. British Patent 34446 ("Improvements in spinning machine").
62. Coleman, *Courtaulds,* vol. II, 51.
63. Notes on Pedder report, 31 October 1931, in CA, SAM.12.
64. Memorandum by Ernst Lunge (Courtaulds) regarding Snia Viscosa, 22 September 1930, in CA, JHW.16
65. Cerretano, *The European Rayon Industry,* 159–175.
66. Bericht ueber die Stapelfaserschnelbidachine des Herrn BLASCHKE und den Vergleich mit dem DRP. 468 315 Beria/Turin, 24. August 1933, in VGF A, SV 179.
67. Cerretano, *The European Rayon Industry,* 204.
68. Coleman, *Courtaulds,* vol. III, 112.
69. Ernst Lunge, "Report on the Cerini Caustic Soda Recovering Plant as Used at Venaria Reale", 14 November 1929, in CA, SNI.4.
70. Cerini Dyalisers, 6 October 1937, in CA, JHW.57.

71. Ibid.
72. Agreement on Lanital, 7 July 1937, in CA, AGR.31.
73. Letter of John Hanbury-Williams to Samuel Agar Salvage (American Viscose Corporation), 15 September 1937, in CA, JHW.3
74. Cable of Samuel Salvage to John Hanbury-Williams, 9 June 1937, in CA, JHW.3.
75. Ernst Lunge (Courtaulds), Memorandum to Samuel Courtauld, Rapallo, 11 April 1931, in VGF A, E7–1–10 bis 14.
76. Coleman, *Courtaulds,* vol. II, 351
77. Transfer of box-spinning technologies from Cologne was, obviously, also agreed with Courtaulds; Letter of Conrad Hermann (VGF) to Franco Marinotti, 5 April 1935, in VGF A, SV 179.
78. Extract from minutes of Board Meetings Courtaulds, 10 March 1939, in CA JHW.4. On cake-washing systems see Coleman, *Courtaulds,* vol. II, 187.
79. Cerretano, *The European Rayon Industry,* 217–222.
80. Ibid.
81. Letter of Balfour-Murphy to John Hanbury-Williams, 1 January 1931, in CA, JHW.51.
82. In the original: "Se con l'intervento straniero la situazione finanziaria può considerarsi pel momento sistemata, non si può, quando si possegga un'ombra di amor proprio, non sentire tutta l'umiliazione di codesto intervento". Note al Duce sull'assemblea generale della Snia Viscosa, 31 marzo 1931, in Archivio Centrale dello Stato, Rome, [hereinafter ACS], SPD, CR, b102,f169/R.
83. Valerio Castronovo, *Giovanni Agnelli. La Fiat dal 1899 al 1945* (Turin, 1977), 339–345.
84. See, in particular, Memoria. Rapporti Snia-Châtillon, 21 ottobre 1939, in ACS, IRI, SR, B15, Fasc: Trattative con Snia Viscosa, 1939–1941 and Memoria. Soc. An. It. per le fibre tessili artificiali già Châtillon 20 ottobre 1941, in IRI, SR, B15, Fasc: Châtillon-Trattative di cessione.
85. In the original: "In una delle conversazioni avute, gli [a Borletti] é stato accennato delle preoccupazioni di carattere nazionale inerenti al rafforzamento del gruppo di maggioranza che, secondo voci diffuse, é controllato da stranieri o rappresenta un interesse straniero. Il Senatore Borletti ha smentito tale controllo. . . . A riprova di ciò, egli ha esibito gli atti costitutivi e gli statuti di due societa: La SAGEPI e la SAFRA . . . é gioco forza comunque riconoscere che le formule eccezionali adottate negli statuti delle due holdings confermerebbero quella che é opinione diffusa, essere cioè il controllo della Snia nelle mani di gruppi stranieri". Azioni Snia, 3 Novembre 1933, in ACS, IRI,SR, B15, Fasc: Trattative con Snia Viscosa, 1935.
86. Coleman, *Courtaulds,* vol. II, 378; Cerretano, *The European Rayon Industry,* 175–183.
87. Ibid.
88. In the original: « Ces modifications n'ont pas été faites pour le goût de changement, ni pour faire de la théorie inutile, mais se sont imposées pour des raisons, voudrais je-dire, politique et d'ordre général . . . cette modification a été proposée uniquement pour moraliser, pour ainsi dire un peu la situation ». Letter of Senatore Borletti to Fritz Bluethgen (VGF), 29 May 1931, in VGF A, E7–1–22 bis 34.
89. Coleman, *Courtaulds,* vol. III, 109.
90. In the original: "In questa industria, la collaborazione tecnica a carattere internazionale, ha portato sempre risultati positivi nel miglioramento produttivo ed economico, attraverso lo sfruttamento delle risorse tecniche via

affioranti in ogni Paese, come pure gli accordi con i gruppi ed i Sindacati nazionali dei vari Paesi produttori, hanno permesso una armonica e progressiva affermazione nel mondo delle fibre sintetiche. Accanto a queste necessitá, è sempre stata ritenuta opportuna la partecipazione finanziaria di gruppi stranieri nelle imprese nazionali dei vari Paesi, e questo per maggiormente facilitare la collaborazione tecnica e commerciale . . . il Ministero delle Finanze ritiene che le partecipazioni estere della Snia non debbano essere eliminate». In Considerazioni e premesse per l'unificazione dei piú importanti organismi Italiani per la produzione dei tessili artificiali". Undated but 1941, in ACS, IRI, SR: Fasc. Châtillon—Trattative di cessione.

5 Big Business, Inter-Firm Cooperation and National Governments

The International Aluminium Cartel, 1886–1939*

Marco Bertilorenzi

Aluminium was widely recognized as one of the most cartelized industries before the Second World War. From 1886, when the modern production process of aluminium was discovered, to 1939, four official cartels appeared one after the other. Much scholarship has underlined the power of these organizations, for better or worse, in controlling the global output of aluminium. Both supporters and detractors pointed out the paradigmatic ability of aluminium cartels to suppress the emergence of outsiders and to maintain control over markets.[1] In this chapter, I will retrace the more intricate interplay between firms, cartels, and governments in order to scrutinize the processes of technology transfer in the industry and the ways in which cartelization reshaped the global diffusion of aluminium production.

William Baumol provocatively pointed out that cartels could have positive effects on innovation and its further dissemination, and vice-versa. According to Baumol, firms could find great advantages in sharing research costs within their cartel frameworks, obtaining decisive gains to compete against outsiders. Furthermore, this transfer of technology could also serve to strengthen the internal cohesion of cartels.[2] Economic literature often views cartels as relatively ephemeral agreements because they are constantly menaced by the individual actions of members driven to maximize their own benefits at the expense of other members.[3] The advantages of sharing technology, Baumol argues, could mitigate the volatility and instability of such agreements. Given this backdrop, how did cartels actually influence technology transfers? What were the interactions in the cartel context, and which actors were involved? Could technology transfers reinforce a cartel agreement? If so, how?

The history of the aluminium industry uncovers many insights into these themes. The high concentration and specific technological features of the industry (heavy capital and energy-intensive production) partially explain its cartelization.[4] For almost fifty years, a few firms managed their industry through cartel structures. Directors of aluminium firms established long-standing relationships and shared common views about the general development of their business. Louis Marlio, the president of aluminium cartels during 1920s and 1930s, claimed proudly that aluminium cartels were a "true co-operation from all points of view—technical, commercial, and financial."[5] From my standpoint, technology was a decisive factor: almost all producers were born from the initial dissemination of the two electrolysis patents (Hall's and Héroult's), cooperated during the arduous initial years to refine the producing process, and shared their know-how to find room for their metal in the difficult non-ferrous metal market dominated by the older businesses of copper or tin.[6]

In the aluminium industry, the historical issue of technology transfers within cartels is more complicated than serving as a simple tool for improving cohesion. Aluminium cartels apparently formed an informal institution, which Douglas North originally posited, as they regulated the life of the industry as a community of actors for many years.[7] In short, technology transfer helped reshape cartel structures in three distinct ways. First, firms implemented individual policies toward technology transfers, international patent licensing, and FDI (foreign direct investment) strategy. Second, cartels amassed technology and transferred it within a collective setup; for instance, they could disseminate expertise to members, refusing to share it externally. Third, governments interacted with firms (and with cartels) in this process by either reinforcing cartel policies in terms of technology transfer or, on the contrary, working to undermine their efforts with more or less effective awareness.

This chapter will provide a concise account of the frameworks in which cartels and technology transfer interacted in the global aluminium industry. In the first part, I will discuss the creation of a technological network of aluminium firms in the 1890s, the subsequent creation of a cartel in 1901, and its evolution through 1914. Moving on, I will focus on the interwar period. Finally, the third part will survey some specific interactions between firm and governments, showing how the economic and political context of late 1930s signified a rupture with the past. Technology transfer was both the source of cohesion and the catalyst of desegregation within the cartel community, depending also on the general conjuncture and international political context. Technology was a tool for a kind of industrial diplomacy that sometimes eroded relationships, even in the robust aluminium cartels.

PATENTS, TECHNOLOGY, AND CARTELS IN THE EARLY ALUMINIUM INDUSTRY (1886–1914)

Aluminium was a new industry at the end of nineteenth century. Electrolysis, which is still used today to produce aluminium, was discovered simultaneously but independently in 1886 by Paul Toussaint Héroult in France and Charles Martin Hall in the United States.[8] Before this discovery, aluminium was a scarce and expensive metal; its global output in 1886 was only around three tons, for example.[9] Electrolysis changed the *status* of the industry, enabling cheap mass production. The first movers in the aluminium industry took advantage of this new producing method by securing control over the two original patents. The Swiss Aluminium Industrie Aktiengesellschaft (hereafter AIAG) was formed in 1887 to use Héroult's patent,[10] while Hall's was adopted by the Pittsburgh Reduction Company (hereinafter PRC, which in 1907 became the Aluminum Company of America, hereinafter ALCOA), incorporated one year later.[11] Both PRC and AIAG first applied electrolysis in smaller laboratories and then proceeded to launch scale and scope strategies.[12]

The first movers also started licensing their patents internationally to diversify the sources of their earnings. After having registered Héroult's patent in all European countries either on the behalf of the inventor or on its ownership,[13] AIAG allowed Héroult to establish an enterprise in France, which he did in 1889 under the name of Société Electro-Métallurgique Française (SEMF),[14] and licensed to another producer in Great Britain, the British Aluminium Company (BACO), in 1894.[15] In both cases, AIAG provided the required machinery to two new firms, supervised their installations, and exchanged stakes with two new firms in order to create stronger bonds with them. AIAG also internationalized its activities at an early stage, investing in Germany (1897) and Austria (1898). By 1891, AIAG had already begun establishing an international network of sales agencies (with agents in Italy, Russia, Austria, Poland, Germany, and Japan) to execute a global commercial strategy.[16]

Although PRC did not have quite the internationalized profile that AIAG did, it shared with its Swiss counterpart the need to extend its earnings through international licensing. Having being forestalled by AIAG to license a producer in Great Britain, PRC licensed a French producer in 1895. Two years later, this firm found itself in a bad financial situation and succumbed. Afterward, this firm was taken over by Produits Chimiques d'Alais et de la Camargue (PCAC, also known as Pechiney), which also secured the Hall's technology.[17] In order to keep its monopoly in the North American markets, PRC also ventured into Canada and formed a subsidiary called the Northern Aluminium Company (NACO) in 1896, although the new company started production in 1901.[18] PRC also created a manufacturing and sales agency in England in order to export the metal that the American market was not yet able to absorb.[19]

These licensing contracts were the first cause of the horizontal transfer of aluminium smelting technology at the end of nineteenth century. Patent protection prevented the formation of outsiders, according with different national legislative constraints, and played an important role in the original structural development of the industry.[20] In my view, this dissemination represented the first step toward cartelization; patent contracts gave a monopoly over both production and sales to the licensees in their own countries in exchange for not exporting. For instance, AIAG granted to both SEMF and BACO a national monopoly on the condition that the licensees would not export. In 1896, the two owners of the electrolysis patents (AIAG and PRC) settled an agreement to stay out of each other's markets (no Swiss exports or investment in North America and no American exports or investments in Europe).[21] In 1901, all the firms involved in this patent network formed an official international cartel, the Aluminium Association (AA).[22]

Without diving too deep into the details of the bargains that preceded the AA, it is sufficient to stress that AIAG led the construction of the cartel and conceived it as a tool to coordinate production, obtain reliable market statistics, and set common policies to govern international sales.[23] The main problem facing the contemporary aluminium industry was a lack of demand despite lower costs. Extensions of aluminium applications required long-term R&D initiatives.[24] Consequently, firms aimed to unify sales under the commercial agents of AIAG that, through a policy of stable prices and a constant flow of information amongst producers, gave the cartel the reach it needed to access a larger number of customers. The AA, acting as an informal agency designed to facilitate the vertical transfer of technology for new uses, became the framework through which players shared know-how.[25]

Cartelization did not halt individual investment strategies, however. By 1903–1904, all firms looked into either the erection of new smelters or the extension of existing ones to satisfy the growing demand.[26] Furthermore, firms invested also to negotiate their positions in the AA during its renewal in 1906 (see Table 5.1). This phase facilitated further diffusion; for instance, BACO contributed to diffuse technology abroad because it invested in Norway in order to exploit cheaper hydroelectric power.[27] However, the economic crisis of 1907 slowed the demand down, while new producers appeared in France, exploiting the expiration of the Héroult's patent. Outsiders also sprouted up in Norway, England, and Italy.[28] In this last case, some German metal traders, hoping to dismantle the AA's sales monopoly, drove technology transfer directly to Italy, where they incorporated joint ventures with electrochemical producers.[29]

AA did not survive the crisis and fell apart in 1908. A new cartel was formed again in 1912 when firms reached a new compromise. The formation of a French national cartel—called Aluminium Français (AF)—was an important factor in the new international scheme. AF was able to lead negotiations thanks to a consistent strategy of technical innovation aimed at recreating cohesion after the failure of the cartel, which was able to end the struggle that followed the termination of the previous cartel. In 1910, PCAC acquired and developed a promising patent called "Serpek" for producing alumina, the mid-product for aluminium, which made it possible to reduce the prices of the metal by about 30%.[30] PCAC involved all other French producers (SEMF and other newcomers appeared after 1906), and AF actually served to exploit this new production method collectively.[31]

Moreover, PCAC also carried out an international strategy. After having forged a commercial alliance with one of most important international traders of non-ferrous metals (Metallgesellschaft),[32] it tried to invest in the United States. With the help of the German firm, AF formed a new company, the Southern Aluminum Company (SACO), to use the Serpek's process to gain a competitive advantage against PRC (which, in the meantime, changed its name to ALCOA). This transfer of technology aimed to force ALCOA to join a new international cartel, after some initial refusals, with a low quota in exchange for access to Serpek's technology.[33] AF also dealt with AIAG to share the same patent on alumina in exchange of a smaller quota in the new international cartel. In 1912, a few days after the incorporation of SACO in the United States and a secret agreement between AF and AIAG on the Serpek's patent, a new Aluminium Association was formed with AF in a leading position (see Table 5.1).[34]

However, the new patent on alumina ended up being unfeasible, and AF lost all its advantages. In 1914, PCAC made a last-ditch effort to start Serpek production in Norway in order to keep its leadership in the cartel, but the initiative ended in failure.[35] The war interrupted AA, anticipating its denunciation raised by AIAG in hopes of breaking its secret agreement with AF. Until 1914, technology was a key element in alliance formation. Thanks to this technical diffusion, firms started their networks at the end of nineteenth century and endorsed cartel schemes afterward. The legal protection of patents precluded the dissemination of technology outside the cartel framework. Thus, the cartels did not take particular initiatives against the diffusion of technology. Technological innovation and its diffusion were a way to compete in a cartelized industry and improve the position of each firm.

CONTROLLING EXPANSION: TECHNOLOGY AND CARTELS DURING THE INTERWAR PERIOD

The Great War transformed the international geography of the aluminium industry, and all firms augmented their output, even investing abroad.[36] For instance, PCAC invested in Italy to supply the Italian government during the Great War and also planned to invest in Russia before the Bolshevik Revolution stepped in.[37] BACO increased its Norwegian production, while AIAG augmented its output, as well. During the war, ALCOA blocked the French investment in the United States and extended its American output to become the greatest world producer, boasting more than half of the world's total capacity.[38] The panorama was also shocked by the creation of a new German company. In 1917, some *Grossen Interessen* from the electrical and chemical branches formed the Vereinigte Aluminium Werke (VAW), which, after the war, was reorganized and put under the control of the German government.[39]

The main outcomes of these investments were the saturation of the principal outlets (the United States and Germany) and relative growth in the output of exporting countries (Switzerland, Norway, and France). In order to manage the resulting overproduction, BACO, AF, and ALCOA explored the possibility of creating an official R&D agency whose goal it would be to carry out joint research on new applications. This would have been useful in promoting a quick transition from war-related to peace-related uses.[40] In

1918, BACO began devising drafts for this type of agency, but the actual formation of such an organization was put on hold by the crisis of 1921 because firms desisted from investing in the structure. Firms were then unable to reach a cartel agreement, which also delayed technical cooperation. The prospects of a joint R&D agency to share patents and innovations were rekindled only when a new cartel agreement was signed in 1926.[41]

Beginning in 1923, European firms worked to resuscitate their cartel, holding regular meetings to coordinate the stabilization of prices after the post-war inflation. However, they found increasingly difficult to involve ALCOA, which refused to take part in the meetings in 1924. ALCOA, after the takeover of SACO in 1915, was again a monopoly and had no free hands to join cartel schemes due to the scrutiny of American antitrust authorities throughout the 1920s.[42] ALCOA also carried out an expansionist strategy during the 1920s that made it too challenging to reach a compromise with the Europeans. In 1925, ALCOA actually succeeded in stopping a very dangerous initiative on the part of Ford and General Electric to come into the aluminium business, taking over a huge investment that those firms started in Canada with the cooperation of Duke and Price for hydroelectric production.[43]

Having taken control of this new smelter, ALCOA owned an enormous excess of production. In order to stimulate sales of this new output, it invested abroad in manufacturing branches (France, Germany, Italy, Japan, Spain, England, and Belgium), thereby simultaneously initiating the technical transfer of know-how. ALCOA also invested in smaller smelters designed to function as "Trojan horses" that would influence tariff policies in order to assist imports from Canada.[44] At the same time, ALCOA created a special division in its managerial structure dedicated to foreign markets (the Foreign Selling Subsidiaries). This structure evolved in 1928 when ALCOA formed a Canadian holding, the Aluminium Limited (ALTED), which took over all foreign activities of the American giant. This choice aimed to penetrate international markets more effectively.[45]

During the 1920s, Europeans were convinced that ALCOA refused to participate in a cartel scheme only for the fear of antitrust persecution. Therefore, European firms tried to cooperate with ALCOA and proposed entry into joint ventures, considering them the first step toward the resurgence of a cartel.[46] AFC shared the stakes of its Norwegian subsidiary with BACO and ALCOA and of its Italian subsidiary with ALCOA.[47] In 1925, AIAG, ALCOA, and AFC invested in a new company in Spain, with a part of the shares going to a Spanish electrical group.[48] These joint ventures were also important for the sharing of new technical improvements; for instance, the Spanish smelter of 1925 was built with a new kind of electrolysis pots called Söderberg pots, whose patents were owed by a Swedish company linked with ALCOA.[49] Through this new company, AFC and AIAG also got involved in using this technical innovation.

Other firms also invested abroad. In 1926, AIAG and VAW invested in Italy. AIAG enlisted the help of an Italian electrical group. VAW formed a joint venture with Montecatini, the leading Italian chemical producer and one of the principal electrical companies of the *Penisola,* in which both firms owned 50% of the shares.[50] The involvement of national interests was conceived as a method to avoid the emergence of free-runners and maintain control over global production capacity. In both cases, technology transfers took center stage. AIAG experimented with new technologies for the erection of dams in order to stabilize the flow of water; VAW, meanwhile, tested the Haglund's patent for the alumina, which was eventually revealed to be less efficient than expected.[51] These activities were also linked to an imminent cartel agreement and aimed at improving relative positions in order to solidify bargaining positions on participation in the cartel (see Table.5.1).

In 1926, European firms formed a new cartel, again called the Aluminium Association (AA). In its contract, the members formalized their attitude toward new investments and technology transfers: FDIs were allowed only when new firms could be fully controlled. The reason for this choice was that companies needed to encourage growth but at the same time also prevent the formation of uncontrolled output.[52] Written into the AA contract were prospective penalties for members that violated its terms (50,000 Swiss francs), but the cartel board never actually enforced this clause.[53] At the same time, AA returned to the idea from 1918 about the establishment of a formal agency for the exchange of know-how. Formed in 1927, the Bureau International d'Etude et Propagande (BIEP) aimed to share technology and patents among cartel members and provide assistance to consumers in order to promote the expansion of demand. The organization also periodically gave out grants for designs and technical innovations.[54]

While AA and ALTED were still achieving their investments planned during the 1920s, an economic crisis took the place of the expansion period. The global consumption of aluminium plummeted, and unsold inventories skyrocketed to alarming levels until a compromise between Europeans and Americans set forth guidelines to reduce global output. In 1931, a new "world" cartel, called the Alliance Aluminium Compagnie (AAC), was created with the involvement of ALTED. This cartel was very different from its predecessors: the AAC was a financial institution for taking control over excess stock, providing a buffer, and reducing production. From a legal standpoint, this form of cartel was acceptable for ALTED.[55] The AAC also took over BIEP, changing its name to the Bureau International de l'Aluminium (BIA), and set up new common R&D programs.[56]

The AAC was built with an anticyclical scope to reduce production while buffering excess inventory, stockpiled because of the economic crisis. The AAC did not prevent new investments, but output was compelled to enter under the AAC's production control. AAC also forbade technical assistance to outsiders.[57] Both these rules and the global economic crisis essentially guarded against technology diffusion outside the cartel without the need to implement agreements with fees. The great overproduction that affected the aluminium industry made increasing production unrealistic. However, these conditions changed rapidly during 1930s, when military rearmament programs ushered in a new season of growth and reasons to invest in new capacities.

THE ALUMINIUM RUSH: POLITICS AND TECHNOLOGY TRANSFERS DURING THE 1930s

Until the end of 1920s, aluminium production was concentrated in a small clique of countries, and, as outlined earlier, the geographical reaches of each producing country was connected via individual firm strategies or international cartel strategies. During the 1930s, a growing number of governments started to explore the possibilities of producing aluminium for strategic reasons; military preparedness and import substitutions were the central motivations behind governmental plans for aluminium. While there were only nine aluminium-producing countries in 1931, world production rose to fifteen countries by 1939, and only World War II stopped further geographic expansion. Even though the AAC aimed to stand in the way of technical aid to newcomers, the cartel was not able to hamper the formation of new "unwanted" producers.

Many governments, such as the Japanese, the Polish, the Czechoslovakian, and the Yugoslavian governments, for instance, asked cartel members to invest in their countries during the market growth process in the 1920s. Only the cartel members had the knowledge to establish efficient and integrated aluminium production. However, cartel members refused to invest in these countries because they were not considered good targets for their respective investment strategies. These countries had neither markets large enough to absorb the full production of a scale smelter nor the optimal factors for obtaining producing costs low enough to export excess output. Firms proposed the creation of strategic stocks instead of direct investments, which appeared irrational from an economic point of view.[58] During the 1930s, political factors became predominant determinants in the choice of providing technology, reversing the past situation.

The first country where the government was able to drive technology transfer was the Soviet Union. Since the middle of the 1920s, the Soviet Union represented an important outlet for AFC, which also formed a dedicated agency called the Comptoir Franco-Russe to establish regular relations with the Soviet market.[59] Amidst the saturated international outlets of the late 1920s, AFC made the decision to provide technical aid to the Soviet Union in order to maintain its commercial position in the country. AFC also forestalled ALTED, which was also bargaining with Soviet authorities for the installation of a national production system, and obtained a priority channel to sell aluminium in the Soviet Union. The country did not want a direct investment from AFC; it asked only for technologies and it aimed to keep a firm grip on production, which was restricted to the domestic market. As a consequence, the Soviet production was neither a risk for AFC, nor a danger for the international markets.[60]

The main problem with Soviet production was the lack of good raw materials, which motivated the government to make attempts at developing alternative technologies. AFC provided decisive know-how on tuning these alternative processes, enabling the country to produce aluminium with its own raw material resources. Raw materials represented a key issue for Japan, as well. Without any source of bauxite in Japan, Japanese firms took control over alternative raw materials in Manchuria after its invasion. The Japanese government provided aid, allowing Showa Denko to launch production in 1934. Two years later, Mitsui took control over some high-quality bauxite deposits in the Dutch East Indies and adopted the Western process.[61] It is not clear how Mitsui obtained its technology because all AAC firms agreed to refuse technical help to Japan. However, it is possible that German authorities helped Japan in order to establish stronger political bonds with its new ally. ALTED also may have provided technology, considering that it created a joint venture with Sumitomo in 1937.[62]

After Russia and Japan set up production, Sweden and Yugoslavia followed suit. In these countries, an AAC competitor played a pivotal role in providing technology and creating FDIs: the German chemical firm Giulini Gebrüder. Giulini had been a leading producer of alumina since the end of nineteenth century and played a key role in the mushrooming of the outsider population after 1906. Thereafter, it supplied both cartel companies and smaller outsiders with its alumina without posing a threat to the AA. The founding of the AAC and its plans to reduce production deprived Giulini of important outlets, which set the company out in search of alternative markets. Giulini started to negotiate with some governments on the construction of aluminium smelters in order to supply them with its alumina. The AAC arrived in extremis to impede Giulini's investment in the Netherlands, delaying the construction of a smelter there, but failed in Sweden and Yugoslavia. ALTED managed to deter Giulini in Sweden,[63] but Giulini succeed in establishing a new firm in Yugoslavia in 1935.[64]

The cartel was very concerned by Giulini's venture in Yugoslavia because the country represented a potential base for further expansions. Actually, Yugoslavia was a military and commercial ally of Czechoslovakia and Romania (the so-called "Petite Entente"). The AAC feared that Giulini might supply these other countries with its Yugoslavian production or, worse, that it posed the risk of starting new smelters. However, the AAC was not able to find a common policy against Giulini: AFC, AIAG, VAW, and ALTED ran separate negotiations with each government, competing with one another to carve out commercial advantages and install local production constructs. Actually, these countries were extending their war demand thanks to new rearmament programs, becoming good outlets for the members of the cartel. Furthermore, tumult on the international monetary scene also changed the relative positions of these countries, rendering them less negative than before.

In this new context, in which globalization faded and national military demand grew, aluminium firms saw the policies of the various countries as opportunities to increase sales, extend the geographical spans of their outlets, and find financial aid for new investments. AFC forestalled AIAG and ALTED in Czechoslovakia and Poland,[65] as well as ALTED and VAW in Romania, in 1937 and 1938. AFC benefited substantially from the diplomatic and military relationships that French authorities had established with these countries. Furthermore, AFC was able to find good national partners, including Skoda in Czechoslovakia and Concordia in Rumania.[66] However, the war interrupted these investments. Political links were also decisive in the creation of the Hungarian aluminium industry; Manfred Weiss started production in 1938, exploiting his personal partnership with Hermann Goering and entering the flow of funds provided by the Four Year Plan.[67]

The failure of the AAC to prevent the formation of new producers was the result of both exogenous and endogenous factors. During the 1930s, the role of governments in the aluminium industry expanded globally at the expense of cartel control over production and trade. In many countries, governments stepped into central roles in the planning of production, in technical research, and in the control of international trade. Research into alternative raw materials were crucial; Japan and Soviet Union, as discussed previously, developed new processes that made use of domestically available raw materials and thus reduced imports. Secondly, the AAC became less effective during the second half of the 1930s also because ALTED became uncomfortable with the AAC after an antitrust process against ALCOA began in 1937.[68] Fearing damage to its sister firm, ALTED led the cartel to end its operations of output control, which was officially suspended in 1938.[69] As consequence, all firms had free hands to invest; all the programs designed to promote technology transfer to new countries arose from this context.[70]

CONCLUSIONS

Firms, cartels, and governments were the main actors in the process of technology transfer in aluminium industry, and their interactions fell into two different phases. Until the 1920s (except for during World War I), technology transfers occurred almost only through the individual strategies of firms and the collective actions of cartels. Few standing firms with global strategies transferred technology across national boundaries to compete and to cooperate in a cartel context. Each technology transfer came from a cartel context that, using the concept expressed by Clemens Wurm and Jeffrey Fear, shaped the rules of the game of competition between firms.[71] An important aspect of the links between cartels and technology transfer is also the way in which firms cooperated in terms of technology; at first, they shared technology informally and, after the consolidation of a cartel, created common R&D agencies.

A second phase occurred during the 1930s: the roles of states in technology transfers developed, and many nonproducing countries (the Soviet Union, Japan, and most Eastern European countries) attracted technology and know-how for military reasons due to the strategic importance of aluminium in modern warfare. While the cartel formally tried to hamper deregulated transfers, in some cases the cartel's firms decided to provide technology for political and strategic reasons. In the context of waning globalization, stagnation in global markets, and the development of autarkic policies, which took hold during the 1930s, sharing expertise with foreign governments provided a great boost to sales and created preferential trade channels. However, these practices deeply affected the cohesion of the cartel, reducing its effectiveness. In many cases, new alliances (states with firms) generated tension among AAC members, which competed in settling agreements with foreign governments.

In conclusion, technology transfer is not always a functional way to strengthen the internal cohesion of a cartel, but the history of aluminium cartels shows that technical cooperation was the seed of cartelization at the end of nineteenth century. The presence of a cartel considered cohesive and fair by its members helped form the specific structures for sharing technology and R&D amongst members because a certain degree of trust, provided by the cartel, was necessary to such operations. Trust, cohesion, and technological information sharing are in this way strongly linked. On the contrary, a lack of cohesion could provoke technology transfers outside the cartel framework—the case of AFC collaboration in the Soviet aluminium industry, the penetration of ALTED in Sweden, and the competition for technical aid in the 1930s endorse this point. FDIs and transfers of technology were also used for competitive purposes; the main difference between the 1920s and the 1930s is that although the 1920s witnessed competition oriented toward the formation of new cartels, the 1930s saw FDIs and transfers of technology were some of the main causes of cartel failure.

APPENDIX

Table 5.1 The evolution of aluminium cartels' quotas, 1901–1931, in percentages

Firms	AA 1901	AA 1906	AA 1912	AA 1926	AA 1928	AAC 1931[b]
AIAG	47.50	35.52	21.40	23.80	22.40	15.40
BACO	15.60	17.24	16.00	16.00	18.00	15.00
French[a]	16.80	30.00	38.90	33.10	31.00	21.40
NACO[c]	20.10	17.24	16.00	–	–	28.50
VAW	–	–	–	27.10	22.60	19.70
Others	–	–	7.70	–	–	–
Total	100.00	100.00	100.00	100.00	100.00	100.00

Sources: author's elaboration for various archives records.

Notes: [a]=in 1901 and 1906 as SEMF + PCAC; afterward as AF; [b]=AAC did not settled quotas of sales, it allowed quotas of production following stakes owned to each firm in AAC and the percentage refers to each firm's stakes ownership; [c]= NACO in 1931 is ALTED.

NOTES

* This research is part of the French National Research Fund (ANR) "CRE-ALU" (ANR-10-CREA-011). I thank Pierre-Yves Donzé and Shigehiro Nishimura for having asked me to write this article and for their fruitful comments on my first draft. This article is a partial result of my PhD thesis, and I want to express my gratitude to my two directors, Luciano Segreto and Dominique Barjot. I also express my gratitude to Ivan Grinberg and Maurice Laparra of the Institute for the History of Aluminium of Paris: their great support was essential during my research. I would like also to thank all the archivists and librarians from various countries and institutions that helped me over the course of my investigation. Finally, I want to thank Patricia, my girlfriend, for her never-ending support.

1. For instance, aluminium cartels were presented as a model in some official or semi-official publications of the Société des Nations and of the International Chamber of Commerce, such as Société des Nations, Section économique et financière, *Etude sur les aspects économiques de différentes ententes industrielles internationales* (Geneva, 1930) and Chambre du Commerce Internationale, Secrétariat Général, *Ententes internationales—Congrès de Berlin 1937* (Paris, 1937). These examples served as negative models to American observers; see George W. Stocking, "Aluminum Alliance," in *Cartels in Action. Case Studies in International Business Diplomacy,* ed. George W. Stocking, Myron Watkins (New York, 1946), 216–273; Charlotte Muller, *Light Metals Monopoly* (New York, 1946); and Donald H. Wallace, *Market Control in Aluminum Industry* (Cambridge, 1936).
2. William J. Baumol, "Horizontal Collusion and Innovation," *The Economic Journal,* vol.102, n. 410 (January 1992): 129–137.
3. George Stigler, "A Theory of Oligopoly," *Journal of Political Economy,* vol. 72, n. 1 (1964): 44–61; Mancur Olson, *The Logic of Collective Action: Public Goods and the Theory of Groups* (Cambridge, 1965); Margaret Levenstein and Valery Suslow, "What Determines Cartel Success?" *Journal of Economic Literature,* vol. 44, n. 1 (2006): 43–95.
4. Dominique Barjot, "Introduction," in *International Cartels Revisited (1880–1980)—Vues nouvelles sur les cartels internationaux (1880–1980),* ed. Dominique Barjot (Caen, 1994), 9–70.
5. Louis Marlio, *The Aluminum Cartel* (Washington DC, 1946), 116. For more on Louis Marlio, see Henry Morsel, "Louis Marlio: Position idéologique et comportment politique d'un dirigeant d'une grande entreprise dans la première moitié du XXc s," in *Industrialisation et societies en Europe occidentale de la fin du XIXe siècle à nous jours: L'Âge de l'Aluminium,* ed. Ivan Grinberg, Florence Hachez-Leroy (Paris, 1997), 53–70.
6. Karl Erich Born, *Internationale Kartellierung einer neuen Industrie: Die Aluminium-Association 1901–1915* (Stuttgart, 1994); Florence Hachez-Leroy, "Le cartel international de l'aluminium du point de vue des sociétés françaises, 1901–1940," in *International Cartels Revisited,*153–162. See also Marco Bertilorenzi, "L'Alliance Aluminium Compagnie, 1931–1939 : Organisation et gestion de la branche internationale de l'aluminium entre Grande crise et Guerre mondiale," in *Contribution à une histoire des cartels en Suisse,* ed. Alain Cortat (Neuchâtel, 2010), 219–253.
7. Douglass C. North, *Institutions, Institutional Change and Economic Performance* (Cambridge, 1990). For the importance of institutional structures, see Peter Hall and David Soskice (eds.), *Varieties of Capitalism: The Institutional Foundations of Comparative Advantage* (Oxford, 2001).

8. Today the aluminium production method is called "Hall-Héroult." Warren S. Peterson and Ronald E. Miller (eds.), *Hall-Héroult Centennial: First Century of Aluminum Process Technology, 1886–1986* (Warrendale, 1986); Ivan Grinberg, *Aluminum: Light at Heart* (Paris, 2009).
9. Jacques Bocquentin, "La Fabrication de l'aluminium par électrolyse," in *Histoire technique de la production d'aluminium : Les apports français au développement international d'une industrie,* ed. Paul Morel (Grenoble, 1991), 29–30.
10. AIAG took this name in 1888 when AEG merged with Schweizerische Metallurgische Gesellschaft, which was formed an year earlier in 1887 by Escher Wyss, Oerlikon, and Nehers. "AIAG" is used here to ensure simplicity. For more on the history of SMG and AIAG, see AIAG, *Geschichte der Aluminium-Industrie-Aktiengesellschaft Neuhausen, 1888–1938,* 2 vols. (Zurich, 1942); Carl Dux, *Die Aluminium-Industrie-Aktiengesellschaft Neuhausen und ihre Konkurrenz-Gesellschaften* (Luzern, 1911); Cornelia Rauh, *Schweizer Aluminium fur Hitlers Krieg? Zur Geschichte der Alusuisse 1918–1950* (Munich, 2009); Adrian Knoepli, *From Dawn to Dusk: Alusuisse—Swiss Aluminium Pioneer from 1930 to 2010* (Zurich, 2011).
11. Charles C. Carr, *ALCOA: An American Enterprise* (New York, 1952); George David Smith, *From Monopoly to Competition: The Transformations of Alcoa, 1888–1986* (Cambridge, 1988).
12. Margaret B. W. Graham and Bettye H. Pruitt, *R&D for Industry: A Century of Technical Innovation at Alcoa* (Cambridge, Mass., 1990); AIAG, *Geschichte.*
13. About patents strategies of Héroult and AIAG, see Marco Bertilorenzi, "From Patents to Industrialisation: Paul Héroult and International Patent Strategies, 1886–1889," *Cahiers d'Histoire de l'Aluminium,* n. 49 (2012).
14. Institut pour l'Histoire de l'Aluminium, Paris (IHA), Documents Henri Morsel, n.c., SEMF, Rapports SEMF/Neuhausen, "Convention avec M. Dreyfus et Sté Métall-Suisse," 26.10.1888; "Rapports avec Ste de Neuhausen," 20.10.1890.
15. University of Glasgow Archives, BACO archives (hereafter BACO archives), UGD/347 21/27/14, "Agreements between the Société Anonyme pour l'Industrie de l'Aluminium de Neuhausen and British Aluminium Company Ltd.," 26.7.1894; UGD/347/21/46/7, "Notes on the Formation of the British Aluminium Company Ltd.," 1.5.1894; "The British Aluminium Company—Memorandum," 13.1.1896. For more on the history of BACO, see Andrew Perchard, *Aluminiumville: Government, Global Business and the Scottish Highlands* (Lancaster, 2012).
16. Alcan Riotinto Archives Zurich, AIAG archives (hereafter KAA), S2, T2, Aiag—Geschichte, "Verkauf Büro—Berlin," 1896.
17. Rio Tinto Group Archives, Paris, Pechiney archives (hereafter Pechiney Archives), 00-1-20029, "Rapport du Conseil d'administration de la Société Industrielle de l'Aluminium et des Alliages Métalliques," 1896. See also Claude J. Gignoux, *Histoire d'une entreprise française* (Paris, 1955), 92.
18. Heinz History Center, MSS #282, ALCOA records (hereafter ALCOA Archives), United States v. Alcoa, Equity 73–85, Exhibits, Ex. 478, "PRC Annual Report, 1895," 17.9.1896. Naco became Aluminium Limited in 1928 and changed its name to ALCAN in the 1950s. For more on the history of ALCAN, see Duncan Campbell. *Global Mission: The History of Alcan,* 3 vols. (Montréal, 1985–1990) and Mathias Kipping, Ludovic Cailluet, "Mintzberg's Emergent and Deliberate Strategies: Tracking Alcan's Activities in Europe, 1928–2007," *Business History Review,* n. 84 (Spring 2010): 79–104.
19. ALCOA Archives, box 37, fold 3, BACO, 1895–1901, Letter of Arthur Vining Davis (PRC) from Paris, 2.6.1896. A small amount of information

on the Aluminium Selling Company can be found in the BACO archives, 351/21/26/10, Wilfried S. Sample, *The Manufacture of Aluminium,* 1894.

20. The date of expiration of Héroult's patent varied according to different national laws. While it expired in France in 1901 (fifteen years), legal protection covered it until 1906 (twenty years) in Germany and the United Kingdom. In the United States, meanwhile, patent protection lasted seventeen years, but Hall's patent expired in 1909 because PRC took control over other patents after a suit for patent infringement against Cowles Electric Company, an American producer of metals alloys. Carr, *Alcoa,* 52–57; Smith, *From Monopoly,* 35–40.
21. AIAG, *Geschichte,* 94; Ernst Rauch, *Geschichte der Huttenaluminiumindustrie in der westlichen Welt* (Düsseldorf, 1962), 23; IHA, Paul Toussaint, *Historique de la Compagnie* (Paris, 1955), 18 vols. not published, vol.4, 806. This agreement was also confirmed in the annual meeting of ALCOA in 1896, ALCOA Archives, United States v. Alcoa, Equity 73–85, Exhibits, Ex. 478, "PRC Annual Report, 1895," 17.9.1896.
22. Pechiney Archives, 00-2-15940, Aluminium-Association, Recueil des conventions, "Convention 1901" and "Marché commercial," 1901.
23. Pechiney Archives, 00-2-15942, AA, Correspondence, AIAG to SEMF 14.6.1901; Technosium Mannheim, Archiv, AIAG documents (hereafter AIAG Archives), folder 223, "Convention, Proposal Agreement," 6.7.1901.
24. Graham and Pruitt, *R&D for Industry.* About Pechniey see Muriel Le Roux, *L'Entreprise et la Recherche: Un siècle de recherche industrielle à Pechiney* (Paris, 1998).
25. AIAG Archives, fold. 225, "Aluminium-Verkäufe," 1902; Pechiney Archives, 00-2-15940, Aluminium-Association, "Rapport de Gestion, Exercise 1902," 1903.
26. The cartel's sales indeed passed from around 3,000 tons in 1901 to around 7,000 in 1905.
27. BACO Archives, UGD/347/21/46/2, "On Loch Leven Scheme Agreement," 1904; "On Loch Leven Water Power Scheme," 12.9.1905; "On Visit to Norway," 14.7.1905.
28. AIAG Archives, 20/157, "Procès-Verbal AA, séance 22.9.1905"; 22/166, "Reklamation des Franzosischen," 1908; letter of BACO to AIAG, 4.11.1907. See also Wallace, *Market Control,* 36–37.
29. Pechiney Archives, 00-2-15942, Aluminium-Association, AA to members, 7.7.1905; Archivio Storico Intesa San-Paolo, Fondo Banca Commerciale Italiana, Società Italiana per la Fabbricazione dell'Alluminio, 1906–1921. See also Maurizio Rispoli, "L'industria dell'alluminio in Italia nella fase di introduzione: 1907–1929," *Annali di Storia d'Impresa,* n. 3 (1987): 281-322; Marco Bertilorenzi, "The Italian Aluminium Industry: Cartels, Multinationals and the Autharkic phase, 1917–1943," *Cahiers d'Histoire de l'Aluminium,* n. 41 (2008): 43-72.
30. Archives Crédit Lyonnais, DEEF 30181, Note N. 3940, "Note sur la Société Générale des Nitrures," September 1913.
31. Florence Hachez-Leroy, *L'Aluminium-Français: L'invention d'un marché, 1911–1983* (Paris, 1999), 33–36.
32. Pechiney Archives, 500-1-17767, Aluminium-Français, Les convenstions 1910–1923, "Conventions avec Metallgesellschaft pour les ventes d'aluminium hors de France," 25.11.1910. For more on Metallgesellschaft, see also Susan Becker, *Multinationalität hat verschiedene Gesichter: Fromen internationaler Unternehmenstätighkeit der Société Anonyme des Mines et fonderies de Zinc de la Vielle Montagne und der Metallgesellschaft AG* (Stuttgard, 1999), 275–277.

33. Pechiney Archives, 500-1-17770, Aluminium-Français, Southern Aluminium Co., "Note. 2.06.1912. Southern Aluminium Cy"; Some information on SACO can also be found in Mira Wilkins, *The History of Foreign Investment in United States, 1914–1945* (Cambridge, 2004), 33–34; Mira Wilkins, *The History of Foreign Investment in United States to 1914* (Cambridge, 1989), 283–284; Rondo Cameron, Valerij I. Bovykin, *International Banking 1870–1914* (Oxford, 1991), 240.
34. Pechiney Archives, 00-2-15942, AA, correspondance, "Projet de contrat 'Nitrures' pour la Société de Neuhausen," 3.2.1912; AIAG Archives, box 229, "Besprechung mit Herrn Dreyfus am 23 Mai 1911 in Paris."
35. Pechiney Archives, 001-14-20486, SNN—Origines, Louis Marlio, "Note Historique," June 1918; René Bonfils, "Pechiney au pays des Vikings, 1912–1958," *Cahiers d'Histoire de l'Aluminium,* n. 27 (2000/2001): 18–42; Espen Storli and David Brégaint, "The Ups and Downs of a Family Life: Det Norske Nitridaktienselskap, 1912–1976," *Enterprise and Society,* vol. 10, n. 4 (December 2009): 763-790.
36. James E. Collier, "Aluminium Industry of Europe," *Economic Geography,* vol. 22, n. 2 (April 1946), 75–108; Wallace, *Market Control,* 43–45.
37. Ludovic Cailluet, *Stratégies, structures d'organisation et pratique de gestion de Pechiney des années 1880 à 1971* (PhD thesis, Université de Lyon III, 1995); Hachez-Leroy, *L'Aluminium français.*
38. G. D. Smith, *From Monopoly to Competition,* 126–127.
39. Hessische Wirtschaftarchiv, Metallgesellschaft documents (hereafter Metallgesellschaft Archives), Abteilung 119/814, "Geschichte der VAW," 1939, 75–77, 220–224; Ernst Rauch, *Geschichte der Huttenaluminiumindustrie in der westlichen Welt,* Vereinigte Aluminium Werke, Dusseldorf, 1962, 120–124. In 1923, VAW passed under the control of VIAG (Vereinigte Industrieunternehmungen Aktien-Gesellschaft), the German state's holding. See Manfred Pohl, Andrea Schneider, *Viag Aktiengesellschaft 1923–1998: Vom Staatsunternehmen zum Internationales Konzern* (Munich, 1998).
40. Pechiney Archives, 00-1-0-11335, Correspondance de M. Marlio, "Conférence ave M. Davis," 2.12.1918, 00-2-15942, "Déjeuné avec M. Davis," 15.11.1918 and 500-1-17772, "Situation actuelle de l'Aluminium (avant 11-11-1918)."
41. BACO Archives, UGD/347/21/19/1, "Annual Report of the British Aluminium Company," 1922; Pechiney Archives, 001-0-11332, "Note sur la crise actuelle de l'Aluminium," 2.8.1921.
42. Spencer Weber Waller, "The Story of Alcoa: The Enduring Questions of Market Power, Conduct, and Remedy in Monopolization Cases," in *Antitrust Stories,* ed. Eleanor M. Fox and Daniel A. Crane (New York, 2007), 121–143.
43. G. D. Smith, *From Monopoly to Competition,* 138–142; David Massell, *Amassing Power. J.B. Duke at Sanguenay River, 1897–1927* (Quebec City, 2000), 176–177.
44. ALCOA Archives, US v. Alcoa, Equity No. 85–73, Exhibits, Ex. 1092, "C. Mortiz to A.V. Davis, Re: European Manufacturing Subsidiaries," 12.7.1926.
45. Usually, studies about the formation of ALTED pointed out that it aimed also to help to establish a cartel with Europeans. Muller, *Light metals;* Stocking and Watkins, "Aluminum Alliance"; Hachez-Leroy, *L'Aluminium Français*; Kipping and Cailluet, "Mintzberg's Emergent and Deliberate Strategies". However, an international cartel was formed only in 1931; during these three years, Europeans and ALTED competed in some international markets. See Marco Bertilorenzi, "L'Alliance Aluminium Compagnie" and Marco Bertilorenzi, *Il Controllo della sovrapproduzione: I cartelli internazionali nell'industria*

dell'alluminio in prospettiva storica 1886–1945 (PhD Thesis, Università di Firenze—Université Paris-Sorbonne, 2010), 211–215.

46. Pechiney Archives, 00-2-15941, AA, Notes, "Note sur nos relations avec l'Aluminium Company of America," 1925.
47. About Norway, see Pechiney Archives, 001-0-11333, "Note sur la SNN," March 1922; BACO Archives UGD/347/21/35/6/2, Private and Confidential, "Report on visit to Norway and Inspection of Det Norske Nitrid company's factories," June 1922; Claude J. Gignoux, *Histoire d'une entreprise française,* 168; Storli, Brégaint, "The ups and downs of a family life." For more on Italy, see Pechiney Archives, 056-00-12348, Alluminio Italiano, "Note sur la situation de l'Aluminium italien et les proposition à faire en vue d'une augmentation de capital et d'une collaboration," 19.8.1924.
48. Réné Bonfils, "Pechiney en Espagne, 1925–1985," *Cahiers d'Histoire de l'Aluminium,* n. 38–39 (2007): 77–92; Ludovic Cailluet, Matthias Kipping, "Ménage à trois: Alcan in Spain, 1950s to 1980s," *Cahiers d'Histoire de l'Aluminium,* n. 44–45 (2010).
49. ALCOA Archives, box 6 fold 3. "Draft, Alcoa and Elkem: Some Notes on a Long and Rewarding Association. Elektrokemisk," 1926.
50. Franco Amatori and Bruno Bezza (eds.), *Montecatini, 1888–1966: Capitoli di storia di una grande impresa* (Bologna, 1990), 42–45.
51. Bertilorenzi, "The Italian Aluminium Industry." AIAG started the construction of mountain tanks, which during the 1920s represented the avant-garde of electrical production in Italy.
52. Pechiney Archives, 00-2-15940, AA, "Contract 11.9.1926, 3eme cartel"; KAA, S9, Berichte u¨ber die Allgemeine Geschaftslage, 1920–1929, "Verwaltungeretsitzung von 25 Dezember 1926."
53. For instance, the VAW-Montecatini Italian firm was not fully controlled by VAW, which owned only 50% of shares. The AA never complained against VAW, nor imposed penalties, and preferred to find a strategy to put the entire production of the new firm under AA control. Bertilorenzi, "The Italian Aluminium Industry."
54. Pechiney Archives, 00-2-19540, Aluminium Association, "Procès Verbal de la Cinquième Réunion," 4.5.1927; "Statut du Bureau de Propagande & Reinsignements," s.d. but 1927.
55. ALCOA Archives, Records of Alcoa, US v. Alcoa, "Draft Project of AIC"; Pechiney Archives, 00-2-15928, Alliance Aluminium Compagnie, Préliminaires, 1931–1932 (et 1939), Murray-Morrison, "Memorandum Re Document for the Proposed Formation of a Finance Company by Aluminium Producers, Private and Confidential," 19.5.1931.
56. Various common R&D programs showed a division of tasks among different firms' R&D laboratories; afterward, individual results were amassed and consolidated at special meetings of the BIA. Pechiney Archives, 00-1-20035, Alliance Aluminium Cie Bale. Bureau International des Applications de l'Aluminium.
57. Pechiney Archives, 00-2-15928, Alliance Aluminium Compagnie, Contrat 1931, "Contrat des Associés de l'Alliance Aluminium Cie, Section 'D,' Fonctionnement de l'AAC," 3.7.1931; 00-2-15933, Alliance Aluminium Compagnie, Correspondance Générale, "Aide Techniques aux Outsiders: Extraits de procès-verbaux des réunions de l'Alliance Aluminium Compagnie," 7.7.1936.
58. IHA, Travaux d'auteur, 180.3, René Bonfils, "Etude assistance technique—ventes de technique, relations, contracts avant 1945."
59. Pechiney Archives, 001-14-20501, Relations Etrangères—sociétés filiales, participations et divers renseignements par pays, Urss 1931/35, Possibilités

de règlement des marchés avec les Russes, "Note sur l'accord commercial avec les Sovietiques," 11.1.1934; Hachez-Leroy, *L'Aluminium Français*, 167; Espen Storli, "Trade and Politics: The Western Aluminium Industry and the Soviet Union in the Interwar Period," in *From Warfare to Welfare: Business-Government Relations in the Aluminium Industry*, ed. Hans Otto Frøland and Mats Ingulstad (Throndeim, 2012), 69–100.

60. Réné Bonfils, "Pechiney au pays des Soviets: Le contrat russe de 1930," *Cahiers d'Histoire de l'Aluminium*, n. 29 (1998).
61. Pechiney Archives, 00-1-20047, Aluminium, Rélations avec les pays étrangers, Japon, "Marché du Japon—Aspects du Marché," 1933; 00-2-15932, Alliance Aluminium Compagnie, AIAG Correspondance au sujet du Japon, M. Bruce (Alted (V)) "Memorandum on the Present Status of Various Schemes for Producing Aluminium in Japan," September 1933; Jerome B. Cohen, *Japan's Economy in War and Reconstruction* (Minneapolis, 1949), 230–231; John G. Roberts, *Mitsui: Three Centuries of Japanese business* (Ney York, 1973), 261, 327.
62. John A. Krug and James Boyd, *The Japanese Aluminum Industry* (Washington DC, 1949), 5–6. No information about how Japan got started using Western methods for producing alumina during the 1930s is available, neither in Akira Kudo, *Japanese-German Business Relations: Cooperation and Rivalry in the Inter-war Period* (London, 1998), nor in Takeschi Yuzawa and Masaru Udagawa, *Foreign Business in Japan before World War II* (Tokyo, 1990). Kudo, however, claims that Germany collaborated with Japanese aluminium production during the Second World War (153). D. Campbell describes the Sumitomo-ALTED joint venture on transformation business and the strategy of ALTED for Japan as focused on increasing imports in Japan. However, he does not explain if ALTED was involved in the Sumitomo production of primary aluminium in the late 1930s; Campbell, *Global Mission*, 215–218. Metallgesellschaft also provided some patents in the transformation industry to Furukawa in 1928, but archives did not contain information about technical help for aluminium or alumina; Metallgesellschaft Archives, Juristischen Büro, n. 4/150, Kopie Furukawa, Patent agreement 17.7.1928.
63. Pechiney Archives, 00-2-15933, Alliance Aluminium Compagnie, Notes diverses, "Questions dans lesquelles l'Attitude de l'Aluminium Lminited apparait un peu trop personelle," 3.1.1934.
64. Pechiney Archives, 00-1-20047, Pechiney, Aluminium, Relations avec les pays etrangers, Yougoslavie, "Fabrication de l'Aluminium en Yougoslavie. Rapport établi par M. Lacreon à la suite de son voyage en Yugoslavie," 1.3.1938; "Note sur l'Aluminium en Yugoslavie," 1.2.1939.
65. KAA, Allgemeiner Bericht an den Welwaltungsrat der AIAG Neuhausem, Sitzung vom 8 Juli 1936; Pechiney Archives, 00-1-20047, Relations avec les pays etrangers, "Note: Projet de Fabrication d'aluminum en Pologne et en Tchecolosvachie," 4.11.1936.
66. Pechiney Archives, 00-1-15933, Alliance Auminium Compagnie, Correspondance et dossier divers, "Etat de la question Aluminium et Alumine vis-à-vis de l'Alliance Aluminium Compagnie," 6.7.1938; 00-1-20047, Relations avec les pays etrangers, Tchécoslovacquie, 1936/38, "Note: Aluminium. Marchés de l'Europe Centrale. Tchécoslovacquie, Pologne, Roumanie, Hongries," 20.10.1938.
67. Pechiney Archives, 00-1-20047, Aluminium: Relations avec les pays étrangers, 1937–1938, Hongries, "Création d'une industrie de l'aluminium en Hongrie: Reisignements généraux," 28.1.1937; I. Berend, Gy. Rànki, "Die deutsche wirtschafliche Expansion und das ungarische Wirtschaftleben zur Zeit des Zweiten Weltekriegs," *Acta Historica Academiae Scientiarum*

Hungaricae, vol. 5 (1958), 313–359; David Turnock, *The Economy of East Central Europe, 1815–1989: Stages of Transformation in a Peripheral Region* (New York, 2006), 277.

68. Pechiney Archives, 00-2-15928, Alliance Aluminium Compagnie, Autres Conférences, 1935, 1936 et 1938, fasc. 5, "Conférence des produceteurs européens d'aluminium tenue à Londres le 11 Juillet 1935."
69. Pechiney Archives, 00-2-15933, Alliance Aluminium Compagnie, Notes diverses, "Reforme de l'AAC," 4.12.1935; 00-2-15928, Alliance Aluminium Compagnie, Protocoles, "Protocole," 1936.
70. Pechiney Archives, 00-2-15933, Alliance Aluminium Compagnie, Notes diverses, Philippe Level, "Note sur l'Alliance," 12.1.1938.
71. Jeffrey Fear, "Cartels," in *The Oxford Handbook of Business History,* ed. Geoffrey Jones and Jonathan Zeitlin (London, 2009), 268–292; Clemens Wurm, *Business, Politics and International Relations. Steel, Cotton and International Cartels in British Politics, 1924–1939* (London, 1988).

6 The Swiss Watch Cartel and the Control of Technology Flows toward Rival Nations, 1930–1960

Pierre-Yves Donzé

INTRODUCTION

Together with multinational enterprises (MNEs), cartels played a key role in the global flow of technologies during most of the twentieth century. Indeed, technology appears as a key component of cartels, whose traditional functions include regulating innovation and the spread of technologies. Even though technology transfers are more often examined in conjunction with MNEs than cartels,[1] the latter play an essential role in many industrial sectors (e.g., chemicals, electrical appliances, textiles and telecommunications), where they control the spread and transfer of technologies to other countries by strictly regulating foreign direct investment (FDI) and manufacturing under licence. The goal is to maintain on the world market the competitive edge conferred by the mastery of technologies.[2] At the national level, cartels are also instrumental in regulating technology, in particular through the adoption of measures governing production (methods, quotas, R&D, etc.). However, the question of technology transfer usually does not arise in cartels organized at the national level, because a single national industry rarely enjoys a technological advantage on the world market that it seeks to maintain through cartel agreements aimed at limiting or even preventing the transfer of technology to other nations. One of the rare examples is that of British industry in the second half of the eighteenth century and the early nineteenth century. At the time, the English authorities sought to prevent the transfer of technology to other countries by prohibiting craftsmen from emigrating and banning machine exports.[3] In the twentieth century, the creation of I. G. Farben in 1924 can also be seen as a way for German chemical manufacturers to use concentration within an industry, a policy that favours exports of finished goods rather than FDI.[4]

The Swiss watchmaking industry is an example of a nationwide cartel designed among other things to control technology transfer.[5] This was not the sole purpose of the cartelization of the Swiss watchmaking industry, a process also aimed at maintaining an industrial structure in the form of district.[6] Between 1930 and 1960, it had to cope with the emergence of newcomers, primarily in the United States and Japan, whose success was partly due to technologies imported from Switzerland. The respective policies adopted by the Swiss cartel authorities towards these two countries highlight the challenges posed by the existence of this kind of special cartel.

THE CARTELIZATION OF THE SWISS WATCHMAKING INDUSTRY

At the beginning of the twentieth century, the Swiss watchmaking industry had a virtual monopoly on the world watch market, with a share estimated at 90% in 1900.[7] Yet despite this dominant position, in the early twentieth century the Swiss watchmaking industry witnessed the arrival of new competitors who started making watches relying on technology transferred from Switzerland. This took the form of what is commonly called *chablonnage,* that is, exporting disassembled watches (movements or movement parts) and assembling them in the countries in which they are sold.[8] The main purpose is to avoid paying high customs duties on finished watches. Swiss watchmakers viewed *chablonnage* as a threat insofar as the technologies (specific parts such as springs and jewels, machine tools, know-how) transferred via watch assembly workshops set up abroad would allow new competitors to emerge. The rise of customs protectionism after the First World War boosted *chablonnage* and made Swiss watchmakers aware of the need to take steps to put an end to such practices.

On the basis of Swiss foreign trade statistics, it is possible to determine movements' share of watch exports (number of units) and to evaluate the spread of *chablonnage* after the First World War. Up until 1914, Swiss watchmakers were not unduly concerned about the practice (see Figure 6.1). Exports of movements showed a steady increase, rising from 297,000 units in 1890 to 1.2 million in 1914. In relative terms, however, this growth was not that significant: watch movements' share of Swiss watchmaking exports (number of units) rose until 1906 (13.6% as against 5.9% in 1890), then fell during the years leading up to the war. After the war, however, movement exports began to pose a problem. Such exports not only rose sharply in absolute terms (2.4 million units in 1918, peaking at 5.6 million units in 1929) but above all tended to become a dominant practice in exports (their relative share of watchmaking exports went from 11.9% in 1914 to a high of 31.6% in 1926). In general, movements averaged 25.1% of watchmaking exports from 1920 to 1935, as compared with 11.5% for 1900 to 1920.

In fact, *chablonnage* was limited to a small number of countries up until the mid-1920s, when it became more widespread worldwide (see Table 6.1) as a result of customs protectionism. Before 1930, North America (United States and Canada), Germany, Russia and Japan alone absorbed nearly 90% of Swiss exports of watch movements. In these four parts of the world, the practice of *chablonnage* reinforced the national watchmaking industry. These technology transfers were particularly problematic in the case of the United States and Japan, where they helped such companies as Bulova Watch, Gruen Watch, Hattori (Seiko) and Citizen Watch to develop.

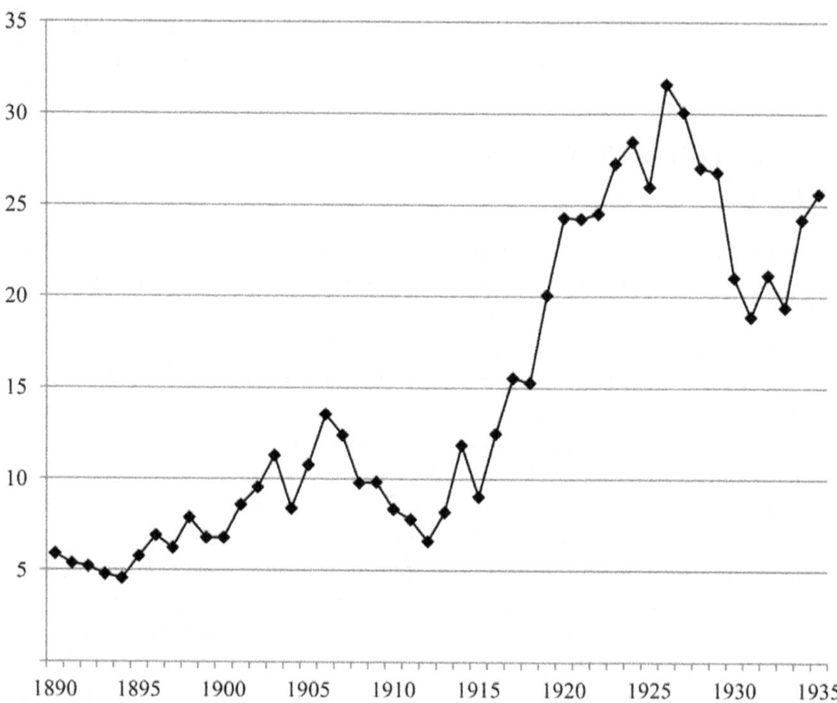

Figure 6.1 Swiss watchmaking exports (volume) as a percentage of movements, 1890–1935

Source: *Statistique du commerce de la Suisse avec l'étranger* (Berne, 1890–1935).

Table 6.1 Main destinations of movement exports for Swiss watches, 1900–1930

	1900	1910	1920	1930
Movements exported, no. of units	498,892	873,522	3,340,982	3,421,959
United States (%)	40.7	29.1	70.3	36.3
Russia (%)	15.3	21.4	–	–
Japan (%)	19.8	10.3	10.9	8.6
Germany (%)	9.8	7.7	–	8.7
Canada (%)	9.6	21.6	9.1	11.2
Other (%)	4.9	10.0	9.7	35.2

Source: *Statistique du commerce de la Suisse avec l'étranger* (Berne, 1900–1930).

To combat *chablonnage* and prevent industrial relocation, during the interwar period the watchmaking sector introduced sweeping cartelization, which obtained State backing in 1934 (see Figure 6.2). As Swiss watchmaking was organized in the form of industrial district—federal surveys

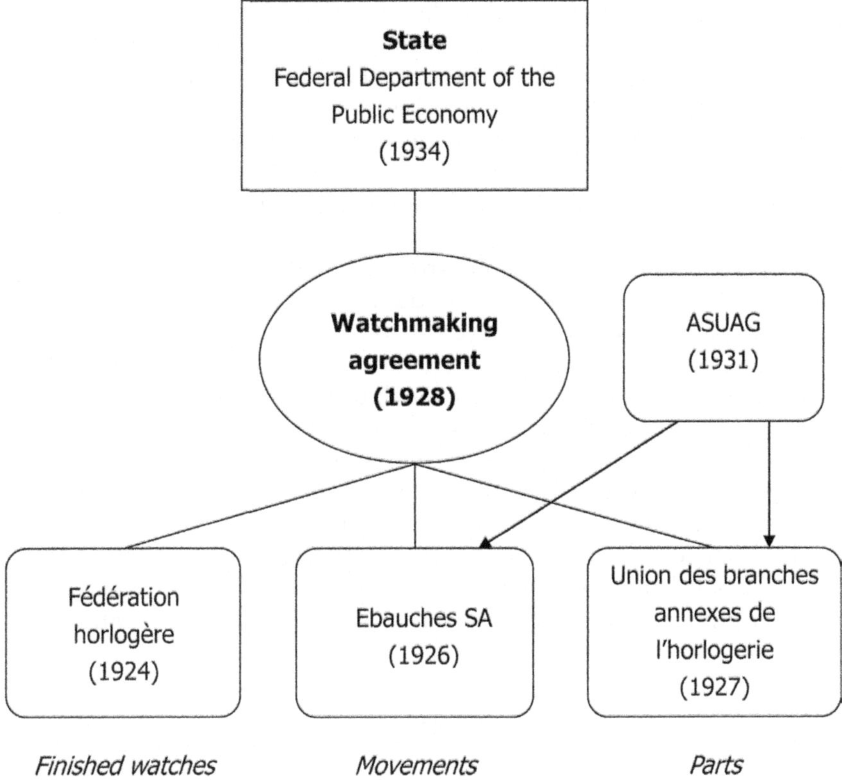

Figure 6.2 Organizational structure of the Swiss watchmaking cartel, 1934
Source: drawn up by the author.

listed 663 companies in 1901 and 1,134 in 1929[9]—the ultimate goal of cartelization was to control the activities of all watchmaking companies. It was a two-stage process. First of all, the various watchmaking companies banded together according to their branch of activity: watch manufacturers within the Fédération horlogère (FH, 1924) and producers of *ébauches* (movement-blanks) within the company Ébauches SA (1926), while the other subcontractors came together in the Union des branches annexes de l'horlogerie (UBAH, 1927).[10] Subsequently, in 1928 these three groups signed a series of agreements known as the *watchmaking conventions,* whereby they undertook to do business exclusively with each other, to respect the minimum prices for the purchase of watch components and above all to avoid resorting to *chablonnage*. However, the cartel did not intervene with regard to production quotas and shared commercial outlets. To tighten control over the production of watch movements, the banks and the federal authorities backed the establishment in 1931 of a holding company, ASUAG, which bought up virtually all manufacturers of movement parts.[11] This organizational structure was strengthened by State intervention in the early 1930s designed to consolidate these agreements by making them binding, as breakaway firms were their weak point. In 1934, the Swiss federal government adopted a federal decree making the watchmaking conventions binding. Activities of watchmaking companies (prices, recruitment of workers, mergers, production techniques, etc.) were strictly controlled by the Swiss Federal Department of Public Economy. *Chablonnage* became illegal and exports of machine tools were henceforth subject to governmental approval.

Thus, from the mid-1930s onwards, the Swiss watchmaking industry had a powerful tool for controlling the transfer of technologies abroad. Moreover, the 1920s and 1930s were marked by a sea change in the nature of watches, which reinforced Switzerland's dominance. The main development was the shift from the pocket watch to a multifunctional wristwatch (calendar, chronograph, automatic mechanism, etc.) (See Figure 6.3).[12] Watches became both smaller and more complex, requiring the use of new, ultra-precise machine tools. In addition, new materials that were cheaper and longer-wearing were adopted, especially for manufacturing springs and jewels.[13] Whereas the main watchmaking nations (Germany, United States, Japan) retooled their own watchmaking industries for arms production, these innovations (machine tools, parts) were developed in Switzerland,

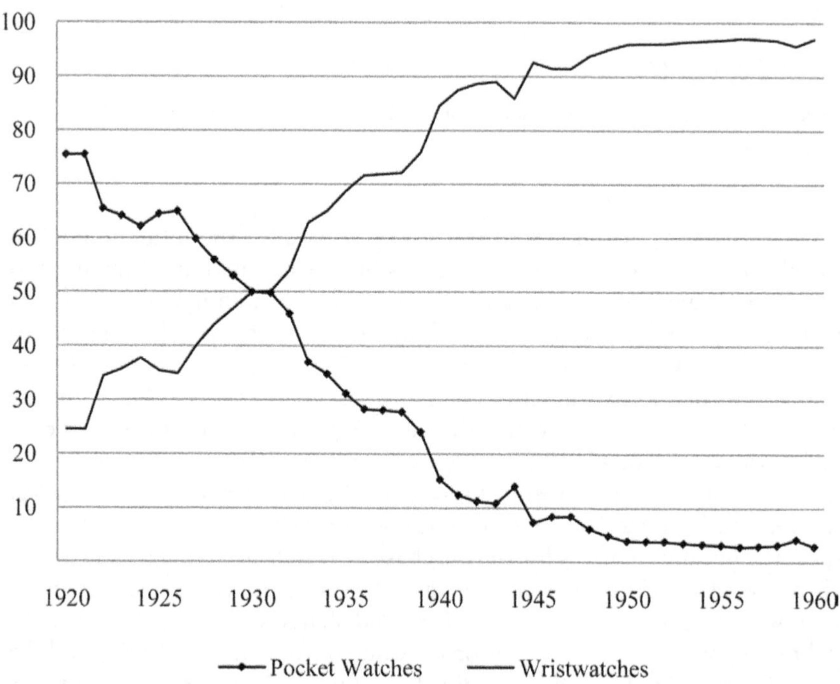

Figure 6.3 Types of Swiss watches exported as a percentage, 1920–1960
Source: Ritzmann Heiner (ed.), *Statistique historique de la Suisse* (Chronos, 1996), 627.

making the country a technological leader from the 1930s onwards. However, the cartelization of the Swiss watchmaking industry did not prevent the rise of American and Japanese rivals, who developed after 1945 thanks to technologies imported from Switzerland. Technology transfers to these two countries took place according to special arrangements and on specific grounds.

THE UNITED STATES

The cartelization of Swiss watchmaking had no impact on *chablonnage* towards the US market. Movements accounted for 87.4% of watch exports to the United States during the 1930s. Even though this proportion fell after the war (64.0% in 1950; 50.2% in 1960), it remained high, averaging 65.3% between 1945 and 1960. In Switzerland, the cartel authorities did not manage to contain the trend. On the contrary, they discreetly encouraged it by signing agreements with the main US firms actively involved in *chablonnage*. This policy, which may appear surprising at first sight, was due to the huge expansion of the US market from the mid-1930s onwards (seeing Figure 6.4). Between 1930 and 1945, the US market developed considerably,

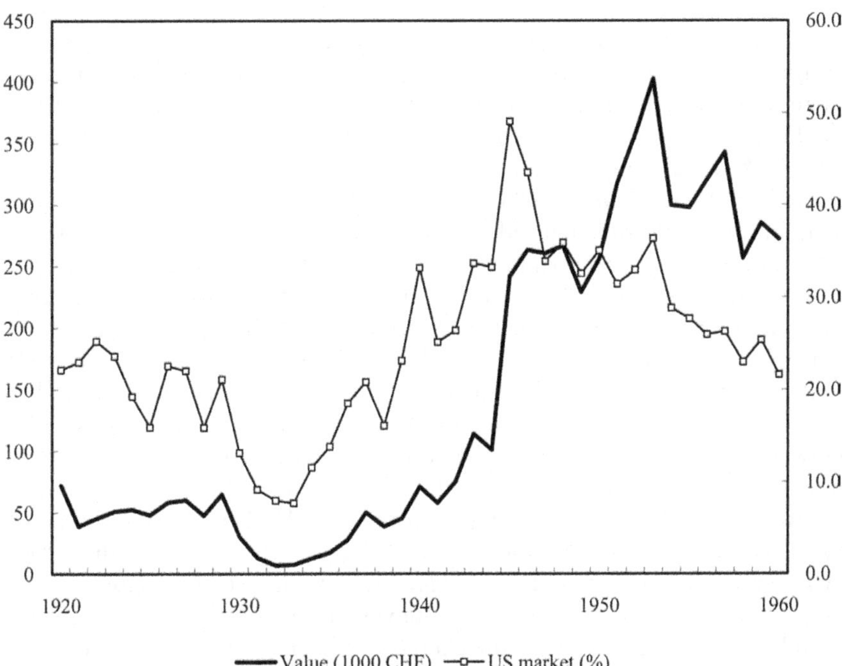

Figure 6.4 Value of Swiss watch exports to the United States in 1,000 CHF, 1920–1960

Source: Statistique du commerce de la Suisse avec l'étranger (Berne, 1930–1960)

accounting for a record 49.1% of the value of Swiss watch exports in 1945. Even though this share fell after the war, it remained high (29.3% in the 1950s), so much so that the United States was the number one market for Swiss watchmakers.

The continuation of *chablonnage* to the United States was due to the fact that cartel regulations did not totally prohibit exports of movement-blanks and parts. Sales to former customers were tolerated, which is why Ébauches SA and UBAH kept a list of foreign clients up to date. Two types of firms were major actors as far as *chablonnage* was concerned. First of all, there were American firms with a branch in Switzerland, mainly Bulova and Gruen.[14] *Chablonnage* enabled these firms, which had previously specialized in distribution, to establish themselves as watchmakers on the US market through the acquisition of new know-how. By opening branches in Switzerland, they managed to put an end to the virtual monopoly of Waltham Watch and Elgin Watch on the US market. The case of Bulova is quite representative of the impact of these multinationals on the boom in Swiss watch exports across the Atlantic.[15] The firm was founded by a Czech immigrant, Joseph Bulova (1852–1935), who opened a watch and jewellery shop in New York in 1875 and began importing Swiss watches in 1887. A branch was opened in 1911 in Bienne, Switzerland to source Swiss products directly, which was soon turned into a watchmaking workshop. By the mid-1910s, Bulova had a dual organizational structure: it produced watches in Switzerland then marketed them in the United States. However, rising US customs duties led the firm to transfer part of its production to America, thereby cutting the umbilical cord with Swiss production facilities. During the 1920s, it developed a strategy for acquiring specific watchmaking know-how with the aim of becoming "independent of Swiss manufacturing" as quoted an official report in 1939.[16] Bulova bought up an assortments workshop in the 1920s and engaged in 1929 as a technical chief a swage maker who until then had been running his own company (F. Guinand and Co.) and who had been trained at the Tavannes Watch Co., one of the biggest Swiss watch factory before the war. Moreover, in the 1930s, Bulova opened in neighbouring France a machine tool workshop to be able to export freely to its American plants.[17] With this newfound technical mastery, it was able to open a movement-blank plant in the United States in the early 1930s. However, it continued to produce some movements on Swiss soil which were then assembled in America. In the 1930s, Bulova also distributed Swiss brands in the United States, acting as an agent for Vacheron-Constantin and taking over Longines-Wittnauer. It is not clear exactly what role these two Swiss manufacturers played in *chablonnage* exports to the United States, but it seems likely that the ties with Bulova led these two prestigious Swiss brands to assemble watches in the United States, enabling them to overcome serious financial difficulties during the Depression.

Gruen Watch followed a similar path.[18] The firm was founded in Cincinnati in 1874 by a German watchmaker, Dietrich Gruen (1847–1911). He began by importing movement-blanks from Glashütte, in Germany, which he finished in his workshop, before moving into start-to-finish production on US soil via the company Columbus Watch Co., which he established with an associate in 1882. Gruen then left the firm to start up his own company with his son, Gruen and Son (1894). The latter firm specialized in assembling watches using movements imported from Germany, then Switzerland with the opening of a branch in Madretsch and a workshop in Saint-Imier (1904). This dual production system flourished in the interwar period, with nearly 1.4 million movements imported from Swiss factories.[19] As was the case with Bulova, some production facilities were transferred to the United States in the 1930s, under conditions that are unclear.[20] Moreover, having a branch in Switzerland meant that Gruen Watch was very receptive when it came to innovation. For example, in 1908 it was the second US firm to produce wristwatches, partly manufactured in Switzerland, one year after Elgin Watch.[21]

Setting up the watchmaking cartel in Switzerland did not put an end to *chablonnage* towards the United States. Companies like Bulova and Gruen continued to supply their US factories with Swiss movements and parts, taking advantage of regulatory loopholes. Moreover, it was particularly difficult to oppose such practices because these companies, especially Bulova, were major customers of the Swiss watchmaking industry. Furthermore, as an importer and distributor of finished watches on the American market, Bulova was an important intermediary for several powerful Swiss watchmakers such as Longines. Bulova and Gruen were also usually considered as Swiss companies. Since the 1920s, the Swiss subsidiary of Bulova was managed by a Swiss citizen and benefited from the financial support of the Cantonal Bank of Bern, a local bank involved in many watchmaking firms.[22] As for the Swiss branch of Gruen Watch, it was also managed by a Swiss citizen in the 1940s and not deemed a foreign firm.[23] Both companies had signed the watchmaking agreement of 1928 and were members of the cartel. As they were considered to be 100% Swiss, they did not appear on UBAH's list of foreign companies, which meant that the company could not obtain export licences for the United States. This absurd situation led to intense negotiations with the Fédération horlogère during the 1930s.

Gruen Watch signed a contract with the watchmaking organizations (FH, UBAH, Ébauches SA) in January 1943.[24] Under the agreement, Gruen Watch undertook to buy finished watches and movements (at least 300,000 units) every year in Switzerland in order to guarantee the smooth operation of its factory in Bienne. It promised not to manufacture parts in the United States and to ensure that more than 20% of all movements were purchased in Switzerland. Finally, it agreed to only manufacture two calibres on US soil and provided the watchmaking organizations with the technical specifications. In exchange, the Swiss watchmaking organizations agreed to grant the necessary export permits.[25] As for Bulova, it is said to have signed a secret agreement with the ASUAG in the late 1930s, authorizing the production of two types of calibres on US soil.[26] A formal agreement was signed in 1948.

The Swiss watchmaking organizations authorized the company to manufacture watches in its US plants and undertook to secure the necessary export permits for the supply of spare parts from the Bienne plant. In exchange, Bulova agreed to limit its expansion and transfer of technology. It signed a three-year agreement stipulating that its production volume in the United States would not exceed two-thirds of imports from Switzerland. Moreover, it promised not to manufacture jewels in the United States "as long as the traditional Swiss jewel manufacturers continued to supply its Bienne plant with the necessary quantities".[27]

Second, a reference should be made to the role played by Swiss watchmaking plants in containing *chablonnage* towards the United States. Although ASUAG's policy of concentration was effective with regard to factories manufacturing movements and parts, the organization did not control the activities of watchmakers, who produced both movements—in principle for themselves—and finished watches. Yet watchmaking manufactures, following the lead set by Longines and Vacheron-Constantin, actively exported disassembled movements to some of their agents, particularly those in the US market, on which they depended. Consequently, in 1948 the Swiss Federal Department of the Public Economy informed delegations at a meeting that Wittnauer and Co. SA and Rolex SA "both intended to operate a watchmaking factory in the United States", reminding them that the practice was strictly forbidden by the watchmaking agreements.[28] Little is known about the conditions in which Swiss watchmakers moved part of their production facilities to the United States. Given its business ties with the American importers for Longines and Vacheron-Constantin, a company like Bulova no doubt played a decisive role in this process.

Chablonnage affected not only the Swiss watchmaking industry but also US watchmaking (see Figure 6.5). Imports of foreign parts and movements, of which 74.1% came from Switzerland between 1926 and 1955, allowed the new manufacturers to become the leading watchmakers on the US market. The average yearly volume of US watches equipped with foreign movements was 4.2 million units for 1926–1929, as compared with 11.2 million watches entirely manufactured in the United States. After a downturn due to the Depression (less than 500,000 watches equipped with foreign movements in 1932 and 1933, as well as yearly domestic production that dropped below 6 million units), the number of watches equipped with foreign movements increased steadily over a twenty-year period, totalling 1.2 million units in 1935, 9.4 million in 1945 and 10.9 million in 1955. Since 1951, as during the Second World War, such products even outstripped US domestic output. Through *chablonnage,* American MNEs such as Bulova and Gruen Watch Co were able to compete with established watch manufacturers (Waltham Watch, Elgin Watch, Hamilton Watch) which controlled the domestic production of watches until the First World War.[29] These three firms reacted to the growth of their rival newcomers by successively engaging in an intense lobbying activity in Washington, pushing for an increase in custom tariffs before the war.[30]

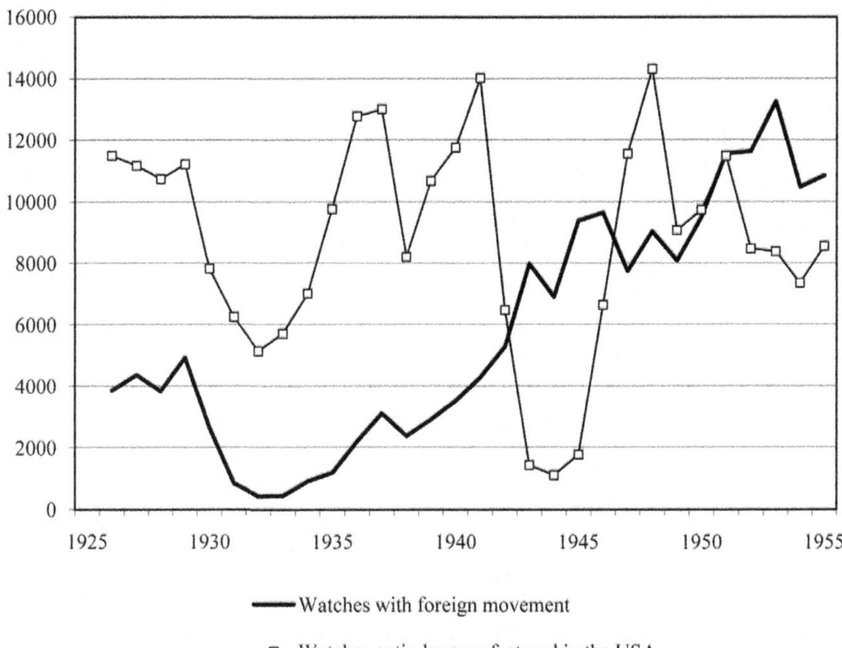

Figure 6.5 US watchmaking production, number of units, 1926–1955
Source: David S. Landes, *L'heure qu'il est: Les horloges, la mesure du temps et la formation du monde moderne* (Paris, 1987), 589.

JAPAN

Japan is completely different from the United States.[31] It is a perfect example of what Swiss watchmaking elites feared as far as *chablonnage* was concerned: the emergence of a rival industry and the loss of a market. Swiss foreign trade statistics clearly illustrate this trend. Whereas Japan was a major sales outlet for the Swiss watchmaking industry in the first half of the 1920s (8.2% of the value of exports for the period 1920–1924), sales dropped from the end of the decade onwards and did not pick up again until the 1950s: by 1938, its share of Swiss exports had fallen to less than 2%. This poor showing can be traced to the emergence of a national industry that developed thanks to *chablonnage* via Switzerland, and is the reason why the cartel oversight authorities strictly applied the watchmaking conventions to Japan.

The development of the firms Hattori and Co. Ltd. (Seiko, which was founded as a watch shop in 1877 and started making watches in 1895) and Citizen Watch Co. (founded in 1930) was boosted from the 1930s onwards by an extremely protectionist policy, in force until 1961. The policy went through two phases. First, from 1930 to 1945, protectionism stemmed from political and military considerations: the goal was to limit

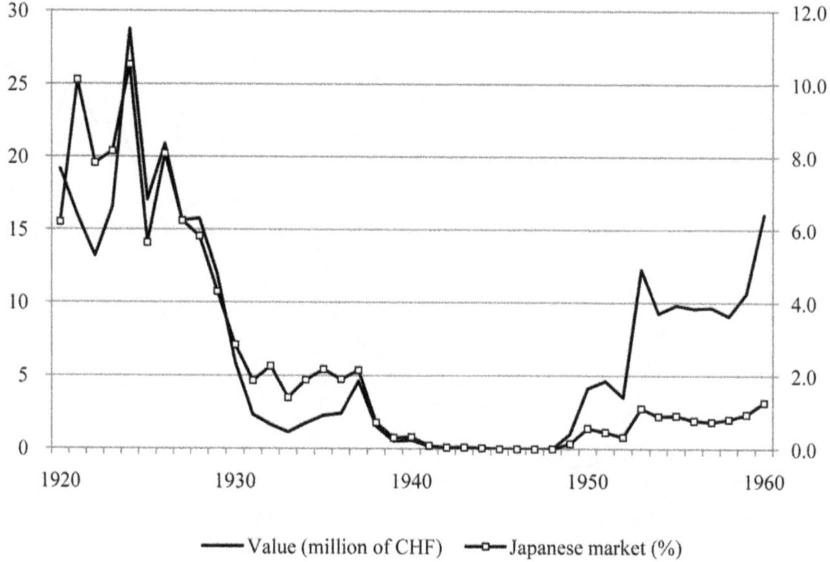

Figure 6.6 Swiss watch exports to Japan, in millions of CHF, 1920–1960
Source: *Statistique du commerce de la Suisse avec l'étranger* (Berne, 1930–1960).

imports and purchases of luxury goods to a minimum in order to devote the nation's wealth to the war effort. Japan's share of Swiss watch exports did not exceed 1.0% during the 1930s and was virtually nil during the war (see Figure 6.6).

Second, a new protectionist policy was adopted in 1945 and left in place until 1961, with a view to facilitating the reconstruction of a national watchmaking industry capable of competing on the world market. Accordingly, watch imports to Japan were prohibited until 1952, with a few rare examples (sports timekeepers for schools; stores reserved for US soldiers; etc.). In 1953 the ban was lifted, but watch imports remained subject to stringent regulations (quotas, import duties) until the sector was deregulated in 1961.[32] Consequently, Japan was of little importance to Swiss watchmaking, accounting for a scant 1.3% of Swiss watch exports in the 1950s.[33] The Swiss cartel authorities were therefore able to adopt a rigorous policy in which deliveries of movements, parts and machine tools depended on the opening up of the Japanese watchmaking market.

In the 1950s, Japanese watch exports were virtually nil (see Table 6.2). The domestic market provided a basis for rebuilding the domestic watchmaking industry, primarily composed of Seiko and Citizen. After the war, the two firms depended on Swiss technology (springs, jewels, incablocs, machine tools, etc.) which the cartel authorities refused to export, especially

Table 6.2 Japanese watchmaking industry, watches and movements (number of units), 1950–1960

	1950	1955	1960
Production	694,000	2,240,000	7,147,000
Exports	38,000	214,000	145,000
Imports	700	219,000	205,000

Source: *Nihon gaikoku boeki nenpyo* (Tokyo, 1950–1960) and *Nihon tokei nenkan* (Tokyo, 1950–1960).

since the Japanese market was closed. Over time, however, this policy merely accelerated the process of technology transfer because it encouraged the Japanese to gear up rapidly for domestic production. Watchsprings and machine tools provide a good illustration of this trend.

In 1949, Japan was added to the official list of countries to which exports of watch parts and movements were forbidden, which meant that Swiss component manufacturers were unable to fill the many orders that Seiko and Citizen placed with them between 1949 and 1953. The watchmakers' dominant position within the cartel helped them to prevail over the parts manufacturers, who underscored, as far back as 1950, the need to "prevent this clientele from turning to other suppliers in the US and elsewhere".[34] Even though they were aware that Seiko and Citizen could source such parts from other countries or by other means, the Swiss cartel authorities made exports of watch parts to Japan contingent on the opening of the Japanese watchmaking market, a rigid position which did not stop the firms in questions from acquiring these parts by two means.

The first strategy of Japanese watchmakers was to import these parts via other countries. Foreign trade statistics clearly reflect this trend (see Table 6.3). Imports of watch parts from Switzerland were not completely forbidden. Japanese dealers carrying Swiss watches could obtain various parts for after sales service. In the 1950s, however, the volumes involved were quite small and Switzerland's share of this trade was marginal compared to what it was before the cartel was set up. In the period 1928–1930, Switzerland accounted for 91.6% of Japanese imports of dissembled watch parts, far ahead of its main rival, the United States (2.5%).[35] Between 1952 and 1957, Switzerland's share of this trade declined sharply, falling to third place (17.9%), behind Germany (47.2%) and France (309.4%). In the specific case of watchsprings, sourcing was from Germany. Relations between Seiko and Germany watchspring-makers were established in 1953, when two executives from the firm toured Europe.

The second means of procuring watch parts was to produce them in Japan, an approach that was used widely in the case of watchsprings. The firm Daini Seikosha (a Seiko watch factory) began working together in 1954 with the University of Tohoku and Professor Hakaru Masumoto, from the Centre for Research on Metallurgical Materials (Kinzoku Zairyo Kenkyujo), in an

Table 6.3 Japanese imports of watch parts, 1950–1960

Year	Value, 1,000 ¥	Switzerland (%)	France (%)	Germany (%)	United States (%)	Others (%)
1950	0	0	0	0	0	0
1951	298	65.7	0	0	34.3	0
1952	9,626	10.3	11.2	78.6	0	0
1953	17,550	18.3	32.6	27.0	22.1	0
1954	18,972	20.0	48.6	31.2	0	0.1
1955	48,061	14.9	21.8	60.8	2.5	0
1956	58,117	19.4	31.1	48.9	0.6	0
1957	88,352	24.8	37.2	36.8	0	1.2
1958	102,863	41.8	31.9	22.6	0	3.8
1959	106,802	58.1	33.0	8.2	0	0.8
1960	134,709	62.2	29.9	0.9	0.2	6.7

Source: *Nihon gaikoku boeki nenpyo* (Tokyo, 1950–1960).

effort to find a new alloy suitable for producing high-quality watchsprings like those of the Swiss industry. A prototype was developed in 1956 (coelinvar). The following year, Seiko opened a new plant in the city of Sendai for mass-producing the springs, thereby throwing off the Swiss yoke.[36]

Machine tools were the second key technology as far as watch manufacturing was concerned. They were also subject to strict control by the Swiss watchmaking cartel from the mid-1930s onwards. In 1934, the cartel authorities drew up a list of machines which were first subject to stiff export duties, and subsequently to the issuing of official export licences from 1939 onwards.[37] After the war, the Swiss authorities set up a special body to monitor purchases or sales of such machines. The company, Machor SA, whose shareholders came from the watchmaking sector, the machines industry and the workers' trade union FOMH, was established for this purpose in 1946.[38] It leased machine tools for watchmaking, but only to countries that had signed a watchmaking agreement with Switzerland. However, as the Japanese watchmaking industry was not deregulated until 1961, Machor refused to deliver the machines which Seiko and Citizen ordered in the early 1950s. The watch manufacturers that controlled Machor were aware that their restrictive policy was ineffective but maintained it as leverage to force open the Japanese watchmaking market. The director of Ebel, Charles Blum, cogently summed up the position of the Swiss watchmakers in 1959: "The said restrictions could however be maintained, in any event as a negotiating tool".[39] In the meanwhile, the Japanese undertook to copy these machines. Seiko in particular sent its engineers on study tours to Switzerland and Germany in the early 1950s and set about copying Tornos automatic lathes in cooperation with Tsugami Machine Manufacturing.

The "Japanese Tornos" (*wasei torunosu*), as these lathes were called at Seiko, were developed during the period 1956–1957. They were then produced by the hundreds to equip the Japanese watchmaking industry and later versions were even exported to Switzerland.[40] The R&D centre which Seiko set up in the early 1950s to handle this technology transfer was quite successful and was spun off in 1964 to form Seiko Seiki Ltd., a firm that began producing machine tools for clients outside the watchmaking industry in the late 1960s.[41] In 1965, however, when trade in watchmaking machine tools was deregulated in Switzerland, the Japanese watchmaking industry no longer needed the Swiss connection and stopped ordering large quantities of machines.

CONCLUSION

The transfer of watchmaking technologies from Switzerland towards the United States and Japan between 1930 and 1960 took different forms depending on the receiving country. With the United States, transfer took place within American multinationals with branches in Switzerland. This is the traditional model as presented in classical economic analysis, whereby multinationals appear as the best means of benefiting from know-how localized in the territory.[42] On the other hand, the case of Japan shows that identical Swiss watchmaking technology was acquired not through FDI or technical assistance contracts but via a more traditional mode: imitation. The difference between the United States and Japanese cases illustrates the point that technology may be transferred under very different conditions for a given product. This example shows that the form of transfer does not depend on the nature of the technology.[43]

With watch manufacturing, the decisive factor was not only the existence of an actor who controlled the circulation of technologies but also specific changes in market conditions. Ideally, the Swiss watchmaking cartel, as it was established at the end of the 1920s and recognized by the State in 1934, was aimed at putting an end to technology transfer and promoting exports of finished products. Yet changing market conditions required the adoption of a pragmatic technology policy. In the case of the United States, it was quite easy to accommodate *chablonnage* and the transfer of some production facilities to US soil, because these changes were accompanied by a boom in the US market, the number one outlet for Swiss watchmakers. Accordingly, agreements were signed with such firms as Bulova and Gruen Watch in order to set the conditions for the continuation of *chablonnage*. With Japan, however, technology transfer led to a loss of market for Swiss watchmakers and the cartel authorities strictly banned exports of parts to Japan until the Japanese watchmaking market was deregulated. This pragmatic application of the policy to combat technology transfer does, however, obey a certain logic, that of watch manufacturers, who were interested in access to markets, whether for exports of finished goods, as with Japan, or for movements, as with the United States. Their interests diverged sharply from those of manufacturers of parts and machine tools, who had great trouble honouring orders from foreign watchmaking firms.

For the Swiss watchmaking industry, however, the cartel had a negative impact insofar as it prevented both industrial concentration in Switzerland and expansion abroad in the form of direct investment or licensed manufacturing. For example, Rolex and Wittnauer were barred from opening factories in the United States in 1948 even though agreements were signed during the same period with US multinationals. Driven by this desire to avoid globalization, the Swiss watchmaking industry retained the structure of industrial districts up until the major restructurings of the 1980s, which saw the birth of watchmaking groups, primarily SMH in 1983 (which went on to become the Swatch Group in 1998). More than the quartz revolution, a technology which the Swiss mastered just as well and just as early as their Japanese and American rivals, it was this refusal to modernize structures that seems to be the root cause of the great difficulty the Swiss watchmaking industry has had in adjusting to globalized capitalism.[44]

NOTES

1. On multinationals and technology transfer, see the introduction of this book.
2. Akira Kudo and Terushi Hara, *International Cartels in Business History* (Tokyo, 1992).
3. Jeremy David, "Damming the Flood: British Government Efforts to Check the Outflow of Technicians and Machinery, 1780–1843", *Business History Review* 51 (1977): 1–34.
4. Alfred D. Chandler, *Scale and Scope: The Dynamics of Industrial Capitalism* (Cambridge, 1990), 563–584 and Akira Kudo, *Japanese-German Business Relations: Cooperation and Rivalry in the Inter-war Period* (London/New York, 1998).
5. Pierre-Yves Donzé, *History of the Swiss Watch Industry from Jacques David to Nicolas Hayek* (Berne, 2011).
6. There is also a second goal of watchmaking cartelization, not taken up here, which consists of combating industry-wide concentration in Switzerland and retaining the industrial districts that keep companies in the villages and the existence of small-scale employers, with a view to maintaining social order and checking the rise of trade unionism. See Christophe Koller, *L'industrialisation et l'Etat au pays de l'horlogerie: Contribution à l'histoire économique et sociale d'une région suisse* (Courrendlin, 2003).
7. Hans W. Uttinger and D. Robert Papera, "Threats to the Swiss Watch Cartel", *Western Economic Journal* 3/2 (1965): 206.
8. For the practice of *chablonnage*, see Christophe Koller, *L'industrialisation et l'Etat au pays de l'horlogerie: Contribution à l'histoire économique et sociale d'une région suisse* (Courrendlin, 2003), 374–380.
9. *Feuille fédérale* (FF), 1931: 193.
10. FF, 1950: 68.
11. Société générale de l'horlogerie suisse SA (ASUAG), *Historique publié à l'occasion de son vingt-cinquième anniversaire, 1931–1956* (Bienne, 1956).

12. For the example of Longines, see Patrick Linder, *De l'atelier à l'usine: L'horlogerie à Saint-Imier (1865–1918)* (Neuchâtel, 2008).
13. Information kindly provided by Jean-Michel Piguet, deputy curator at the International Watchmaking Museum at La Chaux-de-Fonds.
14. David S. Landes, *L'heure qu'il est: Les horloges, la mesure du temps et la formation du monde moderne* (Paris, 1987), 458.
15. Christophe Koller, *L'industrialisation et l'Etat au pays de l'horlogerie: Contribution à l'histoire économique et sociale d'une région suisse* (Courrendlin, 2003), 419–431.
16. Confidential report on Bulova Watch Co. addressed to E. Pequignot, head secretary in the Department of Public Economy, quoted by Christophe Koller, *L'industrialisation et l'Etat au pays de l'horlogerie: Contribution à l'histoire économique et sociale d'une région suisse* (Courrendlin, 2003), 423.
17. Christophe Koller, *L'industrialisation et l'Etat au pays de l'horlogerie: Contribution à l'histoire économique et sociale d'une région suisse* (Courrendlin, 2003), 423.
18. Swiss federal archives (AFS), E 7004, 1967/12, 80, Historique de la Gruen Watch Mfg. de Cincinnati, no date, and Michael C. Harrold, *American Watchmaking: A Technical History of the American Watch Industry, 1850–1930* (Columbia, 1984).
19. AFS, E 7004, 1967/12, 80, letter from Gruen Watch Co. USA to the Swiss consul in New York, 22 January 1940.
20. Jura cantonal archives (ACJ), Fonds Péquignot, 100, contract between the watchmaking organizations and Gruen Watch, 11 January 1943.
21. Michael C. Harrold, *American Watchmaking: A Technical History of the American Watch Industry, 1850–1930* (Columbia, 1984), 51.
22. Christophe Koller, *L'industrialisation et l'Etat au pays de l'horlogerie: Contribution à l'histoire économique et sociale d'une région suisse* (Courrendlin, 2003), 421–423.
23. AFS, E 7004, 1967/12, 80, note of Department of Public Economy, 6 May 1958.
24. AFS, E 7004, 1967/12, 80, Historique de la Gruen Watch Mfg. de Cincinnati, no date.
25. ACJ, Fonds Péquignot, 100, contract between the watchmaking organizations and Gruen Watch, 11 January 1943.
26. Christophe Koller, *L'industrialisation et l'Etat au pays de l'horlogerie: Contribution à l'histoire économique et sociale d'une région suisse* (Courrendlin, 2003), 423.
27. ACJ, Fonds Péquignot, 100, contract between the watchmaking organizations and Bulova Watch, 7 April 1948.
28. AFS, E 7004, 1967/12, 80, letter from Péquignot to the delegates' meeting, 31 May 1948.
29. Amy Glasmeier, *Manufacturing Time: Global Competition in the Watch Industry, 1795–2000* (New York, 2000), 119–129.
30. Jean-Jacques Bolli, *L'aspect horloger des relations commerciales Américano-Suisses de 1929 à 1950* (La Chaux-de-Fonds, 1956). The adoption of protectionist custom tariffs for watches by the United States between 1954 and 1967 mostly results from the difficulties encountered by American watchmaking firms, Bulova included, in shifting from wartime to domestic production after 1945. See Dominique Dirlevanger, Sébastien Guex and Gian-Franco Pordenone, *La politique commerciale de la Suisse de la Seconde Guerre mondiale à l'entrée au GATT (1945–1966)* (Zurich, 2004), especially Chapter 4 on the "watch war".
31. Hoshimi Uchida, *Tokei sangyou no hattatsu* (Tokyo, 1985) and Pierre-Yves Donzé, "Le Japon et l'industrie horlogère suisse : Un cas de transfert de

technologie durant les années 1880–1940", *Histoire, Economie et Société*, 2006: 105–125.

32. *Yunyu tokei no ayumi: Nihon tokei yunyu kyokai 30 nen shi* (Tokyo, 1985).
33. *Statistique du commerce de la Suisse avec l'étranger* (Berne, 1950–1959).
34. International Watchmaking Museum (MIH), La Chaux-de-Fonds, CHS, letter from UBAH to the delegates' meeting, 23 November 1950.
35. *Nihon gaikoku boeki nenpyo* (Tokyo, 1950–1960).
36. *Nihon Keizai Shimbun,* 3 February 1957.
37. Christophe Koller, *L'industrialisation et l'Etat au pays de l'horlogerie: Contribution à l'histoire économique et sociale d'une région suisse* (Courrendlin, 2003), 468.
38. FF, 1950, p. 71.
39. ACJ, Fonds Péquignot, 122, minutes of the "Watchmaking Status" working group, 14 August 1959.
40. *Tsugami* (Tokyo, 1971), 116.
41. *Daini Seikosha,* 272 (1976): 28.
42. John Cantwell, "The Globalisation of Technology: What Remains of the Product Cycle Model?" *Cambridge Journal of Economics* 19 (1995): 155–174, Raymond Vernon, "International Investment and International Trade in the Product Cycle", *Quarterly Journal of Economics* 80 (1966): 190–207 and Mark Casson, "Contractual Arrangements for Technology Transfer: New Evidence from Business History", *Business History* 28 (1986): 5–34.
43. According to traditional analysis, the more complicated a technology is, the more likely it is that it will be transferred via MNEs. See, for example, Farok J. Contractor and Tagi Sagafi-Nejad, "International Technology Transfer: Major Issues and Policy Responses", *Journal of International Business Studies* 12/2 (1981): 113–135 and W. H. Davidson and Donald G. McFetridge, "International Technology Transactions and the Theory of the Firm", *The Journal of Industrial Economics* 32/3 (March 1984): 253–264.
44. The number of jobs in the Swiss watchmaking industry went from 89,000 in 1970 to less than 30,000 in 1987. Convention patronale, *Recensement 2007* (La Chaux-de-Fonds, 2008), 12.

Part III

Learning from Foreign Firms

The third part of this volume deals with technology transfer between firms, looking at how enterprises imported and exported technologies from and to each other. The paths and processes of technology transfer through MNE (multinational enterprise) activities differed among different periods of globalization and different countries. The cases of Latin America in the early 20th century, of a European country in the middle of the 20th century and of China in the last decade of the 20th century and the first decade of the 21st century can bring us broader comprehension of the phenomenon.

Argentina was one of the leading recipient countries of foreign direct investment during the first third of the 20th century. American and European MNEs went into the Argentine market and transferred their technologies to the country, but little scholarship has explored how these corporations went about doing so. María Inés Barbero analyzes the technological transfer process in Argentina during the interwar period, focusing on the firm level. She emphasizes the different ways in which technologies were transferred to Argentina at the time, particularly in the industrial sector, and posits a general typology of the processes (foreign direct investment, joint ventures, license agreements, capital goods imports and new management and marketing methods) involved. For Argentine companies, immigrants—especially entrepreneurs and engineers—played a very relevant role during the 1920s and the 1930s. The author uses several case studies, including those of Algodonera Flandria (textiles), Grimoldi (shoe industry), Siam Di Tella (mechanical goods) and Compañía Italo Argentina de Electricidad (power), for illustrative support.

The issue of knowledge transfer highlights the issue of the different ways in which firms may acquire knowledge. In some cases, knowledge transfer occurred on a private basis between MNEs and their local partners. Pierre Lamard depicts this process with his contribution on the French electrical company Alsthom, a firm in which GE held a stake since its foundation in 1928. Both these firms adopted numerous agreements on the transfer of soft technologies, especially after World War II, within the context of Americanization. After having imported equipment and machines through technical assistance programs in the 1930s and 1950s, Alsthom sent several observation missions across the Atlantic to the United States in the 1960s with the aim of acquiring new management practices to improve the efficiency of work, such as programs for managerial training or dealing with relations among group partners. This Americanization of management, as can also be observed elsewhere in Europe and in Japan, appears to have made a major contribution to the growth of firms in the capitalist world after 1945, offering them some knowledge of soft technologies that were not available within domestic national systems of innovation (NSIs).

Finally, the Chinese automobile industry has since the late 1990s witnessed the rise so-called independent enterprises—firms without foreign capital—able to compete with MNEs. As Zejian Li emphasizes in his chapter, these domestic automobile makers, largely funded by public capital from either the central state or regional governments, acquired technologies from MNEs indirectly by, for example, hiring both foreign and Chinese engineers trained by major global automobile companies as experts or sourcing parts from subcontractors that also worked for the MNEs. These technological facilities enabled these Chinese carmakers to launch the sale of cheap cars for the fast-growing lower end of the market, a segment where foreign carmakers are largely absent and prospects for high growth are good.

7 Technological Transfers in Argentina's Early Industrialization
Agents and Paths, 1900–1930

María Inés Barbero

INTRODUCTION

Several historical studies on technological transfer processes have underscored both their complexity and the multiple ways in which innovation has flown from early-industrialized countries to late-industrialized economies. Available literature reveals the role played by a number of agents that have served as technology transfer drivers over time. On the one hand, scholars have emphasized the role of multinational companies (MNCs) in trade, foreign direct investment (FDI), or several other types of agreements with local companies in host countries, including joint ventures, technology licensing contracts, production-sharing agreements, and more.[1] Many authors view MNCs as a primary technology transfer agent due to both their abilities to create and deploy innovations and the advantages created by their knowledge and market power. On the other hand, scholars have also noted the key role traditionally played by qualified workers and technicians who emigrate from more- to less-developed areas either to work as full-time employees or to build their own ventures.[2] Indeed, people have been instrumental in these processes, as technological transfers involve not only the flow of readily accessible information but also the sharing of largely tacit knowledge that can only be conveyed in direct, face-to-face interactions among social actors. Trade has also been cited as one of the mechanisms used to disseminate technologies across national borders.[3] Finally, authors have also highlighted the role played by public policies to promote technological transfers, particularly in the period starting in the 1970s.[4]

Historical studies already recognized as classics have also pointed to the existence of multiple ways to foster and carry out technological diffusion, including individual endeavors, ad hoc organizations, pressure groups, and tariff schemes, while emphasizing the role of individual initiatives.[5] These studies have also shown how shifts in consumption habits have driven the adoption of new technologies.[6]

This study intends to examine some of the specific mechanisms used for technological transfers in Argentina's early industrialization period, spanning from 1900 to 1930, and focus on how this process unfolded by analyzing the specific experiences of some companies with available information. This analysis draws on the notion that business history relies on the study of technological transfer patterns to complement contemporary research efforts by other disciplines, challenging theories or, at the very least, providing relevant information for conceptualizations.

In addition to this introduction, this chapter comprises three sections. The first zeroes in on the role of MNCs as technological transfer agents. The second section describes how immigrant engineers helped disseminate technologies, and the third offers a number of concluding remarks.

MULTINATIONAL COMPANIES AS TECHNOLOGICAL TRANSFER AGENTS

During the first global economy, Argentina ranked as one of the world's leading recipients of FDI with a share of fixed capital stock value that ranged between 32% and 48% from the 1900s to the 1930s and peaked right before World War I (WWI).[7]

During all the periods analyzed in this chapter, Argentine government favored foreign investment, which the political elite positioned as one of the pillars of economic growth due to the scarcity of internal capital supply. Although Argentina had no foreign investment law (the first one was passed in 1953), there were no limits on the entry of capital or profits remittances between 1900 and 1930.

Throughout this period, MNCs played a key role in technological transfer via innovation in products, processes, business organization patterns, and management practices. Up until WWI, British investments prevailed, using freestanding companies to focus primarily on railways, urban infrastructure, and financial operations. Starting in the early twentieth century, however, American and European MNCs began to settle in Argentina and invest in a broader range of industries, including industrial goods production, sales, and assembly. This process gathered momentum after WWI as American firms took the lead and steered their investments largely toward the marketing and production of industrial goods both in traditional industries (food and beverages) and in more dynamic businesses (chemical products, cars, pharmaceuticals, and electrical appliances). Overall, these companies mostly produced newly emerging consumer goods and established wholly owned affiliates in Argentina to enhance their reach in Latin America's largest market and neighboring countries, as well.[8]

In the earlier decades of the twentieth century, FDI adopted many patterns that, in turn, translated into several means of technology innovation transfer. FDI operated on two basic mechanisms: the creation of commercial affiliates and the establishment of production plants. Still, FDI also came via other intermediate means.

Building Commercial Affiliates: Supplier-Based Innovation

The information currently available on MNCs settling in Argentina in the early 1900s does not distinguish between commercial and manufacturing affiliates. While this may curtail the ability to characterize MNCs' individual strategies, it should be noted that the creation of commercial branches too might drive innovations; thus, production affiliates are not the only means of transferring technologies to host countries. Neither should the importance of building a marketing affiliate be underestimated, for it is often both the first step in an MNC's expansion process and part of a deliberate strategy to penetrate a market. It also implies a greater investment and risk than operating through commercial agents.[9]

Technology transfer via commercial affiliates unfolded primarily through machinery and intermediate goods vendors. According to Pavitt's taxonomy,[10] this process largely involved supplier-dominated sectors and specialized suppliers. In the first case, suppliers of machinery and other industrial inputs are the primary drivers behind innovation, with capital goods and intermediate supplies flowing to manufacturing firms. This includes the more traditional consumer and intermediate goods industries like textiles, apparel, furniture, leather, footwear, ceramics, and simple metallic products. The specialized supplier sector, meanwhile, includes most mechanical engineering and instrument producers, such as machinery for specialized industries (machine tools, for example), and features great supply diversification, significant economies of scope, and a remarkable potential for product innovation.

Given the structure of Argentina's industry after WWI, with traditional industries dominating the scene,[11] suppliers of capital goods and intermediate goods played a key role in innovation processes. The establishment of commercial affiliates by companies manufacturing machinery for traditional sectors helped modernize some of these industries, particularly when offensive market penetration strategies made it easier for users to access capital goods.

The United Shoe Machinery Corporation (USMCo) provides the most documented example thus far. Although UMSCo opened a commercial branch in Argentina in the early going, the company started brisk international expansion in the beginning of the twentieth century. By the onset of WWI, UMSCo had subsidiary companies in Canada, the United Kingdom, France, and Germany, and delegations or machinery depots in Switzerland, Denmark, Norway, Sweden, Belgium, Australia, New Zealand, and Spain.[12]

After launching a commercial affiliate in Buenos Aires in 1903, UMSCo not only provided modern machinery for footwear manufacturing but also offered machine sales and leasing, thereby reducing entry barriers and promoting mechanization. As footwear-manufacturing processes involved a large number of operations, companies were able to choose to mechanize just a few of them, making for a lower investment. In addition to machinery, USMCo also imported spare parts and accessories and provided technical support to shoe manufacturers. By incorporating machines for all or some operations, local businessmen managed to reduce costs and production times in order to compete in terms of price and quality with handmade or imported footwear.[13] As a US Department of Commerce official put it, "the facilities offered through its leased-machine system had made lack of capital not an insurmountable obstacle in the establishment of new shoe factories in Argentina."[14]

These changes also came as a result of the training system implemented by UMSCo, under which its managers and mechanics instructed local manufacturers on how to use the new machinery. In 1925, 416 of the 450 shoe factories across the country used UMSCo's machinery.[15] Along with new machines, these firms also introduced more systematic cost-control methods and finishing improvements, adopted better distribution systems, and adapted American advertising techniques to local conditions.

In 1906, Singer Sewing Machine Co., another US company that had been exporting its products to Argentina since the 1870s, opened a number of affiliates in Buenos Aires and cities in the hinterlands to sell and repair its machines and train customers to use them at factories, workshops, and workers' homes—primarily to bind instep parts together (sewing).[16] Singer was one of the oldest American multinational enterprises, and it had become a truly global company before the WWI, drawing almost 85% of its sales from outside its home market. As Andrew Godley explains, "Already by the late 1870s the center of gravity of Singer's business had shifted decisively away from the United States and moved to encompass Western, Central, and Southern Europe."[17] By 1895, the company controlled perhaps 80% of the world market and had opened its first factories in Canada and Europe.[18] As new markets emerged, Singer broadened its geographical coverage, reaching Russia (which emerged as the most important market at the turn of the century) and expanding into parts of Asia and Africa.[19]

Commercial affiliates often provided minor assembly and technical support services. United Shoe Machinery Corporation owned a workshop to repair and adjust its machines, an outfit that employed thirty to forty employees in the early 1930s. Singer Sewing Machine Company also offered minor assembly services and technical support for its products, as International Harvester Company did, too.[20]

An early adopter of UMSCo's machinery in Argentina was Grimoldi Hermanos, a family business founded in 1895 that opened its first factory in 1904 with a complete forty-five-machine set to manufacture fine men's footwear. Grimoldi Hermanos relied on Goodyear's welted system, a production method introduced by UMSCo to manufacture superior footwear mechanically. Grimoldi had been created by the sons of an Italian immigrant who owned a shoe repair and manufacture workshop. He taught his craft to his sons, who used that knowledge to partner with their brother-in-law to start their own firm. The Grimoldi brothers combined traditional shoemaking with the use of imported machinery, initially with the McKay system and, later, with Goodyear's welt. By building a factory and incorporating UMSCo's machinery, Grimoldi was able to quadruple its output from 1905 to 1910, going from 500 pairs a day to 2,000 and becoming a large player in its industry.[21]

Machinery-importing companies' operations could bear a direct influence on local firms' factory construction and innovation adoptions—not only in equipment but also in workshop design. Electrical motor manufacturers provided a very illustrative example. They offered users advice on plant installations as part of their market entry strategy. European companies had their own engineers, who made themselves readily available to potential customers, competing with freelance engineers for market control. Large companies provided their engineers' advice for free—even for the design of entire plants. Another widespread practice involved the assignment of foremen to oversee new plant construction or machinery setup, while workers were often recruited from suppliers' local or headquarters' staff.[22]

Manufacturing Companies

Foreign companies building production affiliates in Argentina in the 1920s adopted a number of operating schemes—from complete production to packaging commodities imported in bulk—that bore an impact on the local economy. When a company chose to establish a full-production affiliate, technology transfers could translate into both product and process innovations, effectively shaping the local industry's output capacity.

The most prominent example comes from American meatpacking companies, which arrived in Argentina in the early 1900s, introducing not only their chilled system but also more modern production and labor organization methods. These firms were the first to use the mass production system, as they shipped their products to foreign markets. Swift's local affiliate purchased an Australian meatpacking outfit in Berisso (a town near Buenos Aires) in 1907 and refurbished its original building to accommodate the company's Chicago plant standards. These companies also employed the same production methods they used in their plants in the United States, organizing labor with a Tayloristic workflow method. In addition to incorporating their parent companies' production techniques, local affiliates also introduced incremental innovations. Their technical and industrial departments, staffed with engineers, technicians, industrial designers, and draftsmen,[23] performed research and development tasks to adapt machinery, improve tools, and elaborate increasingly complex workflow programs.

As a result of the local market's limited size, mass manufacturing practices were not the rule but the exception, largely used in sectors that shipped their output to foreign markets. However, even when production serviced the domestic market and maintained a smaller scale, FDI favored innovation and drove learning and training processes for both local technicians and workers.

Railway Workshops: From Repairs to Production

Transportation and utility companies' subsidiaries produced parts and also provided assembly and repair services. From early on, British railway companies operating in Argentina as freestanding companies owned repair workshops that gradually incorporated increasingly complex operations. By 1913, these British companies operated fifty-six workshops, employing nearly 15,000 people (10,192 workers and 4,598 laborers) who serviced 149 locomotives, 177 passenger cars, and 5,681 cargo cars that year. Railway workshops employed roughly 50% of Argentina's metal-mechanic industry personnel, and its production accounted for 15% of the industry's overall output.[24]

Workshops started operating at the same time as railway companies and originally served to repair rolling stock, which had been imported duty-free since 1907. However, transportation costs and local resource availability soon drove workshops into assembly and manufacturing operations. When WWI broke out, workshops with previous training were able to strengthen these operations to offset import restrictions. For instance, Ferrocarril Central Argentino's Gorton workshops, built in 1912–1917, were viewed as the largest and best-equipped locomotive workshops in South America by the 1920s. They repaired all Central Argentino's locomotives, assembled new locomotives, and built and refurbished steel cargo cars. These workshops included a foundry, locomotive and car assembly shops, forging and mechanization workshops, boilers, a welding shop, a wheel shop, a timber sawmill, a carpentry shop, a painting workshop, and warehouses. They were equipped with the machinery required to manufacture all locomotive parts. Operating with a modern organization, these facilities featured an engineering department and a planning department or "control office." A team of inspectors, consisting of trained locomotive assemblers, submitted daily reports to this control office, which recorded the information on a schedule board. Central Argentino's car repair shops only handled repair work, but their organization was world class, as these workshops used state-of-the-art production planning and control methods.[25]

Production Partnerships with Local Firms

Some multinational companies did not own or operate production plants in Argentina. Rather, they manufactured their products via agreements with local firms that handled production operations under their supervision. This arrangement was used to manufacture radios, refrigerators, and road-building molds. Although there was no local company that owned the necessary equipment to handle all production operations, agreements were forged with several firms to manufacture specific parts in order to assemble end products.[26]

Pharmaceutical companies often relied on this arrangement. In some cases, agreements only included exclusive rights to manufacture a product with the formula and brand used in the foreign company's home country, requiring royalty payments. At the other end of the spectrum, some agreements focused on production under the direct supervision of a headquarters' representative, with foreign companies controlling raw materials, equipment, production processes, formulas, and, often, sales of end products. Between these two poles, there were many options with differing production, distribution, and control roles for both foreign and local firms.[27]

One example of these arrangements was the several-year-long partnership built by Colgate Palmolive-Peet Company and Compañía de Productos Conen to manufacture Palmolive soaps. Conen's factory assigned one of its sections to Palmolive soap production alone, relying on modern equipment acquired based on recommendations from Colgate Palmolive, which also provided the necessary raw materials and carefully monitored manufacturing operations via its representatives. This foreign company paid Conen for every soap manufactured. In other cases, a local or foreign company manufactured products for several firms. De Valle Ltd. was an Argentine firm that manufactured products for J. B.Williams Co., Kolynos Co., A. S. Hinds, and Perfumería Gal from Madrid. Under the agreement signed by De Valle and Hinds, De Valle's factory manufactured, in just a few days and under the supervision of a Hinds representative, enough products to satisfy a year's demand. The products were stored at De Valle's plant to be shipped as ordered. The equipment used to manufacture these products belonged to A. S. Hinds Company and, after use, was stored until it was needed again. Hinds also rented a share of De Valle's factory for its intermittent production and product storage requirements.[28]

Foreign Licenses and Patents

From 1900 to 1919, 1,243 foreign patents were registered in Argentina, but the number of new patents rose to 8,731 in the 1920s.[29] At the same time, local companies started to use more foreign licenses. In an open economy, characterized by fluent exchanges with more developed countries and consumption habits following trends set by more industrialized societies, domestic companies were forced to adapt their production schemes to accommodate these requirements. As industrial operations diversified, the use of licenses and patents became more intense.

Multinational companies influenced this process in several ways. By setting up commercial and manufacturing affiliates in Argentina, they disseminated the use of new goods, driving their demand and encouraging competition from local producers. In some cases, multinationals ushered their products into the Argentine market by granting licenses to domestic businessmen. The most innovative local entrepreneurs often kept close ties with American and European companies, periodically traveling abroad to update their knowledge on production, management, and distribution practices. For both companies that produced consumer goods and firms that manufactured supplies and machinery, the use of foreign licenses was a means to access new process and product technologies. For these companies, using a license could pave the way to manufacturing their own models. Other companies copied imported products, and these strategies often formed a combined solution.

SIAM Di Tella clearly illustrated this approach. A metal-mechanic company founded in 1910 by three Italian immigrants to produce bakery machinery, SIAM Di Tella became one of Argentina's topmost industrial firms under Torcuato Di Tella's leadership. Born in Italy, Di Tella settled in Argentina with his family when he was fourteen years old and, after working at several jobs, partnered with two fellow Italians to start the company. After WWI, he studied engineering in Argentina.[30] In the 1920s, SIAM started to produce gas pumps with a license from Wayne Pump Co., a US firm. This licensing agreement remained in force from 1923 to 1927. Demand grew as the use of motor vehicles spread in Argentina; several local businesses tried to develop proprietary designs for gas pumps but ran into severe difficulties. As a result, Di Tella decided to look for a foreign license in order to build gas pumps with local and imported parts. When the Wayne license agreement was cancelled, SIAM started to manufacture pumps with its own brand, hiring an engineer from Fiat. In the 1930s and 1940s, SIAM continued to pursue its foreign license-based strategy, entering into agreements with several companies, including Kelvinator and Westinghouse, for refrigerator manufacturing.[31]

IMMIGRATION AND TECHNOLOGICAL TRANSFER: THE ROLE OF ENGINEERS

As in many other newly settled countries, technological transfers in Argentina in the late nineteenth century and for a period thereafter were closely associated with immigration from Southern and Eastern Europe.[32] Several available case studies provide information about how immigrant craftsmen and businessmen drove industrialization and technology dissemination in the last decades of the nineteenth century and onward.[33] Recent research studies have also highlighted the role that immigrant engineers played in fostering technological transfers in the electric industry, a pillar for the Second Industrial Revolution.

Argentina's electricity network-building process started in the late 1880s, when electrical systems became increasingly widespread around the world.[34] In Buenos Aires, Compañía de Electricidad del Río de la Plata, a British freestanding company, was in charge of power generation and distribution. In 1898, a new AEG-funded company and a group of associated investment banks called Compañía Alemana Transatlántica de Electricidad (CATE-DUEG) entered the scene. In the early twentieth century, CATE built its own power plant in Buenos Aires and acquired the electric facilities owned by

British companies operating in the city to become the sole power producer and distributor in the nation's capital.

The creation of Compañía Italo Argentina de Electricidad (CIAE) in 1911 put an end to CATE's monopoly, bringing a consortium of Swiss and Italian investors into Argentina's local electric business. Italian engineer Giovanni Carosio took the initiative to build CIAE, first engaging a group of Italian businessmen who had settled in Buenos Aires. Next, he recruited two Italian manufacturers of electric supplies—Pirelli and Franco Tosi—as well as a group of private investors in Italy. Finally, he managed to bring in a Swiss group consisting of the Motor holding company (created as a result of the efforts made by Brown Boveri—a manufacturer of electrotechnical products—with the support of Swiss and German banks) and two banks—Leu and Co. and UBS.[35]

Specialized studies have underscored the role played by engineers in the creation of electric companies. Engineers promoted the creation of new firms or served as consultants to assess project feasibility, given the technical complexity of constructing and managing power-generation and distribution companies.[36] As Argentina largely lacked technical and managerial resources in the late nineteenth and early twentieth centuries, engineers functioned as representatives of European companies and participated in ventures with investors from several countries.

In the decade preceding the onset of WWI, Buenos Aires played host to the endeavors of two Italian engineers, Giovanni Carosio and Mauro Herlitzka, who rallied groups of local and foreign investors to build power-generation and/or distribution companies in several cities across the country. Venture promoters not only secured management positions in the companies they helped to create but also received rewards for their involvement, often in the form of equity shares. They were also able to meddle in the acquisition of equipment and supplies with their own importing firms. Thus, they combined their technical and managerial skills with new business opportunities.

Both Carosio and Herlitzka had vast technical knowledge and experience in the creation and management of power plants. In addition to being familiar with the local market and its requirements, the two also boasted a large contact network that spanned across European manufacturers of electric supplies, the Buenos Aires business community (particularly—though not exclusively—Italian businessmen), and public officials at the municipal, provincial, and national levels. In the early 1910s, Carosio and Herlitzka embarked on separate efforts to start a new power company to service Buenos Aires, an ever-growing city where public officials seemed eager to grant concessions to companies that would put an end to the existing German monopoly.

Carosio first arrived in Argentina in 1899 as a representative for Franco Tosi, a company that manufactured electrotechnical products and had employed Carosio in Italy. In Buenos Aires, Carosio also represented AEG and joined the board of Compañía Industrial de Electricidad del Rio de la Plata

(1900), a company that manufactured arc lamps and marketed electric supplies manufactured by AEG and Franco Tosi in Argentina. At the smaller power plants in outlying cities and rural areas, Tosi's medium- and low-power engines competed with an edge, enabling Carosio to create electric companies in several Argentine provinces. In 1911, when CIAE was created, Carosio managed both Compañía Industrial de Electricidad del Rio de la Plata and Compañía de Electricidad de la Provincia de Buenos Aires.

Mauro Herlitzka graduated as an engineer in Turin. After working at Siemens and Halske in Germany for two years, he returned to Italy and joined Pirelli to head up the company's electrotechnical lab. A year later, he returned to Berlin's Siemens and Halske before joining AEG as engineering head of the power plant construction department. In 1897, he was sent to Buenos Aires to look into the possibility of setting up a power plant; this project would eventually lead to the creation of CATE, where Herlitzka served as executive director from 1901 to 1910. Like Carosio, he promoted the creation of electric companies, collaborating with local and foreign investors to start seven electric companies in Argentina's hinterlands—most of them managed by a parent company, Compañía Anglo Argentina de Electricidad.

As a result of his drive and the strength of his contact network, Carosio managed to engage several investor groups in Argentina and Europe in a project to create Compañía Italo Argentina de Electricidad, a feat he accomplished in August 1911. The active role played by Italian engineers did not end when these companies were founded; rather, it continued to prove instrumental throughout their history. Carosio served as CIAE president from its inception until his death in 1959. Another engineer who had a leading role in this process was Agostino Zamboni, who was born in Italy (in 1883) and graduated from Politecnico di Milano. Zamboni managed Usinas Eléctricas del Estado in Montevideo from 1907 to 1914 and then joined CIAE, where he served as general manager until 1964. Upon Carosio's demise in 1959, Zamboni took over as CIAE's president and remained in the position until his death in 1969.

Both Carosio and Herlitzka transferred their knowledge and social networks to Argentina, forming bridges between the Argentine market and European multinational companies. Technological transfer took place through different channels. The most direct route was the introduction of imported machinery and inputs for the inception and operation of electric plants. In some cases, foreign companies opened production facilities in the Argentine market; in 1917, for example, Pirelli created a Buenos Aires-based affiliate devoted to the production of electrical wires for CIAE.[37] Electrical companies also hired European engineers and technicians as managers in charge of technological decisions. CIAE's boards during the 1920s included several Italian and Swiss engineers, mostly specialized in the electric sector: Giovanni Carosio (chairman), Agostino Zamboni (CEO), Agostino Nizzola (chairman of Motor Columbus starting in 1925), and Vittorio Valdani.[38] The building and operation of electrical plants and networks demanded sophisticated technical skills. From the outset, CIAE adopted the alternating current system; this system enabled it to compete well with other electrical companies settled in Argentina that employed the direct current system and had to reconvert their facilities.[39]

CONCLUDING REMARKS

The empirical evidence presented here corroborates how relevant both multinational companies and individuals were in the technological transfer processes in Argentina in the early twentieth century. FDI proved crucial for the dissemination of new products and new production, distribution, and management methods. Manufacturing and commercial affiliates too played a remarkable role in technology transfers. Also noteworthy is the variety of production strategies pursued by multinationals since early on and the effects borne by their agreements with local firms on Argentina's adoption of modern industrial methods and plants. FDI patterns also contributed to training local human resources and fostering incremental innovations.

Immigration also drove technological transfers. On the one hand, immigrant professionals and specialized technicians, particularly engineers, played a key role in this process, as CIAE's case illustrates. On the other hand, craftsmen who settled in Argentina brought their knowledge on specific trades and later incorporated new products and processes, as was the case for Grimoldi. In turn, the case of SIAM reveals how the use of licenses granted by foreign companies largely depended on the ability of immigrant businessmen to spot opportunities for innovation and approach multinational companies via their contact networks.

Another important consideration is that endeavors by multinational companies and immigrant professionals were once closely linked. Multinationals relied on teams of engineers in charge of transferring know-how from their home countries. At CIAE, Italian engineers promoted FDI flows from multinational companies. Their social capital proved instrumental in attracting foreign investors, as they liaised between investors overseas and the local market, thus fostering innovation and facilitating technological transfers.

Finally, this analysis of the evidence currently available on Argentina from 1900 to 1930 indicates that technological transfer processes were largely driven by market mechanisms in an open, deregulated economy that favored the incoming flow of goods, funds, and people, while enabling the construction of networks engaging domestic and foreign agents.

Argentine policies regarding FDI and multinational companies continued to be friendly until the 1940s, but the introduction of exchange controls, local currency devaluations, and restrictions on foreign currency remittance in the 1930s all had a negative impact on returns for foreign companies. However, this scenario created new investment opportunities in industrial activities that were becoming more and more profitable within a new prevailing protectionist context. The economic policy developed by the military government in 1943–1945 and, later, by the Peronist administration (1945–1955) brought deep changes, mostly because of the massive nationalization of transportation and public utilities formerly owned by foreign companies that occurred during the period.

NOTES

1. N. Mohan Reddy and Liming Zhao, "International Technology Transfer: A Review," *Research Policy* 19 (1990): 285–307; Rajneesh Narula and Antonello Zanfei, "Globalization of Innovation: The Role of Multinational Enterprises," in *The Oxford Handbook of Innovation,* ed. Jan Fagerberg, David C. Mowery, and Richard R. Nelson (Oxford: Oxford University Press, 2005), 318–345.
2. See, for example, seminal works like Nathan Rosenberg, "Economic Development and the Transfer of Technology: Some Historical Perspectives," *Technology and Culture* 11, no. 4 (October 1970): 550–575; David Jeremy, "British Textile Technological Transmission to the United States: The Philadelphia Region Experience, 1770–1820," *Business History Review* 47, no. 1 (Spring 1973): 24–52; and Sidney Pollard, *Peaceful Conquest: The Industrialization of Europe, 1760–1970* (Oxford: Oxford University Press, 1981).
3. Wolfgang Keller, "International Technology Diffusion" (Working Paper 8573, NBER, October 2001, http://www.nber.org/papers/w8573), 21–25.
4. Reddy and Zhao, "International Technology Transfer"; Alice Amsden, *The Rise of "The Rest": Challenges to the West from Late-Industrializing Economies* (Oxford: Oxford University Press, 2001).
5. Jeremy, "British Textile Transmission."
6. Rosenberg, "Economic Development."
7. Norma Lanciotti and Andrea Lluch, "Foreign Direct Investment in Argentina: Timing of Entry and Business Activities of Foreign Companies (1860–1950)," *Entreprises et Histoire* 54 (April 2009): 37–66.
8. Andrés Regalsky and María Inés Barbero, "Las inversiones extranjeras y el comercio exterior," in *Nueva Historia de la Nación Argentina,* ed. Academia Nacional de la Historia (Buenos Aires: Planeta, 2002), 117–149.
9. Typically, a foreign company's expansion process starts with its exports through an agent, continues with its establishment of a commercial affiliate, and finally moves on to the creation of a production affiliate, which often combines imports with local manufacturing before focusing on manufacturing. See Mira Wilkins, *The Maturing of Multinational Enterprise: American Business Abroad from 1914 to 1970* (Cambridge, MA: Harvard University Press, 1974).
10. Keith Pavitt, "Sectorial Patterns of Technical Change: Towards a Taxonomy and a Theory," *Research Policy* 13 (1984): 343–373.
11. According to the 1914 *Censo Industrial,* Argentina's food, beverage, and tobacco industry accounted for 53% of the nation's industrial product, while the textile and leather industry contributed 11%. Combined, the industries accounted for 64% of Argentina's industrial product.
12. José Antonio Miranda, "American Machinery and European Footwear: Technology Transfer and International Trade, 1860–1939," *Business History* 46, no. 2 (2004): 195–218.
13. Felipe Fortunato Delrío, *Las grandes industrias: Curtido, calzado y afines* (Buenos Aires: Cámara Argentina de la Industria del Calzado [Footwear Industry Argentine Chamber], 1935), 54–55.

14. Herman Brock, *Department of Commerce, Special Agents Series, No. 177, Boots and Shoes, Leather and Supplies in Argentina, Uruguay and Paraguay* (Washington DC: Government Printing Office, 1919), 52.
15. M. A. Phoebus, *Argentine Markets for United States Goods* (Washington DC: Department of Commerce, 1926), 11.
16. Delrío, *Las grandes industrias,* 397.
17. Andrew Godley, "Selling the Sewing Machine around the World: Singer's International Marketing Strategies, 1850–1920," *Enterprise & Society* 7, no. 2 (June 2006): 274.
18. Fred V. Carstensen, *American Enterprise in Foreign Markets: Studies of Singer and International Harvester in Imperial Russia* (Chapel Hill: University of North Carolina Press Books, 1984), 25–26.
19. Godley, "Selling the Sewing Machine," 275–276.
20. Dudley Maynard Phelps, *Migration of Industry to South America* (New York: McGraw Hill, 1936), 11–12.
21. Arthur Butman, *Department of Commerce, Special Agents Series, No. 37, Shoe and Leather Trade in Argentina, Chile, Perú and Uruguay* (Washington DC: Government Printing Office, 1910), 9. In any case, innovations were gradually introduced, as Grimoldi continued to produce handmade, pegged, bootie, McKay-stitched, and Goodyear-welted shoes. For more on Grimoldi's history, see María Inés Barbero, "Construyendo activos intangibles: La experiencia de una empresa fabricante de calzado en la Argentina en la primera mitad del siglo XX," in *Revista de Historia de la Economía y de la Empresa* (2011), 151–176.
22. Philip Smith, *Electrical Goods in Argentina, Uruguay and Brazil* (Washington DC: US Department of Commerce, 1919), 18.
23. Mirta Lobato, *La vida en las fábricas* (Buenos Aires: Prometeo/Entrepasados, 2001), Chapter 2.
24. Adolfo Dorfman, *Historia de la industria argentina* (Buenos Aires: Solar/Hachette, 1970), 297–298.
25. George S. Brady, *Trade Promotion Series, No. 32, Railways of South America. Part I: Argentina* (Washington DC: Department of Commerce, 1926), 50–51.
26. Phelps, *Migration of Industry,* 4–5.
27. Ibid., 6–9; E. L. Thomas, ed., *Latin American Markets for Soaps and Soap Ingredients* (Washington DC: US Department of Commerce, 1931), 37.
28. Phelps, *Migration of Industry,* 7–8.
29. Javier Villanueva, "El origen de la industrialización argentina," *Desarrollo Económico* 12, no. 47 (October–December 1972): 451–476.
30. Nicolás Cassese, *Los Di Tella: Una familia, un país* (Buenos Aires: Aguilar, 2008), 20–27.
31. Thomas Cochran and Rubén Reina, *Entrepreneurship in Argentine Culture* (Philadelphia: University of Pennsylvania Press, 1962).
32. Nathan Rosenberg, *Inside the Black Box: Technology and Economics* (Cambridge: Cambridge University Press, 1982), 249.
33. For more on Argentine business history, see María Inés Barbero and Raúl Jacob, eds., *La nueva historia de empresas en España y América Latina* (Buenos Aires: Temas, 2008).
34. William Hausman, Peter Hertner, and Mira Wilkins, *Global Electrification: Multinational Enterprise and International Finance in the History of Light and Power, 1878–2007* (New York: Cambridge University Press, 2008), Chapter 2.
35. The information on the role of engineers at Compañía Italo Argentina de Electricidad has been drawn from María Inés Barbero, Norma Lanciotti, and

María Cristina Wirth, "Capital extranjero y gestión local: La compañía Italo Argentina de Electricidad: 1912–1950," mimeo (2009).

36. Hausman, Hertner, and Wilkins, *Global Electrification,* 56–59.
37. María Inés Barbero, "Grupos empresarios, intercambio comercial e inversiones italianas en la Argentina: El caso de Pirelli (1910–1920)," *Estudios Migratorios Latinoamericanos* 5, nos. 15–16 (1990): 311–337
38. Compañía Italo Argentina de Electricidad, *Memorias y Balances, 1926–30.*
39. Barbero, Lanciotti, and Wirth, "Capital extranjero y gestión local," 20.

8 American "Soft" Technologies and French Big Business after World War II

Alstom and GE

Pierre Lamard

In the specific area of electrical energy, there were numerous early transfers of technology. Indeed, from the late 19th century onwards, some international exhibitions focused exclusively on electricity with a view to developing trade, competitiveness and innovation. Moreover, the unique universal system introduced for electrical units in 1881 favoured the establishment of dedicated international centres tasked with sharing scientific, technical and industrial knowledge.[1] At the international meetings in question, various agreements were signed to boost industries' competitiveness in a growing market.[2] In France, companies like SACM (Société Alsacienne de Construction Mécanique[3]) and Schneider started to develop their electrical building activities in 1888, initially relying on foreign patents to strengthen their development strategy. This was also the case for Als-thom (known as Alsthom since 1932, and Alstom since 1998),[4] which has since become a global player in the energy and railway building areas. The firm came into being in 1928 when SACM and the Compagnie Française Thomson-Houston (CFTH) were merged to run the Thomson-Houston processes (at the time, CFTH was a major manufacturer of French electrical materials). Some 15,000 employees worked for this new company comprising seven production sites.[5] In the merger, CFTH Company gained the right to use American techniques under the cooperation agreement signed in 1919 with General Electric Co. in the electromechanical building field. At the time, GE was the first firm to introduce scientific results into industrial activities. A laboratory was set up in 1900 in Schenectady, New York, which employed the leading American researchers. For 63 years, CFHT took advantage of GE patents for a fee and could open its own offices in all departments of the US firm, allowing it to benefit from the latest electrical building innovations. Moreover, exclusive agreements were signed covering various markets, including mainland France and its overseas territories. This cooperation long affected the nature of the relationship between GE and Als-thom, because the extension of their cooperation agreement gave Als-thom access to the immense technical and commercial resources of GE, the world's leading electromechanical builder.[6] GE bought 4,000 shares in Als-thom. Because of this relationship between GE and Als-thom, the direct French competitor, Schneider, rapidly developed close ties with Westinghouse, leading concretely to a subsidiary company: SW Electrical Materials. This also marked the arrival of American technology in France and the beginning of interaction with European capitals.

The challenge was finding how to cope with German competition from such renowned groups as Siemens and AEG. On the contrary, American firms were very interested in transferring patents to other companies—whether or not they were subsidiaries—so as to reinforce their own positions on new and fast-growing European markets. Subsequently, from 1920 onwards, major electrotechnical groups like GE gave European engineers an opportunity to train in American industries to study their working processes,[7] As a result of which the US presence and interests grew steadily. The first agreement between GE and Als-thom was subsequently renegotiated in 1969 due to antitrust laws. Relationships were retained only in a few areas where the US company was a technical leader (continuous current transport, power semi-conductor drives and gas turbines).[8]

IMPORTING THE AMERICAN MODEL

As early as 1930, Als-thom took advantage of GE's support to modernize its productive structures. Technological assistance was concentrated in three main fields: (1) knowledge of technical information from laboratories and offices; (2) management and procedural cooperation; and (3) commercial support in some markets. Als-thom paid a 1.8% per year rental fee covering all sales related to US patents. Engineers were seconded to North American factories. This comprehensive agreement enabled Als-thom rapidly to make a name for itself in the French market. It even obtained an interest in General Electrica Espagnola set up by GE and CFTH, whose biggest factory was located in Bilbao (Spain).

Unfortunately, the economic crisis hit. The considerable drop in orders for both electrotechnical building and major electrical equipment[9] required the development of a new industrial strategy. Even though it purchased a large volume of more efficient materials, Als-thom was fully aware of the need to familiarize itself with such new working methods as management controls and financial forecasting. During this period, major constructors like Raoul Dautry, Albert Pestche and Auguste Detoeuf realized that such technical rationalization also had to take such new working and management methods, including the human factor, into consideration.[10] The point should be made that the question of technological transfer already went beyond a strictly technical framework. Als-thom imported hardware technology but was also exposed to different management and administration methods. This initial cooperation intensified after World War II as a result of the French government's push in favour of modernization.

Immediately following the Second World War, French industry embarked on a productivity battle through its large industrial groups. This economic modernization campaign, which began with Jean Monnet's blueprint and was subsequently boosted by the Marshall Plan, was strongly influenced by the American model. Fordian and Taylorian methods were largely applied during World War I because of constraints imposed by the war economy but concerned only a few industries. During the interwar period, these specific industries did not hesitate to implement rationalization principles but failed to look into mass production. This is why rebuilding was the main priority, followed by economic and technological Americanization, in order to compete with the East bloc.

The rebuilding years can be broken down into two specific periods: the first was devoted to retrieving and repairing machines appropriated by Nazi Germany, while the second marked the arrival of the first American machine tools provided under the Marshall Plan: lathes, drills bearing the brands Cincinnati, Sunstrad, Bullard and so on. From 1945 onwards, 75 million French francs were invested in outfitting factories in Belfort, the group's largest production site.[11] It was necessary to invest in national rebuilding. As a consequence, the two main energy sectors, namely, production and distribution on the one hand and electrical traction on the other hand, became priority areas for the State.[12] This entailed the manufacturing of a larger quantity of more efficient material. Simultaneously, the superintendent of the plan proposed, in the French programme for productivity improvement, several steps such as training in the United States. In 1949, seven Alsthom representatives travelled to America in conjunction with the "experimental action of large electrical machines" and spent six weeks studying factors specifically related to high industrial productivity. As for the Belfort firms, four representatives received similar training: two engineers (R. Damisch and R. de la Harpe), a draftsman (A. Guldmann) and a specialized technician (J. Franchi).[13]

The conclusions were evident from a technical point of view, with the necessary modernization, standardization and work simplification, as well as from a human perspective. Indeed, this training revealed the importance of psychological factors for improving productivity. Recommendations advocated strengthening cooperation between departments as well as developing manager training, "the first link involving the working class that should be constantly well maintained to favour the best possible relationships in each enterprise".[14]

Even though Alsthom staff were well documented on this subject,[15] numerous technicians went to America for training or courses through AFAP, the French Association for Productivity Increase. As a result, ties between French and American industries were tightened from 1957 onwards, especially with regard to General Electric. This American firm shared information on its technological performances and working methods with French companies. Subsequently, some major technical changes were made to the new equipment, leading to a fourfold or fivefold increase in productivity but requiring both workers and technicians to learn new skills. From 1958 to 1962, more than 50% of Alsthom's investments were for the Belfort site.

From 1958 to 1963, 110 million French francs were spent on modernizing equipment and tools. At the time, Alsthom supplied virtually all types of electrical materials (turbo alternators, hydraulic alternators, large power motors and engines.[16]

TRAINING: A NECESSARY OBLIGATION

Parallel to these large-scale investments, management endeavoured to encourage staff training, introducing a massive refresher course training programme. Starting in 1953, each production site (industries of Belfort, Lecourbe, Saint-Ouen and Tarbes) as well as the head office in Paris (avenue Kleber) developed its own programmes validated by the corresponding management team. Subsequently, a central department for social relationships was set up, primarily to discuss the question of professional staff training. A committee was specifically tasked with training skilled workers, engineers and managers. In 1960, this body expanded, leading to the establishment of an engineering management unit within the overall management structure and thereby allowing the clear identification of this type of staff. The committee had a mandate to recruit, train, select and oversee the career development of these engineers, and was backed by another committee interested in introducing measures consistent with the general tendency in this area, such as offering a broad choice of engineer training programmes outside the enterprise.

The return to a global strategy, developed for all of Alsthom's productive groups, was largely influenced at the time by American methods, especially as far as management was concerned. For example, a look at a training note shows that references were clearly similar to those used in American industries (Westinghouse and GE). Cooperation was strengthened in 1960: there were 16 missions to GE industry in 1961 and 19 in 1962. Of these missions, 26 focused on technical material while the others concerned organization, scheduling, working conditions and relations. Between 1953 and 1964, some 60 engineers travelled to Schenectady, New York, for training lasting from two weeks to six months.

> The managers must receive the same training. . . . We are really impressed by the distinction made between the technical point of view and the management. . . . We refer to all the analyses concerning the management philosophy, corporate communication or the capitalism and communism concepts . . . which represent some fields for thought far from the day-to-day worries of a department manager: when he came back from Crotonville, this manager was enthusiastic about his training and his working behaviour was different.[17]

Improving internal relations and promoting social cohesion were as important as mastering the new technologies introduced to increase productivity, even if the rationalization of work processes was of great interest. Along with such measures as briefings, it was proposed to circulate an internal publication in order to "create and to develop a 'home spirit' necessary for improving the atmosphere in the different departments".[18] This in turn led to the publication of a news bulletin for managers and skilled workers (five bulletins were published between 1954 and 1955, with a total print run of 2,000), featuring short articles (20 numbers corresponding to 50 specimens) as well as a bulletin for commercial staff news and relations between 1951 and 1953.

At the outset, each industrial site had to list all of its actions in order to understand their impact and thus harmonize the various utilizations. As of 1958, the management of the Belfort industries were pursuing the following avenues:

- Developing training courses on work relations for all manufacturing staff[19] (leaders, induction of new workers, notion of responsibility, safety, etc.);
- Introducing the study about rationalization of work processes aimed at engineers, method agents and designers;
- Organizing some general news briefings.

Even though cooperation involving skilled or management staff was relatively good, only 20% of all agents applied the methods recommended for work relations effectively and consistently. Subsequently, in order to strongly encourage staff to put relevant principles into practice, some practical exercises were carried out in the various departments under the supervision of the department leaders themselves, giving rise to so-called confident collaboration.

After an initial phase of comparing experiences, the company's general management decided to run training courses suited to the level of its workers. As a result, foremen were required to undergo specialized training on work relations, rather similar to that proposed by the TWI system, and to attend lectures on general topics. As for engineers, the system distinguished between training for new engineers (to identify their work-related skills); improvement expressed in terms of study circles, the specialized training circles directly linked to promotion; and, finally, feedback on the impact of the various training courses.

The improvement methods developed in the social relations area and geared to managers were dispensed by various nationwide organizations such as Cégos (Commission Générale de l'Organisation Scientifique du Travail), Study Centre of Training and Improvement, Study and Organization Centre or other organizations like the Centre universitaire de coopération économique et sociale (CUCES), which was primarily responsible for training people capable of moderating and organizing more internal meetings. Thorough training on the scientific organization of work was provided by the School for the Scientific Organization of Work and by the Graduate Institute of Technical Organization, both of which were recognized by the French Ministry of Education.

With regard to the further training of the new engineers, 10 days of external seminars were devoted exclusively to issues pertaining to industrial life: man at work, cost, organization, law, general economy, etc. In the Belfort industry, 47 recruitment processes of young engineers were organized in 1955, 24 in 1959, 65 in 1960 and 91 in 1961, for a workforce of nearly 6,000 employees.

In 1961, high-level courses were offered by the Centre of Research and Study of Leaders, to coach expert engineers in management functions. The programmes developed were intended to diversify these engineers' skills; acquaint them with general problems relating to company management; and further their personal development "to better assume their future leadership function".

> As leaders, we have the responsibility to create and to maintain friendly relationships with our employees and workers in addition to ensure high-quality manufacturing. This responsibility is the cornerstone of satisfactory relations with our workforce (January, 1952).[20]
>
> The American attempts to study and to establish management direction are one of the main reasons of the high productivity and economic domination of the United States (April, 1958).[21]

The operators providing the training came from either training offices or the higher echelons of big companies like Electricité de France (EDF) and Société nationale d'étude et de construction de moteurs d'aviation (SNECMA). It should be noted that only a few sessions relative to scientific and technical improvements were held during this 10-year stretch.

OBJECTIVE: MANAGEMENT EFFICIENCY

In the early 1960s, several missions and research projects were carried out to encourage Alsthom's engineer management team. In particular, one of these mission reports was discussed in some length at GE because it compared the productivity of French and American companies.

The analysis stated that 8,500 hours were required to manufacture the mechanical parts of a diesel locomotive in French industry as against 3,500 hours in America. This worrying conclusion led to the creation of a department specialized in manufacturing studies within the Belfort Traction group. In order to ensure widespread acceptance of cost reduction efforts, the help of a so-called White Cabinet was enlisted to create the necessary frame of mind for success. This entailed the training of 80 managers, engineers and technicians and 150 supervisors, requiring strong ties between the departments and a great many staff members.

> The suggestions provided by the workers and the efforts made by the purchasing department in relation to the suppliers combined to improve these results, in addition to the simplification of both manufacturing and standardization. Finally, the calculated estimations of expenditure and savings as well as their subsequent monitoring were the most important measures designed to cut costs. This also corresponded to the working methods applied in the United States.[22]

Training was then focused on work methods rather than a specific technology. The effects were spectacular indeed, leading to (a) cost savings of some 2 million with regard to the mechanical parts of locomotives in 1965; and (b) a 14–17% reduction in manufacturing delays!

Parallel to this large-scale campaign that concerned only a small share of the Belfort industry's activities,[23] the general management started to research the management of technicians, designers and supervisors. It appeared that supervisors (a) were relatively old—more than 50% were over 50—and (b) had a low basic educational level (66% had stopped with the general aptitude certificate, or CAP). In 1964, for example, out of the average technical managers in Belfort enterprises, 707 of them were not qualified and 423 held a CAP, accounting for almost 80 % of manpower (1,416 persons); 188 average managers held a BEI certificate (Brevet d'Enseignement Industriel); 54 a BP certificate (Brevet Professionnel), and 44 another certificate.

Despite a training push covering a 15-year period, the results were inadequate and recruitment methods had to be improved to cope with a twofold problem: (1) it was necessary to increase the number of technical agents; and (2) they had to be able to perform some engineering tasks. These conclusions were of particular concern to the Belfort management because of its large number of employees: a total of 7,780 persons whose 1,416 mid-level managers and 438 engineers accounted for almost 46% of management staff for all the departments. This was why training courses were stepped up at the Belfort firms. In 1961 and 1962, 276 employees (technical agents, technicians and supervisors) either studied to obtain a BP, BTE (Brevet Technique en Electricité)or DEST (Diplôme d'Etudes Supérieures Techniques) certificate or followed advanced courses. This figure represented 20% of mid-level management or 3.5% of overall manpower.

Finally, development prospects existed for all of the group's departments: "60% of French coal is mined by Alsthom machines, 746 locomotives are delivered and 266 of these locomotives are exported, 100 power stations are built in the world, 335 large turbo-alternators are built and 115 are exported." The activities of the group were summed up by Georges Glasser when General de Gaulle came to Belfort in December 1959.[24]

Problems relating directly to recruitment and skills training were very real, and the managers of the Belfort firms were interested by methods applied by companies in other industries, such as Renault or Peugeot. They sought to become involved in major, inter-sectoral projects with a view to boosting investment.

CONCLUSION

During the period in question, Alsthom set an example in the region for all matters relating to post school training, especially with regard to new work methods and social relations.

At the time, French modernization of productive activities was not only implemented from a technical point of view but also benefited from the introduction of human engineering and management, also developed in American enterprises with an initial impetus provided by the Chicago School. The transfer of new work methods concerned the research and training linked to the new skills in both technology and personnel management.

This "Americanization" introduced by Alsthom in Belfort, specialized in mechanical and electrical manufacturing, set a significant example as far as technology transfer was concerned. The development strategy implemented by the management of this national enterprise was strongly influenced by the firm's productivity missions in the late 1940s. On the one hand, investment in efficient machine tools from the United States was stepped up, and on the other hand, the use of this new industrial equipment required new skills in the different departments. The company made special efforts to recruit qualified workers and to train its technicians and engineers in the methods employed in the United States. Not only were some important technical training programmes conducted, but the supervisors themselves had to be familiar with management methods, including the human factor in industrial development. This in turn led to the development of new relations within the firm.

At this stage, technology transfer, driven by the economic takeoff of the so-called Trentes Glorieuses (postwar boom) went beyond mere equipment imports to include methods directly related to social technologies. Yet these industrial results were conclusive. In 1960, Alsthom was the largest French company in the field of electrical building and large mechanical equipment. Its export turnover exploded, reflecting the company's ability to respond to large international markets without increasing its workforce. Even though the initial agreement was renegotiated in 1959, the relationship with GE continued, especially in the nuclear[25] and gas turbine sectors. In 1989, these relations were further strengthened when Alsthom and General Electric merged their power system activities.

NOTES

1. The International Society of Electricians in particular as well as the International Congress of Electricians played a key role in international and industrial competition. François Caron and Fabienne Cardot (eds.), *L'histoire de l'électricité en France, Espoirs et conquêtes (1881–1918)*, vol. 1 (Paris, 2005), 29–33, 317.
2. Voir, "La mise en place d'un système électrotechnique", ibid., 308–376.

3. Alsacian Mechanical Building Society.
4. Als-thom society became Alstom following its 1998 listing on stock exchanges in Paris, New York and London.
5. Robert Belot and Pierre Lamard (eds.), *Alstom à Belfort: 130 ans d'aventure industrielle* (ETAI, 2009); Jacques Marseille (ed.), *Alcatel-Alsthom: Histoire de la Compagnie Générale d'Electricité* (Paris, 1992).
6. Joseph Kennet, "Belfort/Alsthom (1879–1970): Hommes et technologie chez un grand constructeur" (PhD diss., Université de Paris I Sorbonne-Panthéon, 1993), 172.
7. Maurice Lévy-Leboyer, Henri Morsel (ed.), *L'histoire de l'électricité en France, L'interconnexion et le marché (1919–1946),* vol 2, (Sèvres, 1994), 244.
8. Groupe d'anciens de GEC Alsthom, *Histoire d'Alsthom à Belfort* (Mulhouse, 1997), 130.
9. Ibid., 79, 268.
10. "The greatness of America doesn't correspond to the reality: its wealth is not only gold or raw materials, but also comes from people and management". Ibid., 245.
11. The activities in Belfort factories account for 58% of turnover and 80% of the exports of the Alsthom group.
12. The nationalization of Société Nationale des Chemins de fer Français (SNCF) in 1937 and that of Electricité de France (EDF)'s electrical production reinforced the State's determination with regard to equipment and infrastructure. At the time, some dams were built on French rivers for hydroelectricity production. Some large thermal power stations were also constructed, and the rail network was electrified. All these developments were supported by the French Government. SNCF ordered over 140 Alsthom engines for Paris-Lyon line.
13. Departmental archives of Belfort Territory, 109 J, "First Mission to the United States on Electrical Building (Equipment)," report, August–September 1949, 5.
14. Fonds privé de l'Association Interprofessionnelle, CJP file, minutes, January 1950. Pierre Lanthier, "French and US Industrial Know-How: The Case of Electrical Engineering, 1945–1960", in *Catching Up with America,* ed. Dominique Barjot (Paris, 2002), 305.
15. A catalogue in the Als-thom technical library mentions numerous books on trips or study missions related to productivity questions, for example. Library of Belfort factories, works catalogue, 1 July 1960.
16. A world speed record of 331 km/h was set on 28 March 1955 by an electric locomotive (CC 7121) built in the Belfort factories. Also in 1955, the same model set a world endurance record of 438,324 km covered in seven months.
17. Departmental archives of Belfort Territory, 109 J 1614, excerpts from the conclusion of the mission report "Crotonville and Training for Senior Management at General Electric", 28 June 1961.
18. Departmental archives of Belfort Territory, 109 J 1596, minutes of the meeting of training for foremen, engineers and management staff, 30 December 1952. This led to the drafting of an officers' report (5 reports of 2,000 copies were published between 1954 and 1955) and of brief news (20 reports of 50 copies). Also significant was the information report of the commercial management, published between 1951 and 1953.
19. In 1951–1952, 216 persons participating in 25 master circles took part in such sessions. Departmental archives of Belfort Territory, 109 J 1596, report of 19 June 1952.
20. Departmental archives of Belfort Territory, 109 J 1596, taken from the preface to the manual on problems relating to the positions of foreman and line manager.

21. Departmental archives of Belfort Territory, 109 J 278, communication on management problems in a large decentralized company, 15 April 1958.
22. Departmental archives of Belfort Territory, 109 J 1621, information meeting for senior management on 14 June 1966, excerpt from the presentation by Mr. de la Harpe on reducing industrial costs.
23. At the time, as far as products were concerned, the activities of the Belfort factories depended on four groups: Large Electrical Material and Large Electrical Rotating Material (turbines for example) came under the Large Electromechanical Material Department, Industrial Engines and Medium Dynamos of the Industrial Material Department, Electrical and Mechanical Buildings of the Traction Department. These departments corresponded to decentralized structures, copied from the American model and considered as profit centres, Jacques Marseille (ed.), *Alcatel Alsthom, Histoire de la Compagnie Générale d'Electricité* (Paris, 1992), 283.
24. When General de Gaulle visited in Belfort Alsthom on 19 December 1959, Georges Glasser's comments summed up the group's activities. Groupe d'anciens de GEC Alsthom, *Histoire d'Alsthom*, 128.
25. Henri Morsel (ed.), *L'histoire de l'électricité en France: Une œuvre nationale: L'équipement, la croissance de la demande, le nucléaire (1946–1987)* (Montrouge, 1996), 729–749.

9 Foreign Technologies and Domestic Capital

The Rise of Independent Automobile Makers in China, 1990s–2000s

Zejian Li

INTRODUCTION

The purpose of this study is to investigate the chaotic but progressive emergence of independent Chinese automobile manufacturers (ICAMs). It will also provide an academic view of the relationship between the emergence of ICAMs and international technology transfer, from the points of view of both of the firms involved in the joint ventures (JVs), that is, from both the major foreign automobile manufacturers' (i.e., VW, etc.) and the Chinese domestic automobile manufacturers' (i.e., FAW, etc.) perspectives.

Many studies have documented the relationship between international technology transfer and the development of the Chinese automotive industry. For example, Guo and Zhang discovered that technological transfer from multinational companies has not brought a substantial improvement to the Chinese passenger vehicle industry but rather made manufacturers even more dependent on foreign technological transformation.[1] Focusing on the changing investment behavior of multinational corporations over time, Lei and Xu concluded that the investment atmosphere has changed from one of monopoly to one of competition, which has helped improve the international competitiveness of China's automotive industry.[2] Jia reached a similar conclusion.[3]

However, most of these studies have focused on the transferring side (multinationals), not on the recipient side (Chinese companies). The findings of the aforementioned studies indicate that expectations for international technology transfer exist in China, as does the belief that the competitiveness of China's automotive industry has improved through advanced technology transfer and investment behavior transformation. However, as industrialization is neither spontaneous nor caused by an outside ripple effect alone, this chapter will focus on the internal aspects: the nature of the "Chinese learning mechanism" and the role of international technology transfer in the growth of ICAMs. These ICAMs represent the new force driving Chinese automotive manufacturing, standing in contrast with existing state-owned automobile makers in terms of international technology transfer since 2000.

To clarify these issues, this chapter will attempt to answer the following questions. (1) How and why did ICAMs enter the passenger vehicle market? Why was their emergence chaotic but progressive for the Chinese automotive industry? (2) What role has international technology transfer played in the emergence of ICAMs? What effects, if any, has international technology transfer had on the development of ICAM competitiveness? (3) What are the largest barriers that international technology transfers from automotive Sino-foreign joint ventures to ICAMs face? These questions are followed by an exploration of whether the key factors indispensable to the growth of ICAMs into world-class automobile makers are present in the current situation.

To answer these questions, I have divided this chapter into three parts. Firstly, I distinguish between independent and nonindependent Chinese automobile makers. I elaborate on the background and origin of ICAMs and outline the key factors that affected their emergence, especially in the passenger vehicle market. Although new entrants were banned by the industrial policy a few years after the implementation of the Automotive Industry Policy 1994, some indigenous Chinese enterprises, such as CHERY and Geely, entered the passenger vehicle market successfully. I also consider the question of what changed after the emergence of ICAMs. Secondly, I review the history of international technology transfer to the Chinese automotive industry through the end of the 1990s. Finally, I analyze the dynamic changes of the relationship between international technology transfer and the growth of ICAMs.

DEFINITION OF ICAM: WHAT DOES "INDEPENDENT" MEAN?

"ICAM" corresponds to an automobile maker that satisfies two conditions: (1) it has developed its own indigenous brand; and (2) all the technologies necessary for R&D and the manufacturing process were *not* introduced through a form of joint venture with a foreign company. CHERY Automobile, Geely Automobile, Great Wall Motors, Zhongxing Auto, and so on all fall into the ICAM category.

Nonindependent Chinese automobile makers simply introduce their foreign joint venture partners' existing models as their own new ones even though some kinds of design changes might be taken. Companies such as Beijing Automotive Industry Corporation and Guangzhou Automotive Industry Corporation were provided with brands, passenger vehicle models, and all the necessary technologies, thereby making them dependent on their foreign partners in the early 2000s.

With this definition, over 20 enterprises (or brands) can be recognized as ICAMs. Because of the industry protection policy (that also served as a strict entry restriction for the passenger vehicle market), most ICAMs concentrated on trucks (including pickup trucks) and SUVs (sport utility vehicles) as their main products in the early 2000s. Another problem faced by the newcomer ICAMs was weak design and innovation capabilities, especially in the case of advanced engines and system integration. Thus far, only eight ICAMs have successfully begun passenger vehicle manufacturing:[4] CHERY, Geely, BYD, Brilliance, Lifan, Great Wall, Hafei, and Jianghuai (see Figure 9.1).

Figure 9.1 illustrates that only a few ICAMs have reached a suitable scale (assuming a minimum level of 50,000 units per year) in their early stages. Moreover, most ICAMs' annual sales are still not comparable to those of Sino-foreign joint venture companies (see Table 9.1).

The word "independent" seems to mean "technically independent" in the case of ICAMs. Compared to Sino-foreign joint venture enterprises, most ICAMs did not have either sufficient resources to design all-new models or the necessary manufacturing skills. Sino-foreign joint venture enterprises surpass ICAMs in such aspects as technology, qualified human resources, facilities, and capital.

However, most Sino-foreign joint ventures lack one important characteristic—an "autonomous brand." This makes the introduction of new models of their own almost impossible. Further, these *nonindependent* automobile makers (most of which are state-owned enterprises) have no opportunities to develop inter-competitiveness because most of them are engaged only in the assembly process. The Chinese media claims that state-owned automobile makers are satisfied with the current state of affairs, in which they assemble foreign models from imported parts instead of launching their own brands. Most state-owned automobile makers are supported by the central government and are protected by industrial policies from the competition of new entrants; these automobile makers enjoy being joint ventures and have lost the ability to become "independent." In the other words, they are *nonindependent*.

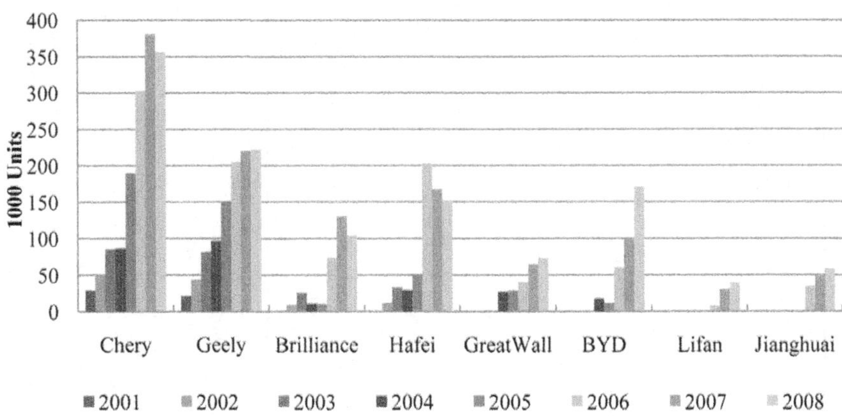

Figure 9.1 Passenger car sales by ICAMs

Source: *Automotive Information* 2002–2009, China Automotive Technology & Research Center (CATARC).

Table 9.1 Sales of top 10 passenger vehicle manufacturers in the Chinese market, 2001–2008

	2001		2002		2003		2004		2005		2006		2007		2008	
1	Shanghai Volkswagen	241	Shanghai Volkswagen	301	Shanghai Volkswagen	396	Shanghai Volkswagen	354	SAIC-GM	325	SAIC-GM	406	SAIC-GM	495	FAW-Volkswagen	499
2	FAW-Volkswagen	125	FAW-Volkswagen	208	FAW-Volkswagen	298	FAW-Volkswagen	300	Shanghai Volkswagen	250	Shanghai Volkswagen	349	FAW-Volkswagen	461	Shanghai Volkswagen	478
3	Tianjin Automobile	80	SAIC-GM	111	SAIC-GM	201	SAIC-GM	252	FAW-Volkswagen	240	FAW-Volkswagen	345	Shanghai Volkswagen	456	SAIC-GM	445
4	SAIC-GM	58	Tianjin FAW	95	Guangzhou Honda	117	Guangzhou Honda	202	Beijing Hyundai	234	**CHERY**	302	**CHERY**	381	FAW TOYATO	366
5	DPCA	53	DPCA	85	Tianjin FAW	114	Beijing Hyundai	144	Guangzhou Honda	230	Beijing Hyundai	290	Guangzhou Honda	295	**CHERY**	356
6	Guangzhou Honda	51	Chang'an Suzuki	65	DPCA	103	Tianjin FAW	130	Tianjin FAW	190	Guangzhou Honda	260	FAW TOYATO	282	Dongfeng Nissan	351
7	**SAIC CHERY**	28	Guangzhou Honda	59	Chang'an Suzuki	100	Chang'an Suzuki	110	**CHERY**	189	FAW TOYATO	219	Dongfeng Nissan	272	Guangzhou Honda	306
8	**Geely Automobile**	22	**SAIC CHERY**	50	**SAIC CHERY**	85	**Geely Automobile**	97	Dongfeng Nissan	158	**Geely Automobile**	204	Beijing Hyundai	231	Beijing Hyundai	295
9	–	–	Aeolus Automobile	41	**Geely Automobile**	76	DPCA	89	**Geely Automobile**	150	Dongfeng Nissan	203	**Geely Auto-mobile**	220	**Geely Automobile**	222
10	–	–	**Geely Automobile**	40	Aeolus Automobile	65	**CHERY**	87	DPCA	140	DPCA	201	Chang'an Ford	218	Chang'an Ford	205

Source: China Internal Combustion Engine Industry Association, "Annual Vehicle Sales and Production of China 2001 (2001 Nian 1-12 Yuefen Qiche Shengchan Xiaoshou Qingkuangbiao)," *Internal Combustion Engine Parts*, 1 (2002): 41–44;*Automotive information* 2002–2009. China Automotive Technology & Research Center (CATARC).

Note: 1. In June 2002, when China FAW Group Corp acquired Tianjin Automotive Xiali Co., the abbreviated name of Tianjin Automotive Xiali Co. was changed to Tianjin FAW.

2. Since SAIC sold its stock back to CHERY in 2004, the abbreviated name of CHERY changed from SAIC-CHERY to CHERY.
3. The sales of Geely Automobile are the sum of all its related subsidiaries, including SMA (Shanghai Maple Guorun Automobile).
4. Sales of crossover vehicles are not counted.
5. DPCA is the abbreviation of Dongfeng Peugeot Citroen Automobile Co., Ltd.
6. Since the data-sources for 2001 and 2002–2008 are different, there may be some inconsistency in the figures for 2001 and after 2001.

BACKGROUND OF THE EMERGENCE OF ICAMs: WHAT STIMULATED NEW ENTRIES?

This section provides an insight into the history of the Chinese automotive industry. As one of the key components of the Chinese economy, the automotive industry was strictly controlled by the central government until the "Reform and Open Policy" was implemented in 1979. At that time, all production activities related to automotive initiatives (such as R&D, manufacturing, and delivery) had to adhere to the annual plan issued by the central government, which provided no independence or management rights to the manufacturers. In this context, the Chinese automotive industry grew mostly out of a policy of self-reliance. The main product lines were trucks and buses. The use of passenger vehicles (regarded as symbols of a bourgeois lifestyle) was limited to official business purposes and remained unsupported until 1987. The first family cars (or "private cars") came out in 1989. Figure 9.2 shows that, in comparison with trucks, the production of basic passenger vehicles increased very slowly in the 1980s.

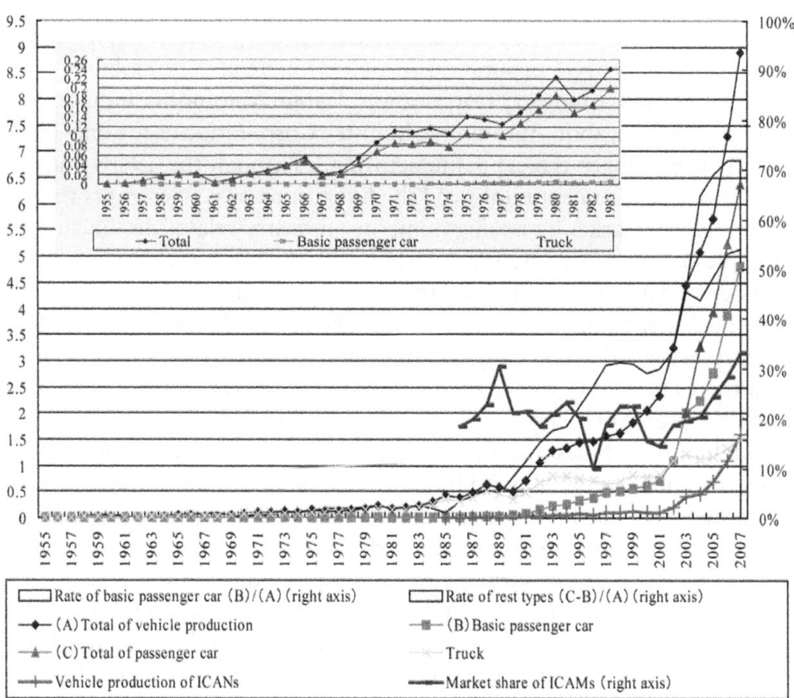

Figure 9.2 Vehicle production in China, 1955–2007

Source: *History of China Automotive Industry 1901–1990* (Beijing: China Communications Press, 1996); *Automotive information* 2002–2009, China Statistical Yearbook 2001–2008.

At a glance, the Chinese central government did not promote passenger vehicle manufacturing until 1987. Beijing-AMC and Shanghai-Volkswagen received permission to launch joint venture projects in 1983 and 1984, respectively. This was somewhat contradictory to the policy of product restriction. By granting this permission, the central government hoped to achieve the objective of import substitution.

The self-reliance policy, which had been in effect for approximately 30 years before the "Reform and Open Policy," kept the Chinese automotive industry completely isolated from the rest of the world. For this reason, vehicles produced by Chinese automobile makers could not satisfy user needs in terms of either quantity or quality. The import rush, especially for passenger vehicles, began after 1980. Although passenger vehicle importing began in the 1950s, the volume increased rapidly in the 1980s, exceeding even the central government's expectations. For example, 183,000 passenger vehicles (of total value, US$ 850 million) were imported from 1981 to 1986. In comparison, the average annual production of domestic automobile makers over that same period was a mere 4,000 units. The import of passenger vehicles became the country's main expenditure in foreign currency.

For this reason, the Chinese government decided to launch an import substitution mechanism. In 1987, the government issued the *Notice from State Council of PRC on the Reinforcement of Controlling the Importation of Passenger Vehicles* to authorize China Faw Group Corporation (FAW), Shanghai Automotive Industry Corporation (SAIC), Dongfeng Automobile Company, Beijing Automotive Industry Corporation, Tianjin Automotive Industry Corporation, and Guangzhou Automotive Industry Corporation as the only domestic players in passenger vehicle manufacturing.[5] Through the 1980s and 1990s, the Chinese government reinforced the limitations of new entrants to the passenger vehicle market by issuing numerous industry-related acts in succession. Examples of these acts are the Notice on the Regulations of Controlling the Number of Passenger Vehicle Manufacture 1988, Decisions Concerning the Main Points of China's Current Industrial Policy 1989, Outline of the State of Industrial Policy in the 1990s, and Automotive Industry Policy 1994.

In the early 1990s, the Chinese automobile market was thus an oligopoly led by a few authorized players and strictly protected by both industrial policy and high import duties. All the authorized players intended to raise productivity through joint ventures with foreign corporations. This import substitution policy met with partial success. However, the prices of the products made by these joint ventures exceeded those in the rest of the world and far surpassed the income levels of the normal Chinese household (see Table 9.2).

For this reason, in the early 1990s state officials and state-owned companies—not regular households—drove automobile demand. The high prices of vehicles were the largest constraint on household demand. The average price of most vehicles was topped RMB 130,000, which was more than 20 times the GDP (gross domestic product) per capita in 1997. In addition, the number smuggled-in passenger vehicles exceeded the number of legally imported vehicles by a considerable margin in the 1990s (see Figure 9.3).

Table 9.2 Prices of some short-lived models in the Chinese market in the 1990s

Model	Price (Year)	Rate of price via GDP per capita*(= RMB 6079)
Audi 100	289,000 ('94)	45.54
Rex	62,800 ('94)	10.33
Hongqi CA7560	520,000 ('95)	85.54
Xiao Hongqi	220,000 ('97)	36.19
Cherokee 2021	188,000 ('97)	30.93
Santana 2000	165,000 ('97)	27.14
Santana	135,000 ('97)	22.21
Jetta	135,000 ('97)	22.21
Fukang (Citroën ZX)	135,000 ('97)	22.21
Peugeot 505	135,000 ('97)	22.21
Charade	66,500 ('97)	10.94
Alto	60,000 ('97)	9.87

Source: Chen Jin, *Chugoku jyoyosha kigyo no seicho senryaku* [Growth Strategies of the Chinese Automotive Manufacturers] (Tokyo: Shinzansha, 2000), 64. National Bureau of Statistics of China.

Note: *means data of 1997.

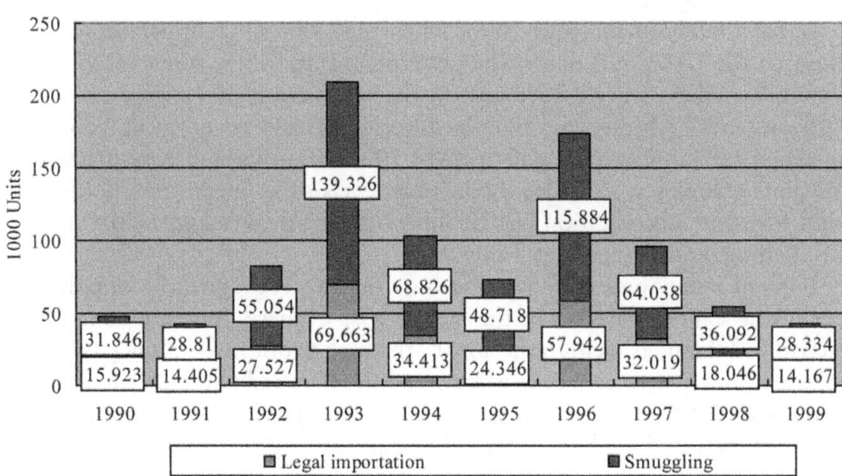

Figure 9.3 Importation in China through the 1990s

Source: Zuoshi Zheng. *Qiche fengzi lishufu* [The Madman for Automobile: LiShufu] (Beijing: China Citic Press, 2007), 75.

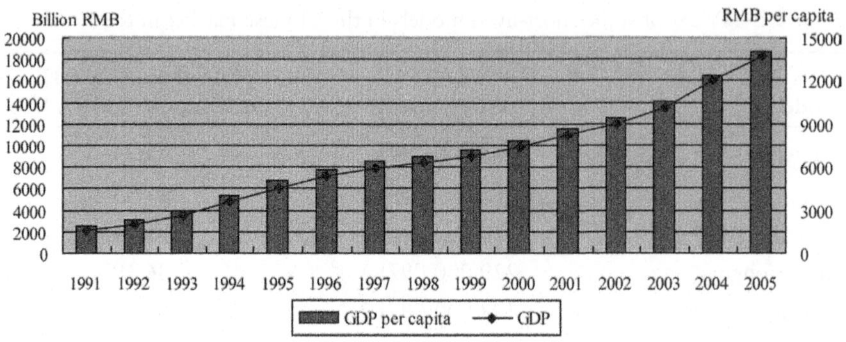

Figure 9.4 GDP and GDP per capita in China, 1991–2005
Source: National Bureau of Statistics of China.

Generally speaking, the motorization of a country is quite smooth after its GDP per capita surpasses US$1,000. After 1994, the Chinese GDP and GDP per capita experienced rapid growth (see Figure 9.4).

In the late 1990s, the Chinese market attracted the attention of global automobile makers, who revealed plans to enter the market because of its high growth potential. In 1998 and 1999, Honda and GM (General Motors) successfully used their last opportunities to enter the Chinese market before the country's admission to the WTO (World Trade Organization). Honda founded a joint venture with Guangzhou Automotive Industry Corporation, and GM, in cooperation with its partner, Shanghai Auto, located one of its plants in Shanghai.

In the middle of the year 2000, when the Chinese GDP per capita was close to the US$1,000 mark, the government and most joint venture automobile makers started to focus on the production of "family cars" (or "private cars"). Many automobile makers planned to promote products specified as "family cars," worth RMB 100,000, to influence motorization in China. However, in 2001, the income levels of Chinese households still were low, and motorization was possible only in advanced areas like Shanghai, Beijing, and Tianjin (see Table 9.3).

Foreign companies were not the only ones to recognize the opportunities in the Chinese market in the late 1990s; Chinese domestic companies recognized them, as well. In the 1990s, the high profit rates in the passenger vehicle industry attracted domestic companies that had potential capabilities (see Figure 9.5). Additionally, the high prices of the joint venture products on the market and the high potential demand from households gave domestic producers optimal opportunities to enter the segment of vehicles priced under RMB 100,000, a realm that joint venture automobile makers did not intend to enter (see Table 9.3).

CHERY and Geely had been planning to enter the passenger vehicle market since 1997 with products priced at under RMB 100,000 (which was half

Table 9.3 Possibility analysis of China's motorization

	The beginning of motorization in depended countries		
	United States	**Germany**	**Japan**
Period of speeding up	1910s–1920s	1950s	1960s
Price of public car Ⓐ	550 Dollars-Ford Model T	4,500 DM VW1200Exp	410,000–430,000 Yen Corolla, Sunny
Annual average per capita income Ⓑ	500 Dollars average of 1914–1923	3800 DM (1958)	380,000 Yen (1966)
Ⓐ/Ⓑ	1.1	1.2	1.1

Case study of China around 2000					
Price of promotion car by joint venture①	**About RMB 100,000 (Toyota Vios RMB 105,000, Honda Fit RMB 99,800)**				
Price of ICAMs' vehicles②	**About RMB 40,000 (Geely HaoQing RMB 29,990–42,990)**				
	China	**Beijing**	**Tianjin**	**Shanghai**	**Guangdong**
GDP per Capita (RMB)③	8622	25523	20154	37382	13730
①/③	11.60	3.92	4.96	2.68	7.28
②/③	4.64	1.56	1.98	1.07	2.91

Source: *Weekly Economist* (September 28, 2004): 25; National Bureau of Statistics of China, author edited

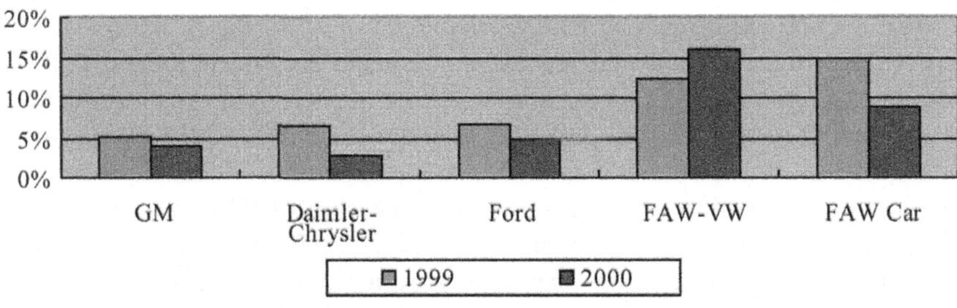

Figure 9.5 Profit margins in the United States and China

Note: Here, Profit margin is calculated as total profit as a percentage of total sales.

Source: Chunhui Gan, Dai Rong, and Li SuRong. "The Industrial Organization Analysis of Chinese Car Industry." *China Industrial Economy* 8 (2002): 15–22.

to two-thirds of the price of the models produced by joint venture automobile makers). Although these domestic companies were not authorized as automobile makers due to the limitations of the Automotive Industry Policy 1994, before China's entry to the WTO, they tried nevertheless to enter the market by gaining support from local governments (CHERY's strategy) or by taking over small state-owned automobile makers (Geely's strategy). Both strategies would give the domestic companies authorization to produce buses and trucks, but not to produce passenger vehicles. Under these conditions, some companies tried to produce and sell passenger vehicle models legally registered as microbuses.

ICAM STRATEGIES AIMED AT ENHANCED COMPETITIVENESS: HOW DID THEY BUILD THEIR "KNOWLEDGE"? (CASE STUDIES OF CHERY AND GEELY)

As mentioned earlier, joint venture automobile makers neglected the market for vehicles priced under RMB 100,000 in the late 1990s; the potential demand from households, fueled by the gradual growth of the national GDP per capita, gave domestic companies an entry opportunity. On the other hand, the entry of domestic automobile makers into this low-end market, coupled with their intentions to produce cheap products, provoked price competition among manufacturers. The low-price strategy also further escalated competition in the entire market, triggering price drops and rapid market expansion.

Since 2000, the Chinese passenger vehicle market has become one of the world's fastest-growing automobile markets—annual sales of new vehicles grew from 2.06 million units in 2000 to 7.27 million units in 2006, demonstrating a 23.4% average annual growth rate—and has attracted automobile makers from the world over with its potential for growth and profits. Due to this growth, the number of domestic automobile makers, including CHERY and Geely, has expanded rapidly.

This section explores how ICAMs managed to build their "knowledge." I focus on how international technology transfer has strengthened ICAM competitiveness. First, let us examine CHERY and Geely more closely.

According to its website, CHERY, officially known as CHERY Automobile Co., Ltd., "was founded in 1997 by five of Anhui's local state-owned investment companies, with an initial capitalization of RMB 1.752 billion. Plant construction commenced on March 18, 1997, in Wuhu (City), Anhui Province, China. The first car was produced on December 18, 1999. This represents a milestone in Chinese manufacturing history because it was the first car produced by a totally Chinese-owned and managed company."[6] CHERY sold 3,810,000 units in 2007, up from just 87,000 units in 2004. In 2007, CHERY Automobile sold 119,800 units in overseas markets, including Russia. Overseas expansion, especially in Russia, Southeast Asia, and the Middle East, has become a very important determinant of CHERY's growth.

Geely, official known as Geely Group Co., Ltd., was founded on November 6, 1986. According to the company's official website,

> Geely made its debut in manufacturing parts of refrigerator-evaporators. It was located in Huangyan, Luqiao, Taizhou city, Zhejiang Province. In 1989, Geely entered the production of advanced decoration materials and manufactured the first magnalium bent board in China. In April 1994, Geely entered the motorcycle industry, and in June of the same year, it manufactured China's first scooter motor. Its total sales volume reached 60,000 units in 1995 and 200,000 units in 1996. Geely thus became the main motorcycle manufacturer in China.[7]
>
> In May 1996, Geely Group Co., Ltd was re-organized. In March 1997, Geely entered the higher-education industry. The Group now has three colleges, including Beijing Geely University—one of China's privately-owned universities that possesses the independent right to authorize the High Education Diploma in Beijing city.[8]

The company's website continues, explaining that in 1997, "Geely entered the automotive industry. On August 8, 1998, the production of the first Geely Car was launched in Linhai City, Zhejiang Province. On November 9, 2001 and December 26, 2001, China State Economic and Trade Commission (hereafter SETC) approved the Geely Automobile JL6360, HQ6360, MR6370, and MR7130 series to be listed in the SETC automobile products public catalog. Geely Automobile became the first private enterprise approved as an automobile manufacturer in China."[9]

Most of CHERY and Geely's first generation products were thought of as either copies of existing models or hodgepodges of different products (see Tables 9.4 and 9.5), which was especially true for exterior design. Both companies fell under the scrutiny of intellectual property disputes with foreign automobile makers. As I will explain, this point of view was based on empirical observation and strongly affected by visual likeness. What, then, was the cause of the resemblance between the ICAMs' products and other existing models? The new entry limitations forced domestic companies to take an unusual approach in entering the passenger vehicle market. Without the necessary technology accumulation required for original R&D, qualified human resources, or capital, the ICAMs, including CHERY and Geely, designed new models by using reverse engineering tools, outsourcing design, and introducing technology and know-how through product line acquisition. As mentioned above, this imitative design method sparked numerous intellectual property rights problems before 2003.

In order to avoid conflicts with foreign automobile makers, it became extremely important for all ICAMs to enhance their original designs and

Table 9.4 HQ6360 (Geely) vs. TJ7101 (Tianjin Xiali)

Parameters	HQ6360	TJ7101
Photo		
Maker	Geely	Tianjin Xiali
Length-width-height (mm)	3650/1615/1410	3680/1615/1385
Wheelbase (mm)	2340	2340
Engine	376Q	TJ376QE
Engine displacement (cc)	993	993
Weight (kg)	1170	815

Source: Zejian Li, "Relation between Chinese Auto-Product Management and Entry to the Automobile Industry of Domestic Companies, CHERY and Geely," *The Journal of Asian Management Studies* 13 (2007): 207–220.

Table 9.5 QQ (CHERY) vs. Matiz (GM-Daewoo)

Parameters	QQ	Matiz
Drive System	FF	FF
Length-width-height (mm)	3550/1508/1491	3495/1495/1482
Wheelbase (mm)	2348	2340
Engine	SQR372MPI/DA–465QMPI	M-Tec/B1OS1
Engine displacement (cc)	812/1051	796/995
Weight (kg)	850	840
Top speed (km/h)	135	140
Tire	175/60R13 77H	155/65R13
Suspension (Front)	MacPherson Strut	MacPherson Strut
Suspension (Rear)	Independent suspension	Nonindependent suspension
Fuel consumption (L/100 km)	4.2 (60 km/h)	4.0 (90 km/h)

Source: Zejian Li, "The Growth Strategy of Emerging Chinese Domestic Automakers: Focus on CHERY and Geely," master's thesis, Kyoto University, Japan, 2006.

concepts. Next, I will explore the case of CHERY to illustrate how ICAMs managed to bolster their original product design and R&D faculties. Geely essentially followed the same path.

The Recruiting of High-Quality, Proficient Experts

The first stage of knowledge acquisition (especially design and R&D expertise) included using "headhunters" and other types of intermediaries to hire

Chinese engineers who were working for major global automobile makers and related companies.

The companies also invited a number of foreign experts to work in China. For example, CHERY invited about 30 overseas experts with broad experience in such companies as GM, Ford, Visteon, Daimler Chrysler, Du Pont, TRW, and Motorola before 2004. These experts brought advanced technologies and know-how to CHERY and then diffused their knowledge throughout the company via on-the-job training. This was especially effective for young engineers, who tend to be capable of absorbing useful knowledge directly and quickly.

In addition to bringing in 30 foreign experts, CHERY invited more than 150 Chinese experts and engineers from FAW, which had supposedly employed more engineers than any other state-owned automobile maker. These highly skilled professionals commenced work in the R&D and manufacturing departments of CHERY. By the end of 2006, CHERY had 18,000 employees, 20% (approximately 4,000 people) of whom were engineers and 1,500 of whom were directly related to R&D (see Table 9.6).

Joint Development Projects and Design Outsourcing

Besides the human resource policy, CHERY also acquired technology and know-how via cooperative joint development projects and design outsourcing. Most ICAMs operated in a similar fashion, preferring the tie-up cooperation of joint development projects and introducing the necessary knowledge from foreign professional engineering corporations.

For instance, in 2001, CHERY initiated a joint development project with Anstalt für Verbrennungskraftmaschinen List (AVL) for 18 high-level engines. AVL is the world's largest privately owned independent company engaged in the development of power-train systems with internal combustion engines and instrumentation and test systems.[10] In this joint development project, for the purpose of improving its capabilities, CHERY wanted to acquire not just the 18 ready-made engines but also the knowledge of how to design an original high-level engine and how to manage the project.

AVL organized a special training program for CHERY's specialists and brought a group of guest engineers to acquire technical knowledge of the process. After a full day's work, the engineers had to recall all the details, record them, and report to CHERY's head office. Based on the working records of these guest engineers, CHERY established its own development standards and launched the development of its own original engine.

For design outsourcing, CHERY chose to cooperate with an outsourcing destination by sending a team of CHERY engineers to the outsourcing company. As soon as CHERY's engineers were able to understand and master certain aspects of a project, they were entrusted to fulfill these functions by themselves; CHERY outsourced only the operations that their engineers could not fully comprehend. After repeating this process several times,

Table 9.6 List of high-level proficient experts in CHERY

Name	Post	Job experience
Oversea Chinese experts—about 30 people		
Xu, M.	Director of Automotive Engineering Institute of CHERY, Chief Leader of R&D	Engine Expert, Ph.D. of Engineering (Hiroshima University), worked for GM, Ford, Visteon
Xin, J.	Vice Director of Automotive Engineering Institute of CHERY, Leader of Engine Durability and Hybrid Car	Worked for Honda (United States)
Gu, L.	Vice Director of Automotive Engineering Institute of CHERY, Leader of Digital Crash Test	Crash Test Expert, Ph.D. of Modern Mechanics (University of Science and Technology Beijing, Northwest University), worked for Ford
Yuan, T.	Vice President (Parts Procurement)	Studied in Beijing University of Aeronautics and Astronautics, Ph.D. of Engine (Centre National de la Recherche Scientifique)
Qi, G. J.	Vice Director of Automotive Engineering Institute of CHERY, Leader of Automotive Body-in-White	Worked for DaimlerChrysler AG
Sun, G. C.	Vice President (CFO)	Worked for DuPont (China) as CFO
Yuan, Y. B.	Chassis Research	Worked for TRW Automotive
Li, M.	Electronic Driving Research	Worked for Motorola
Zhu, X. C.	Transmission Research	Back to CHERY from Australia
Gu, Y.	Vice President of CHERY Subsidiaries (Die & Molt)	Worked for Fuji Japan
Chinese Experts from FAW—about 150 people		
Kang, L. M.	Chief Engineer, Engine Project Manager	FAW

Hu, F.	Vice Chief Engineer, Project Leader of Engine Co-project with AVL	Gratitude from Automotive Engineering (Tsinghua University), FAW, retired from DongFeng Motors in 1995
Feng, J. Q.	Vice Chief Engineer, Designer of CAC372 Engine for QQ0.8L	The first engine designer of New China, he designed 6102 gasoline engine for JieFang 141 Truck
Foreign Experts—about 40 people		
Terada, S.	Plant Manager, Operation Management	Worked 30 years for Mitsubishi Motors as Plant Manager
Kawano, K.	Director of Plant KAIZEN	Worked 40 years for Mazda Motors
Kim, U. S.	Vice Chief Engineer	Ricardo Company
German experts	Manufacturing Technology Support	Unknown
Others Domestic Engineers		
Lu, J. H.	Vice President (R&D)	Gratitude from Automotive Manufacturing (Tsinghua University)
Li, F.	Vice President (Sales)	Worked for Foton Motors sales Co. as Vice President
Total		
In 2006, CHERY had 18,000 employees, including nearly 4,000 engineers. Fifteen hundred engineers were directly involved in R&D.		

Note: Each rank/title corresponds to the year 2004 position.

Source: Zejian Li, "Analysis on the Competitiveness of CHERY Automobile: Focus on Aspect of Reinforcement in R&D," *Annals of the Society for Industrial Studies* 23 (2007): 103–115.

CHERY acquired more of the knowledge and technology required to enhance its original design capabilities.

Original Affiliated Supplier Chain Construction

When CHERY and Geely made their first attempts to enter the passenger vehicle market with their first generation products, they depended on existing parts suppliers that were subordinated to joint venture automobile makers. For example, in 2002, Geely relied on parts from Tianjin Xiali's suppliers (at a maximum rate of 95%) to produce HaoQing.[11] CHERY procured parts from suppliers affiliated with Shanghai-Volkswagen for its first generation sedan product, which was called WindCloud.

However, the procurement of essential parts from competitors' affiliates caused a dilemma for CHERY and Geely because it forced them to compete with the very companies from which they procured essential parts like engines and chassis. As new entrants, they depended on a low-price strategy to establish competitiveness in the passenger vehicle market. The relatively high prices of parts from competitors, however, reduced their potential profits. This motivated CHERY and Geely to build their own network of affiliated suppliers as quickly as possible.

By the end of 2004, there were approximately 200 parts suppliers that had business relationships with Geely. Meanwhile, Geely gained 50% control of 100 companies and successfully founded its own stable system of parts suppliers. As a result, the company's dependence on Tianjin Xiali affiliates for supplies decreased from 95% to 1% by 2004.

Using these methods, ICAMs gained the opportunity to enhance original design capabilities and improve competitiveness. What is remarkable is that although ICAMs were not at the same growth level, given the facts that they had entered the market at different times and had different management structures, the need to gain and enhance original R&D capabilities was common to all of them. In light of the fierce competition between the joint venture automobile makers and their forerunners, there was no room in the passenger vehicle market for new local participants like CHERY and Geely, especially considering that their strategy was to copy and market existing low-end models.

DISCUSSION: THE ROLE OF INTERNATIONAL TECHNOLOGY TRANSFER

ICAMs demonstrated rapid growth rates in both the domestic and the international markets. In 2007, ICAMs accounted for a 31% share of the domestic market, which was the highest such mark in history. A good example is CHERY, which boasted sales of 3,810,000 units in 2007 compared to just 87,000 units in 2004. In 2007, CHERY also sold 119,800 units to overseas markets, including Russia (see Figure 9.6).

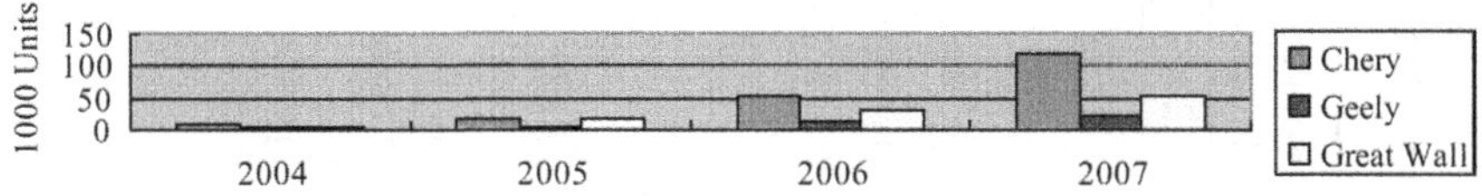

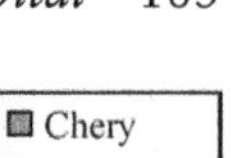

Figure 9.6 Top three car exports

Source: *Automotive information* 2002–2009, China Automotive Technology & Research Center (CATARC).

There is no doubt that the expansion in both the domestic and overseas markets, especially those of Russia, Southeast Asia, and the Middle East, was made possible by the growth of CHERY'S original capabilities in design and R&D. At the same time, global automobile makers achieved further expansion through the establishment of Sino-foreign joint ventures (see Table 9.7).

A look at the sales of 14 global automobile makers in the Chinese market indicates that 2008, Volkswagen was the top seller with approximately one million units. Toyota, GM, Honda, and Hyundai sold 500,000 units each—half of Volkswagen's sales. In the same year, Nissan sold 361,000 units, approximately the same volume as that of CHERY. In 2008, CHERY, the top ICAM automobile maker, reported a slight decrease in sales (356,000 units in 2008, down from 379,000 units in 2007). Geely, the second largest ICAM automobile maker, sold 221,000 units in 2007.

The data suggests that despite the rapid expansion that ICAMs have achieved in recent years, global automobile makers operating Sino-foreign joint ventures still dominate ICAMs in their markets. The economic activities of these Sino-foreign joint ventures remain the key factor in the Chinese market. Their operations, which mainly involve international technology transfer to China, have a strong and consistent effect on the development of the Chinese automotive industry.

In conclusion, as outlined in Table 9.8, I have outlined the methods by which ICAMs acquired their own design and R&D capabilities, using the example of CHERY. The role that international technology transfer played in this process cannot be ignored. In this section, I will analyze the roles of both direct and indirect international technology transfer.

Firstly, it is impossible to distinguish clearly the positive and negative effects of international technology transfer; thus, Table 9.8 is based only on empirical analysis.

Before GM obtained permission to create Shanghai General Motors Corp., a JV between GM and SAIC, other global automobile makers such as Volkswagen and Peugeot were motivated purely by profit to operate in the Chinese market. Only nonsignificant knowledge related to R&D was transferred with their products to their Chinese operations. Local state-owned automobile makers, meanwhile, were looking for short-term profits and, as a result, were satisfied with this position. Though technologies were rare during this period, skills in manufacturing, parts supply, and sales were

Table 9.7 Global automakers' operations in China (up to 2008)

	Sino-foreign joint venture				
				Sales, locally produced passenger vehicles	
Global automaker	**Ownership**		**Models produced**	**2008**	**2007**
BMW AG	JV: BMW Brilliance Automotive Ltd.		BMW 3 series, 5 series	35,164	32,249
	BMW AG	50%			
	Brilliance China Automotive Holdings	50%			
Daimler Chrysler AG	JV: Beijing Benz-Daimler Chrysler Automotive Co.		Mercedes-Benz C class, E class	14,356	6,882
	Beijing Automotive Industry Holding Co.	50%			
	DaimlerChrysler AG (DCAG)	39%			
	Northeast Asia Ltd.	11%			
Chrysler	No longer has any JV, but has licensed two companies to produce its vehicles		Chrysler 300C, Grand Voyager, Sebring; Dodge Caravan	11,200	9,277
	Chrysler LLC	100%			
Fiat	Fiat no longer has any JV's in China		No models produced in China	–	15,525
Ford Motor	JV: Jiangling Motors Corp.		Ford Transit, New Generation Transit; JMC Baodian, Baowei, Qingka	161,758	180,476
	Jiangling Holding Co.	41%			
	Ford Motor Co.	30%			
	Others	29%			

	JV: Changan Ford Mazda Automobile Co.		Ford Fiesta, Focus, Mondeo, S-Max; Mazda2, Mazda3; Volvo S40, S80L		
	Ford Motor Co.	50%			
	Changan Automotive Co.	35%			
	Mazda Motor Co.	15%			
General Motors	JV: Shanghai General Motors Corp		Buick Excelle, Excelle HRV, LaCrosse, Park Avenue, Regal; Cadillac SLS	485,545	528,260
	SAIC Motor Corp.	50%			
	General Motors	50%			
	JV: Shanghai GM Dongyue Motors Co.		Chevrolet Aveo, Cruze, Epica, Lova		
	Shanghai General Motors	50%			
	Shanghai Automotive Co.	25%			
	General Motors China	25%			
	JV: Shanghai GM (Shenyang) Norsom Motors Co.		Buick GL8		
	Shanghai General Motors	50%			
	Shanghai Automotive Co.	25%			
	General Motors China	25%			
	JV: SAIC-GM-Wuling Automobile Co.		Chevrolet Spark; Wuling Hongtu, Rongguang, Single & Double pickup, Sunshine, Xingwang		
	Shanghai Automotive Co.	50%			
	General Motors China	34%			
	Wuling Automotive	16%			

(*Continued*)

Table 9.7 (Continued)

	Sino-foreign joint venture				
				Sales, locally produced passenger vehicles	
Global automaker	Ownership		Models produced	2008	2007
Honda Motor	JV: Honda Automobile (China) Co.		Honda Jazz (for export)	470,033	422,345
	Honda Motor Co.	55%			
	Guangzhou Automobile Industry Group	25%			
	Honda Motor Investment Co.	10%			
	Dongfeng Motor Group Co.	10%			
	JV: Dongfeng Honda Automobile (Wuhan) Co.		Honda Civic, CR-V		
	Dongfeng Motor Corp.	50%			
	Honda Motor Co.	40%			
	Honda Motor Investment Co.	10%			
	JV: Guangzhou Honda Automobile Co.		Honda Accord, Fit, New City, Odyssey		
	Guangzhou Automobile Industry Group	50%			
	Honda Motor Co.	40%			
	Honda Motor Investment Co.	10%			
Hyundai Motor	JV: Beijing Hyundai Motor Co.		Hyundai Accent, Elantra, Elantra HDC, Sonata, Sonata Lingxiang, Tucson	450,163	345,425
	Hyundai Motor Co.	50%			
	Beijing Automotive Industry Holding Corp.	50%			

	JV: Dongfeng Yueda Kia Automobile Co.		Kia Carnival, Cerato, Cerato H/B, DYK Sportage, Optima, Rio		
	Kia Motors	50%			
	Dongfeng Motor Industry Investment Co.	25%			
	Jiangsu Yueda Co.	25%			
Mitsubishi Motors	JV: Hunan Changfeng Motor Co.		Liebao, Liebao Feiteng	21,170	41,475
	Changfeng Group	50%			
	Others	34%			
	Mitsubishi Motors Corp.	16%			
	JV: Soueast (Fujian) Motor Co.		Delica, Freeca, Galant, Lancer, Landio, Lioncel,New Space Wagon, Veryca		
	Mitsubishi Motors Corp.	25%			
	Fujian Motor Industry Group	50%			
	Taiwan China Motor Corp.	25%			
Nissan	JV: Zhengzhou Nissan Automobile Co.		Nissan MPV, NT400 Cabstar, Paladin, Pickup, Rich, SUV	361,015	281,520
	Dongfeng Motor Group Co.	51%			
	Dongfeng Motor	29%			
	Nissan Motor Co.	20%			
	JV: Dongfeng Nissan Passenger Vehicle Co		Nissan Bluebird Sylphy, Geniss, Livina, Qashqai, Teana, Tiida, X-Trail		
	Nissan (China) Investment Co.	50%			
	Dongfeng Motor Group Co.	50%			

(*Continued*)

Table 9.7 (Continued)

Global automaker	Sino-foreign joint venture				
				Sales, locally produced passenger vehicles	
	Ownership		Models produced	2008	2007
PSA Peugeot Citroen Group	JV: Dongfeng Peugeot Citroen Automobile Co.		Citroen C2, C-Elysee, C-Quatre, C-Triomphe, Picasso, New Xsara; Peugeot 206, 207, 307	178,308	207,255
	PSA Peugeot Citroen	50%			
	Dongfeng Motor Industry Investment Co.	50%			
Suzuki Motor	JV: Jiangxi Changhe Suzuki Automobile Co.		Liana, Landy, North Star (Suzuki Wagon R+)	178,853	160,849
	Changhe Group	51%			
	Suzuki Motor Corp.	25%			
	Suzuki Motor China Investment Co.	21%			
	Okaya	3%			
	JV: Chongqing Changan Suzuki Automobile Co.		Suzuki Alto, Gazelle, Swift 1.3, Swift 1.5, SX4		
	Changan Automobile Co.	51%			
	Suzuki Motor Corp.	25%			
	Sojitz Corp.	14%			
	Suzuki Motor (China) Investment Co.	10%			

Toyota Motor	JV: Tianjin FAW Toyota Motor Co.		Toyota Corolla EX, Vios, Toyota Crown, Reiz, Toyota Corolla	543,106	455,140
	Toyota Motor Corp.	40%			
	FAW Xiali Automobile Co.	30%			
	First Auto Works	20%			
	Toyota Motor Investment Co.	10%			
	JV: Sichuan FAW Toyota Motor Co. (SFTM)		Toyota Coaster, Prado		
	FAW Group	50%			
	Toyota Motor Corp.	45%			
	Toyota Tsusho Corp.	5%			
	Changchun Fengyue Company of SFTM		Toyota Land Cruiser, Prius		
	FAW Group	50%			
	Toyota Motor Corp.	45%			
	Toyota Tsusho Corp.	5%			
	JV: Guangqi Toyota Motor Co.		Toyota Camry, Yaris		
	Guangzhou Automobile Industry Group	50%			
	Toyota Motor Corp.	31%			
	Toyota Motor Investment Co.	19%			
Volkswagen AG	JV: FAW-Volkswagen Automotive Co.		Models produced: Audi A4L, A6L; VW Bora classic, New Bora, Golf, Magotan, Jetta, Sagitar	983,436	898,588
	China FAW Group Corp.	60%			
	Volkswagen AG	20%			
	Volkswagen Investment Co.	10%			
	Audi AG	10%	Models produced: VW Lavida, Lingyu, Passat, Touran, Polo, Cross Polo, Santana, Santana Vista; Skoda Fabia, Octavia		
	Shanghai Automotive Industry Corp.	50%			
	Volkswagen AG	40%			
	Volkswagen Investment Co.	10%			

Source: "Guide to China's Auto Market.," *Automotive News* (2009), last modified January 22, 2013, http://www.autonews.com/assets/PDF/CA61057424.PDF.

Table 9.8 Role of international technology transfer in the Chinese automotive industry

			Receiving side	
			Positive effect	Negative effect
Spreading side	Indirect pathway (Spillover)		CHERY, Geely (R&D, Manufacturing, Sales)	
	Direct pathway	Type 1	Sino-foreign JV (Manufacturing, Sales)	state-owned automakers(R&D)
		Type 2	CHERY, Geely (R&D, Manufacturing)	

Note: Type 1 refers to interior technology transfer in multinational enterprises (MNEs). Type 2 refers to technological consulting and outsourcing.

developed through FDI (foreign direct investment). I consider this a Type 1 positive effect, as listed in Table 9.8.

On the other hand, this FDI caused a suspension of R&D activities at existing local passenger vehicle automobile makers. For example, SAIC had to abandon its original product under its Shanghai brand in order to meet the localization standards required for the Santana. After the founding of Shanghai GM, the competition among Sino-foreign JVs quickly escalated. Some of the R&D projects undertaken by Sino-foreign JV projects were limited to product adaptation and localization. Due to the absence of original passenger vehicles for R&D projects at Sino-foreign JVs and state-owned automobile makers, engineers directly involved in R&D shifted to ICAMs like CHERY and Geely. I consider this a Type 1 negative effect of international technology transfer.

The spillover of technological and R&D capabilities to ICAMs is a positive effect. For example, Kaking Technology Co., Ltd., a subsidiary of CHERY, undertook over 60% of CHERY's design work until 2005. Kaking Technology's founders were former team members of the Dongfeng Technology Center, which had undertaken R&D projects for XiaoWangzi (an original passenger vehicle product from Dongfeng Automobile Company) and modification work for Citroen Elysee (a product manufactured by Dongfeng Peugeot Citroen Automobile Co.).

Thanks to the spillover from Sino-foreign joint ventures, ICAMs acquired basic technological capabilities in R&D, manufacturing, and sales. After CHERY successfully entered the passenger vehicle market, it preferred to use Type 2 technological consulting and outsourcing (see Table 9.8) to refine its technological capabilities in R&D and manufacturing.

Even though international technology transfer—an important external factor—had a number of positive effects on the development of ICAMs development, however, the cultivation of managerial capabilities and system integration—an internal factor—became the chief aim of all ICAMs.

NOTES

1. Wenqiang Guo and Shaojie Zhang, "Analysis on Technology Spillover Effect of Multinational Company's Technology Transfer to the Investment of Chinese Car Industry," *Journal of Zhengzhou Institute of Aeronautical Industry Management* 26 (2008): 61–64.
2. Hui Lei and Changsheng Xu, "An Analysis of the Effects of Multinational Corporations' Market Behaviors on China's Automobile Industry," *Nankai Business Review* 9 (2006): 103–108.
3. Qiufeng Jia, "Shilun kuaguo gongsi dui woguo qiche chanye jishu yizhuan moshi zhuanbian," *ShangHai QiChe* 11 (2004): 7–9.
4. In 2001, the Chinese government amended *Motor Vehicles and Trailers—Types—Terms and Definitions* from GB 3730.1–1988 to GB 3730.1–2001. Under this amendment, the definition of "passenger car" was updated to include basic passenger cars (i.e., sedans or saloons), MPVs (multipurpose vehicles), SUVs (sport utility vehicles), and crossover vehicles (minivan/van models). For this reason, some local Chinese SUV or MPV manufacturers, regarded as commercial vehicle manufacturers under the previous definition, have become passenger car manufacturers since the amendment was approved. In this chapter, I do not cover these cases; I am concerned only with the companies that are permitted to manufacture basic passenger cars. That is why I focus only on these eight passenger vehicle manufacturers.
5. State Council of PRC, "Chinese Pinyin: Guanyu yange kongzhi jiaoche shengchandian de tongzhi [Notice on the Regulations of Controlling the Number of Passenger Car Manufacturers]," (1988), last modified April 8, 2013, http://www.gov.cn/xxgk/pub/govpublic/mrlm/201108/t20110830_64019.html.
6. "Overview," last modified April 10, 2010, http://www.cheryglobal.com/about_chery.jsp.
7. "History of Geely," last modified April 10, 2010, http://www.geely.com/english/about/intro.htm.
8. Ibid.
9. Ibid.
10. "Company," last modified April 10, 2010, http://www.avl.com/wo/webobsession.servlet.go?app=bcms&page=view&nodeid=400013015.
11. Zhishan Sun, "Chinese Pinyin: Jili liantiao shangde jingzhengli [Geely's Competitiveness on Supplier Chain]," *China Logistics* 7 (2007): 44–53.

Part IV

Engineers as Intermediaries

The fourth part delves into the complex role of engineers in the transfer of technology, with all of the chapters focusing on one recipient country in a clearly defined period—post–World War II Japan—in order to show how these engineering networks organized technology flows among many different industries and sources of technology. Taking the example of a single country during a short but decisive period is indeed the best way to emphasize the complexity of technology transfer and the involvement of engineers in the intervention of several types of institutional actors (states, armies, firms, universities, etc.).

The diffusion of knowledge and technology from the United States to Japan in the late 1940s and the 1950s did not occur only within the private framework discussed in Part III; it also took place out of the traditional flow from MNE (multinational enterprise) to subsidiary, and the state and public institutions played pivotal roles in integrating such knowledge and technologies into the national systems of innovation and thus helping domestic companies acquire such knowledge. The chapter by Yuki Nakajima on the so-called PB reports in Japan underscores the appropriation of knowledge as a "two-step technology transfer" in a high-tech field, namely, the chemical industry, without using the international patent system or any agreements between MNEs. Rather, it was the state that acted to make foreign information available to domestic firms. In the aftermath of World War II, Japan had access to millions of pages of technical reports drafted by engineers from the Allied armies in Germany—the PB reports—as the result of cooperation between American companies and the state. Indeed, the US government, acting together with private companies, organized the gathering of technological information in Germany just after the end of the war. These reports provided a wealth of information on the production processes and equipment of German firms, especially in the chemical industry (IG Farben), and helped American companies in the late 1940s. The resources were made available at the National Diet Library in Tokyo, through a form of technology scouting, and used by Japanese engineers in the early 1950s. Nakajima also emphasizes that the diffusion of technology and knowledge within a given country is not a natural process consecutive to the physical existence of documents in the country; rather, it requires the input of individuals, like engineers, to use these documents and turn them into "useful knowledge."

On occasion, the state also played a more active role and became directly involved in forging a framework to bolster the acquisition of foreign technologies, which helped small domestic firms compete with MNEs. Concentrating on the transfer of penicillin production technology to Japan after World War II, Julia Yongue stresses that it was possible to acquire know-how in a high-tech industry without using the international patent system or entering into an agreement with an MNE. The occupation years in Japan (1945–1952) were, of course, a special environment that enabled the transfer of technology from American MNEs to Japanese firms through government officials and scientists: in 1946, Merck sent an engineer to organize the mass production of penicillin in Japan at the request of the US occupation authorities due to health care issues. This health policy nevertheless had a major economic impact: it led to the organization of R&D facilities within Japanese companies for the development of penicillin and the mass production of drugs, both of which remained important in the following decades.

The chapter by Stephen B. Adams and Paul J. Miranti on the transfer of quality engineering knowledge to Japan from 1945 to 1955 provides another example of the complex interactions between different kinds of actors in postwar Japan technology transfer. It appears that some engineers from Bell Laboratories played a key role in this transfer, but the move did not occur as a traditional MNE activity. Rather, the Bell System was brought to Japan by the US government and the Supreme Command Allied Powers (SCAP)—public authorities—and then transmitted to Japanese associations and the government, which made it available to domestic firms. This transfer was established by some Bell engineers as part of the SCAP programs designed to rebuild Japan after 1945. Thus, technology held by an American MNE was incorporated into the Japanese NSI (national system of innovation) through inter-governmental cooperation and industrial associations such as the Japanese Federation of Communication Equipment Manufacturers Association (JFCEMA) and the Union of Japanese Scientists and Engineers (JUSE). Public bodies, firms and industrial associations were all key actors in postwar Japan's technological development. Their active involvement in the import of foreign technologies highlights their common desire to strengthen the Japanese NSI through the transfer of technology.

10 The Allied Forces and the Spread of German Industrial Technology in Postwar Japan

Yuki Nakajima

INTRODUCTION

One of the main reasons for Japan's technological development after World War II (WWII) is believed to be the enthusiastic transfer of technology from advanced countries. During the war, Japan was isolated from the international scientific and technological exchange network, and it fell far behind advanced countries. After its defeat, Japan attempted to reintroduce foreign technology into the country. Many studies have focused on the technology licensing between foreign and Japanese companies and its crucial role in improving quality of products and production efficiency in various industries such as iron and steel, electronics, chemicals, and so on, especially from the 1950s to the 1960s.

In order to successfully acquire these technologies, Japanese companies firstly had to make a right choice of them to introduce among various options. Technology historian Tetsuro Nakaoka emphasizes that Japanese engineers were not seeking aimlessly for foreign technologies to introduce; their wartime research activities helped them recognize what technological problems they faced and what technologies they lacked. Based on such experiences, they were able to accurately apply the technologies most suitable to their condition since the 1950s, resulting in a dramatic and immediate improvement in their technological capabilities.[1] Therefore, the R&D activities in Japan during wartime and the rehabilitation period should not be ignored when studying the Japanese postwar technological development.

For some time even after the technical license agreements with the foreign partners were authorized by the Japanese government, given the situation that the Japanese economy was short on foreign currency, the engineers tried taking every other possible measure to obtain technology information from abroad. A precious source for them was the so-called FIAT/BIOS technical reports which were known to Japanese engineers as the "PB reports." The reports were technological documents published by the US and British governments from 1946 onward, most of which had been requisitioned from factories based in Nazi Germany. John Gimbel comprehensively studied the case of the United States and claimed that these technologies were a blessing for not only the military but also the private sectors in postwar the United States.[2] Though this forced technology transfer from Germany to the United States and the United Kingdom was peculiar to the occupation period, the reports were scattered not only in these countries but also in other countries all over the world. Therefore, through the reports, the German technologies were first transferred to the United States and the United Kingdom, then secondly to other countries. Among them was Japan. In such two-step technology transfer process, the latter seems not to have received much attention in previous studies on technology transfer. As mentioned earlier, Japan was one of the countries that tried to obtain the reports and applied them to their postwar industrial recovery. Although science historian Shigeru Nakayama has already mentioned the reports,[3] no research has precisely estimated their value for Japan's postwar technological development. This study describes the dissemination process of the reports in Japan and evaluates its impact.

In considering the process of technology transfer through the FIAT/BIOS reports, it would be not sufficient to focus only on business activities in the Japanese industries. There were other related parties involved in the process, such as politicians, scientists, engineers, academic societies, public and governmental institutions, and business associations, most of which had been conducting R&D activities since the prewar period or had established themselves during the wartime mobilization. Although a comprehensive examination of these players is beyond the scope of this chapter, their activities should be referred to the extent that they relate to the reports. In the next section, mainly based on John Gimbel's work, the outline of the reports will be described briefly. The introduction process of the reports into Japan will be described in Section 3. Some case studies in Section 4 will illustrate their impact on technological development, mainly in the Japanese chemical industry around the 1950s. Following the preceding examination, the mobilization and the systemization of science and technology during and after the war will be emphasized as important factors for the postwar Japanese technology introduction in conclusion.

THE FIAT/BIOS TECHNICAL REPORTS[4]

In 1944 the UK and the US governments created a special military unit the T-forces to gather German technological information, and the Combined Intelligence Objective Subcommittee (CIOS) whose duty was to select targets named the Black list and later expanded the Gray lists for the T-Forces with the support of the Technical Industrial Intelligence Committee (TIIC) on the US side, which consisted of more than 10 subcommittees that represented various industries. A large number of people from the business circles became members and recommended numerous targets to investigate and capture.[5]

When the CIOS was dissolved in the summer of 1945, the American component of it was moved to Washington DC, and the British component was renamed the British Intelligence Objective Subcommittee (BIOS). On the other hand, in June 1945 Supreme Headquarters Allied Expeditionary Forces (SHAEF) created the Field Information Agency Technical (FIAT) in which the US and the UK wings were controlled separately, to keep close relationship to each other.[6] Many technologists who had joined these investigation programs enthusiastically claimed that the technologies they had found in occupied German areas were much superior to those of the industries in their country and that the US government continue its investigation programs. Meanwhile, in August 1945, President Truman ordered the disclosure of scientific and technical information that had been developed with governmental funds. The newly established interdepartmental Publication Board screened the investigations to be released and then put reference numbers on them with the initials "PB" to publish.[7] In contrast to the US Army, which was reluctant to disclose information, the US Department of Commerce was the most enthusiastic to disclose information in order to promote postwar industrial recovery. The department created the Office of Technical Service (OTS) to investigate German technology by themselves. The OTS selected and recruited specialists from various industries through the Technical Industrial Intelligence Branches (TIIB); these specialists were then dispatched to Europe. The FIAT supplied equipment for transportation and communication and helped the OTS in the interrogation of German engineers.[8]

On the other hand, in order to promote the use of the reports, the Publication Board and the OTS offered the information of the reports to the general public through the weekly "Bibliography of Scientific and Industrial Research Reports." Even after the investigation in Germany was completed and the FIAT was closed in July 1947, the Department of Commerce carried the program on till the end of July 1948, when the OTS drastically downsized its operations.[9] The US government maintains the policy of disclosing research results developed with governmental funds and continues to issue technical report series and bibliographies, as shown in Table 10.1.

By the early 1950s, the volume of the reports reached over 100,000 comprising 7.4 million pages. The documents requisitioned in Germany accounted for an overwhelming majority (Table 10.2). The release of reports on German technology peaked in 1948 and drastically decreased from 1949 onward.[10] Even at the time that the operations of the FIAT and the OTS were terminated, there still remained a large volume of the reports to be analyzed. To complete their mission, the OTS gave up checking all the reports one by one and assigned PB numbers not to each report, but to "microfilms" that contained about 100 reports each. The total volume

Table 10.1 Bibliography of technical reports issued by the US government

The data of first issue	Title
1946, January	Bibliography of Scientific and Industrial Reports
1947, January	Bibliography of Technical Reports
1954, October	U.S. Government Research Reports
1965, January	U.S. Government Research & Development Reports
1971, March	Government Reports Announcement
1975, April	Government Reports Announcement & Index

Source: National Diet Library in Japan, Web search system (Standards, Technical Reports, etc).

Table 10.2 The total number of PB reports and their pages from January 1946 to January 1952

	Reports		Pages	
Countries	Number	%	Number (1,000 pages)	%
Germany	55,772	52.2	5,255	70.3
United States	44,629	41.8	1,762	23.6
Japan	3,262	3.1	322	4.3
United Kingdom	1,600	1.5	47	0.6
Others	1,582	1.5	91	1.2
Total	106,845	100	7,477	100

Source: Morio Uehara, "PB ripoto ka Beikoku Seifu Kenkyu ripoto ka [the PB reports or the US government research reports?]," Saiensu Laiburary [Science Library], 5/4–5 (1959, May), 55.

of microfilm was over 5,000 reels, which contained numerous reports to be disposed of without complete analysis or detailed abstracts. Therefore the bibliographies issued around this period were also useless and caused engineers inconvenience in locating the appropriate reports.[11] In Japan as mentioned later, however, persons and organizations cooperated to solve this problem.

The reports dealt with a variety of technological subjects, mainly chemistry, electricity, aeronautical engineering, and mechanical engineering. Moreover, the reports contained not only abstract or scientific knowledge but also concrete industrial technology such as descriptions of manufacturing methods that contained precise designs of equipment. For example, the German engineers at IG Farben, who were interrogated by a US investigation team, had served the company in important positions (Table 10.3).

Table 10.3 German engineers interrogated by the investigation team

Company and Factory	Person's name	Position
Anorgana G.m.b.H. Gendorf	Dr. Tapperman	
I.G. Farben Höechst	Dr. Spiker	Chemist in the Division of Technical Applications
	Dr. Otto Wegwitz	Head, Electrolytic Plant, Inorganic Division
	Dr. Fritz Bachran	Chief, Inorganic Division
	Dr. Rothweiler	Head, Methyl Plant
	Dr. Eggert	Assistant, the Methyl Plant
	Dr. Huber	Head,Caustic Dehydration
I.G. Farben Rheinfelden	Dr. Carl Liebich	Plant Manager
	Dr. A. Hermann	Superintendent, Elrctrolysis
	Dr. H. Heres	Superintendent, Caustic Concentration
	Dr. E. Renshler	Superintendent, Liquid Chlorine and Bleach
	Dr. J. Jung	Superintendent, Organic Division
I.G. Farben Ludwigsahfen	Dr. Pfannmuller	Director, Inorganic Division Ludwigshafen
	Dr. Honsberg	Superintendent, Chlorine Electrolysis
	Dr. Hans Retschy	Superintendent, Liquid Chlorine and Caustic Soda
	Dr. W. Huhn	Superintendent, Alcl Electrolysis
I.G. Farben Huels	Dr. Paul Bauman	Plant Manager
(chlorine operation)	Dr. Oswin Nitzchke	Division Head
	Dr. Ing. Erich Buttgenbach	Superintendent, Cl2 and NaOH
I.G. Farben Leverkusen	Dr. August Wingler	Head, Azo Department
	Dr. Bencker	Superintendent, Chlorine Electrolysis
	Dr. Klebert	Head, Inorganic Division

Source: PB Report No. 7747.

The information they provided was received with surprise not only by the Americans but also by the Japanese.

INTRODUCING THE REPORTS TO JAPAN

A series of bibliographies, not original FIAT/BIOS reports, might have been distributed by the US government to Japan in 1948. Though the National Diet Library (NDL) in Japan received and stored these bibliographies, they were not made public right away.[12] It is unclear why they were kept unpublicized or who first received the reports in Japan. Mitsubishi Chemical Company was considered to be the first that received the information about the bibliographies from the NDL in the summer of 1949. A researcher from the company recognized the value of these bibliographies on the first reading; the researcher then transcribed these bibliographies at the research institute. After exploring the bibliographies, they selected some reports and put a purchase orders for copies of them to the US government in the winter of 1949. The company utilized the purchased reports to reduce the production cost of the sulphonamide antibacterial sulfadiazine, an effective medicine for bacterial diseases such as pneumonia, gonorrhea, and suppuration.[13]

Meanwhile more than a few Japanese engineers were becoming aware that a lot of academic studies published in the United States referred the FIAT/BIOS reports. They frequently visited the library which was established in Tokyo in November 1945 by the Civil Information and Education section (CIE), General Headquarters Supreme Commander for the Allied Powers (GHQ/SCAP). The main purpose of the library was to make foreign magazine back issues available to Japanese citizens. For some time after the war, the engineers could access foreign journals only here.[14] Among the engineers in the chemical industry, Eiji Nakabachi, a technical official at the Tokyo Industrial Research Institute (TIRI), visited the CIE library almost daily to check the latest technological articles and found that many of them referred the reports with PB numbers. At first, he could not figure out what these reports were or how to obtain them in Japan. One day in 1950, however, he accidentally got hold of a copy of the report; he was surprised to discover that the report contained important factory data from IG Farben and precise production know-how of an organic dye. He made several copies to distribute to Japanese chemical companies.[15] However, there was still no way for him to check other reports. In February 1952, he heard that a relevant department to patent management in the GHQ/SCAP had presented the bibliographies to the Japan Patent Office (JPO). He immediately visited the JPO to check the bibliographies and discovered that there were many other reports that contained top German manufacturing secrets. For example, he recognized the existence of 60 microfilms on operating procedures in the IG Farben factory; the original documents contained over 50,000 pages. He also found some reports that had the seal "Streng Vertraulig" (strict secrecy) which dealt with an important analytical method. The TIRI decided to import a copy of over 10,000 pages.[16] The TIRI was Japan's foremost national research institute and had a long R&D tradition in the chemical field, dating back to prewar days. Under Nakabachi's instructions, the dyestuffs laboratory at the TIRI imported several hundred reports and issued reference summaries for the Japanese chemical industry.[17]

Some other engineers got a chance to go to the United States on a technology inspection tour. A technical official at the chemical department in the Ministry of International Trade and Industry (MITI) went to the United States in 1950 and brought back several reports related to plastic technology. He did his official duty by distributing them widely in the Japanese plastic industry; the information was received with surprise.[18] In the soda industry, Tatsuzo Okada, a professor at Kyoto University, visited the United States from September to December in 1950 and brought some reports back to Japan. The Japan Soda Industry Association (JSIA) delivered copies of these reports to member companies and organized a joint-research group to study them.[19]

These cases are probably the earliest encounters with the FIAT/BIOS reports by Japanese engineers. After that, the reports gradually became known in the society of Japanese engineers and scientists. However, it was still not easy for individual Japanese to purchase reports in foreign currency. Therefore the package purchase of all the reports by the Japanese government was appealed by some engineers, among which was Masamitsu Yoshimura, a chemical consulting engineer, who was considered to be one of the key persons behind this initiative. Yoshimura had visited the JPO at the same time as Nakabachi did and had also recognized the importance of the reports. He was also a column writer of scientific and technological topics for NIKKEI news, and his article in May 1952 introduced the FIAT/BIOS reports as the "PB reports." As a result of his petition to purchase all the reports from the US government, the NDL organized a committee to investigate and evaluate the reports.[20]

Whilst there were two other organizations that were related to this process, the Science Council of Japan (SCJ) and the Scientific and Technical Administration Commission (STAC), both were established in 1949. According to science historian Tetsu Hiroshige,[21] Japan's scientific system was severely criticized as the main cause of Japan's defeat: critics stressed the inconsiderate scientific bureaucracy, the factional strife by scientist themselves, and so on. On the other hand, it was also pointed out that the newly postwar science system should be the main contributor for postwar economic recovery and the birth of a cultured nation. Under the initiative of scientists who had close connections with Harry C. Kelly at the Scientific and Technical Division, Economic and Scientific Section (ESS/ST), GHQ/SCAP, the Committee for Reform of Science Research Structure decided to establish the SCJ.[22] The SCJ aimed to discuss important matters on science and technology and recommend desirable policies to the government on behalf of the scientists of the country.

The STAC was established under the Prime Minister's Office to strengthen the administrative cooperation between ministries on the scientific issues. Some influential scientists such as physicist Seiji Kaya, Ryokichi Sagane, and chemist Naoto Kameyama at Tokyo Imperial University were keen to participate in the governmental policy-making in order to reform Japan's science system and eager for a powerful scientific administrative agency in which scientist could play a principal role. But as a result of heated discussion with an opposition group who emphasized that scientists should try to distance themselves from politics, the SCJ and the STAC couldn't get biding force to government and became only a consultative agency.[23]

However in terms of introducing the FIAT/BIOS reports into Japan, the SCJ and the STAC were influential with the government. The SCJ, at an administration committee held in June 1952, resolved to recommend that the Japanese government purchase all the reports. It then filed a petition with Prime Minister Shigeru Yoshida. This idea had been suggested by the Chemical Society of Japan headed by Kameyama, who was previously mentioned, and also the president of the SCJ.[24] On the other hand, at the STAC meeting, as the representative of the SCJ, Kaya requested for a budget to purchase all the reports to the Ministry of Finance.[25] He emphasized that the "PB reports" contained so much important technical information that he was worried that the US government would stop issuing them before the Japanese government's decision to purchase them came through. The Ministry of Finance replied that they would consider this subject and shortly come to a conclusion.[26]

The Japanese National Diet responded quickly to the request from the SCJ. Before the discussion on purchasing the reports began, Hideo Maki, a professor in the Faculty of Engineering at Tokyo University, had mentioned the reports on vat dye technology at the House of Councilors held in March 1952. He explained that research on vat dye had progressed dramatically in recent years because the reports had revealed all the secrets of German chemical technology, which Japanese companies could apply domestically.[27] In July, just after Yoshimura's article had received much attention, the House of Representatives passed a resolution to request the government to purchase all the reports immediately.[28] A few days later, the librarian of the NDL mentioned that he was aware that many concerned parties such as the MITI, the JPO, and the SCJ had been enthusiastically studying the bibliographies. He said that the NDL had also been considering importing all the reports from the US government.[29] A proposal for their budget was presented to Parliament at the end of the month.[30] As a result, by the end of the year, over 69 million yen (more than US$191,000 worth at that time) from a supplementary national budget for fiscal year 1952 was assigned for the import of over 110,000 reports in microfilm format from the US government, 10,000 a month of which arrived since then. The Japanese government opened them to the public from the September 1953 onward at the NDL.[31] This political measure enabled all Japanese citizens, that is, those from both big chemical companies and small companies in various industries, to utilize them for their R&D activities.

CASE STUDIES

Although it is nearly impossible to comprehensively investigate the usage pattern of the reports in Japan at the time, according to the survey conducted by the NDL in 1955, 60% of the users comprised scientists and engineers in the field of chemical technology.[32] The following cases show how the reports were applied to the postwar technological development in Japan.

In the dyestuffs industry, the TIRI continued reviewing many reports, especially those related to IG Farben's products. Among them was "PB report No. 25652: I.G. FARBEN INDUSTRIE A.G. Manufacturing method of preparation of dyestuff, as directed through T.E.A Büro documents."[33] According to the bibliography, the report was contained in "FIAT Microfilm, Reel No. C185, frame 1–1100," and explained as follows: "This reel consists of complete direction for the production of about 400 dyes and intermediates. In most cases the direction includes of structural formulas or correct chemical names for the intermediates. The directions for the individual dyes are briefly abstracted below in German."[34] By utilizing them, of the 149 kinds of acetate rayon dye sold by the company under the trade name "Celiton," the TIRI analyzed 140 kinds for their chemical structure, mixture of dispersant, and production techniques.[35]

The reports were also indispensable to other researchers in the Japanese chemical industry. A researcher in a major chemical company, Nippon Kayaku Company, recollected that his main job at the time had been to decipher German chemical technology through the reports.[36] In the prewar days, Japanese companies had only been able to produce low-quality direct dyestuffs. The German company Bayer had been the lone supplier of high-quality products, under the brand name "Sirius." However after the war, Nippon Kayaku Company began to develop high-quality dyestuffs by collecting the reports, which helped them to understand the chemical structure of Sirius dyestuffs and to develop effectively new dyestuffs. The company continued collecting reports and other foreign patents about dyestuffs, which made them recognize the usability of an intermediate product stocked in their factories for improving light fastness. On the other hand, they had problems with the black direct dye used for machine-sewing cotton; it did not have enough color fastness for washing and easily ran color on shirts.

Having obtained technological information from the reports, they began developing a new black dye with high washing fastness. They consequently expanded their market to the spinning industry, and their domestication of Sirius-level high-quality dyestuff rapidly progressed after the 1950s. Due to their R&D activities, the company was awarded the Okochi prize in 1964, which is given for distinguished achievement based on excellent inventions and ideas.[37] In another case, a report revealed new production technology for dye intermediate which reduced the consumption of sulfuric acid and caused dramatic declining of production costs.[38]

The Japanese caustic soda industry recovered rapidly after 1950 from wartime damage.[39] As shown in Table 10.4, their manufacturing plants were converted from an ammonia soda process to an electrolytic soda process in the 1950s. The electrolytic process generated chlorine as a by-product, which could be used as a raw material in producing vinyl chloride, whose demand was growing very fast during this period. On the other hand, caustic soda, which had been used for producing rayon, did not expand its market as large as that of vinyl chloride. As a result, the sales of chlorine products became more important than those of caustic soda for the industry. Therefore, Japanese chemical companies expanded their production capacity by introducing the electrolytic process.[40] The most important equipment used in the method was the electrolytic cell. There are basically two types of the cells, the mercury process cell and the diaphragm process cell. Professor Okada pointed out that the diaphragm process cell had developed mainly in the United States and accounted for over 95% of the

Table 10.4 Production capacity of caustic soda

		(1000 t)		
		Electrolytic		
Year-end	Ammonia	Total	Mercury	Diaphragm
1939	415.8	236.9		
1949	261.0	199.0	85.8	113.2
1950	261.0	226.0	92.7	133.3
1951	301.0	261.0	112.9	148.1
1952	301.0	297.2	134.3	162.9
1953	301.0	327.5	164.5	163.0
1954	301.0	361.1	197.9	163.1
1955	301.0	389.1	220.3	168.7
1956	390.6	492.6	299.9	192.7
1957	390.6	626.5	418.0	208.5

Source: Japan Chemical Industry Association ed., *Nihon no Kagaku Kogyo Sengo 30-nen no Ayumi [A thirty-year History of Japan Chemical Industry after the war]* (Tokyo, 1979), 65.

production capacity in the country just after the war. On the other hand, the lower price of mercury prompted the development of the mercury process cell in Germany. IG Farben had enthusiastically developed this type of the cells in response to the growing demand for chlorine during the wartime.[41] Table 10.4 indicates that the mercury process cell became popular in Japan. Although the mercury process cell created less impurities and an exceedingly better product, this technology consumed more electric energy, which would have been reduced by expanding its electric capacity.[42] As mentioned earlier, Professor Okada had visited the United States in 1950 and brought back the reports on soda technology. He had visited Dr. W. C. Gardiner at the Mathieson Alkali Company and Robert B. MacMullin, a chemical consultant who had worked for the U.S. Chlorine Industry Team (which had been dispatched to Germany under TIIB).[43] Okada had been studying IG Farben's mercury process cell since 1946. Then some soda companies, such as Ajinomoto and Mitsui Chemical Company, cooperated with Okada under the auspices of the JSIA. In prewar days, domestic soda companies kept their technology secret, and little technology disclosure and exchange between them was allowed. However as the wartime economy deepened, some technological research council and informal gatherings started in April 1941 so that the companies in the industry could make use of domestic highest technologies developed by others in the same industry to reduce the consumption of scarce materials. Soon after JSIA was established in 1948, technological expert committees were founded in the field of ammonia soda process and electrolytic soda process, which were renamed and expanded in 1950.[44] JSIA became a base of technological exchange for domestic soda companies which longed to get foreign newest technology information through the reports. An engineer at Ajinomoto recollected that the reports he could obtain were full of originality in the operation data, the design specifications, and the improvement technology. He gleaned most of the ideas and knowledge in the field of electrolytic techniques from the reports.[45] On the basis of technology developed by IG Farben and Mathieson Alkali Company, Japanese companies improved the mercury process cell and their technology came to be regarded as the world's highest level around 1955.[46]

In addition to the chemical industry, a case of electronics industry provides us an example that the reports contributed to the development of Japanese small firms in a provincial areas. During the war, a German company Bosch Corporation had been successfully developing the Metalized Paper (MP) Condenser, which was smaller than existing one by 70% in volume and had a "Self-Healing Action," an innovative recovery mechanism from damage. In Japan, captain Ito Yôji of the Naval Technical Research Institute ordered to investigate it in 1944. Professor Yukio Saitou of the Tokyo Institute of Technology and some big electronics companies such as Hitachi also started investigating them, but couldn't achieve practical use before the end of the war.[47] On the other hand, there were a lot of small firms which produced electronics components as subcontractors of big companies which produced radio wave weapons. After the war, with upsurge of demand for electronics components assembled in radio receivers, not a few companies began developing their original technology.[48]

Among such small companies, Matsuo Electronics Company founded in 1949 with only seven employees started their business by producing condensers for radio receivers. Having been located in Osaka prefecture, western Japan, the company firstly expanded its customers inside the area such as local merchants. However, the company recognized that the MP condenser would have had high potential demand because reduced size components were suitable for assembling a more precise electronics instrument such as television set, and tried to develop it by solely depending on the report.[49] The company successfully started to put the MP condenser on the market from January 1954 and obtained a massive order from Sony in the same year, which contributed to their business rapidly expanding from the 1950s onward.[50] This episode implies that even the small company could get a chance to develop and keep up with larger electronics company in their R&D activities by utilizing the reports.

CONCLUSION

As we saw in the case of the chemical industry, the FIAT/BIOS reports supplied important information to Japanese engineers. On the contrary in Germany, the dyestuff industry was unable to develop new products and remained at the same technology level as that in the reports even at the end of the 1950s.[51] In that sense, the reports reduced the technology gap between Japan and Germany. In order to estimate the significance of the reports more precisely, more case studies in various industries should be gathered. In some technology fields that progressed rapidly after WWII, such as electronics and petro-chemistry, the reports seem to be less reliable.

It should be noted that the US investigation team requisitioned not only the documents but also numerous machines and equipment. Moreover, they took many German technologists back to the United States.[52] The US government and industries could comprehensively utilize this technology information. On the other hand, all the information the Japanese engineers could obtain was in document form. With these constraints, they made their best effort to utilize the reports.

First of all, a few engineers in various fields, such as universities, public and national institutes, and consulting businesses, recognized the importance of the reports. Some technical officials and academicians especially played an important role by never trying to withhold information. On the contrary, they actively delivered the reports to the concerned people. Such openness seems to have been a result of their official positions.[53] Moreover their research experience during wartime must have contributed for their prompt response to the reports. The following questions have yet to be answered: on what subjects was research conducted, and how they recognized the limits of their research capabilities during the period of the wartime science and technology mobilization.

In addition to the individuals, the SCJ and the STAC requested the Japanese government to purchase all the reports immediately. These institutions were established in the democratization process of Japanese science and technology, which was promoted by GHQ/SCAP after Japan's defeat in WWII. Such process was motivated by Japanese scientists' wish for the modernization of science system. However, as Hiroshige claimed, their wish for and criticism of the Japanese science system goes back to the wartime science mobilization in which they required the Japanese government to modernize the Japanese science system for the development of weapons.[54]

Joint research in the JSIA also goes way back to the wartime. Some recent studies have pointed out that a number of joint research studies—not only between companies but also between companies and universities and between military and other governmental institutes—played a very important role in technological development, especially in the postwar Japan; many of these research studies had been organized during wartime.[55] The social changes between wartime and the reform period or the systemization of science and technology should not be ignored in an understanding of Japanese postwar technology development.

Finally, as the reports were fairly open to the rest of the world and must have been used in various countries and areas,[56] more studies of the diffusion and utilization of them, especially in relatively poorer countries, should be explored. David Edgerton, in his study of a global history of "technology-in-use," claims that nations acquire more new technology from abroad than they innovate themselves, and in the poor world there were many cases of late adoption and long use of rich-country technologies.[57] The wartime technology rapidly has become out-of-date since 1950s in advanced countries. However, the reports may still have been valuable technological resource for the countries which were behind in technology. Therefore comprehensive study of the reports enables us to understand more accurately how seemingly old German technologies contributed to the technological and economic development in the postwar world.

NOTES

1. Tetsuro Nakaoka, "Gijyutsu Donyu [Technology Introduction]" in *Nihon Sangyo Gijyutushi Jiten [The Encyclopedia of Japanese History of Industrial Technology]*, Japan Society of Industrial Technological History (JSITH) ed. (Kyoto, 2007), 24–25.
2. John Gimbel, *Science, technology, and reparations: exploitation and plunder in postwar Germany* (Stanford, 1990).

3. Sigeru Nakayana, "Kagaku Jouhou no Kokusai Kouryu [The International Exchange of Scientific Information]," in *Tsu-shi Nihon no Kagaku Gijyutsu [The Social History of Science and Technology in Contemporary Japan]*, Sigeru. Nakayama et al. eds., Vol.1 (Tokyo, 1995), 161–169.
4. As mentioned later, Japan imported FIAT/BIOS reports mainly from the US government. Therefore the publication process of the report only in the US is described in this paper. For the British case, see Carl Glatt, *Reparations and the Transfer of Science and Industrial Technology from Germany: A case study of the Roots of British Industrial Policy and of Aspects of British Occupation Policy in Germany between Post-World War II Reconstruction and the Korean War, 1943–1951* (Ph.D. thesis, the European University Institutes, 1994), Chap. 2. I am indebted to David Edgerton and Frances Lynch for obtaining the thesis.
5. Gimbel, op. cit., Chap. 1. Arnold Krammer traced the requisition process of German synthetic fuel technology and revealed close cooperation between the US government and petroleum industry; see Arnold Kramer, "Technology Transfer as War Booty: The U.S. Technical Oil Mission to Europe, 1945," *Technology and Culture,* No.22, 1981, 68–103.
6. Glatt, op. cit., 137–138.
7. This is the reason Japanese people called them "PB" reports.
8. Gimbel, op. cit., Chap. 2.
9. ibid. Chap. 4.
10. Morio Uehara, "PB ripoto ka Beikoku Seifu Kenkyu ripoto ka [the PB reports or the US government research reports?]," *Saiensu Laiburary [Science Library]*, 5/4–5 (1959, May), 55.
11. Sigeharu Isobe, "PB Ripoto ni Tsuite [An introduction to the PB reports]," *Gakuto,* 49/11 (1952, Nov.), 57–58.
12. Masamitsu Yoshimura, *Kin no Tou [A Tower of Gold]* (Tokyo, 1953), 322.
13. Masamitsu Yoshimura, "PB Ripoto ni Himitsu ha Nai [There is no secret in the PB reports]," *Cyuo Kouron,* 67/10 (1952, Sep.).
14. Nakayama, op. cit., 162.
15. Eiji Koike, "PB Ripoto Tono Deai [My encounter with the PB reports]," *Jouhou Kanri [Journal of Information and Processing and Management]*, 33/2 (1990, May), 174–177.
16. Eiji Nakabachi, "PB Repoto no Tebiki [A guide to the PB reports]," *Kagaku Kogyo Shiryo [Chemical engineer's digest]*, 20/3 (1952, Jul.) 33–34.
17. The TIRI, *PB (BIOS, FIAT, CIOS) Kagaku Kogyo Bunken Syoroku [The bibliography of the PB (BIOS, FIAT, CIOS) reports on chemical technology]* (Tokyo, 1953).
18. Yoshimura, op. cit., 1952, 98.
19. JSIA, *Nihon Soda Kogyo 100-nen shi [A 100-years History of Soda Industry]* (Tokyo, 1982), 718–729.
20. Yoshimura, op. cit., 1952, 99.
21. Tetsu Hiroshige, *Kagaku no Syakai shi: Kindai Nihon no Kagaku Taisei [The Social History of Science: The Scientific Structure of Modern Japan]*, (Tokyo, 1973), Chap. 10.
22. For further details about the relationship between Japanese scientists and the ESS/ST and the establishment process of the SCJ, see Bowen C. Dees, *The Allied Occupation and Japan's Economic Miracle Building the Foundation of Japanese Science and Technology 1945–1952*,(Richmond,Sur rey,1997), chap. 6, 8.
23. Hiroshige, op. cit., 266–269.
24. The SCJ, "PB Ripoto ni Tsuite Youbou [A request on the PB reports]," *Nihon Gakujyutsu Kaigi Geppou [The monthly journal of SCJ]*, 2/6 (1952, Jun.), 9.

25. STAC, "Dai 41 kai Kagaku Gijyutsu Gyosei Kyougikai Youshi [The official record of the proceedings of the STAC 41st meeting]," (1952, Jun.).
26. The STAC, "Dai 42 kai Kagaku Gijyutsu Gyosei Kyougikai Youshi [The official record of the proceedings of the STAC 42nd meeting]," (1952, Jul.).
27. "Sangiin Okura Iinkai 27 gou [The Japan House of Councilors, 27th committee on finance]," (March 20th, 1952). All minutes of the National Diet were cited from the website "On-line Search System (http://kokkai.ndl.go.jp/)".
28. "Syugiin Toshokan Unei Iinkai 3 gou [The Japan House of Representatives, 3rd Library Management Committee]," (June 18th, 1952).
29. "Sangiin Toshokan Unei Iinkai 4 gou [The Japan House of Councilors, 4th Library Management Committee]," (June 20th, 1952).
30. "Syugiin Hon-Kaigi 63 gou [The Japan House of Representatives, 63rd Plenary Session]," (June 30th, 1952).
31. "Sangiin Toshokan Unei Iinkai 2 gou [The Japan House of Councilors, 2nd Library Management Committee]," (Feb. 3rd, 1954).
32. JDICA, *Kaseihin Kogyo Kyokai 50-nen shi [A fifty-year History of Japan Dyestuff and Industrial Chemical Association]* (Tokyo, 1998), 155–157.
33. Yoshie Bansho et al., "Senryou [dyestuffs]," *Yuki Gousei Kagaku [The Journal of the Society of Organic Synthetic Chemistry, Japan]*, Vol.10 No.10 (1952, Oct.), 37–38.
34. The U.S. Department of Commerce, *Bibliography of Scientific and Industrial Reports,* Vol.7 No.4 (1947, Oct. 24th), 287.
35. Yoshie Bansho et al., op. cit.
36. JDICA, *Gousei Seni Gijyutu no Rekishi [A history of synthetic fiber technology]* (Tokyo, 1997), 9.
37. Nihon Kayaku, *Kayaku kara Kayaku made Hara Yasuzaburo to Nihon Kayaku no 50-nen [From gunpowder to chemical agent, A fifty-year History of Nihon Kayaku]* (Tokyo, 1967), 206–222.
38. Sirou Yamaguchi, "Senryo Kogyo no Saikin no Shinpo [The progress of the dye industry in recent years]," *Nikka kyo Geppou [Japan Chemical Industry Association monthly]*, 7/7 (1954, Jun.), 26.
39. JCIA, *Nihon no Kagaku Kogyo Sengo 30-nen no Ayumi [A thirty-year History of Japan Chemical Industry after the war]* (Tokyo, 1979), 63.
40. Touru Takamatsu, "San and Arukari [acid and alkali]," in JSITH, op. cit., 132.
41. Tatsuzo Okada, "Tategata Kaitenshiki Suiginhou Denkaisou ni tuite [An introduction to Vertical Rotary Mercury process cell]," *Nichikakyo Geppou [Japan Chemical Industry Association monthly]*, 45 (1952, Feb.), 27–29.
42. JCIA, op. cit., 65.
43. JSIA, op. cit., 724–725.
44. JSIA, op. cit., 423–426.
45. Toshiyuki Sugino, "Soda Kogyo Gijyutu no Hensen -Kako kara Mirai e-Sono1 PB Repoto to Suiginhou no Kindaika [A change of soda technology: from the past to the future Vol.1, a modernization of mercury process and PB reports]," *Soda to Enso [Soda & chlorine]*, 42/6 (1991, Jun.), 10–17.
46. JCIA, op. cit., 66, 240.
47. MP condensers were carried to Japan from Germany by submaline; see Saburo Hayashi, "Condenser no Ayumi 2 [The development of condenser part 2]," *Denshi Zairyou [Electronic material]*, 1962 Nov., 76.
48. Yuki Nakajima, "Sengo Nihon niokeru Senmon Buhin Meka no Hatten -1945~60: Denshi Buhin Sangyou no Jirei [The Progress of Specialty Components Makers after Wold War 2 in Japan: Electronic Components

Industry from 1945 to 1960]," *Keiei-shi Gaku [Japan Business History Review],* 33/3 (1998, Dec.).

49. Though the title and the number of the report is unclear, the report "BIOS 226: Metallized Paper Capacitors" may be the one the company consulted.
50. Sanjyu-Go Nenshi Hensan Incai [35 years history editorial committee], *Matsuo Denki Sanjyu-Go Nenshi [A thirty-five year history of Matuo Denki]* (Osaka,1985), 48–52.
51. Eiji Koike, "Sekai no Senryo Kogyo (1) [The dyestuff industry in the World Part 1]," *Senryo to Yakuhin [Dyestuffs & chemicals],* 4/12 (1959, Dec.), 697.
52. Gimbel, op. cit., Chap. 3, Chap. 6.
53. In his comprehensive historical analysis of Japanese R&D system, Minoru Sawai emphasizes that from the inter-war period to the middle of high-growth era in 1950s the governmental sector such as the Naval arsenals and Railway Technical Research Institute was the major driving forces of Japanese technological development. He also points that the governmental technical institutes became open to public after the defeat of the war; See Minoru Sawai, *Kindai Nihon no Kenkyu Kaihatsu Taisei [The Research and Development System in Modern Japan],* (Nagoya, 2012), 526–527.
54. Hiroshige, op. cit., 252–253.
55. See Hiroshige, op. cit., 204–206; Hiroshi Aoki and Atsushi Hiramoto, "Kagaku Gijyutsu Douin to Kenkyu Tonarigumi: Dainiji Taisen Ka Nihon no Kyodo Kenkyu [The Mobilization of Science and Technology and 'The Research Neighborhood Groups': Research Collaboration in Japan During World War II]," *Shakai-Keizaishi Gaku [Socio-Economics History],* 68/5 (2003, Jan.); Minoru Sawai, "Senjiki Nihon no Kenkyu Kaihatsu Taisei: Kagaku Gijyutsu Doin to Kyodo Kenkyu no Shinka [Research and Development in Wartime Japan: Mobilization of Science and Intensification of Joint Research]," *Osaka Daigaku Keizaigaku [Osaka Economic Papers],* 54/3 (2004, Dec.).
56. Glatt points out that there is considerable evidence that Russian Embassy in London purchased BIOS reports; Glatt, op. cit., 177.
57. David Edgerton, *The Shock of the Old: Technology and Global History Since 1900* (New York, 2007), 43, 111.

11 The Introduction of American Mass Production Technology to Japan during the Occupation

The Case of Penicillin

Julia Yongue

The transfer of penicillin technologies to Japan is not a typical case for two reasons. First, although multinational enterprises generally act as the driving forces of technology transfer in high-tech industries, one being pharmaceuticals, in the case of penicillin their role was negligible. Instead it was scientists and government officials who worked in close collaboration to oversee the transfer and diffusion of penicillin technologies to the Japanese industry. The absence of multinational activities in the beginning of the transfer process can be explained by Japan's isolation during the War and its early aftermath. It was only at the end of the Occupation when industry would begin to take a more central role in the transfer of new technologies for the semi-synthetic derivatives of penicillin.

Second, government allowed Japanese companies to manufacture penicillin until the end of the Occupation without a patent. Although penicillin was never patented, the technologies used in mass production and semi-synthetic derivatives were. In the early years of the Occupation, all patent rights were waived, as the concern for saving lives far outweighed all economic considerations. The situation drastically changed, however, at the end of the Occupation with the enactment of new legislation regarding patent rights. As will be shown here, the changes in Japan's legal environment had a marked and lasting effect on the relationship between enterprises, scientists and the state.

Although the case of penicillin was in two ways atypical, it can also be seen as representative and illustrative. The transfer of technologies for this single drug demonstrates the full range of forms—both formal and informal—that technology transfers took in the postwar development of the Japanese pharmaceutical industry. Moreover, if one considers all of the types of penicillin technologies including the various semi-synthetic derivatives, this drug has a remarkably long lifecycle, providing the business historian with a rich source of information for analysis. Viewed from a broader perspective, the transfer of penicillin technologies was of great consequence to Japanese business as it sparked the development of a research-based pharmaceutical industry while also setting in motion the process of globalization in the postwar period.

This chapter will focus on two types of transfer over two phases: mass production technologies in the first phase (1944 to 1951) and licensing agreements for innovative penicillin derivatives in the second (1951 to the early 1960s). While exploring the two phases, the writer will also examine the roles and relationships of the three driving forces of technology transfer: government, industry/entrepreneurs and scientists. Through this analysis, it will be possible to draw some conclusions regarding the environment for technology transfer and the characteristics of the pharmaceutical industry at that point in its development.

THE ROLE OF TECHNOLOGY TRANSFERS IN THE DEVELOPMENT OF THE JAPANESE PHARMACEUTICAL INDUSTRY

Mass Production Technologies

Though its role is often underemphasized in the literature on the development of the Japanese pharmaceutical industry, technology for the mass production of medicines was vital for three reasons. First, mass production technology provided an impetus for enterprises to improve product quality. Thanks to the profits accrued from penicillin, sales companies were able to begin to modernize their operations by constructing and upgrading their plants. Improved production technology and equipment helped to reduce contamination. The efforts to improve plant facilities would take on an even greater significance in the 1960s, when the issue of safety would come to the fore, as well as in the early 1970s, when international manufacturing standards (Good Manufacturing Practices) were introduced in Japan.

Second, mass production technologies helped to increase the volume of penicillin in circulation and pave the way for the large-scale production of other drugs. Thanks to the transfer of submerged culture or tank method technology, penicillin became available throughout Japan as early as 1948.[1] In 1949, Japan became one of only three nations to attain self-sufficiency in this drug and went on to become an exporter.[2] With a modern infrastructure for mass production in place, manufacturers were also better prepared to meet the rise in demand for all types of medicine that would occur after the implementation of a national health insurance system in 1961.

Third, the transfer of mass production technologies gave rise to numerous innovative applications. One spinoff was asepsis technologies, which were necessary to prevent contamination. This technology had multiple applications, which went beyond the scope of medicine into other fields such as electronics. In addition, enzyme technologies, notably amino acid, had wide applications in the pharmaceutical as well as the food industries.[3]

Licensing Agreements

The significance of licensing agreements to the postwar development of the Japanese pharmaceutical industry is unquestionable: licensing was the most expedient and efficient means for manufacturers to procure innovative technologies from abroad. Licensing was of capital importance to Japan's pharmaceutical manufacturing enterprises at that time, as it provided opportunities for both economic growth and learning in new disciplines such as chemical engineering.

Considered from a long-term perspective, the transfer of penicillin technology and its derivatives provided the "seeds" of future innovation. Japanese pharmaceutical manufacturers were able to build on this knowledge and later apply it to their own endeavors to develop new antibiotics. For a number of Japan's research-oriented companies, including Yamanouchi and Fujisawa (Astellas, since their 2005 merger), antibiotics were among their first internationally marketable drugs.

One can easily highlight the positive effects of licensing on the growth of Japan's pharmaceutical industry, yet there was also a notable downside. At the time of the transfer of mass production technologies, existing Japanese pharmaceutical companies conducted little research and functioned above all as manufacturers and marketers of medicines. Few would begin to undertake research in real earnest until the 1960s when the first laboratories were constructed.[4] Consequently, many Japanese pharmaceutical manufacturers used licensing as a substitute for in-house research and development and became overly dependent on foreign technology.

When licensing was not feasible, many companies simply "reengineered" existing drugs by slightly modifying the development process. This practice brought a spate of lawsuits but remained the general tendency until the patent reform of 1976, when product patents were finally recognized. Licensing thus provided Japanese pharmaceutical manufacturers with a source of novel technology during a phase in the industry's development when the legislative environment was not conducive to innovation and investment in in-house research was well out of reach for most manufacturers.

THE DRIVING FORCES OF TECHNOLOGY TRANSFER

Government

What were the main drivers of the transfer of penicillin technology, and what were their roles? Scholars, including the writer, have examined the role of government and its importance in the economic expansion of the pharmaceutical industry from the postwar to the present. Consequently, there now exists a growing literature on policy as a catalyst or hindrance—depending on one's interpretation—in the industry's development.[5] Though the existence or type of an industrial policy for the pharmaceutical industry may be debatable in some periods of postwar business history, it was decisive to the successful transfer of penicillin technologies during the period in question and contributed the long-term development of the industry.

According to Arai Katsuhiro, "when Japan resumed technology exchanges with Western countries after the war, Japanese technology was estimated to be around twenty years behind the most advanced nations."[6] Japan did lag far behind the United States and Britain in many technological areas. However, Japan's technological deficiencies at that time were not in the basic fields of science such as organic chemistry but in their industrial applications. Chemical engineering technologies necessary to developing mass production equipment were lacking. Without the government's technical assistance and financial support of industry via the transfer of penicillin technology, that gap might have widened even further.

The legislative environment was also favorable to Japan's catching up. During the first period, the government prioritized penicillin development, as it was considered essential to the recovery. Pharmaceuticals were among the industries designated for special assistance along with coal, steel and ammonia sulfate. The government initially set the price of penicillin, but in 1950, policy makers reintroduced the drug pricing system first established during the War. Drug prices were calculated according to the bulk-line formula, a system that allowed even the least innovative firms to profit from the sale of medicines.[7]

Few would dispute the importance of government as the driving force in the transfer and diffusion of penicillin technology or the positive effects the sale of penicillin had on the business operations of Japanese pharmaceutical manufacturers in the immediate postwar years. However, there were limitations to its support of industry. The government's stance as a promoter of industry would gradually begin to evolve from the late 1950s due to the increased incidence of adverse drug reactions. In 1956, one particularly well-publicized case of anaphylactic shock resulted in the death of a professor from the prestigious Faculty of Law at the University of Tokyo. Following the incident, the general public and physicians alike began to question penicillin as a true panacea. The government would not however assume its role as regulator until the Thalidomide incident in the 1960s.

Entrepreneurs

While government played a central role in the transfer of technology, particularly in the first phase, it was not the only driving force of industrial development. As many of those who have written on this industry have noted, entrepreneurship was also crucial.[8] Business leaders were important catalysts, particularly after the Occupation when licensing agreements with foreign enterprises became the main source of new technology transfers to Japan.

Ironically, the existing and most experienced pharmaceutical manufacturers were not particularly entrepreneurial. Indeed, most of the penicillin producers in the first phase were not pharmaceutical enterprises. Though representatives from the pharmaceutical industry took part in government-organized training sessions, most were initially reluctant to embark on production.[9]

There was, however, one notable exception, Banyu Pharmaceutical, founded in Tokyo in 1915. Banyu became Japan's very first postwar manufacturer of penicillin and a leader among pharmaceutical enterprises in establishing licensing agreements. In the second phase, Iwadare Koichi, the son of the first president of the company, traveled to the United States to negotiate the transfer of a penicillin derivative, Procaine G. Moreover, he and the founder, Toru oversaw the establishment of an agreement that would allow other domestic producers to manufacture this product under the same license.

Initiating licensing agreements in the early post-Occupation period presented a formidable challenge to most of the existing Japanese pharmaceutical manufacturers. Because of the country's isolation during the War, their ties with foreign pharmaceutical manufacturers had been severed or severely weakened. Most managers lacked the linguistic skills and international expertise necessary to carry out successful negotiations. Without contacts or an introduction, the representatives of some companies had little choice but to visit the headquarters of foreign manufacturers in the hope of being granted a meeting.

After the Occupation, government policy began to take a less central role. Although Japanese firms had to obtain government approval to establish licensing agreements with foreign enterprises due to ownership restrictions, it was nonetheless businessmen who actually instigated these negotiations. The transfer of the latest technologies via licensing agreements with foreign enterprises was essential to the development of the Japanese pharmaceutical industry and would remain the dominant means of procuring expertise in the decades to follow.

Scientists

Existing literature explores the importance of policy and entrepreneurialism in the development of the pharmaceutical industry, yet often overlooks the third actor, scientists, who played an indispensable role in the transfer of penicillin technology in both phases. Scientists undertook research before the official transfer of penicillin technology got underway. Based on the dearth of information they were able to gather from journal articles, they even succeeded in developing methods to produce small quantities domestically. In the early aftermath of the War, they continued to play a vital role as intermediaries by "translating" knowledge and know-how from abroad as well as across disciplines to key figures in government and business.

Although there were many outstanding scientists, Umezawa Hamao stands out. In the first phase, he played a key role in Japan's attainment of self-sufficiency, while in the long term, he aided in the emergence and growth of a research-based Japanese pharmaceutical industry. Perhaps the most significant scientific achievement of his career was the discovery of an antibiotic, kanamycin in 1956, a cure for diseases such as tuberculosis that were not treatable with penicillin. Sales of kanamycin contributed to the economic growth of the domestic industry and offered proof to the international community that Japanese scientists were on par with those in other developed nations despite the long period of isolation.

TWO PHASES OF TECHNOLOGY TRANSFERS

The Organization of Penicillin Research during the War

Before delving into the official transfer of mass production technology via the Occupation government, it is useful to provide an overview of Japan's wartime progress in penicillin research and production. The purpose of this overview is to offer an assessment of the level of penicillin development. At the same time, it will demonstrate that a well-organized system of research was already in place even before the arrival of the Occupation forces.

In Japan, just as in many other countries, Alexander Fleming's discovery of penicillin did not spark much initial interest. It was not until 1943 when an article by Manfred Keise of the University of Berlin reached Japan that research on penicillin began in earnest. According to the work of Kakuta Fusako, the most comprehensive account of Japanese penicillin production during the War, it is likely that the Keise article reached Japan clandestinely aboard a submarine.[10] Inagaki Katsuhiko, the army physician in charge of the penicillin project, obtained the article from Nagai Willy, an official in the scientific section of the Ministry of Education and son of the famous scientist, Nagai Nagayoshi. Inagaki then passed the article along to Umezawa, who translated it into Japanese.

With sufficient funding from the Japanese Army but extremely scarce resources available at that time, Inagaki summoned all of Japan's best scientists for a special meeting in Tokyo. In January 1944, he established the Penicillin Committee for the purpose of finding a method to produce penicillin. The search for penicillin would become a national cause, as is reflected in the change of the committee's name from penicillin to the newly coined word "hekiso" to avoid the use of a foreign (enemy) term. Thanks to much hard work and Inagaki's close coordination of the project, in only nine months' time, several research groups had managed to produce small quantities of penicillin with varying degrees of efficacy and purity.

It is interesting to note that in late 1944, contrary to the wishes of Inagaki, measures were taken by the Japanese Army to establish a secret patent for penicillin. The Japanese Army took this step in response to an initial move made by the Japanese Navy to apply for a patent so as to prevent misuse by manufacturers. After much deliberation, a final draft of the patent was drawn up according to which no individual could claim ownership of the rights for penicillin. However, because the decision to submit a request was followed by heavy bombings of Army facilities and the close of the War, the patent application was never submitted.[11]

The Production of Penicillin during the War

Having discovered a method for producing penicillin in 1944, Inagaki wasted no time in embarking on production. Although the manufacturing of penicillin is referred to as "mass production" in Japanese documents, because the surface culture method (producing cultures in glass recipients) was employed, volume was nominal. Morinaga Confectionery Company and Banyu Pharmaceutical Company were the first companies to receive official authorization to produce penicillin. In 1945, these two companies were capable of manufacturing 20,000 units per month,[12] scarcely enough to meet the nation's needs.

By contrast, America's largest manufacturer of penicillin, Pfizer, opened the world's first plant in 1943 for the express purpose of mass-producing it using tanks (submerged culture method). Though the volume produced at Pfizer reached 4,000 million units in January 1944, it quickly jumped to 100,000 million units per month by the end of the same year.[13] Thus by 1945, America was producing enough penicillin to fill the needs of the entire population. At the same time, research and limited production of synthetic derivatives of penicillin were already underway. By 1945, new discoveries would make even the most advanced mass production methods obsolete, thus widening Japan's technology gap with the United States even further.

The United States and Japan were not the only nations where the search for penicillin was underway. Many countries including Germany, the Netherlands, France and even China were also conducting research during the War. However, these projects were small-scale and did not have a well-organized national network that Japan or the United States did. The American model of collaborative research involving government, scientists and industry is well documented.[14] One major difference in the two programs is that the two Japanese companies needed no persuasion from Inagaki to engage in penicillin production during the War. On the other hand, Howard Florey experienced some initial difficulties during his visit to the United States in his efforts to convince companies to manufacture penicillin. Because of the strong cooperation between government, scientists and industry that officials were able to foster in the United States, it is likely that they had this model of collaborative research in mind when they decided to establish a similar organization in Occupied Japan.

Phase One: Mass Production

The Introduction of Penicillin via the Occupation Government

As mentioned earlier, penicillin is a unique case in the history of technology transfers to Japan, as mass production technologies were made freely available in every sense of the word to any manufacturer with the desire to manufacture it. All patent obligations were thus waived. The American government's interest in ensuring that penicillin would be rapidly and widely available in Japan was twofold. The first was to aid in Japan's postwar recovery, and the second to protect troops stationed in Japan from contracting sexually transmitted diseases.[15]

For the transfer of mass production technology in the first phase, Japan received the best possible assistance. The Supreme Commander of the Allied Forces, General Douglas MacArthur, solicited the advice of George Merck on how to transfer mass production technology to the Japanese industry. In November 1946, Merck sent one of his employees, Jackson W. Foster, to Japan. Foster had studied microbiology under a future Nobel laureate, Selman Waksman, and would spend four months giving lectures and hands-on technical assistance to the newly established penicillin industry.

The 1947 inaugural issue of the *Journal of Penicillin,* a scholarly publication on penicillin research in Japan, contains a preface written by Foster himself, which sets the tone for the great mission the Japanese had embarked upon. He wrote,

> A tremendous mobilization is requisite for this peacetime battle. So complex is the task that each phase demands the concerted efforts of separate specialists. And yet, the affairs of one are the affairs of all. In this project the industrialist and the academician share responsibility equally. The factory man will find himself dealing with curious theoretical problems and the scholar will be confronted with the expediencies of mass production. Representatives of virtually every aspect of modern technology will be participating in this unique enterprise: the microbiologist, the chemist, the engineer, management, and through these a host of subsidiary activities. Each must know that his role is no less essential than any other. . . . How successful you are depends on your exploitation of three watchwords: organization, cooperation, action.[16]

Foster strove to systemize research activities by establishing two groups to promote the diffusion of penicillin. The first was the Japan Penicillin Association, or JPA, consisting of manufacturers. At its first meeting in July 1946, government officials designated four companies to represent industry: Banyu Pharmaceutical, Wakamoto Pharmaceutical, Yashu Chemical and Iryotosei. As penicillin production got underway more companies joined. The second group was the Japan Penicillin Research Association, whose membership consisted of prominent scientists from a variety of disciplines as well as several Health Ministry officials.

Having two associations whose functions were different yet complementary provided the necessary framework for the production and diffusion of penicillin technology in Japan. At the same time, they also helped to reinforce a spirit of cooperation and openness. The functions of the two were well defined: government oversaw the technology transfer process, while scientists from different fields carefully pooled their knowledge and know-how to ensure that the new technologies transferred to Japan would be properly implemented. Scientists diffused the latest domestic and international research findings and offered direct assistance to various industry representatives during their visits to factories. For their part, JPA members worked closely with scientists and government officials and even shared their observations with rival enterprises in order to increase the volume and quality of penicillin throughout Japan.

The Systemization of Research

Foster began his mission by surveying production sites where the surface culture method was already being employed in order to make assessments of the quality of Japanese penicillin. He opted not to introduce the submerged culture method employed in the United States, as he reckoned that building a full-scale plant would take at least three years and instead decided to build a pilot plant equipped with small-volume tanks. To promote the development of basic research in Japan in the long term, Foster also proposed the construction of a central laboratory.

The two Japanese associations deliberated on the idea of establishing a central laboratory at length. Although the idea itself was welcomed, funding was a major obstacle. It was initially decided that JPA would finance the construction of a facility through the collection of dues. Had the profits from the sales of penicillin remained high, this idea might have been feasible; however, the price of penicillin quickly plummeted due to excessive competition.[17]

In 1947, the project of establishing a central laboratory was finally realized. However, because the problem of inadequate funds remained unresolved, a new structure was not constructed, and the central laboratory was housed in an existing facility at the University of Tokyo. Moreover, the purpose of the laboratory was not for conducting basic research as initially intended but for carrying out inspections of penicillin quality. Finally in 1950, it was government, rather than industry, that erected a central laboratory, the precursor of the National Institute of Infectious Diseases.

The Diversity of the Entrants

Companies from a variety of sectors joined the pharmaceutical industry in the first phase. Some examples include chemicals, synthetic fiber and foods; yet there were many others. There are several explanations for the diversity of the entrants. The first is cost: some firms were able to avert start-up expenditures since they already possessed equipment that could be easily adapted to penicillin production. Such companies were at an advantage at that time since financial as well as material resources were extremely scant. Meiji Milk was one of the first firms to produce penicillin by using glass milk bottles.

The second reason is the eclectic set of technologies necessary for mass production. Technologies such as fermentation were not new but their applications were. For that reason, sake brewing companies as well as confectioners had an edge over pharmaceutical enterprises thanks to their long practical experience in using this technology. Surprisingly, however, the site of the first pilot plant was that of a company with no such experience, Toyo Rayon (now Toray), a synthetic fiber manufacture. According to its seventy-year history, Toyo Rayon produced penicillin from 1947 to 1953 at its plant in Shiga Prefecture then withdrew from the JPA in 1954.[18] Mitsubishi Kakoki Kaisha and Hitachi also worked with scientific experts to manufacture the tanks to be used for penicillin production. Their efforts enabled the Japanese to use domestically manufactured equipment rather than import from abroad. At the same time, their participation in penicillin production helped them to gain valuable knowledge in chemical engineering, which could be applied to other types of manufacturing.

The third, and dominant, explanation for the large number of entrants is that penicillin production offered the opportunity for rapid postwar recovery with the sale of a single product. Because penicillin was the most effective treatment of infections, demand was initially high. On the other hand, entry barriers to the early postwar pharmaceutical industry were extremely low: firms could procure technology without a patent and receive production assistance directly from American experts. These circumstances made it possible for businesses with no prior experience in the field of medicine to become pharmaceutical manufacturers.

One such example is Daito (Sugar) Company, which lost all of its overseas holdings after the War. In 1950, Masuda Katsunobu, Daito's vice president, became the Penicillin Association's third chairman of the board of directors. The following remark was made at the commemoration of the tenth anniversary of the founding of JPA. "Penicillin is widely known for saving the lives of so many people; however, we will be eternally grateful to this drug for saving our company."[19] This was no understatement: for a number of Japanese companies, penicillin was a godsend for their efforts to rebuild their operations in early aftermath of the War.

The Penicillin Producers

In the history of the development of the Japanese pharmaceutical industry, one can observe waves or "booms," as they are known in Japanese, during which new or existing firms from various sectors entered production en masse for the first time. The technologies for penicillin sparked one such wave. During the so-called penicillin boom, one can identify three types of participants. The first type, the largest of the three, is enterprises that joined the industry for a relatively short time. Examples of this type are Japan Steel, Toyo Rayon, Shinagawa Electric, and so on. These firms participated in penicillin production during the initial boom years then returned to their primary business.

The second type describes the opposite: enterprises that joined the industry as penicillin manufacturers and remained over the long term. Among them are the "dual-function" (*kengyo*) enterprises, that is, firms that combined pharmaceutical manufacturing with their existing business. The first example is Meiji Seika, a confectionery company. This company was able to continue producing pharmaceuticals in the decades after the War thanks to a joint licensing agreement for streptomycin with Kyowa Hakko (*hakko,* meaning fermentation) and the close relationship that its corporate scientists cultivated with Umezawa. This company still continues to manufacture pharmaceutical products today. The second example, Toyo Jozo, a small-scale sake brewer, joined the industry as a penicillin producer and still exists as the pharmaceutical branch of Asahi Kasei.[20] The third, Kaken, founded in Tokyo in 1917 initially as a research laboratory (Rikagaku Kenkyujo), built a twenty-ton tank for the production of penicillin and became the leading producer in Japan in 1949 with 11.8 percent market share.[21]

The third type included the existing Osaka-based medicinal manufacturers, specializing (*sengyo*) in pharmaceutical production. Many of these enterprises originated as medicinal merchants whose businesses can be traced back to the pre-Meiji period.[22] Representatives from Takeda, Japan's largest pharmaceutical manufacturer, attended Foster's lectures but, initially at least, took only a lukewarm interest in production.[23] Financial difficulty rather than interest seems to be the most prominent reason for the reluctance of existing pharmaceutical manufacturers to join in penicillin production. Tanabe, one of Japan's oldest pharmaceutical companies, and Yamanouchi (established in Osaka in 1923) suffered sizable losses during the War due to air raids and loss of overseas production sites. As a result, both were unable to make the start-up investments in production equipment. These companies never manufactured penicillin; however they did market it under their own well-known brand names. According to the *100-Year History of Shionogi,* another longstanding Osaka-based manufacturer, the company's late start as an antibiotics producer was caused by severe financial difficulties in the aftermath of the War coupled with a lack of scientific expertise.[24]

The geographical shift of the center of the Japanese medicinal industry from Osaka to Tokyo began during the Meiji period and continued to accelerate during the so-called penicillin boom. All of Foster's lectures and demonstrations were held in Tokyo. Tokyo was also the location of the Central Research Laboratory and the Ministry of Health. Although slow to join, the well-established Osaka-based pharmaceutical companies seem to have made a concerted effort to reverse the shift of the medicinal production capital to Tokyo. In the February 22, 1947, minutes, members of the JPA, many of whom had the headquarters of their operations in Osaka, decided to organize all of their technical meetings in the Kansai region.[25]

Phase Two: The Licensing of Technology for Penicillin Derivatives

High sales of penicillin motivated pharmaceutical enterprises to construct research laboratories; however, until the reform of the patent legislation in 1976, the tendency to rely on technology transfer as opposed to in-house development remained strong. The year 1953 marked the true start of the postwar era of technology introduction for the Japanese pharmaceutical industry.[26] From the end of the Occupation period to the mid-1970s, Japanese pharmaceutical companies would compete furiously to be the first domestic manufacturers to secure key licensing agreements with foreign enterprises. Thus in the first phase of this study, pharmaceutical manufacturers struggled to survive. In the second, however, they enjoyed greater stability and economic growth thanks to military demand from the Korean War, the gradual expansion of the insurance system, which would become universal in 1961, and features of the drug pricing and distribution systems. Pharmaceutical sales were particularly impressive at that time and even overtook those of chemicals.[27]

The Japanese Pharmaceutical Industry in the Early Post- Occupation Period

According to the 1949 Afterwar Remedy Order of the United Nations' Industrial Property, the patents of persons from United Nations member-states who had registered them on the day of the start of the War or within one year thereof would be recognized. This legislation specifically stated that Japanese manufacturers who wished to manufacture medicines including semi-synthetic derivatives of penicillin would have to procure a license, even for products they were already manufacturing without one. At the same time, it bought to an abrupt end the open and collaborative business environment that had existed during the first phase.

During the Occupation, some twenty Japanese manufacturers had begun to manufacture Procaine G, a semi-synthetic derivative of penicillin. Procaine G, which combined oil with penicillin, was an improvement over existing forms of penicillin, as it was longer lasting and injections were only needed once per day. Bristol, the American manufacturer and developer of the drug, applied for a patent in Japan and received approval in September 1953. According to the Afterwar Remedy Order of the United Nations' Industrial Property, all of the companies that wished to continue producing it were required to apply for a license.

With the idea of establishing such an agreement, the president of Banyu, Iwadare Toru (hereafter Iwadare) asked his son, Koichi, who was already travelling in the United States in November 1952, to explore the possibility of licensing Procaine G from Bristol. Through his connections at Wyeth, Iwadare Koichi was able to request an introduction to meet the president of Bristol, who in turn agreed to establish a licensing agreement. However, there were two clauses that were of particular concern to the company. First, Bristol requested that either Banyu or the president, Iwadare, be the sole licensee; the second concern was royalties.

Iwadare considered his options carefully: if Banyu were to become the sole owner of the patent rights in Japan, this would create tension between his company and other JPA member firms. Iwadare knew that because many companies had already begun production during the Occupation, they would resent having a single manufacturer gain control over the entire domestic market for this product. When news of the licensing agreement reached Japan, tensions had already begun to mount as illustrated by the fact that some representatives elected not attend a meeting Iwadare called to discuss the agreement.[28] To avoid further conflict, he asked Bristol to allow all the manufacturers concerned to engage in the production of Procaine G on equal terms rather than to license the product solely in his name.

Regarding royalties, Bristol stipulated that the producers of Procaine G disburse an initial advance of $50,000 and pay 5 percent of all subsequent sales. At that time, excessive competition among manufacturers had already begun, which caused prices to drop precipitously.[29] When Iwadare consulted with the Ministry of Health regarding the stipulations, officials told him that if Bristol did not agree to renegotiate the terms of the licensing agreement, Japanese manufacturers would simply have to abandon production of Procaine G in favor of a less costly substitute. Consequently, Banyu asked Bristol to lower the ratio from 5 to 2 percent.[30]

Although initially apprehensive, JPA members eventually agreed to allow Iwadare to negotiate the license on their behalf. In January 1953, Banyu succeeded in negotiating a less onerous agreement, which was acceptable both to manufacturers and the government. Bristol agreed to the arrangement, and most of the original twenty manufacturers continued to manufacture Procaine G. After the favorable conclusion of the agreement, the JPA even presented Iwadare with a certificate of appreciation for his endeavors.

Thus, in the case of Procaine G at least, direct conflict between rival manufacturers could be circumvented. However, the license for Procaine G would mark the last such amiable arrangement between Japanese manufacturers and the end of the penicillin boom. Trials between Japanese pharmaceutical manufacturers, some of which had originated overseas, became increasingly common.[31] As for penicillin production in Japan, at its peak in 1946 the JPA was comprised of seventy-two members. By 1951, the number had dropped to nineteen and in 1961 ceased to exist entirely.[32] By the mid-1960s, penicillin would be replaced by newer antibiotics, which entered the country not via direct government assistance but through technology transfer agreements between individual Japanese and foreign enterprises. These licenses became the main source of technology transfer as well as innovation in Japan for many years to follow. At the same time, scientists such as Umezawa continued even after the penicillin boom to provide technical guidance and support to corporate researchers. Their contributions to the fostering of domestic research on antibiotics and other drugs aided in the scientific development and economic growth of the Japanese pharmaceutical industry in the long term.

CONCLUSIONS

This chapter explored the sources (German journal article, Occupation government assistance, foreign licensing agreement) and types of technology transfer (mass production, semi-synthetic derivatives) over an extended period of time (mid-1940s to early-1960s). It also illustrated the roles of the three actors in the technology transfer process: government, industry/entrepreneurs and scientists. The role of the first actor, government, was especially significant during the first phase. Without the transfer of mass production technologies and direct technical assistance from the United States, which was facilitated by Japanese officials, the diffusion of penicillin would have been much slower. Government worked closest with industry and scientists during the first phase and was vital in fostering a cooperative and propitious environment for the transfer and diffusion of penicillin technology on a large scale.

The history of drug-induced incidents in Japan got its start with the introduction of penicillin. While semi-synthetic penicillin derivatives with fewer contaminants contributed to the purity and potency of the drug, they did not entirely remedy the problem of safety. Because of the potential risk of adverse drug reactions, the role of government would gradually evolve from promoter of industry to regulator, a responsibility it would fully assume in the 1960s in the wake of the Thalidomide incident.

The second actor, industry/entrepreneurs, also played an important role in the technology transfer process during both phases. In the first phase, they worked in cooperation with government officials, scientists and even other competitors to share information so as to improve the volume and quality of domestically produced penicillin. In the second phase, one entrepreneur, Iwadare, was instrumental in the technology transfer process, as it was he who initiated the negotiations to license Procaine G for the benefit the entire penicillin manufacturing industry.

The transfer of penicillin technologies served as an incentive to industry representatives to modernize their operations by constructing new manufacturing facilities or upgrading existing ones. At the same time, the discovery penicillin and other novel antibiotics provided an impetus to companies to begin in-house research despite patent legislation in place at that time that discouraged it. The fact that many Japanese pharmaceutical manufacturers began to establish their own central research laboratories in the 1960s illustrates this point.

The third actor, scientists, also made a significant contribution to the transfer and diffusion of penicillin technologies during both phases. In the first phase, they worked assiduously with manufacturers in order to help them to engage in the mass production of penicillin as quickly as possible. Cooperation between scientists from different disciplines, information sharing and direct assistance to corporate researchers were essential factors in the postwar recovery of the pharmaceutical industry. Because of the unquestionable correlation between diffusion of penicillin and the decline in deaths from infectious diseases, one can conclude that scientists' support of industry helped to improve not only the economic but also the health conditions of the nation as a whole.

Among the many scientists who engaged in the transfer of penicillin technologies, Umezawa played a particularly significant role. He contributed to the long-term development of Japanese pharmaceutical manufacturers by providing new knowledge and technical assistance to improve the quality of their products and nascent research capabilities. In this sense, his role as an educator went far beyond the boundaries of his university laboratory. Although his relationships with Meiji Seika and Banyu were especially close, he provided expert guidance to many other Japanese pharmaceutical manufacturers throughout his career.

This chapter traced the process by which the transfer of penicillin technologies transformed the business environment in Japan from one of cooperation and openness to a completely new climate characterized by competition and in some cases conflict. The main reason for this change was that after 1949, new penicillin technologies had become patentable commodities. Royalties from patents on innovations provided a strong incentive to companies as well as individual scientists to possess and protect their discoveries, often via long legal battles. The coexistence of cooperation and competition between pharmaceutical companies did not disappear after the penicillin boom, yet never were both as intense as during the two phases examined in this chapter. The cooperative and open environment fostered by the three actors prevailed up until the end of the Occupation and proved to be the key to the successful transfer of penicillin technology to Japan.

NOTES

1. Fusako Kakuta, *Hekiso Nihon Penishirin Monogatari (The Story of Penicillin)* (Tokyo, 1978), 225.
2. Japan Penicillin Association, *Penishirin no Ayumi (Progress in Penicillin)* (Tokyo, 1961), 130–135.
3. Keiichi Takeda, who was working as a young assistant in a laboratory at the University of Tokyo in 1946, describes some of the applications of penicillin-related technologies in the following work. *Penishirin Sangyō Jishi (The Start of the Penicillin Industry)* (Tokyo, 2007), 293–294.
4. In the 1960s, many industries including pharmaceuticals began to build central laboratories. A list of research facilities built by Japanese pharmaceutical manufactures between 1954 and 1970 can be found in the following. Japan Society of the History of Pharmacy (ed.), *Nihon Iyakuhin Sangyō Shi (History of the Japanese Pharmaceutical Industry)* (Tokyo, 1995), 123.
5. One can find many works in both English and Japanese that explore the role of government in the development of the Japanese pharmaceutical industry's development. One interesting comparative study is Jonathan Howells and Ian Neary, *Intervention and Technological Innovation: Government and the Pharmaceutical Industry in the UK and Japan* (London, 1995). Julia Yongue, "Origins of Innovation in the Japanese Pharmaceutical Industry: The Case of Yamanouchi Pharmaceutical Company," *Japanese Research in Business History* 22 (2006). Michael Reich, "Why the Japanese Don't Export More Pharmaceuticals: Health Policy as Industrial Policy," *California Management Review* (Winter 1990): 124–150. For a more critical overview,

see L. G. Thomas, *The Japanese Pharmaceutical Industry: The New Drug Lag and the Failure of Industrial Policy* (London, 2001).

6. See Katsuhiro Arai and Shigeru Nakayama with Kunio Gotō and Hitoshi Yoshioka, *A Social History of Science and Technology in Japan* (Melbourne, 2001), 215.
7. For an explanation of this drug pricing system, see Jonathan Howells and Ian Neary, *Intervention and Technological Innovation: Government and the Pharmaceutical Industry in the UK and Japan* (London, 1995), 111–116.
8. This point is persuasively argued in Hiroyuki Odagiri and Akira Gotō, *Technology and Industrial Development in Japan: Building Capabilities by Learning, Innovation and Public Policy* (Oxford, 1996) and in Johannes Hirschmeier and Tsunehiko Yui, *The Development of Japanese Business, 1600–1980* (Boston, 1975).
9. This point is made by a firsthand observer in the following work, Keiichi Takeda, *Penishirin Sangyō Jishi (The Start of the Penicillin Industry)* (Tokyo, 2007), 257.
10. Kakuta painstakingly investigates the development of penicillin in wartime Japan in Fusako Kakuta, *Hekiso Nihon Penishirin Monogatari (The Story of Penicillin)* (Tokyo, 1978). Her work, which includes numerous interviews with key figures, describes the many hardships Japanese scientists experienced in their quest to produce penicillin.
11. Fusako Kakuta, *Hekiso Nihon Penishirin Monogatari (The Story of Penicillin)* (Tokyo, 1978), 140–141.
12. See Hazime Mizoguchi and Shigeru Nakayama with Kunio Gotō and Hitoshi Yoshioka, *A Social History of Science and Technology in Japan* (Melbourne, 2001), 545.
13. Walter Sneader and Drug, *Discovery: A History* (Sussex, 2005), 294. For more about Pfizer's penicillin production see the following. Jeffrey L. Rodengen, *The Legend of Pfizer* (Ft. Lauderdale, 1999), 65.
14. One such work is Robert Bud, *Penicillin Triumph and Tragedy* (Oxford, 2007). The chapter entitled "Penicillin from Organized Science" describes the situations in England and the United States.
15. Among the sexually transmitted diseases, there were 556,000 cases of gonorrhea, 108,000 cases of chancroid and 436,000 cases of syphilis. Thomas B. Turner, "Japan and Korea," in *Civil Affairs/Military Government Public Health Activities,* vol. viii of Ebbe Curtiss Hoff (ed.), *Preventative Medicine in World War II* (Washington DC, 1976), 680.
16. Japan Penicillin Research Association, *Journal of Penicillin* 1 (1947): Preface.
17. There are numerous examples of "excessive competition" in Japanese business history, a tendency caused by companies that sell similar or identical products and compete by price cutting to gain market share. It is likely that penicillin is the first case of excessive competition in the postwar period.
18. Japan Business History Institute, *Tōre Nanajū Nenshi (The Seventy-Year History of Toray)* (Tokyo, 1997), 200–201.
19. Japan Penicillin Association, *Penishirin no Ayumi (Progress in Penicillin)* (Tokyo, 1961), 5.
20. Keiichi Takeda, *Penishirin Sangyō Jishi (The Start of the Penicillin Industry)* (Tokyo, 2007), 260.
21. Ibid., 261.
22. The origin of the oldest Japanese pharmaceutical industry is unique among developed economies in that companies began not as producers but as large medicinal merchant houses clustered in one area of Osaka (Doshōmachi). One of the oldest firms is Tanabe, established in 1678.

23. Keiichi Takeda, *Penishirin Sangyō Jishi (The Start of the Penicillin Industry)* (Tokyo, 2007), 257. Takeda Keiichi writes that Foster once became slightly irritated while conducting an on-site lecture due to a representative from Takeda Pharmaceutical who continued to boast about his company's vitamin research during his explanations.
24. Shionogi Kabushiki Gaisha (ed.), *Shionogi 100-Nenshi (The One-Hundred-Year History of Shionogi)* (Osaka, 1978), 275.
25. Keiichi Takeda, *Penishirin Sangyō Jishi (The Start of the Penicillin Industry)* (Tokyo, 2007), 25.
26. Japan Business History Institute, *Banyu Seiyaku Hachijūgo Nenshi (The Eighty-Five-Year History of Banyu)* (Tokyo, 2002), 121.
27. Ibid., 118.
28. This is mentioned in the corporate history and proven by letters between Banyu and Bristol as well as by notes (lists of meeting attendees) found in Banyu's archives in Tokyo.
29. Japan Business History Institute, *Banyu Seiyaku Hachijūgo Nenshi (The Eighty-Five-Year History of Banyu)* (Tokyo, 2002), 124.
30. Ibid., 129.
31. The most famous case involving Bristol is the described in John Sheehan, *The Enchanted Ring: The Untold Story of Penicillin* (Boston, 1982). Some disputes between Japanese enterprises (licensees) originated abroad, while others were the result of patent infringements between Japanese and foreign enterprises. The following article states that Japanese companies patented processes for existing drugs with only slight modifications. Kōji Yamakawa and Kiyoshi Nishitani, "Nihon no Seizō Tokkyo Jidai niokeru Iyakuhin Tokkyo Keisō Saiban nitsuite no taiken kenkyō (Empirical Studies on Some Drugs for Patent Lawsuits in the Age of Manufacturing Patents)," *Japanese Journal for the History of Pharmacy* 44, 2 (2009): 77. This practice of patenting slight modifications in the production process was common until the 1976 patent reform and was the underlying cause of the disputes.
32. Japan Penicillin Association, *Penishirin no Ayumi (Progress in Penicillin)* (Tokyo, 1961), 170.

12 Agents of Change

Bell System Employees and Quality Assurance Knowledge Transfer in Postwar Japan, 1945–1955

Stephen B. Adams and Paul J. Miranti

INTRODUCTION

The transfer of industrial knowledge to Japan during the US Occupation after World War II had a lasting impact on that nation's economy and has been fodder for much scholarship. Bowen Deese and Kenneth Hopper have chronicled how CCS (Civil Communication Section) and other SCAP (Supreme Commander of the Allied Powers) subsidiaries promoted US management practices.[1] Stephen Adams and Paul Miranti have evaluated also CCS's role in facilitating the reorganization and restoration of telecommunications transmissions and manufacturing.[2] Alfred D. Chandler has argued that Japanese success in consumer goods is attributable to exploiting first-mover advantages by learning how to integrate managerial and technological capabilities.[3] Richard Pascale and Anthony Athos contend that learning depends on the type of knowledge. They believe that objective matter—that is, strategy, structure and system—proved more adaptable to Japanese business than more subjective social and cultural values affecting organizational staffing and management style.[4] In his study of the Japanese automobile industry, Michael Cusumano notes how receptivity to US practices was conditioned by Japan's perceived effectiveness in addressing home market conditions.[5] Michael Fransman has explained the decisive role of government in giving priority to economic plans that emphasized exports.[6] William C. Tsutsui has examined the sociopolitical factors that fostered Japanese interest in scientific management.[7] Jonathan Zeitlin and Gary Herrigel argue that the acceptance of US management practices resulted from the flexibility of its underlying knowledge base which was adaptable in many dissimilar sociocultural contexts.[8]

This study extends this literature by evaluating the Bell System's influence in transferring knowledge of quality assurance methodologies and management to Japan. The next section surveys the guidance provided by Bell employees who dominated the membership of the CCS in the restoration and improvement of the Japanese telecommunications industry. The third section focuses on the activities of three CCS agents—Frank Polkinghorn of Bell Laboratories, Charles W. Protzman of Western Electric and Homer

Sarasohn of Raytheon Corporation and Crossley Radio—who developed the first training programs designed to cure the Japanese engineering management learning deficiencies uncovered. The fourth section evaluates the educational emphasis of two consultant educators, W. Edwards Deming and Joseph M. Juran, and the influence they exerted on Japanese quality management after the withdrawal of CCS in 1950. The concluding section shows how this unique episode in global knowledge transfer affected the evolution of instructional approaches to quality engineering and management.

CCS AND JAPANESE TELECOMMUNICATIONS REVIVAL

SCAP's initial mission, defined by the terms of the Potsdam Agreement, called for the restoration of Japanese economy to subsistence levels, the elimination of militaristic influences and the promotion of democratic institutions and values.[9] The achievement of economic self-sufficiency began to take on new prominence as a means for alleviating some of the costs imposed on US taxpayers by the Occupation. By 1949, the achievement of the latter goal became more critical to building the strength of a potential ally against the spread of Communism in Asia.

CCS began working with the Ministry of Communications (MOC) in 1945 to reestablish telecommunications capacities. This was a critical precondition for the restoration of the ability to coordinate activities in a complex economy with many interdependent elements. The MOC was a vast conglomerate of loosely connected activities. It controlled the nation's telephone and telegraph system, the national radio-broadcasting network, the postal system with its giant savings and insurance facilities and the Electrical Communication Laboratory which conducted research relating to telecommunications, radio, heavy power equipment and the ionosphere.[10]

The CCS staff of about 100 engineers and technicians, most of them on loan from the Bell System, served as advisers to the MOC in restoring Japan's heavily damaged telecommunications grid. AT&T's president, Walter S. Gifford, had negotiated the "Affiliated Plan," which provided managerial and technical personnel to the US Army.[11] In 1945, Assistant Secretary of War Robert P. Patterson extended the arrangement to include SCAP and the occupation forces. Regular Signal Corps officers remained in overall command CCS. Its first head, Brigadier General Spencer Akin, after his escape from Corregidor, had served as MacArthur's chief of signals intelligence.[12] The CCS staff included experts in traffic, plant and commercial engineering, operational training and human resource management.

A key step in CCS's plan for recovery that was accepted by the Japanese government was the creation of a quasi-independent, for-profit telecommunications enterprise whose growth would be driven by the expansion of telephone service rather than the previously predominant telegraph sector. In 1949, MOC spun off a new Ministry of Telecommunications (MOT), the forerunner of Nippon Telephone and Telegraph, NTT.[13] MOT's planned exploitation of the telephone's potential was attractive to the US advisers for several reasons. First, they were familiar with this technology coming from a nation with 30 million telephones or 25 per hundred population. Second, few Japanese enjoyed access to telephone service with 1.3 million stations or about 1.6 per hundred population. The average number of completed calls per month in Japan amounted to 14 million, about one third of 1 percent of the US average.[14] Third, besides greater convenience in accessing telecommunication services, the leasing of telephone equipment to consumers promised to generate more revenue than the individual message charge arrangement used in telegraph. Fourth, increases in traffic density in urban centers made possible the exploitation of scale economies. Fifth, an increase in demand would result from lowering telephone taxes and initiating consumer advertising.

In spite of shortages, inflation and labor unrest, the CCS advisers proved effective in helping the MOC resolve network problems. They introduced traffic studies for balancing system loads and capacities. They pressed for more intensive maintenance to minimize equipment failure and service outages. They helped to rationalize the organization of the ministry's warehouses and procurement practices. They advised larger manufacturers such as Nippon Electric and Tokyo Shibaura (Toshiba) in the reconstruction of major factories. The Americans introduced new modes of budgeting and full accrual accounting necessary for monitoring activities in a profit-seeking entity. CCS planners assisted in restoring physical facilities in urban centers damaged by wartime bombing. They persuaded the Japanese to reorder their national research laboratories along the lines of the Bell Laboratories.[15] They introduced a statistical quality control (SQC) system like the one pioneered at the Bell System in the 1920s at Nippon Electric which reduced losses from defective vacuum tube production.[16]

Nevertheless, some CCS operatives harbored misgivings about Japanese management practices and production engineering knowledge. In 1947, these issues became the focus of a new addition to the CCS industrial division's staff, Charles W. Protzman, a manufacturing supervisor from Western Electric's Hawthorne plant. For the next two years Protzman worked with Homer Sarasohn, a circuit designer, to study the problems of production management that affected many of the 300 independent manufacturing companies that supplied MOC. That same year Frank Polkinghorn, a Bell Laboratories research scientist, also arrived to study engineering education and the types of learning that connected Japanese industry and universities.

CCS SURVEYS AND KNOWLEDGE INTEGRATION (1947–1950)

Although the methods used by Protzman and Polkinghorn to evaluate weaknesses in Japanese management practice differed, they agreed that improvement could only come through educational reform. Protzman believed the solution was to upgrade managerial skills through training provided by CCS in cooperation with industrial associations. Polkinghorn, on the other hand, militated for university curriculum modification and the establishment of closer connections between the academy and industry.

Protzman visited about 70 factories and concluded that an approach different from the one employed earlier was necessary to strengthen Japanese management capacities. Previously, during factory visits, CCS representatives sought unsuccessfully to inculcate knowledge of modern business methods and concepts in meetings with engineering and production staffs. While Japanese managers frequently implemented CCS suggestions, the full benefit of the consultation was not realized because of a general failure to grasp the underlying principles that might be applied to resolve similar problems in the future. To Protzman, this evinced a lack of practical engineering knowledge. He attributed this to the high prestige universities accorded to theory and research. Japanese graduates prized careers in laboratories or institutes of higher learning rather than in low-status manufacturing. Because of these biases, insufficient emphasis was placed on fundamental manufacturing and management paradigms. Consequently, the operational effectiveness of many firms suffered because of, "loose supervision, lack of knowledge of costs, absence of control techniques, failure to recognize the interrelationships of various company functions and, in many instances, one man domination."[17]

Although Protzman and Sarasohn believed that the solution lay in formal training programs, their superiors at CCS felt that a more detailed study was necessary to win the support of SCAP headquarters and Japanese industrial associations. The result was site surveys with the management of six firms producing either communication equipment, wire and cable, radio or vacuum tubes. Each survey lasted about two weeks and focused on the nature of organizational structure and management and functional effectiveness.[18]

The surveys began with top management interviews, including the president and managing directors, and extended to factory supervisors. The CCS representatives sought to determine how well managerial concepts were understood and how organizational authority and responsibility were delegated. The CCS agents assessed management's ability to recognize and implement sound controls. They searched for evidence of duplication or gaps in authority which might engender conflicts or inefficiency. Through this probing they sought to judge the "nature and effectiveness of organization and structure."[19]

The interviews identified serious managerial shortcomings. The organizational structures were found to be "haphazard, top-heavy and lacked coordination." Basic policies were either not defined or were developed on an ad hoc basis. Job responsibilities remained unspecified. Few supervisors received preparatory training. Top management often seemed to have a poor grasp of their responsibilities.[20]

Protzman also thought that firm performance suffered from shortcomings in the relationship between management and workers. His views doubtless were influenced through his own experience of the "lessons" of the Hawthorne plant experiments sponsored by Western Electric in the 1920s and 1930s. This study led by Professor Elton Mayo of the Harvard Business School concentrated on extending the understanding of the factors that affected labor alienation and motivation.[21] Protzman recognized such issues at work in the Japanese firms he surveyed. He believed that weak leadership undermined factory unity and failed to encourage, "all employees to cooperate in findings ways of bettering the condition of the company." This he felt was reflected "in one-man domination, in the failure of top management to tap the resources of ideas that are available in lower levels, in the absence of two-way communication, in the frustration and lack of cooperation, enthusiasm and morale at lower supervisory and worker levels."[22]

The second part of the survey evaluated functional performance. Protzman and Sarasohn reviewed manufacturing procedures and cost data to learn how the firms planned and scheduled production, monitored the efficiency of labor and material usage, controlled scrap, and utilized overhead information relating to maintenance, inspection, safety, process control and working conditions. The CCS agents also studied supervisory effectiveness including corporate practices for recruitment, training and evaluation of plant foremen. They focused on marketing and steps taken for undertaking surveys, making forecasts, developing advertising, sales training and program planning. They considered the influence of industrial and labor policies as they related, among other factors, to wages, worker grading, union negotiating and health and safety.[23]

The surveyed firms received low marks for functional efficiency for several reasons. The war had contributed to the attrition of supervisory and management personnel, the destruction of business records and the weakening of production routines because of the tremendous demand for output. The companies failed to sufficiently define personnel policies, operational techniques, worker efficiency measures and material controls. Antiquated accounting systems impeded profit planning because of the inability to segment cost information by function, product and operations or to provide useful yardsticks for assessing direct and overhead charges dynamics.[24]

In the meantime Frank Polkinghorn found the local universities and technical institutes ill prepared for correcting the knowledge deficiencies of engineering managers. The universities had long remained aloof from industry. This was reflected in a curriculum which emphasized the theoretical over the practical. Because of the lack of business contact, the schools often did not address bodies of knowledge critical to the functioning of modern industry. Leading programs, for example, failed to consider such topics as development engineering, for which there was not even a word for in the Japanese language at that time. Polkinghorn also faulted lax pedagogical practices including a lack of homework, insufficient testing and excessively long lectures. Shortages of textbooks and laboratory equipment eroded instructional effectiveness.[25]

Polkinghorn concluded that weaknesses in education translated into shortcomings in engineering practice. Engineers frequently lacked clear ideas about planning and implementing telecommunication projects. Research and development often suffered because of unclear specification of purpose. Equipment testing frequently did not trigger necessary design corrections. Poor quality led to high costs of operation and maintenance. Poor planning contributed to excessive production, high inventories and weak operational coordination.[26]

Although Polkinghorn tried to remedy these and other problems through formal conferences with the engineering professoriate during his two-year tenure in Japan, the pace of change was slow. It was not until March 1950 that leaders in education and industry, for example, were persuaded to meet to discuss their mutual interests.[27]

Protzman eventually turned to the Japanese Federation of Communication Manufacturing Industry Associations (JFCMIA) for assistance in promoting management education. Earlier, the Federation had organized instructional meetings in which larger telecommunication firms disseminated knowledge of new manufacturing techniques to their smaller industrial brethren. The learning related to the revival of major facilities for which CCS engineers served as advisers. This primarily included Toshiba's vacuum tube factory at Yobe and Nippon Electric's automatic switching unit at Mita and its automatic switch plant at Tomeagawa.[28]

After receiving authorization from General MacArthur, Protzman and Sarasohn developed a multiday training program that was presented first in Tokyo (September–October 1949) and then Osaka (November 1949–January 1950).[29] The two Americans developed their own instructional materials, which later were translated into Japanese.[30] Each course incorporated 31 four-hour training sessions plus a graduation.[31] Interest in the program grew in response to the publicity given by the Japanese Management Association. Soon, associations representing manufacturers of chemicals, textiles, machines and heavy electrical industries sought training for their membership.

Given Protzman's experience at the Hawthorne plant, it was not surprising that the courses reflected supervisory perspective in a single plant environment. The Osaka instruction, for example, had four broad elements. Two sessions dealt with *Policy,* addressing how the basic objectives of the enterprise could be realized through the definition and enforcement of management and administrative policies and the role of executive leadership. But there was no mention of strategic definition or evaluation. *Organization* accounted for 14 sessions. This involved a discussion of the "zones" of management or factors contributing to the establishment of hierarchical structures. It also included discussion of organizational design and the significance of line, staff and functional arrangements. Much of the organization curriculum was dedicated to evaluating the role of functional specializations including engineering, finance, manufacturing and industrial relations. *Control* topics were the subject of 13 meetings with the greatest emphasis placed on quality (6), including many of the SQC concepts used at Western Electric, and cost (3) control. *Operations* were limited to two conferences that addressed the issues of organizational coordination. The focus centered largely on achieving operational cohesion between the interdependent departments within a factory. Overall, the program did not address the problems of coordinating activities in large multi-location or division enterprises. Instead, it incorporated a report that detailed the successes of a small US firm that was guided by "modern management principles." This provided tests for analyzing organizational effectives and for appraising organizational leadership.[32]

Although the two training sessions were well received, the CCS-JFCIMA educational alliance ended with the departure of Protzman and Sarasohn in 1950. However, a new sponsor, the Union of Japanese Engineers and Scientists (UJSE), soon initiated training that focused more narrowly on addressing the problem of manufacturing quality, a major weakness affecting Japanese global competitiveness. UJSE was a professional organization that among other goals was dedicated to the revival of the national economy. Ichiro Ishihawa, who helped form UJSE in 1946, had been a member of the steering committee for CCS's management Tokyo training program. Although UJSE subsequently sponsored quality seminars, they were only marginally successful because of the over emphasis of the underlying mathematics by academic instructors. Ishikara soon recognized the need to recruit presenters with industrial experience that could make the statistics more accessible to students not heavily steeped in quantitative methods.

THE ADVENT OF STATISTICAL QUALITY CONTROL (SQC) AND MANAGING FOR QUALITY

While UJSE recruited many quality experts during the postwar era, the experience of two—W. Edwards Deming and Joseph M. Juran—provide insight into ways that the new knowledge was evolving. Both men were attracted to consulting at transition points in their own careers. Their Japanese experiences helped in their successful efforts to reinvent themselves as world authorities in the emergent specialization of quality assurance. The nature of their instruction differed. Deming placed greater emphasis on technique. He stressed the analytic method implicit in SQC developed at Western Electric and the Bell Laboratories and adopted by the American Standards Association's Emergency War Standards for defense production. Although part of this tradition, Juran placed greater stress on the context of knowledge application. Drawing on his plant floor experience, Juran's instruction centered more on how statistical knowledge of quality could be integrated more broadly to inform management decision processes across the business enterprise.

W. Edwards Deming's involvement with quality control came relatively late in his career. After graduating from Yale University with a doctorate in mathematical physics, he joined the staff of the Nitrogen Laboratory of the Department of Agriculture in Washington DC in 1927. His first exposure to statistical control came about through his responsibility for developing part of the scientific curriculum for the graduate school that his agency operated during the 1930s. Deming's duties included inviting eminent scientists to Washington to lecture on advances in their fields. Deming's supervisor, Charles R. Kunsman, recommended that he invite Walter Shewhart, who was pioneering the application of probability theory to quality analysis.[33] Both Kunsman and Shewhart had been doctoral students in physical chemistry at Berkeley and had begun their careers at Bell Labs.[34]

To scientists like Deming, statistics and probability theory had become vital in comprehending the uncertainties that permeated the material world. During the modern era, the older Newtonian model of a precisely ordered universe had given way to new perspectives that emphasized the limits of exact physical knowledge and the utility of probabilistic approximations. During the last quarter of the 19th century, James Clerk Maxwell in Britain had, for example, demonstrated through his thermodynamic equations that the measurement of molecular action in gaseous aggregates depended on probabilistic analysis. Similarly, early in the 20th century, Neils Bohr in Denmark and Max Born and Werner Heisenberg in Germany drew on statistical constructs to advance the theory relating to subatomic particle dynamics.[35]

Walter Shewhart shared that new perspective. The Bell scientist who had led the development of SQC had already documented his reasoning in his *Economic Control of Quality of Manufactured Product* (1931).[36] Shewhart's subsequent lectures in 1939 in 1939 provided additional amplification about how SQC revolutionized manufacturing at Western Electric. What impressed Deming was how Shewhart's analysis aided by new conceptions such as the "control chart" greatly facilitated the identification of "specific" or "assignable" (i.e., controllable, nonrandom) causes and common (i.e., noncontrollable, random) causes of variation in statistical aggregates.[37] Deming and his colleague Raymond T. Birge of Stanford University had in 1934 developed a theoretical model to address the problem of error classification.[38] Unlike enumerative approaches characteristic of other contemporary theoretical models, however, Shewhart's system seemed superior to Deming because it was developed from the analysis of dynamic production system. The ability to distinguish between what was random and what was systematic enhanced quality efficiency by enabling managers' ability to specify, among other factors, steady state conditions for production lines, the economic limits of inspection engineering and effective sampling methods. Deming avidly took notes for Shewhart's lectures which were later published under the title *Statistical Method from the Viewpoint of Quality Control*.[39]

This volume benefited from Deming's considerable skills as an editor and his ability to make complex notions comprehensible for general readers.

Deming's understanding grew further through his association with Leslie E. Simon, an officer in the Army's Ordinance Department Ballistic Research Laboratory in Aberdeen, Maryland. Simon had become interested in quality control as a means of overcoming faulty high explosives production at the Picatinny Arsenal in Dover, New Jersey. Simon made contact with Walter Shewhart, who served as a consultant to the Army and lived in nearby Troy Hills, New Jersey. Shewhart encouraged the publication of Simon's, *An Engineer's Manual of Statistical Methods.* Simon also presented his ideas in seminars at the Agriculture's graduate school.[40]

The outbreak of World War II drew Deming closer to quality assurance practice. Although he had transferred to the Census Bureau, Deming played a leading role in the development of training in quality control to strengthen war production.

Deming served on the expert panel of the American Standards Association (ASA) chaired by Harold Dodge, a close associate of Walter Shewhart at Bell Laboratories, that at the behest of the War Department defined wartime standards for quality control.[41] The committee produced three documents known as the American War Standards for Quality Control, derived largely from Shewhart's earlier service during the 1930s for developing standards for quality control for the American Society for Materials and Testing.[42] The three ASA volumes published in 1941–1942 included *Guide for Quality Control, Control Method for Analyzing Data* and *Control Chart Method of Controlling Quality during Production.*[43] These publications were employed in quality education teaching programs for war industries that Deming helped to organize and teach under the auspices of the US Office of Education and the Office of Production Research and Development of the War Production Board. During the conflict, over 7,500 executives received training, each averaging about 60 hours.[44]

Deming's association with Japanese industry began after the war, when released from the Census Bureau through a reduction in personnel. Joining the SCAP staff, he worked as a consultant in planning the Japanese labor census. In 1950, he was engaged by the Union of Japanese Scientists and Engineers on the recommendation of Kenneth Morrow of SCAP's Economic and Scientific Section after Walter Shewhart had declined the opportunity because of poor health.[45]

Although Deming maintained close contact with the Japanese quality community, his teaching in that country only spanned the period 1950–1952. Interest in his teaching was most intense in 1950; this enthusiasm seems to have waned sharply by 1952. In 1950, he taught an eight-day quality-training program at Tokyo (230 participants) and Fukuoka (110). Drawing on many of the materials developed for the US wartime training programs, the primary focus centered on enhancing the comprehensibility of mathematical concepts and the use of the control chart for middle level executives and supervisors.[46]

During the last three days of that year's visit he also was called upon to develop and present a quality course for top managers. The following year he ran four seminars over a 66-day period which addressed quality control (two), sampling methods (one) and quality for senior management (one). In 1952, he cut back his Japanese teaching to 12 days leading a clinic on quality control and a clinic on quality control and markets surveys. The programs relating to sampling and market surveys apparently were not well received. The demand for quality training had shifted from a primary interest in its statistical methods to its managerial dimensions.[47]

Deming's fame, however, also derived from the inspiration that he conveyed to depressed business leaders about the central role of quality in reviving Japanese society. This was communicated in lectures at the Tokyo Industry Club in July 1950 and at a second conclave held at Mount Hakone the following month. Deming believed that a stronger focus on quality assurance, the assessment of consumer wants through market surveys and more responsive product design processes could resolve many of the problems of low industrial productivity and weak export demand in five years. The realization of such a transition, however, required fundamental changes in the ordering of industry. Top managers had to become committed to reform and provide strong leadership in effectuating change. A key part of this involved making more effective use of the nation's endowment in human resources, particularly the linking of the complementary skills of engineers and statisticians in industry.[48] Implicit in this schema was the understanding that quality-driven manufacturing could serve as a powerful socioeconomic mechanism for enhancing wealth while defusing dangerous political tensions that threatened social stability. The new knowledge served simultaneously as a palliative for production problems and labor alienation. Deming argued that Japan must conceive itself a system whose success in a global competitive order depended on achieving quality and restoring trust and cooperation between managers and workers. These ideas registered positively with Japanese business leaders who commemorated Deming's commitment to their cause by naming the UJSE's prize for excellence after him in 1950.[49] While Deming continued to lecture in Japan in the years that followed, his professional focus after 1951 became increasingly divided between consulting in the United States and service on the faculties of Columbia University, New York University and George Washington University.

A second strategy of UJSE to disseminate knowledge of quality assurance was reflected in the consultancy of Joseph M. Juran. Unlike Deming whose experience in quality assurance had been heavily shaped by teaching its statistical methods, Juran's exposure to the new knowledge had derived more from both applying the knowledge on the factory floor and integrating the specialized activities within the firm's administrative hierarchy. He joined the inspection engineering department at Western Electric's Hawthorne plant in Cicero, Illinois, after completing a bachelor's degree in electrical engineering at the University of Minnesota in 1925.[50] Juran pioneered in the development of SQC, serving as a plant representative in negotiations with Bell Laboratories about the integration of the new procedures into production management.[51] In addition he also played an active role in providing instruction in the new specialization in the Hawthorne evening educational program. Juran would rise to high rank in factory administration in the years prior to World War II. During the war, at the behest of E. R. Stettinius, Juran was loaned by Western Electric to the Lend-Lease Administration where he served as a management expert and authored his first book, *Bureaucracy: A Challenge to Better Management.*[52] After the war, Juran left Western Electric and embarked on a career in management consultancy. He was eventually invited by UJSE in 1954 to provide instruction about what he termed "quality management."

UJSE officials had approached Juran because they were interested in broadening the scope of quality instruction to include a fuller explanation of its relationship with other corporate operating functions. They were deeply impressed by Juran's *Quality Control Handbook* (1951), which extended the scope of the discussion of quality beyond statistics to include such dimensions as "economics. . . , specification, organization, inspection, assurance and supplier relations."[53]

In Juran's view statistical evaluation was only one part of the problem of knowledge exploitation. The relevance of quality information was not limited to the manufacturing line but also had important implications for marketing, strategic planning and other critical managerial functions. Thus, deep, firm-specific learning was also required on how product-quality data could be ordered and distributed to inform decision processes within complex administrative echelons.[54] Moreover, Juran believed that quality information provided industry with a second powerful body of knowledge for enterprise management to go along with accounting data.

In 1954 Juran met with industrial leaders in Japan to explain his ideas about quality engineering. During that trip he taught two courses: a two-day seminar for senior managers at Hakone and Kayosan and a 10-day program for middle managers at Waseda University near Tokyo and at Osaka. During the trip Juran also prepared a special report about quality engineering for Japanese industry. He warned against the danger of placing too much reliance on statistical methods alone. He stressed the importance of following a more reasoned approach that also incorporated firm-specific capabilities for economic and organizational analysis, quality planning and the specification of quality goals.[55]

Although by the 1960s UJSE had begun to develop its own quality training capabilities, the connections with Deming and Juran remained close. The new focus shifted from seminars to international conferences in which leading scholars and practitioners shared their research papers and discussed pressing problems confronting the rising quality engineering profession. The leaders of Japan recognized the importance of Deming's and Juran's educational bootstrapping. For their efforts both were awarded, the Second Order of the Sacred Treasure, the highest honor conferrable on individuals who were not Japanese subjects.[56]

CONCLUSION

The effectiveness of transfer of quality knowledge by the Bell System in postwar Japan was shaped in several ways by the nature of the institutional setting. Although CCS identified many problems in industry and tried to implement educational solutions, the impact was limited because of resource scarcity and the agency's limited term. Greater continuity of purpose derived from business and professional associations who thought that the new knowledge represented an important mechanism for strengthening national economic competitiveness. They provided the forums that enabled local industry to decide which among varied pedagogical approaches seemed most efficacious. These organizations also provided valuable feedback to Japanese universities whose previous lack of leadership in these matters had stemmed from aloofness from industry rooted in considerations of social prestige and from beliefs in the importance of the theoretical over the pragmatic inquiry.

The Japanese experience also indicated that there were several different brands of quality assurance. CCS evaluated its utility within the context of broad operating principles for running a single plant. UJSE unsuccessfully tried to comprehend the new knowledge primarily in mathematical terms. Deming facilitated the comprehensibility of the mathematical foundations of SPC and explained its relationship to market research. Juran illuminated quality controls broader managerial implications within complex organizations. This reflected the fundamental adaptability of statistics and mathematics in depicting socioeconomic dynamics. The new expertise was just beginning to become part of engineering curriculums. Walter Shewhart had taught the first course on statistical quality control at Stevens Institute of Technology during the 1930s. The first doctoral dissertation relating to quality control was completed by Armand V. Feigenbaum at MIT in the mid-1940s. The new profession formed its national representative association, the American Society for Quality control (later the American Society for Quality) in 1946. The various Bell-associated initiatives built a foundation for the further intellectual flourishing of the field in both Japan and elsewhere in the decades that followed.

In Japan a greater psychological and pragmatic impact resulted from the actions of independent management consultants with varying degrees of knowledge of Bell practices. Ultimately, Deming's promise in 1950 seemed fulfilled with the eventual rise of Japanese global leadership in consumer electronics, automobiles, steel and textiles. Although the transition resulted partly from trade liberalization and supportive national export policies, economic recovery and social unity would have been difficult to achieve without the radical improvement in manufacturing quality.

Ironically, the beginnings of Japanese superiority over the United States in several industries could trace their beginnings, in part, to the transfer of knowledge from the Bell System representatives and consultants who had learned their trade there.

NOTES

1. Bowen C. Dees, *The Allied Occupation and Japan's Economic Miracle: Building the Foundation of Japanese Science and Technology, 1945–1952* (Richmond, UK, 1997). See also Kenneth Hopper, "Creating Japan's New Industrial Management: The Americans as Teachers," *Human Resources Management* 21 (Summer 1982): 13–34; and by the same author, "Quality, Japan, and the U.S.—The First Chapter," *Quality Progress* (September 1985): 34–41; Kenneth Hopper and William Hopper, *The Puritan Gift: Reclaiming the American Dream Amidst Global Financial Chaos* (New York, 2009), chap. 10 passim.
2. Stephen B. Adams and Paul J. Miranti, "Global Knowledge Transfer and Telecommunications: The Bell System in Japan, 1945–1952," *Enterprise and Society* 9 (March 2009): 98–124.
3. Alfred D. Chandler, Jr., *Inventing the Electronic Century: The Epic Story of the Consumer Electronics and Computer Industries* (New York, 2001).
4. Richard Tanner Pascale and Anthony G. Athos, *The Art of Japanese Management: Application for American Executives* (New York, 1981).
5. Michael A. Cusumano, *The Japanese Automobile Industry: Technology and Management at Nissan and Toyota* (Cambridge, Mass., 1985).
6. Martin Fransman, *The Market and Beyond: Cooperation and Competition in Information Technology Development in the Japanese System.* (Cambridge, Eng., 1990); and by the same author, "Controlled Competition in the Japanese Telecommunications Industry: The Case of Central Office Switches," in *Economics of Information Networks,* ed. Cristiano Antonelli (Amsterdam, 1992), 253–275.
7. William M. Tsutsui, *Manufacturing Ideology: Scientific Management in Twentieth Century Japan* (Princeton, N.J., 1998).
8. Jonathan Zeitlin and Gary Herrigel, *Americanization and Its Limits: Reworking US Technology and Management in Post-War Europe and Japan* (Oxford, Eng., 2000).
9. For discussion of SCAP and its sections see, Takemae Eiji, *Inside GHQ: The Allied Occupation of Japan and Its Legacy* (New York, 2002).
10. Adams and Miranti, "Global Knowledge Transfer," 103.
11. Ibid., 101–102.
12. William B. Breuer, *MacArthur's Undercover War: Spies, Saboteurs, Guerillas and Secret Missions* (New York, 1995).
13. Adams and Miranti, "Global Knowledge Transfer," 100–102. For origins of NTT see also, Marie Anchordoguy, "Nippon Telephone and Telegraph Company (NTT) and the Building of a Telecommunications Industry in Japan," *Business History Review* 75 (Autumn 2001): 507–541.
14. Appendix A, "Briefing of the Visiting Scientists of the Second United States Scientific Mission to Japan," November 28, 1948. Box 299–090–303, American Telephone and Telegraph (AT&T) Archives, Warren, N.J.
15. Adams and Miranti, "Global Knowledge Transfer," 103–107 and 107–114.

16. Wilbur S. Magill, a Western Electric quality engineer serving in CCS's industry division played a key role in implementing the SPQ system at NEC in 1946, see Koji Kobayashi, "Quality Management at NEC Corporation," *Quality Progress* (April 1986): 18–19.
17. C. W. Protzman, "Report on Activity with Occupation Forces in Japan November 1948 to May 1950," n.d., 2. Box 299–090–303, AT&T Archives.
18. Ibid., 2–3.
19. Ibid., 3.
20. Ibid., 3–5.
21. For discussion of the Hawthorne studies, see Richard Gillespie, *Manufacturing Knowledge: A History of the Hawthorne Experiments* (New York, 1991), chap. 8–9 passim.
22. Protzman, "Report on Activity with Occupation Forces in Japan," 4.
23. Ibid., 3.
24. Ibid., 3.
25. Unsigned and undated memo, "Work Done by the Research & Development Division, Civil Communication Section on the Improvement of Telecommunications Engineering Education in the Period 3 August 1948 to 1 May 1950," 1–2. Box 299–090–303, AT&T Archives.
26. Ibid., 1–2.
27. "Relations between Telecommunication Professors and Telecommunication Industry," March 13, 1950, and "Cooperation between University Professors and Industry," March 23, 1950, both by Frank Polkinghorn, Box 3162, Record Group 331, National Archives II, College Park, Maryland.
28. Adams and Miranti, "Global Knowledge Transfer," 117–118.
29. Protzman and Sarasohn encountered opposition from SCAP's Economic and Scientific Section in advancing their educational plan but eventually won the support of General MacArthur; see N. I. Fisher, "Homer Sarasohn and American Involvement in the Evolution of Quality Management in Japan, 1945–1950," *International Statistical Review* (2008): 8–9.
30. Homer M. Sarasohn and Charles A. Protzman, *The Fundamentals of Industrial Management: CCS Management Course* (Civil Communications Section, SCAP 1950, 1998). In the acknowledgements the authors indicated that they drew on contemporary text in the preparation of their volume, including L. P. Alford, *Principles of Industrial Management* (New York, 1947); P. E. Holden, L. S. Fish and H. L. Smith, *Top Management Organization and Control* (Stanford, 1947); and D. S. Kimball, *Principles of Industrial Organization* (New York, 1939).
31. "Synopsis of CCS Industrial Management Course," n.d., n.a., 1–3. Box 299–090–304, AT&T Archives.
32. Ibid., 1–3.
33. Cecilia S. Kilian, *The World of W. Edwards Deming*. (Washington DC, 1988), 55–58.
34. Shewhart completed his dissertation in 1917 entitled "A Study of Accelerated Motion of Small Drops through Viscous Medium" and Kunsman completed his dissertation in 1920 which was entitled "A Study of the Residual Ionization in Gas with Reference to Temperature Effects."
35. See Gerd Gigerenzer et al., *The Empire of Chance: How Probability Changed Science and Everyday Life* (New York, 1989), chap. 5 passim. Lorenz Kruger, "The Probabilistic Revolution in Physics—An Overview," in *The Probabilistic Revolution,* 2 vols., ed. Lorenz Kruger, Gerd Gigerenzer and Mary S. Morgan (Cambridge, Mass., 1986), 2: 373–378. See also in this same volume, Jan van Plato, "Probabilistic Physics the Classical Way," 2: 378–408;

Nancy Cartwright, "Max Born and the Reality of Quantum Probabilities," 2: 409–416; and Nancy Cartwright, "Philosophical Problems of Quantum Theory: The Response of American Physicists," 2: 417–435.

36. Walter A. Shewhart, *Economic Control of Quality of Manufactured Product* (New York, 1931).
37. W. Edwards Deming, *Out of the Crisis* (Cambridge, Mass., 1986), chap. 11 passim. Shewhart used the term "assignable cause" of error while Deming substituted the term "special cause" of variation.
38. W. Edwards Deming and Raymond T. Birge, "On the Statistical Theory of Errors," *Review of Modern Physics* 6 (1934): 119–164.
39. Walter A. Shewhart, *Statistical Method from the Viewpoint of Quality Control* (Washington DC, 1939).
40. Leslie E. Simon, *An Engineer's Manual of Statistical Methods* (New York, 1941), v–vi.
41. "Harold French Dodge, 1893–1976," *Journal of Quality Technology* 9 (July 1977): 96–97.
42. American Society of Testing and Materials, Committee E-11, *ASTM Manual PM Quality Control of Materials* (Philadelphia, 1951), iii.
43. American Standards Association, American War Standards, *Guide for Quality Control ASA Z1.1–1941* (New York, 1941); *Control Chart Method of Analyzing Data ASA Z1.2–1941* (New York, 1941) and *Control Chart Method of Controlling Quality during Production ASA Z1.3–1942* (New York, 1942).
44. Holbrook Working, "Statistical Quality Control in War Production," *Journal of the American Statistical Association* 40 (December 1945): 425–447; and by the same author, "Making Statistical Methods Contribute to the War Effort," *American Statistical Association Bulletin* 3 (May 1943): 2–4.
45. Kilian, *W. Edwards Deming,* 123.
46. Ibid., 126–127.
47. Junji Noguchi, "The Legacy of W. Edwards Deming," *Quality Progress* (December 1995): 35–37. See also Peter Kolesar, "What Deming Told the Japanese in 1950," *Quality Management Journal* 2 (Fall 1994): 9–24.
48. Kilian, *W. Edwards Deming,* 124–128.
49. Ibid., 132–135.
50. Joseph M. Juran, *Architect of Quality: The Autobiography of Dr. Joseph M. Juran* (New York, 2004), 67–69.
51. Ibid., chap. 10 passim.
52. Ibid., chap. 17, passim; and J. M. Juran, *Bureaucracy: A Challenge to Better Management; A Constructive Analysis of Management Effectiveness in the Federal Government* (New York, 1944).
53. Juran, *Architect of Quality,* 247–248.
54. Peter Kolesar, "Juran's Message to Japanese Executives in 1954: Some Lessons for Us in 2004," Decision, Risk & Operations Working Papers, Columbia University Business School, DRO-2004–06 (New York, 2006), 1–11.
55. Juran, *Architect of Quality,* chap. 10 passim.
56. Kilian, *W. Edwards Deming,* 278; Juran, *Architect of Quality,* 296–297.

Afterword

Technology Transfer and the Competitive Advantages of Regions

Takafumi Kurosawa

The twelve chapters of this book elucidate the great importance and wide variety of technology transfers in modern history. The editors of this volume (Pierre-Yves Donzé and Shigehiro Nishimura) presented the core fact findings and implications of the studies in the first chapter. In this last section, I[1] will thus try to provide a possible way to extend these implications from the perspective of industrial history and competitiveness analysis by addressing the historical approach, technology history, industrial history, competitiveness, and the "region" as a potential scope of research.

First, this collection of papers demonstrates how the historical approach can contribute to understanding of the present world. As some methodological studies suggest, the task of historical study is twofold. One is to present cases and their implications to relativize the narrower view of our contemporaries. Often, historical research reveals that presumably general rules are merely ephemeral in nature. On the other hand, some "novel" phenomena believed to be specific to an age, such as globalization since the late 1970s, may turn out to be not new at all. Historical research that achieves "medium-level" generalization to reach the "Erkenntnisgrund"[2] (*cause of knowledge*), as defined by Max Weber, can contribute much to social sciences and related disciplines. The other task of historical research is, of course, to explain why and how the world exists as it does or existed as it did (*historischer Realgrund* [historical "real cause"], also as defined by Weber).

Many of the chapters of this volume uncover an abundance of interesting historical causalities. By positioning nonrepetitive and irrevocable historical events ("actors," "processes," and transformations of "institutions") in the right place and shedding light on age- and location-specific contexts, including a wider sense of "institution," this book successfully illuminates tangible historical causality without reducing it to an insipid concept of *path dependency.* Further, historical causality essentially crosses over the boundaries of individual research disciplines. This volume is full of such examples; the impact of world wars on global technology transfer is the one of the most conspicuous.

Second, several chapters in this book explore a basic characteristic of technology, namely, general versatility. While some technologies are created in a specific industry for specific products and remain so, others can work with different products, find applications in several industries, and evolve further. Technology, together with other categories like goods and markets, is thus an important path through which industries link together. The evolutionary tree of a given technology often shows historical connections among industries. In other words, every technology has its own dynamics, and analyses of industrial and economic history complement investigations of the technology's relations with business.

When a transfer of technology takes place within an enterprise and brings about a new product or new process, creating a new, sustainable foundation for the business, it is called diversification. When it occurs among different actors in a specific location, it might produce clustering in narrow sense. When it happens among geographically separated actors, meanwhile, it constitutes the most typical image of technology transfer—and the special focus of this volume.

At the same time, technology is one of the most important elements to mark an era. In order to clarify age-specific conditions and the aforementioned notion of historical causality, a comprehension of technology history is indispensable.

Third, technology transfer is one of the most crucial concepts underlying the history of various industries. Here, industry signifies the arena for competition and cooperation among economic entities. In other words, an entry barrier for outsiders shapes the boundary of an industry. Technology often constitutes such an entry barrier. Thus, technology transfer plays a major role in explaining the historical dynamics of industries.

The converse is also true. While one can understand some aspects of the various forms and results of technology transfer as outcomes of location- and age-specific conditions, one can also interpret other features as industry specific.

Likewise, because technology transfer is a pivotal strategy for latecomers looking to play catch-up, the industry-specific features of technology transfer may bring about industry-specific catch-up patterns. If that is the case, and if the pattern is closely related to the rise and fall of an entire industry (the formation of a stable entry barrier and its collapse, etc.), many elements of the "industry life cycle"—which can have different forms from industry to industry—can be interpreted via the dominant form and results of technology transfer to a significant degree.

Fourth, technology transfer is crucial in understanding the historical dynamics of competitiveness. Primarily, competitiveness is a concept for specific economic entities (enterprises, individuals, or groups of them) in actual competitive relationships within a given market. As mentioned earlier, "industry" represents an arena for competition among and cooperation between economic entities; thus, any dynamic analysis of economy is, in fact, an analysis of competition in the most general sense.

While it appears to contradict the preceding definition of industry, there may be a competitive relationship between one industry and another; an industry—a pool of certain capability—may find itself in a relationship of substitution with another industry and at risk of being replaced. In these cases, however, it is not common to refer to the relationship as "competitiveness." This phenomenon should merit analysis as a question of the rise and fall of an industry and the temporal changes in the industry's boundaries.

Many experts raised the question of whether the region as a unit could have competitiveness. Some opposed Michael Porter's argument in *Competitiveness of Nations,* asserting that regions and nations themselves were institutional and environmental factors constituting the competitive environment, rather than actors involved in competition. Yet it has remained an obvious fact that two or more regions generating or hosting a certain economic activity are in a competitive relationship. Today, with nation states exerting weaker control and globalization continuing to spread, regions are in more direct in competition around locating economic activities. Even in the case of multinational companies, it is possible to discuss the competitiveness of the "organization" in conjunction with a specific region, given that a major element supporting its competitiveness exists in close relationship with a certain geographical element. Needless to say, we must distinguish between competitiveness as the home country/region and competitiveness as the host country/ region—but still, their interaction deserves ample attention. At any rate, it is indisputable that technology transfer constitutes a key element of this question.

The competitiveness of technology itself—competition among different technologies—is also important. This falls within the scope of the technology history issue described earlier. Some parts of this book deal with cases of such technology transfer, such as competition among multiple processes concerning a certain product.

Fifth, the book provides an opportunity to introduce the "region" as a unique unit or framework for analysis, fitting in between the national and global markets.

On the one hand, the history of geographical transfers of technology exhibits the universality of technology. Even though the technology levels of local societies demonstrate striking disparity, both cutting-edge technology and matured secondhand technology spread and set down roots worldwide. In world history, as this book shows, technology transfer has been the main driver for catch-up efforts by latecomers. Therefore, the variety of technology transfer is, in many ways, the variety of catch-up.

On the other hand, as some authors have illustrated, the flow often moves in two directions instead of one. The process travels through many agents, institutions, and routes in a very intricate way, and each region and nation has different capabilities to introduce new technology from outside. Although technology transfer works in part as a mechanism that flattens out the world, the real world is far from "flat"; the transfer of technology itself is an uneven operation.

In this respect, the introduction of a medium-level analytical unit is useful. This book addresses both national and global phenomena; some of the contributions deal with interaction among multiple nations or the interactions of national and global phenomena. Although not explicitly, these analyses imply that the "region"—Europe, North America, East Asia, and so forth—can be a meaningful, heuristic geographical scope for several reasons.

First, as several chapters argue, geographical, social, and cultural (especially linguistic) proximity have played an important role. For example, the role of immigrants and the importance of written material are contrasted between Japan and other "peripheries" (Argentina and Spain), which are culturally or geographically closer to the global "center" of technology. In this respect, a focus on the "region" is instrumental. Other elements that facilitate technology transfer, such as well-functioning institutions (e.g., patent systems), organizations (e.g., multinational enterprises [MNEs]), and historical developments (e.g., reductions in transportation costs and the development of information technology) also often have "regional" characteristics.

Second, the role of the nation state, the size of the national economy, and the intraregional heterogeneity of the society differ among regions. Geographical technology transfer in Europe has attracted a considerable amount of scholarly attention because the area comprises many nation states with many different languages and different levels of technological development. The context in North America is significantly different in this respect. Cartelization, which this book treats through an entirely new approach, and MNEs, especially the ones based in small but advanced nations in Europe, are the most eminent examples of this contrast. In East Asia, Japan's early rise, imperial expansion, and collapse, as well as the disconnection and late reentry of population-rich China into the world market, again shaped region-specific conditions.

Third, the position in the global history of technology is another important factor that makes the scope of "regions" more meaningful. A few studies in this book underlined the long-term stability of global "centers" of technology, namely, some "core" countries and enterprises in Europe and the United States. Though the leading role of the United States is undeniable, some chapters highlight many exceptions. Japan joined the "club" only after the Second World War and kept its position as the sole "center" in East Asia for several decades. Although Japan was once significantly "backward" in comparison with North America and the core regions in Europe, it can be said that Europe, North America, and Japan (as well as the rest of East Asia, now) have kept their positions as comparable geographical units. In addition, parallel geopolitical developments in Europe and East Asia, including nationalistic movements during the interwar period, attempts to create regional autarky, World War II, occupation periods, and the Cold War, positioned these regions as comparable entities.

Fourth, needless to say, the aforementioned points do not mean that regions are harmonious and autonomous units in the world economy. If the regions have similar factor endowments, institutions, and positions in the world economy, the rivalries among economic entities grows more intense. Smooth technology diffusion in a region not only prompts clustering on the regional level and boosts the competitiveness of the region in the global market but also enhances competition within the region.

All these "regions" are woven closely together in the wider fabric. The heterogeneous allocation of resources and capabilities has enrooted the global division of labor and sustained the flow of technology.

As outlined here, technology transfer is a fertile ground for both industrial history and competitive analysis. The wide-ranging significance of technology transfer this book has emphasized is quite thought provoking for economic, business, and technology history; management studies; and their adjacent disciplines. Above all, the book provides an indispensable springboard for delving into the dynamics of regional competitiveness.

NOTES

1. I was invited to join the session on technology transfer at the XVth World Economic History Congress 2009 in Utrecht as a commentator. The event marked the first milestone of this research project. I then proceeded to launch another international research project on the competitiveness of regions ("CARIS"; http://www.econ.kyoto-u.ac.jp/˜kurosawa/caris/), an initiative of which the editors and three other authors of this book are core members.
2. Max Weber, "Kritische Studien auf dem Gebiet der kulturwissenschaftlichen Logik (1906)," in *Gesammelte Aufsätze zur Wissenschaftslehre* (Tübingen: Zweite durchgehende und ergänzte Auflage besorgt von Johannes Wickelmann, 1951), 235; Hans Kenrik Brunn and Sam Whimster, eds. *Max Weber: Collected Methodological Writings* (London/New York: Routledge, 2012), 151.

Contributors

Stephen B. Adams is an associate professor of management at the Franklin P. Perdue School of Business, Salisbury University. He is the author of *Mr. Kaiser Goes to Washington: The Rise of a Government Entrepreneur* (University of North Carolina Press, 1997) and, with Orville R. Butler, *Manufacturing the Future: A History of Western Electric* (Cambridge University Press, 1999). He is currently working on a book about the development of Silicon Valley, tentatively titled *Before the Garage.*

María Inés Barbero is a professor of economic and business history at the Universidad de San Andrés and the Universidad de Buenos Aires, Argentina. At San Andrés, she directs the Research Center on Business History (CEHDE). The author and editor of numerous books and articles on Argentinean and Latin American business history, Barbero was also Alfred Chandler Visiting Scholar at Harvard Business School during the fall of 2009. Her current research interests are family firms, business groups, and multilatinas in Argentina and Latin America.

Marco Bertilorenzi received his PhD through a "cotutelle" thesis project between Università degli Studi di Firenze and Université Paris-Sorbonne in 2010. In his thesis, he explored the history of the international aluminium cartels from 1886, when the modern aluminium industry was born, to 1945, when the last official cartel underwent liquidation. He is currently a postdoctoral researcher at the Centre Rouland Mousnier of Paris-Sorbonne University and involved in the French national research project "CREALU" (creation and aluminium), ANR-10-CREA-11.

Valerio Cerretano holds an MA (Laurea) from the University of Pisa and a PhD from the University of Cambridge. Before joining the Adam Smith Business School, University of Glasgow, he taught at the universities of Cambridge, Bozen, Glasgow, Manchester, and Birmingham. He has also been a research fellow at Paris Jourdan, now part of the Paris School of Economics, and at the Hagley Museum and Library in Wilmington, Delaware. Valerio's research interests lie in the area of management and international business from a historical perspective; he contributes to both the understanding of the factors underlying the internationalization of large European corporations, the determinants to the international spread of technology and the forms of cross-border corporate cooperation, and the emergence of the industrial state in the Western world after the First World War and the 1929 global financial crisis.

Harald Degner was a member of the scientific staff of the Department of Economics at the University of Hohenheim, Germany, until 2011. His main research interests are the economics of innovation and the economic history of Germany. For his work, Degner won a travel grant from the German Business History Association (GUG) in 2008 and the Alfred D. Chandler Jr. travel grant from the Business History Conference (USA) in 2010.

Pierre-Yves Donzé is an associate professor and hakubi scholar at Kyoto University. He was born in Switzerland and studied history at the University of Neuchâtel, where he obtained his PhD in 2005 before doing stints as a visiting researcher in Japan and the United States. His publications include *History of the Swiss Watch Industry from Jacques David to Nicolas Hayek* (Peter Lang, 2011) and articles in *Business History* (2010 and 2013), *Social History of Medicine* (2010), *Enterprise & Society* (2011), and *Business History Review* (2013).

Geoffrey Jones is the Isidor Straus Professor of Business History at the Harvard Business School. He has written extensively on the history of globalization and multinational corporations, specializing in consumer products, banking, and commodity trading. His recent books include *Multinationals and Global Capitalism: From the Nineteenth to Twenty First Century* (Oxford University Press, 2005), *Renewing Unilever: Transformation and Tradition* (Oxford University Press, 2005), and *Beauty Imagined* (Oxford University Press, 2010), which provides a history of the global beauty industry. He is now researching the history of green entrepreneurship on a global scale over the last 50 years.

Takafumi Kurosawa is a professor in the Graduate School of Economics at Kyoto University in Kyoto, Japan. His dissertation analyzed the Swiss economy and the formation of the cross-border economic region in the 19th century. He translated the final report of the Bergier commission into Japanese and added original research outcomes. His publications in English range broadly in subject matter, exploring multinational enterprises (MNEs) and political risk, industrial clusters, the paper and pulp industry, and industry policy, and his work examines both European and Japanese cases. Since 2012, he has been organizing a large-scale international project on the competitiveness of regions, focusing on industrial history.

Pierre Lamard is a professor at the University of Technology of Belfort-Montbéliard, where he directs the Department of Humanities. He teaches industrial history to engineering students and focuses his research on the analysis of industrial areas, big entrepreneurial dynasties (Japy, Peugeot, Viellard-Migeon, and more), and technological choices within this framework.

Zejian Li is an associate professor in the Faculty of Economics at Osaka Sangyo University and a project researcher at the University of Tokyo's Manufacturing Management Research Center. He has authored numerous articles on strategy, marketing, innovation, and the automotive industry. Li now resides in Osaka, Japan.

Paul J. Miranti is a professor in the Department of Accounting and Information Systems at Rutgers Business School in New Brunswick, New Jersey. He is the author of *Accountancy Comes of Age* (University of North Carolina Press, 1990); *A History of Corporate Finance,* coauthored with Jonathan B. Baskin (Cambridge University Press, 1997); and *The Institute of Accounts,* coauthored with Stephen Loeb (Routledge, 2004). Dr. Miranti has also published extensively on the early application of probability theory and quantitative methods in management. He is currently writing a book tentatively entitled *Risk, Uncertainty and the Origins of Management Science at the Bell System, 1877–1950.*

Yuki Nakajima is an associate professor at Toyo University, Japan. He has conducted research on the history of the Japanese electronics industry and wrote his PhD thesis on the development of the Japanese electronics components industry since 1945. He has also participated in the "History of Japan's Trade and Industry Policy" research project organized by the Research Institute of Economy, Trade and Industry (RIETI), and his article on the Japanese car and material processing industries will be published soon.

Shigehiro Nishimura is associate professor of business history at Kansai University, Osaka, Japan. He was the visiting fellow of the Business History Unit of the London School of Economics and Political Science from 2011 to 2012. He wrote his doctoral thesis on the international patent management of General Electric Company and received his PhD from Kyoto University. In the years since, he has written a series of papers on international patent management at various multinational enterprises.

David Pretel is Max Weber Postdoctoral Fellow in History at the European University Institute in Florence. Prior to coming to the EUI, he was an Economic History Society "Anniversary" Fellow at the Institute of Historical Research (University of London), and a research associate at

Trinity Hall (University of Cambridge). David Pretel has published articles in journals including *History of Technology* (2010 and 2012) and *Empiria* (2009). He is co-editor of *The Caribbean and the Atlantic World Economy: 1650–1914* (Palgrave-Macmillan, forthcoming 2013).

Patricio Sáiz is a professor of economic history at the Universidad Autónoma de Madrid, where he conducts research on patent and trademark management in "backward" economies, especially Spain and Latin America. Since 1999, he has been in charge of a research agreement between the university and the Spanish Patent and Trademark Office. His recent publications include "Did Patents of Introduction Encourage Technology Transfer? Long-Term Evidence from the Spanish Innovation System," *Cliometrica* (2013), and "Catalonian Trademarks and the Development of Marketing Knowledge in Spain, 1850–1946" in the *Business History Review* (2012).

Jochen Streb is the professor of economic history in the Department of Economics at the University of Mannheim, Germany. Streb's research focuses on the innovation history and regulation history of Germany. He has published in the *Economic History Review, Explorations in Economic History,* the *Journal of Economic History,* the *RAND Journal of Economics, Research Policy,* and other journals.

Julia Yongue is a professor in the Faculty of Economics at Hosei University, Tokyo, Japan. Her research focuses on the development of the Japanese pharmaceutical industry from its modernization in the Meiji period to its rise as a global business. Her interests span a wide range of subjects, including business history, the history of pharmacy/medicine, and the impact of healthcare policy on the behavior of pharmaceutical firms.

Index